Happiness and Holiness

Denise Inge studied Thomas Traherne for her doctorate and announced the authorship of the Traherne manuscript discovered at Lambeth Palace in 1997. She has compiled a short Traherne anthology for SPCK's series *The Golden Age of Spiritual Writing* and frequently gives lectures and talks on Traherne. Her book *Wanting Like a God* (SCM Press, 2008) explores the themes of desire and freedom in Traherne's work.

She is married to John Inge, the Bishop of Worcester, and has two daughters.

CANTERBURY STUDIES IN SPIRITUAL THEOLOGY

Happiness and Holiness

Thomas Traherne and His Writings

Edited by
Denise Inge

CANTERBURY
PRESS
Norwich

First published in 2008 by the Canterbury Press Norwich
(a publishing imprint of Hymns Ancient & Modern Limited,
a registered charity)
13–17 Long Lane, London EC1A 9PN

www.scm-canterburypress.co.uk

British Library Cataloguing in Publication data

A catalogue record for this book is available
from the British Library

ISBN 978-1-85311-789-3

Typeset by Rowland Phototypesetting Ltd,
Bury St Edmunds, Suffolk
Printed in the UK by CPI William Clowes
Beccles, NR34 7TL

Contents

Acknowledgements

The shape of this book and some of its chapter titles were first suggested to me in the course of several discussions with the late Jeremy Maule of Trinity, Cambridge, whose idea it first was that there should be a Traherne Reader. True to the generous and wide-ranging mind of its originator, Jeremy's initial plan was more extensive; what I have produced is a much modified and reduced version of that Reader that reflects my own editorial concerns and areas of interest. Nevertheless, it is from Jeremy that the idea for this book derived, and it is to him that credit is due. Along the way I have been much aided by the scholarly enthusiasm of Donald Allchin, David Ford, Jacob Blevins, Julia Smith and Jan Ross, who each in their way have found Traherne's new manuscript discoveries as gripping as I have and who have offered quiet words of encouragement or advice. Anthony Russell has kindly lent me his volumes on George Herbert. Polly Willett has translated incomprehensible bits of Italian. Bridget Nichols, friend and reader, has been the best of critics.

I would like to thank the artist Tom Denny for kindly allowing his new Traherne window at Hereford Cathedral to be used for the cover of this book. Fellow enthusiast Richard Birt has offered helpful information, as has Rosalind Caird, archivist at Hereford Cathedral. I am grateful to Christine Smith for commissioning the book and for her unflagging patience as it was written and compiled, to Tarita Johns and Jane Baker for secretarial support, to Zuzanna Demcakova for the months of childcare. To my husband John whose faith in my work remains unshakable when mine is not and who doesn't mind this other man in my life, my debt of gratitude is both incalculable and, happily for me, forever forgiven.

With thanks to

British Library
Bodleian Library
Folger Shakespeare Library
Lambeth Palace Library
Beacon Press

In memory of
James and Donald Longenecker

Abbreviations

C	*Centuries of Meditations*
CE	*Christian Ethicks*
COH	*Commentaries of Heaven*
CYB	*Church's Year-Book*
EN	*Early Notebook*
FN	*The Ficino Notebook*
ITR	*Inducements to Retiredness*
KOG	*The Kingdom of God*
L	*Love*
RF	*Roman Forgeries*
SE	*Seeds of Eternity*
SM	*Select Meditations*
SV	*A Sober View of Dr Twisse*
TCL	*The Ceremonial Law*

Introduction

Several hundred years ago, a frustrated question was penned on the flyleaf of the large leather-bound unidentified volume, now known to be the work of the seventeenth-century priest and poet Thomas Traherne. It read: 'Why is this soe long detaind in a dark Manuscript, that if printed would be a Light to the World and a Universal Blessing?' A light to the world, a universal blessing – these are bold, almost Christological, claims to make of an unnamed manuscript. How disheartened that anonymous reader might have been to know that this 'light to the world' manuscript was destined to remain in the dark for several centuries more. For Thomas Traherne is only now, at the turn of the twenty-first century, being rediscovered as a serious theologian, and the volume in question was not published until 2005. Being long detained in darkness seems an apt description for much of Traherne's work, most of which the author never lived to see published. After his death at the age of 37, his manuscripts, largely unnamed and sometimes untitled, lay for years in deep obscurity. The story of the discovery of Traherne's manuscripts reads like a novel with astonishing twists and surprises, moments of serendipity, hazard, happenstance, resolve. Volumes rescued from book barrows, from misattribution, from obscurity, from a burning rubbish heap, the flames batted out, the leather smouldering. He is a writer who, if luck were anything to go by, should have disappeared altogether. He so nearly did. There is little chance now that he will.

Two remarkable discoveries (the Lambeth Manuscript in London – five prose works of doctrinal, testimonial and philosophical theology[1]

---

1 Jan Ross, ed., *The Works of Thomas Traherne*, Vol. 1, Woodbridge, UK: Boydell and Brewer, 2005. For details of the manuscript discovery, see Denise Inge and Cal MacFarlane, 'Seeds of Eternity: A New Traherne Manuscript', *Times Literary Supplement* (2 June 2000), p. 14.

– and *The Ceremonial Law*, a long fragmentary poem on Genesis and
Exodus housed at the Folger Library, Washington DC[2]) have sparked
a flash of Traherne publications – anthologies, a modern version of
Centuries of Meditations, critical studies, a new biography, and a collection of essays. An impressive 'Complete Works' is under way. What
has happened to Traherne in the new *Dictionary of National Biography*
is somehow symbolic of what is happening in general: he has slipped
from the catalogue of forgotten persons to take up his rightful place
between the eminent Toynbees and Anthony Trollope with an entry
four pages long.

Traherne is best known for the distinct voice of his poetry of innocence and the infinite, and for his *Centuries of Meditations*, described
by C. S. Lewis as 'almost the most beautiful book . . . in English', from
which he 'could go on quoting . . . forever'.[3] *Centuries of Meditations*
is a collection of meditations, in groups of 100, the fifth of which
remains unfinished, that celebrate the beauty of nature and the innocence of childhood, the infinity of the soul and its capacity for joy.

'The corn was orient and immortal wheat which never should be
reaped nor was ever sown.' 'You never enjoy the world aright until the
sea itself floweth in your veins . . . till evry Morning you awake in
Heaven: See yourself in your father's Palace: and look upon the Skies
and the Earth and the Air, as Celestial Joys.' So the *Centuries* sing,
while his poetry proclaims:

> How like an angel came I down,
> How bright are all things here
> ('Wonder', ll. 1–2)

Because of his preoccupation with the themes of innocence, nature and
the infinite, he has been classed as a pre-Romantic and grouped with
Wordsworth and Blake,[4] though interestingly his work, at the time

---

2 This manuscript was announced by Julia Smith and Laetitia Yeandle in
'Felicity disguisd in fiery Words', *Times Literary Supplement* (7 November 1997),
p. 17. Extracts have been published in Julia Smith, 'The Ceremonial Law', *Poetry
Nation Review*, xxv (1998), pp. 22–8; and in Denise Inge, *Thomas Traherne:
Poetry and Prose*, London: SPCK, 2002.

3 *They Stand Together: The Letters of C. S. Lewis to Arthur Greeves (1914–
1963)*, London: William Collins, 1979, pp. 492 and 369.

4 Dorothy Sayers, 'The Beatrician Vision in Dante and Other Poets', *Notting-
ham Medieval Studies*, 2 (1958), pp. 3–23.

hidden in undiscovered manuscripts, cannot have been known by either. More recently he has become an inspiration to those concerned about ecology and the environment. For Traherne nature, innocence and virtue go hand in hand, and it is true that in many ways Traherne is reminiscent of those other poets of the countryside. 'Donne is a poet of the town; Herbert is a poet of the vicarage; Crashaw is a poet of Rome; but Vaughan, with all his learning and culture, is a poet of the rugged countryside', wrote T. S. Eliot in one of his essays in *The Listener*. One could as easily substitute 'Traherne' for 'Vaughan' in that sentence. The similarities do not end there: like Vaughan, Traherne is much attached to his home in the English/Welsh borders; his main inspiration is the unusual mystical experiences of nature in his childhood, which results, like Vaughan's, in a poetry of innocence and of nature. So similar are Traherne and Vaughan that one early critic mistook Traherne's poetry for Vaughan's and was about to publish it under Vaughan's name before the real identity of the poet was discovered. It could be said of Traherne, as of Vaughan, that 'Much of his poetry is religious, but is not of the Church'.[5] This may be part of what makes Traherne comfortable to many. At first glance he appeals to those who are interested in the spiritual quest but do not want to subscribe to any particular expression of faith. Such a reading of him is misleading. Most recent discoveries show Traherne to be passionate in his defence of English Christianity and deeply concerned with the protection of specific Christian doctrines. Although his fluent account of a personal mystical experience may make him attractive to post-Christian seekers, his 'un-churchy' poetry is, on closer inspection, with his other works, more deeply rooted in the life of the Christian church and in the scriptures than is commonly known.

There is a real value in reading the exultant passages from Traherne such as those quoted above on their own. A single poem or a prose meditation can stand alone effectively and inhabit our memories with piercing eloquence in the same way that, for example, St Paul's much quoted passage on love from 1 Corinthians 13 – 'Though I speak with the tongues of men and of angels . . .' – may do. Beautiful as the 1 Corinthians passage is, it is specific; it does not speak for the whole of Paul's writings, or in other of his varied tones, or to his several

---

5 This and the preceding quote are from T. S. Eliot, 'Mystic and Politician as Poet: Vaughan, Traherne, Marvell and Milton', *The Listener* (2 April 1930), pp. 590–1.

concerns. The whole of Paul may there be hinted, but there are many other faces it does not show. To construe the writer's whole theology or philosophy from one or two sources is likely to lead to half truth; the same can be said of Traherne. What we have known and loved best from his writings are only part of the picture. We are at a time of great discovery in our understanding of Traherne, for the newest manuscript discoveries and unpublished works allow a much richer, more rounded, sometimes less cosy but no less engaging Traherne to emerge. For perhaps the first time we can begin to discover him not just as a metaphysical poet or a spirituality guru but also as a theologian engaged in uncovering God, and seriously addressing widely held public concerns.

This may be a new angle for those familiar with Traherne as a poet of private meditation. It is true that personal memories of early innocence inform his work; his subject is infant innocence remembered and lost, the infinite capacity of every soul, each person's enjoyment of the world. There is much, then, in his writing that is personal – personal to him and appealing personally to his reader. The danger here is to confuse the terms private and personal. As recent studies have suggested, and the newest manuscripts corroborate, whereas Traherne is very often personal, he is hardly ever private. Even his most intimate writings, such as the *Centuries*, which were not dedicated to a large audience but written for a friend, are not exclusive. There may be much in the poetry and in *Centuries* that reads as autobiographical – his highly unusual infant intimations of innocence and eternity may not at all be like our own or anyone else's – but they make no claim to privacy. *Roman Forgeries*, of course, as well as recently available texts such as the *Select Meditations* and *A Sober View of Dr Twisse*, show him to be deeply concerned with public affairs. Even the better-known texts that have an intimate tone may be read as intended for an extending circle. The well-known inscription inside *Centuries of Meditations* that reads

> This book unto the friend of my best friend
> As of the wisest Love a mark I send,
> That she may write my Maker's prais therin
> And make her self thereby a Cherubin.

suggests that the work was intended to be added to by the recipient, thought to be Susannah Hopton. As Raymond-Jean Frontain notes, Traherne, having learned from the psalmist David how to praise God, passes his meditations on to his friend Susannah Hopton, and she to her devotional circle; by historic anomaly, the modern print reader too becomes, in the imaginative act of continuing the unfinished fifth Century, a part of the creative circle to which the work calls us. This is saying more than that a manuscript circulated to a small circle of friends can be a public act, or that conversely a printed text may in fact be intended for a specific individual reader. The whole of Traherne's work exists in the context of a wider debate concerning private and public acts of prayer and praise; his work carries within it the tensions of corporate and individual good. As we will see, for Traherne salvation of the person occurs in the context of the community of faith and indeed of the nation.

Alongside the nature-loving mystic and the visionary poet, then, we also need to note other voices in Traherne: the loyal friend, the theologian, the controversialist who adopts debating positions, the philosopher, the psalm singer, the prayerful meditant, the catechist, the instructor of other ministers, the parson, the amateur scientist, the scholar, the benefactor. Alongside the gentle Traherne, we must read the controversial Traherne; alongside the mystical Traherne we need to see the political divine. We have hailed him as a poet of childhood, a poet of happiness, a nature-loving mystic whose singular vision invites us to a life of joy. He has fed our growing environmental concern and spoken to our human longings, and he has inspired many of our favourite spiritual writers: C. S. Lewis, Thomas Merton, Dorothy Sayers, Elizabeth Jennings, Annie Dillard. But we have not given him a credible theological context. Nor have we commonly seen the full range of his varied styles – poetic, encyclopedic, polemic, political, mystic, musing, confessional – running cheek by jowl. The purpose of this book, then, is twofold: to offer for the first time an introduction to all of his works in a single volume, and to begin to open doors on aspects of his theology.

Studies of Traherne as a theologian have often been beset by problems of Christian orthodoxy. So strong is his love of nature and his confidence in the goodness of creation that some critics have raised the question of whether Traherne is more of a 'nature mystic' than a Christian.[6] Some

---

6 For example, for Alison Sherrington, *Mystical Symbolism in the Poetry of Thomas Traherne* (St Lucia, Queensland: University of Queensland Press, 1970) Traherne's poetry is about mystical union not with Christ, but with the world. Franz Wohrer (*Thomas Traherne: The Growth of a Mystic's Mind: A Study of the Evolution and the Phenomenology of Traherne's Mystical Consciousness*, Salzburg Studies in English Literature, University of Salzburg, 1982) confines Traherne's nature mysticism to an 'irreligious phase' of his life. Keith Salter

have noted a lack of clear Christology,[7] or suggested a Pelagian lack of redemption theology and an absence of passion imagery.[8] The new Traherne discoveries will go some way to correcting these misapprehensions; for instance, in *A Sober View of Dr Twisse*[9] Traherne sets out a correction of Pelagius, and *The Kingdom of God*[10] explores Christ's work on the cross. More importantly than these individual arguments, however, the new manuscripts show us a Traherne who is at once deep and broad in his study of theology, a person devoted both to the minute details of doctrine and to the sweeping philosophical implications of a God who loves and seeks to be loved by his creation. The same Traherne, and not the same Traherne; or rather, the same Traherne seen in different light and from a new angle. This book attempts to make connections between the Traherne we have long known and the one we are now discovering. Arranged according to theme, it seeks to explore several strands of his theology and practice, looking at him not primarily as a poet or mystic or philosopher, though all of these strands inevitably appear, but first of all as a priest engaged in some of the questions that seventeenth-century theology and parish ministry raised. This book is only a beginning. I hope it will invite others to pursue the theological themes about which Traherne showed great intuition in his peculiar blend of poetic image and intellectual exploration.

A huge amount of fine critical study has preceded this book, a good deal by English literature experts whose careful and inspiring work over the years has greatly increased our knowledge of Traherne's poetry, his sources and influences, and the shape of his thought.[11] Among these

(*Thomas Traherne: Mystic and Poet*, London: Edward Arnold, 1964) suggests pantheism, as does Robin Attfield ('Thomas Traherne and the Location of Intrinsic Value', *Religious Traditions*, 6, 1983).

7 In Peter Maitland's *Thomas Traherne's Path to Felicity: The Missing Christ* (MA Carleton University, Canada, 1994), Traherne's experience transcends Christianity. See also Pat Pinsent, 'The Image of Christ in the Writings of Two Seventeenth-Century English Country Parsons: George Herbert and Thomas Traherne', in S. Porter, M. Hayes and D. Tombs, eds, *Images of Christ: Ancient and Modern*, Sheffield, UK: Sheffield Academic Press, 1997.

8 See K. W. Salter, 'Traherne and A Romantic Heresy', *Notes and Queries*, Vol. 200 (1955), pp. 153–6; and Michael Ponsford, 'Traherne's Apostacy', *Durham University Journal*, 76:2 (1984).

9 See *SV*, II, 'the fall'; also 'free grace'.

10 *KOG*, Ch. 14, ll. 145–69.

11 A. L. Clements, Stanley Stewart, Leigh DeNeef, Alison Sherrington, Carol Marks, Malcolm Day, Julia Smith, Barbara Lewalski and Nabil Matar could be

critics and others, there often emerges a detailed way of reading Traherne theologically that has to do with reading him alongside the theological treatises of his day. His writings can be seen as a response to millenarianism nonconformists, Papists, Calvinists, Arminians, Baptists, Quakers; his relationship to his patron Sir Orlando Bridgeman, Lord Keeper of the Seal, and his loyalty to him after he fell out of favour with the Catholic-leaning Charles, raises interesting politico-theological questions. Traherne was a man formed by and informing his world, deeply embedded in his own time, rooted in its cultural past and open to the future it anticipated.

What surprises me as I read these studies is not so much that Traherne the parish priest was also deeply engaged in the politics of his day, but that what comes out of this engagement so resonates with our own time. This volume, therefore, while attendant to the historic context of the seventeenth century, also seeks to place Traherne's theology in the flow of Christian theology as a whole, looking back to his antecedents and forward to our own day.[12] No doubt much of his work was written as a response to specific events of his time. His response, while not necessarily mild, does tend to steer the middle ground in a way that has become typically Anglican, and distilled from his work we find intimations of what it means to be human so that one feels his writing, while it may often be conceived as a response, results in an exploration. What kind of creatures are we? How may we find happiness? What about the problem of sin? How free are we? How should we live? These are the questions from Traherne this volume seeks to address.

---

the beginning of the list. More recently, see the work of Carol Ann Johnston and Jacob Blevins.

12 This work is already begun. See A. M. Allchin, *Participation in God: A Forgotten Strand in Anglican Tradition*, London: Darton, Longman & Todd, 1988; 'The Sacrifice of Praise and Thanksgiving', in A. M. Allchin, Anne Ridler and Julia Smith, eds, *Profitable Wonders: Aspects of Traherne*, Oxford: Amate, 1989; A. M. Allchin, *The Joy of All Creation*, London: New City, 1993; Mark McIntosh, *Discernment and Truth*, New York: Herder and Herder, 2004; David Ford, *Self and Salvation*, Cambridge: Cambridge University Press, 1999; and David Ford, *Christian Wisdom*, Cambridge: Cambridge University Press, 2007.

Traherne's life

The records Traherne left are fewer than any biographer would like. We have a few dates from parish and college records that form a kind of skeleton of his life, which can be fleshed out with scraps disclosed in his own asides, comments of churchwardens, colleagues, gossip writers; and we have the additional information we glean from new manuscript discoveries. From all of these a 'collage' image of the man emerges. His probable year of birth is 1637, six years after fellow poet John Donne's death. We have the dates of his entry into Brasenose College, Oxford in 1652 at the age of 15, of his BA in 1656 and MA in 1661. We know that he was appointed to the rural parish of Cred-enhill in Herefordshire in 1657 and ordained in October 1660. He is believed to have become chaplain to Sir Orlando Bridgeman, Lord Keeper of the Seal, in 1669, although recent scholarship suggests that this may have happened as late as 1673. He published his first work, *Roman Forgeries*, in 1673 and died in the first week of October 1674 at Bridgeman's house in Teddington.

Background and character

The seventeenth-century historian Anthony À Wood describes Traherne simply as 'a shoemaker's son of Hereford'. From this, and from Traherne's own memories of relative poverty, early biographers con-strued a poor and possibly orphaned Traherne; a more recent view is that he was neither, although precise details of his family life remain sketchy. Contemporary gossip writer John Aubrey records a story of Traherne's indicating that there were two apprentices living in the Traherne household,[13] and it is likely that Traherne's cobbler father, who was a freeman of the city, may in fact have been the master crafts-man of a small cottage industry and Traherne a member of the rising middle class.[14] In *The Kingdom of God* Traherne claims to be writing from his own experience when he states: 'One of those Causes that

13 See John Aubrey, *Miscellanies Upon Various Subjects*, 1696, pp. 129–30.
14 For this and additional biographical matter see Julia Smith's entry on Traherne, *Dictionary of National Biography*, Oxford: Oxford University Press, 2004, Vol. 55, pp. 205–8.

made my Father Delightfull to me upon Earth was the Convenient House and Estate I did inherit by descending from him.'[15]

What kind of person Traherne was is less mysterious. Aubrey described him as 'a learned a sober person';[16] his churchwarden calls him 'a Godlie man . . . a devout liver'.[17] He visited the sick and educated the young, a faithful priest who sometimes found the task of loving his flock wearing. He remained unmarried following his own advice, recently discovered, 'To give one Self wholly and Singly to God . . . and love all Mankind in him . . . That is, evry person in the whole World, with as near and violent affection. As I would my Wife, or my Dearest Friend'.[18] He was well educated, and by all accounts affable.

A friend describes him as 'a man of cheerful and sprightly Temper, free from any thing of the sourness of formality, by which some great pretenders of Piety rather disparage and misrepresent true Religion, than recommend it. And therefore was very affable and pleasant in his Conversation'. He was also so 'wonderfully transported with the Love of God to Mankind . . . that those that would converse with him, were forced to endure some discourse upon these subjects, whether they had any sense of Religion, or not'.[19] Well meaning to all, he must have seemed as irksome to the irreligious as he was engaging to the pious.

Traherne confesses that he talked too much. 'Reservation and Silence: are my Desires', he wrote, 'O that I could attain them: Too much proneness to Speak is my Diseas.'[20] He was passionate about what he believed, and the heated debates recorded in the Introduction to *Roman Forgeries* and in *Commentaries of Heaven*, to which we will return later, show Traherne to be a fiery opponent, as emotionally engaged in his work as he was intellectually keen and meticulous. Traherne could argue his point tenaciously, often jumping in with both feet and saying more than, on reflection, he may have liked to have said. He prayed for divine assistance to overcome this fault: 'O my God make me faithfull, lively, constant; and Since thou hast Given me a Tongue . . .

---

15 *KOG*, Ch. 34, ll. 11–14.

16 Aubrey, *Miscellanies*, pp. 129–30.

17 Hereford County Records Office, Registrar's files, 1667 / 349.

18 *ITR*, ll. 412–13, 430–2.

19 From the Preface to *A Serious and Pathetical Contemplation of the Mercies of God, in several most Devout and Sublime Thankgsivings for the same*. London: George Hickes, 1699.

20 *SM*, III, 65.

Teach me to use it moderately Prudently Seasonably to thy Glory. Amen.'[21] And he resolved to improve: 'I will be more silent when they talk of vanitie. And since I cannot accompany their Imaginations and the thoughts of God; I will either overrule their Souls, or Depart the company' (*SM*, III, 2). But verbosity seemed always a thorn in his side.

His arguments with the Roman Catholic Church and with the 'Independents' were equally strident. Where the Roman church was a 'Mother of Lyes' and a black-footed 'Peacock',[22] the independent preachers of his day were 'Ignorant Zealots' (*SM*, I, 85) and 'Narrow Souls' (*SM*, III, 25; I, 87) whose thoughts were so absurd, that it was 'even a part of felicity to detest and hate them' (*SM*, III, 25). Such extreme sentiments were the stuff of seventeenth-century life – the ordinary political and religious parlance in a world in which faith was a matter of life and death – and in speaking so vociferously Traherne is a man of his time. He loved the re-established church in England, speaking possessively of 'the Beautifull union of my Nationall church!' (*SM*, I, 85); and he would defend her vigorously against 'the Ingratitude of Pious persons, that would tear out the Bowels of that church which gav them a Beginning' (*SM*, III, 24).

In common with many writers, he took criticisms to heart, licked the wounds and defended himself.[23] Yet as we now know from new manuscript discoveries, he subjected his work to the eyes of a critical reader who pulled no punches, writing such comments as: 'This is not soe pertinent and profitable as it is daingerous, and Inconvenient and seemingly Arrogant if not Impious' (*ITR*, l. 1016) and: 'This is not well at all for a Junior to say to such a man as this was' (*SV*, XXI,

---

21 *SM*, II, 100.

22 *RF*, Ch. 18 ends: 'Surely the feet upon which this Peacock stands, are very Black' and he concludes his final chapter by suggesting that the Roman Church, a 'Mother of Lyes', 'espoused to the Father of Lyes', has produced an 'adulterate brood' and so is 'defiled with so great an Off-spring of notorious Impostures'. Of Cardinals and Jesuits he writes: 'Cunning Wits such as Cardinals & Jesuits, may perhaps when they are disposed to do it impose upon old Women & ignorant Tradesmen, having no better defence than their narrow reach & shallow Brain' (*COH*, 'Ascension', fol. 139r).

23 'Here I am censured for Speaking in the Singular number, and Saying I. All these Things are done for me ... There it shall be our Glory and the Joy of all to Acknowledge, I. I am the Lords, and He is mine. Every one shall Speak in the first Person, and it shall be Gods Glory that He is the Joy of all. Can the friend of GOD, and the Heir of all Things in Heaven and Earth forbear to say, I' (*SM*, III, 65).

l. 39). He seems to have written as prolifically as he talked, judging not only by the comments of his contemporaries but also by his prodigious output (he was still adding to *Roman Forgeries* as it was going to press). And he wrote for a broad range of audiences: *Roman Forgeries* for the general public, *Commentaries of Heaven* for 'Publick Persons' who were the 'Watchmen & Bulwarks of Christianity' and also for the 'Satisfaction of Atheists', *Inducements to Retirednesss* for 'the pious soul', *Christian Ethicks* for the ordinary layman, *Centuries* for a friend. And yet in the midst of this incessant oral and written conversation, he repeatedly highlights the need for quiet, retiredness, introversion and reflection. It was almost as if he craved solitude as much as he needed an audience.

He lived a relatively simple though by no means penurious life – his living was worth £50 per year. This seems to have been more than enough for him in terms of both wealth and station: 'Exhaltations and Honors, among Riches and Beauties, hav persued me, as much as they hav fled from other men', he wrote in *Inducements to Retiredness*; 'I hav tasted the very Cream of Earthly Delights. And hav had many Treasures under my Hand by way of Eminence' (*ITR*, ll. 248–50). He enjoyed what he had and he was generous. He was a Brasenose bene-factor in 1664, the time at which the college was building its chapel, cloister and library. He owned several houses in Hereford. In his will he gave his books and his best hat to his brother Philip, his second-best hat to his servant, a ring to each of the ladies of the house, and tokens of thanks to all the servants.[24] After his death the several houses he had owned in the city became almshouses for the poor: an entirely appropriate disposal of the estate of one who is recorded as being, while he lived, 'Charitable to the Poor almost beyond his ability'.[25]

Career, friends and associates

His career was mostly though not exclusively parochial. Alongside his parish ministry he worked with the cathedral clergy in Hereford and carried on with his writing. At some point between 1669 and 1673 he became chaplain to Sir Orlando Bridgeman, Lord Keeper of the Seal,

24 For a transcription of the nuncupative will and other biographical details, see Margoliouth's Introduction to *Centuries, Poems and Thanksgivings*, Oxford: Clarendon Press, 1958.
25 See the Preface to *A Serious and Pathetical Contemplation*.

in whose Teddington household he died. In contrast to those ministers who took a living but left the care of the souls to a curate, Traherne seems to have been a 'hands on' clergyman, according to the testimony of his churchwarden (1673): 'Our minister is continually resident amongst us'.[26] The parish records suggest Credenhill to be either small or sparsely populated, with only two baptisms, three marriages and three burials in the most lively year, 1667.[27] Yet Traherne went about his work there diligently; his churchwardens describe him as 'a goo[d] & Godlie man well Learned . . . a good Preacher of gods word',[28] who visited the poor and did duly 'Instruct the youth.'[29] Evidence of his relationships with parishioners and with local clergy can be found in local records as well as in his writings. The parish register is signed in his own hand from 1664 to 1668 and in 1672. His churchwarden's comment in 1673 that he was continually resident challenges an earlier belief that he became Bridgeman's chaplain in 1669. It may be that he was a visitor in Bridgeman's London home and did not move to Bridgeman's household until after Bridgeman's removal to Teddington in 1673–74, or that in fact he was not appointed chaplain until 1673 or thereabouts.

That is not to say that he was intellectually or socially isolated. The fact that he was on book-borrowing terms with the Lady Margaret Professor and Provost of Queen's College, Dr Barlow,[30] suggests that he retained at least some of his Oxford contacts. Other Oxford-educated fellow clergy were within reach of his parish in Credenhill, as were eminent local families. He was close to his younger brother Philip. Somewhere along the way Traherne was admitted to what he describes in *Christian Ethicks* as 'the society and friendship of Great men, where a Nod or a Word is able to prevail more, than the strength of Oxen and Horses'.[31] Some of these friendships went beyond mere sociability; in Bridgeman's household or before it, Traherne discovered, by experience, what it was like to become a most trusted friend. For he writes: 'they [great men] will entrust their Wives and Children in [a friend's] hands, as I have often experienced; their Gold, their Bonds, their Souls, their Affairs, their lives, their Secrets, Houses, Liberties, and Lands; and

26 Hereford County Records Office, Registrar's files, 1673 / 488.

27 One of those buried in 1667, 'Edward Traherne Late of the City of Hereford', may have been a member of Traherne's family.

28 Hereford County RO, Registrar's files, 1667 / 349.

29 Hereford County RO, registrar's files, 1673 / 488.

30 *RF*, p. 90.

31 *CE*, edited Carol Marks, p. 173.

be glad of such a Friend in whom to be safe'.[32] Although Traherne valued these close and trusting friendships, they were never enough to satisfy his need to belong to all humankind and all humankind to belong to him. In *Inducements to Retiredness* he confesses, rather disappointedly, 'I hav reason to believ that I hav had as many Strict and Close Amities, with Persons of the Greatest Principles and Bravest Worth. But all that I hav learned from them was Solomons Vanity.' He had high expectations for friendship, believing it required more intimacy and emotional commitment than marriage.[33] His disappointment with human friendship is directly related to a similarly high ambition to love infinitely as God does, for he adds: 'I must be Beloved of all Mankind. And be the Image of the Dietie, and reign Enthroned in the Bosom of God; or els for ever be Dissatisfied.'[34] But it may also be that he had experienced the breakdown of friendship. 'A Close Illimited Friendship is a Divine Enjoyment: could it be always pure, Sincere and perfect', he writes in *Inducements to Retiredness*; 'But so many thousand Things conspire as Ingredients to compose and make up a Perfect friend, that I shall sooner Expect an Angel to be Conversant here on Earth, then such a Person.'[35] He could be speaking theoretically here, but these comments, while not necessarily bitter, seem to suggest a personal knowledge of human affairs. And 'if the Temper be lively and vigorous in my friend, the Resentments will be: if it be flat and insipid, there is an Abatement of the Pleasure. I confess that a Golden and Complying Humor, will smooth and Polish many Asperities',[36] reads as testimonial. Although Traherne acknowledges the limits of human friendship, he never despairs of it entirely; 'for Man is made a Sociable Creature', he admits a few lines later, 'and is never Happy till His Capacities are filled with all their Objects'.[37] Perhaps once bitten twice shy, and certainly experienced in human relationships, he concludes: 'It is better only to hav an infinit Benevolence toward all the World, a Moderate friendship with the Good and Excellent: an Intire Illimited friendship with God alone.'[38] This is where his confession of the limits of human friendship is leading – to friendship with God.

32 *CE*, edited Marks, p. 200.
33 See *ITR*, ll. 392–405.
34 *ITR*, ll. 252–4, 255–7.
35 *ITR*, ll. 376–9.
36 *ITR*, ll. 384–7.
37 *ITR*, ll. 272–3.
38 *ITR*, ll. 389–91.

As noted above, he worked closely with the clergy of Hereford cathedral; in 1671 and 1672 he acted as surrogate dean for the Dean of Hereford's consistory court. This was no sinecure, but an appointment that at its busiest required him to be present in Hereford as regularly as every Saturday or every other Saturday for months on end.[39] On his death he was described by Thomas Good, Master of Balliol and Prebendary of Hereford, as 'one of the most pious ingenious men' he had known. As well as regular contact with fellow clergy, he found companionship among the county families, in particular with Sir Edward Harley of Brampton Bryan, Herefordshire, who referred to Traherne on his death as 'my worthy friend'. There are also the unknown friends of *Select Meditations*, abbreviated as 'O my T. G. O my S. H. O my brother!'[40] In addition to these friends and colleagues, Traherne seems to have participated in the manuscript culture of his day, offering his work to be read by others. There is the female friend of the *Centuries*, sometimes thought to be Susannah Hopton. More recently a new manuscript reader has been discovered – Traherne's critical reader of *Inducements to Retiredness* and *A Sober View of Dr Twisse*. As we have seen above, this reader could be fierce over Traherne's excesses. However, the critical reader praises him too, with phrases like 'This is a very Accurate and Pertinent description' and 'This is sound and good'.[41] The reader corrected factual errors when they occurred and reprimanded gently: 'all this is Good and True, but you have said it over and over',[42] as well as fiercely. Similarly, the manuscript of the newly discovered unfinished poem *The Ceremonial Law* bears the comments of an enthusiastic reading friend ('I like this mightily but pray prosecute it . . .'). That Traherne submitted his work to such readers indicates something of his seriousness as a writer and affirms earlier suggestions that he wrote in the company of colleagues.[43]

39 The Acts of Office records of the Dean's Court for 1671 [7002/1/5] record Traherne's presiding presence in court in February, March, April, May, August, September and December; in 1672 three times in January, twice in February, May and June, and again three times in July, among other occasions. The Acts of Instance 1661–1672 [7002/1/13] records show a similarly frequent presence. I am grateful to Rosalind Caird for directing me to the relevant records in the Hereford Cathedral Archives.

40 *SM*, II, 38. Could 'T.G.' refer to Thomas Good cited above (or to Theophilus Gale) and 'S.H.' to Susanna Hopton?

41 *SV*, XIX, l. 76 and XVII, l. 120.

42 *SV*, XVIII, l. 18.

43 See Julia Smith's Introduction to *Select Meditations*, p. xxii; and Traherne entry in *DNB*, pp. 206, 207.

Sources and influences

Throughout his writings, Traherne had the habit of quoting freely from what he had been reading, often without citing his sources. Whole passages are lifted, sometimes altered, sometimes simply planted in the middle of his work and woven in alongside other texts and ideas. Often, in this way, his primary sources go unidentified and whole phrases that are not his own are attributed to him. Untangling the problems of source for each work is therefore a complicated process. This interweaving of texts happens most often with Traherne's use of scripture; he passes in and out of scriptural passages interlacing scripture, sometimes in paraphrase, with his own words as if the phrases of scripture have become the language of his mind. This deep indebtedness to the Bible should not be surprising given the deep grounding in scripture he would have received during his education. The principal of Brasenose during Traherne's time was the Puritan Dr Greenwood, of strict governance; and the college grew and flourished during Greenwood's time, the numbers in residence rising from 20 to 120. The Visitors Register gives examples of the religious rigour which held sway in Traherne's day: 'every Tutor ... at some convenient time beween the houres of seven and tenne in the evening' was to 'cause their Pupills to repair to their chambers to pray with them'; and that 'every Lord's Day' all bachelors of arts and undergraduates were to give 'an account ... of the sermons they have heard, and their attendance on other religious exercises on that day'.[44] Perhaps it is because of that strong biblical grounding in his Puritan days that the Bible remains the most prolific and most powerful influence in Traherne's work. We know from his account in the *Centuries* that at the same period in his life Traherne read Logic, Ethics, Physics, Metaphysics, Geometry, Astronomy, Poesy, Medicine, Grammar, Music and Rhetoric. He mentions Albert Magnus, Galileo, Hevelius, Galen, Hippocrates, Orpheus, Homer and Lilly (*C*, III, 36). Alongside scripture there grew up and remained a wide range of other sources and influences, philosophical, literary and scientific.

One much noted group who influenced Traherne were the Cambridge Platonists: Benjamin Whichcote, John Smith, Peter Sterry, Ralph Cudworth, Nathanael Culverwell, John Worthington and Henry More. We know that Traherne read from all the above writers' works, from the

44 *Visitors Register*, July 1653 and June 1653. See Gladys Wade, *Thomas Traherne*, New York: Octagon, 1969, p. 49.

notes in the *Early Notebook* (Bodl. Ms. Lat. Misc. f. 45.) and in the *Commonplace Book* (Bodl. MS. Eng. Poet. c. 42.). Traherne found himself drawn to the same texts to which they were drawn – from the ancient Hermetic writings attributed to Hermes Trismegistus, through to Plato and Plotinus and on to the Renaissance writers Ficino and Pico della Mirandola.[45] Plato and Plotinus appear scattered throughout Traherne's work, especially in the *Centuries*, and Traherne's interest in Ficino and Pico della Mirandola has been well documented.[46] Traherne's imagery of light and vision, the eye and the mirror, resonate with neo-platonic notions that the ultimate reality is perceived by image or reflection. The Cambridge Platonists all held that there existed in each person a 'natural light', placed there by God, which did not disagree with the light of reason.[47] It is to these 'seeds of natural light', God's 'private Law ... engraven on mens Consciences', that Traherne refers when he speaks of the 'pure and virgin apprehensions' of his infancy and of the 'divine light' in which he was born.[48]

There is much, however, in Traherne that is Aristotelian. His extensive writing on happiness and the life of virtue relies heavily on the

45 Certainly Sterry read Plato, Plotinus and Ficino, these texts being cited among others in his possession by Vivian de Sola Pinto (*Peter Sterry, Platonist and Puritan*, Cambridge: Cambridge University Press, 1934, p. 57). For a fuller account of the literary diet of More and the other Platonists see Carol Marks, 'Traherne and Cambridge Platonism', *Publications of the Modern Language Association*, 81 (1966), pp. 521–3.

46 See Marks, 'Traherne's Church Year-Book', *Papers of the Bibliographical Society of America*, 58 (1964), pp. 31–72; 'Thomas Traherne and Cambridge Platonism', *PMLA*, 81 (1966): 521–34; 'Thomas Traherne and Hermes Trismegistus', *Renaissance News*, 19 (1966), pp. 118–31; 'Thomas Traherne's Commonplace Book', *PBSA*, 60 (1966), pp. 458–65; 'Traherne's Ficino Notebook', *PBSA*, 63 (1969), pp. 73–81; and Introduction to *Christian Ethicks*, Ithaca: Cornell 1968.

47 Culverwell, for instance, refers to 'cleare and undelible Principles, some first and Alphabetical Notions', which 'are stampt and printed upon the being of man'. And in Traherne's *Commonplace Book* we find the following: 'And indeed these common seeds of naturall Light are a private Law, which God has deeply engraven on mens consciences, and is universally extensive unto all, though with a latitude of Degrees; it being in some more, in some Lesse, but in all in great measure obliterated, and defaced since the fall. It is also by Divines generally termed the Light, or Law of Nature, because it flows in, and with, and from Human Nature, eyther immediately, or mediately' (*CB*, under the heading 'Reason', fol. 83 col. 1, quoted from Theophilus Gale, *Court of the Gentiles*, Vol. I, part II.

48 C, III, 1.

Aristotelian/Thomist tradition, and he chooses Aristotle's causes as the structure of his most in-depth treatise on philosophical theology, *The Kingdom of God*. In this balance between Plato and Aristotle, as in many of his theological theories, Traherne shares much with his fellow theologian 'the judicious [Richard] Hooker',[49] who was also deeply imbued with the Platonic/Aristotelian combination and with the work of the Church Fathers. Traherne's patristic and medieval sources are many: Gregory of Nyssa, Gregory the Great, Irenaeus, Augustine, Aquinas, Thomas a Kempis, John Chrysostom, to name a few. There are correlations between his work and that of Maximus the Confessor, whose *Four Hundred Chapters on Love* bear a remarkable resemblance to Traherne's *Centuries*.[50] *Seeds of Eternity* adds to the list of Traherne's sources Cicero[51] and Justin Martyr, as well as the Jesuit scholars of Coimbria University in Portugal, whose Latin translations of Aristotle and others who wrote on the soul were very popular among advanced scholars of the seventeenth century.

Traherne was also very much involved in popular theology. As we shall see, Traherne specifically sets *Christian Ethicks*, his major work on virtue, over against Richard Allestree's *The Whole Duty of Man*, the most popular handbook on holy living in its day. Donald Allchin reminds, us that in the *Church's Year-Book*, an unpublished manuscript that both meditates on and expounds the feasts of the church year,[52] Traherne makes use of Lancelot Andrewes, Richard Hooker, Jeremy Taylor, George Herbert, Daniel Fealtry, William Austin and several Commonwealth Prayer Book commentaries. This, coupled with the scholarly digging of *A Sober View*, is indicative of the kind of contemporary theological scholarship that fed his work. Alongside these philosophical and theological sources come the long list of scientists who also fired Traherne's imagination, some of whom are mentioned above,

49 *KOG*, Ch. 22, ll. 1–4. 'The judicious Hooker, that Glorious Beam of the English Church, and the admired Star of all his Nation, wading into the spring and fountain of Laws, and digging neer into the root of things, hath some Sage and important Maxims which he casteth up like Sparkling Jewels.'

50 I am indebted to Sam Wells who first pointed me in the direction of Maximus the Confessor, a link also noted by John Stewart Allit in *Thomas Traherne Il Poeta-Teologo*, Milan: Edizioni Villadiseriane, 2007.

51 Traherne uses the name Tully.

52 For a fuller account of this work see Allchin, 'The Sacrifice of Praise and Thanksgiving' in *Profitable Wonders*, pp. 22–37. For extracts of the *Year-Book* see A. M. Allchin, *Landscapes of Glory: Daily Readings with Thomas Traherne*, London: Darton, Longman & Todd, 1989.

as well as fellow poets: George Herbert, for instance, appears in the *Church's Year-Book* and in *The Kingdom of God*, Spenser in *Commentaries of Heaven*, and Francis Quarles and William Austin in the notebooks.

Traherne's works

Of the many works Thomas Traherne wrote, only his fiercest was published in his lifetime. A second work, which he had been preparing for publication when he died, appeared the year after his death, and another a few years later; then there is a silence until the turn of the twentieth century when his famous *Centuries of Meditations* and his poems were discovered on a shabby book barrow in London. He was hailed as a 'newly discovered' poet; further manuscripts trickled into the public arena in the mid and later part of the twentieth century, and the century culminated with the double discovery, alluded to earlier, of the Lambeth Manuscript works and *The Ceremonial Law*. These most recent discoveries, with other Traherne manuscripts, are still being transcribed, edited and published. As this happens it may be that dates for the works will emerge, but because there is not yet a clear chronology of when each work was written I have listed them here roughly in order of publication. Parts of some of the unpublished works, fragments and notebooks listed below have appeared in articles and anthologies, but none of them has been published entire. *Meditations on the Six Days of Creation* has been published several times, but its authorship remains uncertain. Some critics claim it as the work of Traherne, some as the work of his friend Susannah Hopton.

Early publications:
Roman Forgeries (1673)
Christian Ethicks (1675)
The Thanksgivings (1699)

Twentieth-century publications:
Centuries of Meditations, discovered 1896–97, published 1908
The poetry:
   The Poetical Works, Dobell MS, published 1903
   The Poems of Felicity, Burney MS, published 1910
Select Meditations, discovered 1964, published 1997

Twenty-first century publications:
The works of the Lambeth Manuscript, published 2005:
  Inducements to Retiredness
  A Sober View of Dr Twisse
  Love
  Seeds of Eternity
  The Kingdom of God
Commentaries of Heaven, British Library MS, identified 1981, published 2007

Unpublished works:
The Ceremonial Law, Folger MS, discovered 1997
The Commonplace Book, Bodleian MS
Early Notebook, Bodleian MS
Church's Year-Book, Bodleian MS
The Ficino Notebook, British Library MS

Work in question:
Meditations on the Six Days of Creation, authorship uncertain

Roman Forgeries

This highly political and controversial text, the only book that Traherne published in his lifetime, attempts to prove that many documents, encyclicals, letters and records of early councils held by the Roman Catholic Church are forgeries. These forgeries, claims Traherne, fatally undermine the authority and structures of the Roman Catholic Church. His basic belief is that authority in the early church was not centralized and should not be so now, that national churches should apply their own disciplines locally, their bishops conferring together with bishops of other national churches as equals, that the Bishop of Rome should not have pre-eminence, and that the existing pre-eminence he enjoyed had been won through deceit, expurgation of texts, suppression of dissent and a fraudulent rewriting of history. Using Irenaeus' theory for discerning heresies, he sets out to examine the writings that followed the first 420 years of early, and he would argue idyllic, Catholicism. The treatise is immensely learned: he read widely in early texts in order to compile his arguments, which attack Roman Catholic authority and historicity rather than doctrine. By focusing on the Council of Nicea,

which was honoured by both Catholics and Protestants, as being 'of
great Authority; next to the Holy Bible, the very first, and most indis-
putable [authority] that is' (sig. A7), he allows himself at once to refute
Rome and remain within the teachings of the 'one holy Catholick and
Apostolic Church'. His method purports to be propelled by unity, as
is his vision of the primitive church, but there is a profound dis-ease in
the work, as if the religious anger of his age spills out on the pages. As
one critic has noted, 'his rhetoric is bound by the fury of its own time'.[53]
If his language is no more intemperate than that of his peers, he also,
like many of them, shows in his detailed textual research a wish to
move away from revelation towards reason in matters divine. Traherne
seeks to address the same question as Browne's *Religio Medici*: how
does an intellectually vigorous person of religious conviction arrive at
the truth amid the competing claims of churches? Dismayed by both
the unquestioning obedience of Roman Catholicism and the diverse
independent voices of the 'sola scriptura' tradition, he offers an answer
in *Roman Forgeries* that relies on the scientific collection and presen-
tation of evidence, that simultaneously calls for critical thinking and
demands that the reader think those critical thoughts within the bounds
of an ecumenically accepted creed. In this as in many respects,
Traherne's treatise follows close in the tracks of Thomas James, first
librarian to Sir Thomas Bodley and fellow at Oxford, whose 1611 *A
Treatise of the Corruption of Scripture, Councels, and Fathers, by the
Prelats, Pastors, and Pillars of the Church of Rome, for Maintenance
of Popery and Irreligion* similarly traced forged documents, counterfeit
treatises and texts expurgated. Like Traherne, he approaches his work
as a serious scholar seeking to secure religious faith on reason, and like
Traherne he sets up the atmosphere of a courtroom with his readers as
a jury. Traherne's tone, structure and style of argument are all strikingly
similar to those of James.[54]

The work shares, with *A Sober View of Dr Twisse*, *Commentaries
of Heaven*, and to a lesser extent *Select Meditations*, a passion for the
shape and future of the Church in England. Where once *Roman
Forgeries* was seen as a singular text because of its confrontational
tone, it may now be seen as one link in a chain of Traherne's writings

53 Stanley Stewart, *The Expanded Voice: The Art of Thomas Traherne*, San
Marino: Huntington Library, 1970, p. 30.

54 For deeper analysis of the similarities between these works and for the
fullest study of *Roman Forgeries* I have found see Stewart, *The Expanded Voice*,
pp. 16–44.

whose concern is to define and defend the emerging post-Restoration Church in England.

Christian Ethicks

Intended by Traherne for publication but published posthumously, in the year after his death, *Christian Ethicks* is Traherne's extensive study of the virtues with a stated aim of leading its reader to 'true felicity' in this temporal life as well as in the hereafter. The 33 chapters of this book, though much less well known than *Centuries* or his poetry, are even more explicit about happiness than they are. Traherne operates here as a serious logician persuading his public, rather than as a spiritual philosopher communing with God, with himself, with a friend. Less intimate than *Centuries*, less inclined towards childhood than the poems, in *Christian Ethicks* Traherne addresses himself not, as other contemporary treatises on virtue did, to the simple, pious reader looking for a guide to the dutiful life, but to 'the curious and unbelieving soul', in the belief that the beauty of virtue will prove irresistible. Although the book shows a certain intellectual rigour in its arguments, its refutation of Hobbes's materialism and its nuanced explication of the virtues, Traherne's complete confidence in the irresistibility of virtue means that it reads as somewhat unrooted, optimistic, even incredible to many modern readers. We have lost a sense of what happiness is, let alone where it may be found. We seek it in ecstatic moments, in the satisfaction of superficial desire: for many of us, happiness is really not much more than the dregs of our empty teacup, a by-product of our voracious consumption. We feel it as fleeting, ephemeral, unattainable, even unreliable. Not only does it elude us, we fear it also deludes us. As Margaret Botrall notes of happiness in her introduction to the modern version of *Christian Ethicks*, 'We can neither compass the ethical notion that it is the crown of a wise and noble life, nor the religious notion that it is the fulfilment of the soul's desire for union with the divine.' For Traherne, it is both of the above. His understanding of happiness is altogether more robust than ours; so convinced is he of its solidity that he builds the entire work premised on its eventual inevitability, its essential reality, its place as the soul's origin and home.

Traherne classes the virtues of this happy life as belonging to one of three states through which we pass: the estate of innocency, the estate of misery and grace, and the estate of glory. Those belonging to the first and final estates are eternal, whereas the 'harsh and sour virtues occasioned by the fall', such as patience, fortitude and meekness belong to the second and were not, he contends, initially intended by God. Traherne sees some virtues as the food of the soul, some as medicines only, some as essential to felicity and some accidental to it. His categorizing of virtues in this way, downgrading the grittiest virtues and exalting the loftier ones, reflects the work's concern with the beauty of holiness rather than with straightforward prudential morality. He is holding up the highest virtues as the standard: 'A straight line is the measure both of itself and of a crooked one', writes Traherne in the introduction, 'To the Reader', so the virtues make all vice appear like dirt before a jewel. Virtue, in its rich and alluring forms, is so much more enticing than paltry and squalid vice. It inflames the heart, excites the desire and enriches the mind; happiness lies within the grasp of any who will exchange false values for true ones. There are times when *Christian Ethicks* seems to suggest that right thinking, a kind of cognitive therapy, is the way to happiness, but thinking alone can never cure the soul. Traherne insists that to feel is as necessary as to see. We must be transformed in our hearts if the model of virtue is to take root: 'Covet a lively sense of all you know of the excellency of God and of Eternal Love, of your own excellency. And of all objects whatsoever. For to feel is as necessary as to see their glory' (*CE*, introduction).

In its emphasis on human liberty, volition and act, *Christian Ethicks* touches one of the central intellectual questions of Traherne's day: freedom or necessity. This question is treated in much more detail in *A Sober View of Dr Twisse*, which gives its whole attention to the Calvinist/Arminian debate on election and free will. However, while the free choice/predestination debate runs alongside *Christian Ethicks*, the work's recurring treatment of liberty, volition and act has a more pointed purpose than moderating an internal Christian debate; it offers a specifically Christian answer to secular morality. Resisting the Hobbesian and Grotian view of morality as a contract between equals, Traherne ignores questions of conduct, not because he is unaware of the problems of sin and the practical benefits of morality, but because he wants to redress the balance that had, in Hobbes and Grotius, reduced morality from an issue of the will to a description of a person's movements. He writes a treatise that will inflame the reader and excite desire for virtue precisely because for him the will is central in matters moral. *Christian Ethicks*, his treatise on virtue, is perhaps less misty-eyed and rosy than has hitherto been thought.

The Thanksgivings

The Thanksgivings are nine long prose/poems of gratitude reminiscent in style of Lancelot Andrewes' *Preces Privatae*. They comprise 'Thanksgivings for the Body', '. . . for the Soul', '. . . for the Glory of God's Works', '. . . for the Blessedness of God's Ways', '. . . for the Blessedness of his Laws', '. . . for the Beauty of his Providence', '. . . for the Wisdom of his Word', '. . . for God's Attributes', and 'A Thanksgiving and Prayer for the Nation'. Traherne explores in detail the reasons to be thankful by listing, reflecting, distinguishing one reason from another, enumerating, linking, quoting from scripture. It is not uncommon for a single Thanksgivings to go on for nine or ten pages; and, as Andrewes does, he organizes his ideas using brackets, indentation and varied types of verse form in order to keep the wide-ranging ideas poised. *The Thanksgivings* show a devotional and prayerful Traherne, steeped in scripture, especially the Psalms, whose thanksgivings are as instructive to the person praying or reading as they are praising of God. He often speaks in the first person, but his eye is also on the general and parochial, the needs of his congregation and of his nation. He prays that each 'creature of his habitation' might be made an image of God to him:

In every one of those,
As the Sun shineth both naked to mine eye
Again in a mirror
Hast thou given me thy self
A second time.

He also revels in the vastness and in the infinite capacity of his soul made in the image of God. *The Thanksgivings* also reveal a good deal about Traherne's political and social ideals, his love of the infinite, his distress at his own failings and the failings of others, and his capacity for joy in a pitched blend of penitence and praise, humility and exaltation not unlike the psalmist David whom he seeks to emulate.

Centuries of Meditations

Commonly known simply as the *Centuries*, these prose meditations, together with the poetry, are Traherne's best known and some would say finest work. Written in groups of 100, there are four complete Centuries exploring his themes of childhood, a good creation, the capacity of the soul, its proneness to love, its astute desire, enjoying the world, his thirst for felicity, and the active nature of the soul. The fifth Century, in which Traherne investigates infinity, remains unfinished. Here, in the *Centuries* more than anywhere else except perhaps *The Kingdom of God*, Traherne is master of the Affirmative Way. The world is full of God's glory and life, the *Centuries* say. We come to know God's nature and his love through the creation, which is essentially good. It is partly from the lack of emphasis on sin apparent in *Centuries* that Traherne has inherited a Pelagian label. Diverging strongly from the tradition of mystics such as St John of the Cross, for whom the world is that from which the soul must free itself, Traherne calls his reader to embrace every part of creation as fully as possible, to desire and aspire, and to trace, in the thirsts that cannot be quenched, the thirst of God. 'Never was any thing in this World loved too much', he insists, 'but many Things hav been loved in a fals Way: and all in too short a Measure.' 'You must want like a God that like God you may be satisfied.' The *Centuries* are ecstatic, autobiographical, repetitive and rich. In his vision of the whole world present in a grain of sand we may hear echoes of Julian of Norwich, who saw the whole world in a hazelnut shell, and Traherne's moments of ecstatic abandon reverberate sonorously with the spontaneous abandonment of Teresa of Avila. It is not surprising that many readers of the *Centuries* have considered Traherne's voice to be more mystic than theologian.

This is not a work to be read at a single sitting; the prose is so rich that one has to moderate one's intake or suffer an intellectual fate not dissimilar to the physical discomfort of the gourmand. Yet this use of repetition and layering in *Centuries* is part of its strength. Not unlike Augustine's *Confessions* and *De Trinitate* or St Bonaventure's methods of meditation, Traherne's repetition of the known draws the reader towards knowledge of the unknown.[55] His meditations on desire and on the cross in the first Century are remarkable for their repetitive

55 See Louis Martz, *The Paradise Within: Studies in Vaughan, Traherne and Milton*, New Haven and London: Yale University Press, 1964.

effectiveness. What saves the work from being a handbook to personal satisfaction is Traherne's reiteration of the interconnectedness of souls, his ecstatic vision of happiness found in mutual giving and receiving: 'We never enjoy ourselves but when we are the Joy of others', he writes, 'Till you lov Men so as to Desire their Happiness, with a Thirst equal to the zeal of your own: till you Delight in GOD for being Good to all: you never Enjoy the World' (C, I, 30).

The Poetry

Traherne is often at his most poetic in his prose writing, and there are moments in his poetry that could be called prosaic. Poems occur in most of his prose manuscripts, and there are forms like the *Thanksgivings* that waver between poetry and prose. Separating out his poetry into a discrete unit could therefore seem a bit arbitrary. There are, however, two main manuscripts that have provided lengthy collections of poems and it is from these that most of what has been spoken of as his poetry derives. They are the Dobell and the Burney manuscripts, discovered and published at the turn of the twentieth century as *The Poetical Works* and *The Poems of Felicity*. Much critical study has gone into discussing the differences and similarities between the manuscripts; the Dobell manuscript is often taken to be the more authoritative of the two, since the Burney manuscript was altered by Traherne's brother Philip in preparation for publication, but many of the same poems occur in each.

The poems of the Dobell and Burney manuscripts celebrate original innocence: what the child is as a model of what humankind is meant to be. We start in silence and come again to silence as wisdom; in between we fall away largely through learning, with the advent of speech, the ways of the world. The pre-verbal child and the post-verbal enlightened adult each have a particular wisdom to offer and each revel in a world that is alight with divine life. 'Eternity was Manifest in the Light of the Day, and som thing infinit Behind evry thing appeared', he writes (C, III, 3). Once we are freed from 'custom' (which is the false sight that sees only the temporal and desires only the material) the divine becomes visible in the ordinary. This linking of sight and speech, right sight, silence and ebullience is characteristic of the poetry. What Traherne is aiming at is self-knowledge. Joy is consequent to it, freedom is consequent to it, gratitude, compassion, mercy, humility and goodness follow in its wake.

There is in his poetry in general, as in *Select Meditations* and elsewhere, an attempt to discover 'naked Truth', by 'Simple Light' bringing 'down the highest Mysteries to sense', so that the 'Soul might see / With open Eys' its great felicity, view its eternal objects and trace the way to bliss both here and hereafter. As A. L. Clements notes, the traditional values of poetry – truth and pleasure – join in Traherne when he aims at 'naked truth' so that his readers might find 'highest bliss'. He eschews what he calls 'curling metaphor' in favour of an unadorned catalogue of words used literally and repetitively, hoping for a clarity of language that has led many readers to find his poetry somehow prosey.

What we see most clearly in the poetry is a mystic who realizes that truth is beyond words, who knows the necessity of silence and the real though finite power of metaphor, caught in the dilemma of wishing to pass on what he has learned while admitting that the way to what he has learned is ultimately beyond words. Traherne reaches for the concealing, revealing ambiguity of symbols perhaps sensing what Thomas Carlyle writes: 'in a Symbol there is concealment and yet revelation: here therefore, by Silence and by Speech acting together, comes a double significance'.[56] The infinite embodied in the finite, visible and attainable – this is what Traherne seeks to convey in much of his work, and especially in his poetry. Perhaps it is partly his frustration with the whole business of language that makes him so reliant on the image of the eye. The 'Ey' is his most frequent symbol, and its siblings sight, vision and light draw his reader, in the poetry most particularly, though also elsewhere, to apprehend. Seeing is believing, not because sight casts out doubt, but because to see is to be transformed.

In the Dobell and Burney poems, Traherne finds a place in the long line of poets, from Dante through Wordsworth and Blake to, more recently, Edwin Muir, who have retained and reinvigorated for us the vision of childhood. More generally, in his poetry we see Traherne as a visionary striving to make the ineffable comprehensible and the essential real. We may see origins and our destiny.

56 Thomas Carlyle, *Sartor Resartus*, New York, 1937, pp. 219–20, in A. L. Clements, *The Mystical Poetry of Thomas Traherne*, Cambridge, MA: Harvard University Press, 1969, p. 43.

Select Meditations

Identified at Yale by James Osborn in 1964,[57] and published in 1997 (edited by Julia Smith), this is thought to be the work of a young Traherne, written not long after leaving university and taking up his post at Credenhill. *Select Meditations* gives readers an exciting new window into Traherne since here we see not so much the lofty flights of mystical vision but the wranglings of a thoughtful, devout and passionate young man with a vocation to priesthood finding his way in a time of particularly intense political and ecclesiastical conflict. It is both a deeply private and a very public work: private in the extensive self-examination of his spiritual reflection, which is distinctly more aware of the problem of sin than, for example, *Centuries*[58] and the poems; public in his political/ecclesiastical concerns which, recurring frequently as they do, remind us that his public considerations are never far from his thought. His political comment is sometimes explicit – his delight in the return of the king, for instance, is pronounced; but there are many other comments, couched in the seventeenth-century common parlance of biblical quotation and allusion, that may be less obvious to the twenty-first-century reader. For Traherne, speaking through scripture, as well as lending an air of authority to what he had to say would have had the double advantage of avoiding possible political censure while at the same time associating England with Israel, God's chosen people.

The *Select Meditations* are written, like the *Centuries*, in groups of 100. The manuscript has been badly mutilated and some meditations are missing, so that the first group begins with meditation 81 and there are subsequent numerical gaps. Textual references to the king, a

57 James Osborn, 'A New Traherne Manuscript', *TLS*, 9 October 1964, p. 928.

58 Traherne's concern with sin in the *Select Meditations* is a concern about both private and public sin. Just two of many examples of private confession are: 'And Since my Baptisme, and Since my Repentance I have Grieveously Sinned' (I, 34) and the even more passionate 'As a prisoner returning from the pitt, as a Malefactor Saved from the cross, yea as a Devill taken out of Hell, I return O Lord to the Glory of thy Kingdom. For my crime hath been wors then Satans' (II, 36). And of the sins of humanity and of his particular parishioners he writes: 'Gods Eternite is a Bottle like the Heavens Wherein the Tears of Penitents Glitter like the Stars' (I, 93). 'Tho they have been and are Rebellious against Thee and will be, yet let me Continually Intercede for them' (I, 84).

restored church beleaguered by dissenters, and a nation at peace suggest that this was written not long after the Restoration. The recent editor of this work, Julia Smith, suggests a date between 1660 and 1665,[59] which would make it a product of Traherne's early twenties. This sits well with the work's exploration of vocation and ministry and with the confessional tone of many of his meditations, which would have read as familiar to the Puritan mentors of his youth.

Although firmly rooted in the concerns of his day, the Traherne of *Select Meditations* seems surprisingly modern in his soul-searching introspection. He is gloriously human: verbose and affable, penitent and jubilant, a man of vigorous affections and vehement oppositions who experiences moments of both frustration and joy; he is full of hope and deeply concerned about the welfare of his nation, desiring always to love and be beloved.

The Works of the Lambeth Manuscript

Inducements to Retiredness

In the opening words of the first work, *Inducements to Retiredness*, Traherne invites his reader to retire from the world 'for the better Introversion of Spirit' and in so doing sets the tone for the work as a whole. For Traherne's concern is particular; his invitation to a life set apart is not an invitation to denial for the sake of mortification, but for the sake of greater joy and fruitfulness. His denial is, if you like, a kind of spiritual and physical pruning in which everything is ordered to its proper place so that the soul may be 'sweetly disposed and Composed for Devine Enjoyments'.[60] In its praise of strict solitude and prayerfulness *Inducements to Retiredness* echoes the traditional mon-

---

59 See Smith's introduction to *Select Meditations*, p. xii: 'Many references to the political situation in England seem to date its composition (though not necessarily the manuscript copy) shortly after the Restoration of Charles II in 1660. The king had clearly returned, as we see from prayers such as "Soften our Kings Heart, Teach our Senators Wisdom" (*SM*, I, 8), but the memory of turmoils which preceded the Restoration is fresh, and Traherne's anxiety about the precarious settlement of the national church and the "Disobedient Hereticks" (*SM*, III, 23), the Protestant nonconformists who opposed it, suggests a date not long after 1660.' The reference 'As long as our nation continueth in peace' (I, 86) may refer to the approaching war on the Dutch, which was declared in March 1665.

60 Lines 5–6 of the abstract to the first section of *ITR*.

astic wisdom of Thomas à Kempis' *The Imitation of Christ*.[61] In fact, he cites, Thomas à Kempis in the first Century when he considers the religious impulse to condemn the world that does not sit easily alongside his famous admonitions to enjoy the world. 'Give all (saith Thomas à Kempis) for all. Leave the one that you may enjoy the other',[62] writes Traherne.

Traherne's aversion to marriage in *Inducements*, and his insistence on celibacy as the better way for clergy, is reminiscent of St Paul. However, there is no sense in Traherne that it is 'better marry than burn';[63] Traherne is not concerned with marriage as a means of sexual containment. His concern is purely practical: marriage is a distraction. Like St Paul, Traherne regards celibacy as a gift that affords freedom to belong to all and to be concerned with many that is the strength of the public minister. Traherne's discussion of singleness in *Inducements* may also be traced in the voluminous extracts and notes from Bacon found in Traherne's *Early Notebook*. Among the extensive notes on Francis Bacon's *De augmentis scientiarum* and fragments of *Apotegms* and *Essays* that appear over 101 pages of the *Early Notebook* are extracts from Book II in praise of Queen Elizabeth's celibacy.[64] This sentiment Traherne expands in *Inducements*, concluding that although celibacy is not a universal rule, yet 'it holdeth infallibly in Publick Ministers'.[65] Celibacy for ministers, and retirement for Christians in general, is desirable not because the public life is inherently evil, but because it is a distraction from the aims of eternity, infinity, felicity. Retirement is a Freedom and a Glory, 'the Paradice or Palace of Pleasure'.[66]

Inducements to Retiredness is written in five relatively short sections.

61 See, for instance, 'If thou wilt stand as thou oughtest, and make a due progress, look upon thyself as a banished man, and a stranger upon earth' (Book I, Ch. XVII); 'Seek a proper time to retire into thyself, and often think of the benefits of God . . . The greatest saints avoided the company of men as much as they could and chose to live to God in secret' (Book I, Ch. XX). These are two among very many such admonishments.

62 C, I, 7.

63 1 Corinthians 7.9.

64 EN, p. 113; Bacon, II, 485. As Marks has noted, Traherne had 'a talent for extracting the pith of Bacon's argument, as well as a frequent disregard for Bacon's main points and priorities' (Carol Marks, 'Thomas Traherne's Early Studies', *PBSA*, 62 (1968), pp. 511–36).

65 ITR, l. 461.

66 ITR, ll. 805, 926.

Section I is an invitation to withdrawal from the world. Section II calls for a stable resolution in dedicating oneself to God. In section III the will is transformed so that the holy person becomes qualified for service in the world. Section IV considers retirement as the citadel of truth and the centre of rest, the necessary home of the holy. Section V studies the example of holy persons. The work is a study of holy living, and in its structure we see a pattern familiar in spiritual writings about holiness in which the person who would be holy is called away from the world that he/she may re-enter it more usefully, and in which the holy person, though called to separateness, is called in a community of saints and fellow-seekers. All of this sounds deeply theoretical, but in *Inducements to Retiredness* one feels that Traherne is speaking from experience, his own as well as that borrowed from the monastic tradition. However, its tone is testimonial rather than confessional; what he is saying is prepared, poised as if intended to instruct. *Inducements to Retiredness* treats issues of celibacy, friendship and public ministry that are of particular concern to clergy, but addressed to 'the pious soul'; the work also invites a wider audience. In the midst of his clerical concerns, he has a great deal to say about human nature and human relationships. *Inducements to Retiredness* is rich with practical wisdom, like the suggestion, in the fourth section, that it is not scarcity but service that maketh jewels and that 'we are to grow Rich, not by seeking what we Want, but by Enjoying what we have'.[67]

A Sober View of Dr Twisse

The second work in the Lambeth manuscript, *A Sober View of Dr Twisse*, is a long work (28 sections) of academic theology covering the Calvinist/Arminian debate, that highly charged dispute concerning predestination and free will – do we choose God or does God choose us? – with Calvinists on the side of election or predestination, and Arminians arguing for human choice. *A Sober View* shows Traherne engaged in the messy business of working out, alongside his fellow theologians, the way forward for the newly restored English Church. The texts to which Traherne refers in *A Sober View* are Samuel Hoard's *Gods love to mankind. Manifested by dis-prooving his absolute decree for their damnation* (1633, 1656, 1658), William Twisse's posthumous

---

67 *ITR*, ll. 859–60. References are made here to the line numbers only.

The riches of Gods love (1653), which answers Hoard, and Henry Hammond's *Pacific Discourse* (1660), containing long extracts from a letter by Robert Sanderson.

This was an intellectual battle about God's decrees, the decisions God had made before the foundation of the world, but it mattered so much precisely because at its heart lay burning questions about human choice and liberty, and the position of the individual in the scheme of things, questions that had implications for the whole way in which the country was to be governed. This is where the debate gained its electricity and the ground on which the Calvinist/Arminian debate was staged was littered with retaliatory discourse of the most heated variety.

During the first five sections of *A Sober View* Traherne focuses his attentions on the writings of strict Calvinist Dr Twisse;[68] then, less than a quarter of the way through the work, he leaves Twisse and moves on to a consideration of Henry Hammond and the much more moderate Robert Sanderson. Essentially he has jettisoned staunch Calvinism, and now hones in on the finer points of moderate Calvinism versus universalism; that is, the doctrine that all persons are saved. He contrasts Article 17 of the Anglican Thirty-Nine Articles, which allows that God does choose or elect some, with Article 2, which suggests that God's grace is extended to all, and the Comfortable Words said before communion, a prayer from Ash Wednesday and the Thanksgiving at a public baptism, all from the *Book of Common Prayer*. Traherne was a conforming minister, and it is a testament to his commitment to the Restoration Church that he judges the orthodoxy of his sources against the doctrines of the Church of England rather than against any other creed or against his own isolated reasoning: 'He [Dr Sanderson] had the Advantage on Dr Hammond in that he perfectly conformeth to the Ch. of England,' Traherne writes. And yet, he will dismiss neither

68 Twisse (1578–1646), of English and German descent, educated at Winchester and Oxford, was appointed by James I to be chaplain to Princess Elizabeth in Heidelberg in 1612. He made his reputation as a rigid Calvinist for his defence of the Sabbath, his report on the Synod of Dort, and his defence of the Calvinist doctrine of predestination. His attack on the Jesuits brought him fame in Europe. Ever one to arouse passions, he was buried with great pomp in Westminster Abbey, but his bones were exhumed and tossed into a communal grave outside at the Restoration. On Twisse's attack on Thomas Jackson (1631) that accused Jackson of Arminianism leading to Pelagianism, see Sarah Hutton, 'Thomas Jackson, Oxford Platonist, and William Twisse, Aristotelian', *Journal of the History of Ideas*, 39:4 (1978), pp. 635–52.

reason nor experience; he continues: 'for he that denieth the Article of Election, loppeth away one great Branch from the Doctrine of the Ch. of England: as he that denieth the Gift of Liberty doth violate a great part of Experience and Reason.'[69] We may see him firmly placed in the Anglican position of deriving authority from a balance of scripture, reason and tradition.

'All verity fitteth in the Golden Mean',[70] says Traherne, and to err on either extreme is equally dangerous. However true to church doctrines he remains, he is not comfortable with the darker side of the doctrine of election – that God hates some just as he loves and chooses others – and says we should not think about election in those terms or it will drive us to despair. To those who quote Romans chapter 9, a central text in the argument for election – 'Jacob have I loved, Esau have I hated'[71] – Traherne replies that one must be wary of how one applies a particular text. Using an image of Sanderson's, he writes: 'Fire is the same, put it where you will: yet in the Chimney it will warm you, or roast your meat; if you apply it to a Weinscoat Wall, it will consume the Dwelling.'[72]

There is a tension here with which Traherne must live. Repeatedly he returns to the principle 'that above all things in the World God desires that men should turn of themselves and that having all Means and Motives thereunto, should repent and believ of their own Accord.'[73] God's action in drawing people to himself, though prevenient, is not exclusive. In the case of either the Elect or the Reprobate, the end of divine initiative is that the human soul should act of its own accord. 'For that they may herafter do Good Works of their own Accord are the one [the Elect] now Invaded: and that in this Act the other might be righteous of their own Accord are the other omitted.'[74]

The intense examination of doctrine in *A Sober View* may draw scholars back to reconsider *Roman Forgeries*, not only because the two works signal a similar interest in matters ecclesiastical, but because they

---

69 *SV*, VII, ll. 19–22.

70 *SV*, VI, l. 44.

71 Romans 9.13; see also Malachi 1.2–3.

72 *SV*, XXVII, ll. 113–15. In his sermons, Sanderson describes Puritan zeal as 'a kind of fire' whose right use is valuable, though 'blind or indiscrete zeal, like fire in the thatch will soon set all the house in a combustion', *Thirty-four Sermons*, 5th edition of the 1657 collection of sermons (London, 1671), pt 2, p. 159.

73 *SV*, IV, ll. 196, 197.

74 *SV*, IV, ll. 28–30.

both make the same kind of claim to an earnest pursuit of the truth. They also both indicate the degree to which Traherne was willing to engage in inseparably linked theological/political controversies of his day that have been the subject of much study by Tyacke and others.[75] In the combination of these two works, as elsewhere, Traherne criticizes Roman Catholicism and nonconformity alike, and taken together they may chart a middle way between extremes. As one can see even from the very brief description offered here, *A Sober View* is a highly technical work. It will be of primary interest to specialists concerned with placing Traherne securely within post-Dort theology[76] of the Church of England. However, the questions he raises, and the parts of the questions he chooses to emphasize, highlight his overarching philosophical concerns regarding freedom, choice and action seen elsewhere in his work. In *A Sober View* Traherne is more detached than in many of his other works. There are no rhapsodic exhaltations, no lofty flights into mystical vision. He is concentrated, busy, trying to find a simple answer, though simplicity eludes him. Calvinism and Arminianism – in *A Sober View* Traherne puts two pins in the map of post-Reformation theology and charts a tricky path between them as he asks the question: How free are we?

75 See Nicholas Tyacke, 'Arminianism and English Culture', in A. C. Duke and C. A. Tamse, eds, *Britain and the Netherlands, Church and State since the Reformation*, The Hague, 1981, pp. 94–117; 'Puritanism, Arminianism and the Counter-Revolution', in Conrad Russell, ed., *The Origins of the English Civil War*, London: Palgrave Macmillan, 1973, pp. 119–43; *Anti-Calvinists: The Rise of English Arminianism: 1590–1640*, Oxford: Clarendon Press, 1990; *Aspects of English Protestantism 1530–1700*, Manchester, UK: Manchester University Press, 2001. See also Dewey Wallace, *Puritans and Predestination*, Chapel Hill, NC: University of North Carolina Press, 1982; Peter White, 'The Rise of Arminianism Reconsidered', *Past and Present*, 101 (1983), pp. 34–54; and Patrick Collinson, *From Cranmer to Sancroft*, London: Continuum, 2006.

76 That is the theology that followed the Synod of Dort (1618–19) convened by the Netherlands to end the bitter controversy over Arminianism, in which followers of Arminius (d.1609) were summoned as offenders rather than as representatives. At the synod the Five Points of Arminianism were condemned and the Five Points of Calvinism were stated explicitly. Representatives from England were present; the Decrees of Dort gained wide approval in the Reformed Churches. For a concise account see J. T. McNeill, *A Dictionary of Christian Theology*, London: SCM Press, 1969, p. 99.

Love

A beautiful and engaging fragmentary start to a larger unfinished prose work, *Love*[77] begins with the words, 'To Speak fully and distinctly concerning Lov is impossible.' Traherne wisely sets parameters for the work: 'Four Cares and concerns it has, which abov all other I shall chuse to speak of,'[78] he writes. But here the reader is teased, since not only does he get no further than the first concern, which is that love desires to beautify itself, but he also fails to tell us what the other three concerns were going to be. What we have is a tantalysing beginning. He starts by contemplating 'the illimited Sweetness of Tyrannical Love',[79] in which an Empress, admired and adored by many, surrenders herself to the love of one, greedily desiring his embraces and prodigally bestowing her own. Traherne is telling a story that reads as remarkably real for one who claims to disown such experience: 'Such fancies and descriptions have I seen in Playes and vain Romances.'[80]

The themes in *Love* are similar to the ending of *The Kingdom of God*, where in an extended metaphor in the final chapter we also see the soul as the bride. This image of the soul/bride is not unusual in Traherne, recurring several times in *Commentaries of Heaven* and in *Select Meditations*, and less forcefully, in Chapter 18 of *Christian Ethicks*. In each of these works, the soul is the beloved wooed by a divine Lover, but here in *Love* the allegory is sharper. Gone are the notions of benevolence and complacency that mark the relationship of God to the soul in *Christian Ethicks*; superseded are the distant longings of *Select Meditations*. Instead we have greedy desire and wild abandon as the lovers surrender to their great passion. The exploration of the theme is striking in its intensity, making this fragment particularly interesting to those concerned with Traherne's theories of desire in the love of God. That Traherne's God yearns is not only a reflection of the divine desire for a lost creation, but a comment too on the very character of a God who, in the persons of the Trinity, is essentially relational. Traherne's defence of Trinitarian doctrine is powerfully made elsewhere; here in this picture of God the lover, we see the deeply Trinit-

77 The treatise is untitled in the manuscript. *Love* is the modern title given it by Jeremy Maule.
78 *L*, ll. 5–6.
79 *L*, ll. 35–6.
80 *L*, ll. 71–2.

arian nature of God revealed in ecstatic love that goes out of itself and seeks reciprocity. Traherne's God is a God who risks all for love, who knows in Godself as well as in God's relationship with the created order, the bliss of union and the pain of separation. He is writing not only about the soul and God, but also about the character of God whose nature is to love.

Seeds of Eternity

Seeds of Eternity is a short theme (12 pages) exploring the powers of the soul, by the greatness of which the human is made capable of union with the divine. It was this phrase, 'seeds of eternity', under the heading 'Three theological treatises of the 1660s',[81] that caught the eye of Jeremy Maule as he perused the Lambeth catalogue of acquisitions in 1997, hoping for a find. The phrase struck him as reminiscent of Traherne and he asked to inspect the manuscript; so it is in some part to this short treatise that a whole discovery is due.

Seeds of Eternity opens with the words: 'Humanity, which is the Handmaid of true Divinity, is a noble Part of Learning, opening the best and rarest Cabinet in nature to us, that of our Selvs'.[82] In many ways this is just what the treatise is – an exploration of the self. The soul, says Traherne, 'naturaly desires to see the Lineaments of its own face',[83] but he was largely disappointed in learning because it did not answer his thirst for knowledge of the soul. The lectures he heard on humanity were unsatisfactory; his reading of Aristotle on the soul was not much better. Like the Oxford Platonist Thomas Jackson, who derided Aristotle for dealing with neither 'the first cause or last end of all things',[84] Traherne also grew impatient with Aristotle's treatment of the soul, which left it 'like a broken monument whose fragments are seen, but lying in the Rubbish',[85] which outlined the faculties and powers

81 E. G. Bill, *Catalogue of Manuscripts in Lambeth Palace Library: MSS 1222–1860*, Oxford, 1972, pp. 78–9.

82 See also *C*, III, 41–42, in which Traherne discusses the excellence of 'Humanity': 'By humanity we search into the powers and faculties of the Soul ... Whereby we come to know what man is in this world.'

83 *SE*, l. 18.

84 *The Eternal Truth of the Scriptures* (1613, 14) 112; see also *Treatise of the Divine Essence and Attributes* (1628, 29), 31. Jackson is one of the sources in Traherne's *Commonplace Book*.

85 *SE*, ll. 191–2.

of the soul, but did not show 'the uses of those Faculties'.[86] He longed
to see the end for which the powers of the soul were created. This, he
says, Aristotle 'buried in Silence'.[87] In *Seeds of Eternity*, Traherne asserts
that the powers and inclinations of the soul – the desire to see the
excellence of things and the covetousness that longs to have possession
of them – are two high and soaring inclinations coming 'from GOD to
GOD'[88] that make us capable of bliss. This flow or 'communication' is
central to the project of *Seeds*. The two inclinations – to see the excellence of things and to desire the possession of them – are implanted in
order that they might be satisfied by a God willing to communicate
himself to his creation. 'He [God] desires to be Delightfull, and to be
enjoyed: he is infinitly Good and communicative', writes Traherne,
'that therfore we might be capable of all Enjoyments, in communion
with him, he made us like him self',[89] who also desires the most excellent
things, and enjoys them. Nothing can be a treasure that is not possessed,
says Traherne, and the divine nature therefore 'desires Application, as
well as Excellency'.[90] For a thing may be capable of being a treasure
that is not a treasure until it be enjoyed.

What Traherne wants to do is to reach a clear understanding of the
soul's capacity for union with the divine that resonates with experience
– to *feel* the things that Humanity declares.[91] The soul is infinitely
communicative in the image of God, Traherne argues, thus the Classical
admonition 'know thyself', given famously at Delphi, becomes an
oracle of deepest wisdom, for 'in the knowledge of one self, the Knowledge of God, and all things appeareth'.[92] *Seeds of Eternity* goes on to
consider the body as a glorious companion to the soul and to assert
the Classical notion of the superiority of humankind over animals. The
treatise ends with the inquisitiveness and restlessness of human nature
that needs to know the Original and End of creation. It concludes by
stating briefly that it is by all the powers of the soul and superiority of
the human position that the soul is made capable of union with God.

86 *SE*, ll. 155–60. Similarly, Traherne's disappointment with his scholastic
education is recorded in C, III, 37.
  87 *SE*, l. 183.
  88 *SE*, l. 187.
  89 *SE*, ll. 93–4, 96–7.
  90 *SE*, ll. 100–1.
  91 This is similar to his complaint in C, III, 37 that what he studied at university
was always studied 'as aliena'. Information was gained but meaning was missed.
  92 *SE*, ll. 299–300.

In *Seeds of Eternity* Traherne expounds Christian humanism using a long line of ancient and patristic sources and in so doing he quotes freely, often not identifying his source until some lines later, if at all; many of his sources are quoted second hand.[93] *Seeds of Eternity* resonates with Traherne's exposition of the utility of humanity and the surpassing significance of felicity in the third Century,[94] and with parts of *Christian Ethicks*;[95] in its high view of man *Seeds of Eternity* echoes the neo-platonist ideals we see in his poetry and prose, particularly in his quotations from Pico in the *Centuries*.[96] In its themes of insatiability and the capacity of the soul, *Seeds of Eternity* is reminiscent of the lofty 'Thanksgivings for the Soul'. But although his subject is marvellous, in *Seeds of Eternity* Traherne refrains from ecstatic utterances. Just as *Christian Ethicks* aims to draw the reader towards a life of virtue by considering the beauty of the virtues, so *Seeds of Eternity*, in its consideration of capacity, studies the glory of the soul rather than its capacity for evil; it aims to draw the reader to repentance by focusing not on his or her sins but on the great beauty of the original that has been marred.

The Kingdom of God

The title of the work suggests that it may have a place among those millenarian writings common in the seventeenth century that explored the biblical promise of God's 1,000-year reign on earth, though the phrase from the Lord's Prayer 'Thy kingdom come' was by no means exclusively in Commonwealth millenarian parlance. It was preached and prayed over in Traherne's day[97] by both aspiring millenarians and

---

93 He quotes at length the Coimbran scholars – Jesuits from Coimbra University in Portugal whose Latin translations of Aristotle were popular among advanced scholars in the seventeenth century. For further examples of Traherne's borrowing, see Ross, Introduction to *The Works of Thomas Traherne*, Vol. 1, p. xxiii.

94 See C, III, 41–46.

95 See most significantly *CE*, Ch. 4, 'Of the Powers and Affections of the Soul', and to a lesser extent Ch. 20, 'Of Prudence'.

96 See C, III, 74–78.

97 Millenarians believed the approaching thousand-year reign of Christ on earth prophesied in scripture would be ushered in by divine and often by apocalyptic means; but their interpretations of how and when this would occur, who would benefit or suffer from the arrival of the 'new heaven and new earth' or

post-Restoration divines who reflected that perhaps the reign of God was, after all, to be best expressed as a kingdom rather than a common-wealth. It may well be that Traherne had a political point to make that anchors the work in this millenarian or anti-millenarian discourse, but what also fascinates a twenty-first-century reader is how much of what he says about the self, the world and God seems apposite today. This is Traherne's longest work of philosophical theology: a 42-chapter study of God and his creation – God as creator first of all, then the creation as an expression of Godself. It is a story of divine disclosure and of divine goodness extending in love. What Traherne is saying about the world first is that it reveals God to us, that in it we may come to know both the nature of God and something of the great longing God has for all that he has made; second, he is saying that this world is heavenly because here we may begin to live the life of heaven. Both of these statements resonate profoundly with Maximus the Confessor's assertion that immediately and without change, the created world is filled with uncreated grace.

Traherne begins *The Kingdom of God* with careful clarity, setting out the Efficient (Chapters 1–16), Material (17–30), Formal (31–42) and Final Causes of God's kingdom.[98] He is aware of the enormity of the work he has set himself, admitting from the start that neither he nor anyone else is sufficient to the task; and it is in a spirit of endearing humility that he sets about this demanding project. The kingdom he is about to consider is not just the kingdom of God on earth, all of creation animate and inanimate; but rather it is a kingdom that marries earth with heaven and time with eternity. It is a kingdom of angels as well as of men in which all ages are present together and all territories animated with the divine life. Well then may he be daunted by the task ahead of him. It is as if he is already expecting the work to exceed the careful boundaries he has set for it before he begins and it may be this

---

the 'new Jerusalem' differ widely. At different points the millenarian banner was taken up by puritans, radicals, restoration divines and latitudinarians alike.

98 The terms 'Efficient', 'Material', 'Formal' and 'Final' refer to Aristotle's four causes necessary for producing a result. They concern questions of origin and process as follows: (1) Efficient – where things come from, or that which originates the process; (2) Material – of what they consist, the matter from which a thing is made; (3) Formal – how things operate, what form they have, the shape or design that is imposed on the materials; (4) Final – the end towards which they aim. In the case of a house, for example, the Efficient Cause might be the builder or architect, the Material Cause the bricks, the Formal Cause the archi-tect's drawings or the builder's plans, the Final Cause shelter and comfort.

anxiety that, throughout the work, draws his thoughts back again and again to the scholastic framework with which the work opens. Traherne knows he is attempting an immeasurable and untameable magnificence; and although the first chapter begins with the firm structural foundation, it ends with the searching question: 'What footing Can we Expect, what limit, what foundation, what Shore . . . where all is Infinit and Eternal?'

Nevertheless, Traherne feels bound to attempt this consideration of the kingdom of God, 'for that which discourages Timorous Spirits, animates the Couragious'.[99] It is the very incomprehensibility of God's kingdom that is part of its allure. In this he echoes the voices of Gregory of Nyssa (whom he cites also in *Centuries*) and Gregory the Great (cited in *Commentaries of Heaven*), who each conceived God as essentially unknowable. Here too we may hear echoes of the 'Som great thing' of the first Century that also allures Traherne and his reader, though here, as in *Centuries*, the call that Traherne is answering is more than curiosity. He wants to 'consider and feel, and see, and prie into the Bottom',[100] as far as he can, not just because he loves prying but because, along with many fellow theologians, he believes that this kingdom is a mirror of the divine essence in which 'God himself, and the Eternal Generation of his Son, are made Known by his Works'.[101] This kingdom of God is, he writes, 'the Center of our Union, and the sphere of our Communion with GOD'.[102] Clearly Traherne is hoping for more than knowledge as the fruit of this project. In *The Kingdom of God*, as elsewhere, what he seeks to find and to convey is an unfolding of the mystery of divine abundance and divine longing.

The chapters on the 'Efficient Causes' (1–16) explore the nature of God's kingdom as deduced from our human needs and experience of God, and from his attributes. Under the heading of 'Material Causes' (Chapters 17–30) Traherne considers the kingdom by examining parts of the physical creation. The extent of Traherne's interest in the new sciences is made clear primarily in the chapters in the twenties, the 'scientific' chapters of the work, that consider the atom and the stars, the sun, the moon, the circulation of the blood – all the interior and exterior discoveries of microscope and telescope that were shaking and inspiring the thinking world of his day.

99 *KOG*, Ch. 2, ll. 4–5.
100 *KOG*, Ch. 2, ll. 64–5.
101 *KOG*, Ch. 2, ll. 54–5.
102 *KOG*, Ch. 2, ll. 57–8.

Under 'Formal Causes' (Chapters 31–42) Traherne considers how the kingdom is constituted, its laws, the relationships between creatures and their creator, and their relation to each other. In the kingdom all things find value in their relation to each other. The sun, for instance, matters because of its influence on earth and earthly creatures: 'if it be not Good to other things it is good for Nothing' (Ch. 31, ll. 145–6) he writes; 'Use gives to things their Worth' (Ch. 31, l. 165).

Curiously, the promised 'Final Causes' never materialize. This could be because, since the first and final causes are the same – 'The Efficient and the final Cause is God himself' (Ch. 1, l. 10), writes Traherne at the outset – the whole category of 'Final Cause' is by implication included in the first discussion of the 'Efficient Cause'. Or it is possible that the work is simply unfinished, though as Jeremy Maule noted in his first lecture on the discovery, the work shows the kinds of editing that are consonant with an intention to publish – hints that are not conclusive.

A philosophical study of divine interaction with creation, *The Kingdom of God* is at points didactic, a treatise designed to correct specific theological misconceptions and to convince its readers of the possibility of the life of heaven beginning here on earth. It is also in another sense a love story that begins with a display of a king's dominion and ends with his betrothal – a revelation of God's outstretched longing to communicate his love, and a desire that his love should be reciprocated. In this work God always longs to reveal himself as fully and intimately as it is possible he should. It is interesting to note that *The Kingdom of God* reads as less testimonial than some of Traherne's other works. Only in the two chapters on 'love' and 'life' does Traherne allow himself an overflow of rapture. The moments of annunciation or epiphany that we find in *Select Meditations* or *Centuries* are largely absent here. The revelation is of Godself in the world, the world to the self, God to the self, the self to God. In Chapters 16, 17 and 27 the creation is God's body by which he seeks to show himself. In Chapter 41 Traherne conceives the creation as a love letter from God to the human soul, personal but not exclusive, written and copied, as were most works in the manuscript culture in which Traherne wrote, to be distributed to humankind, his bride. For God had 'made an Epistle of his Lov. He had written it upon the Earth in knots and flowers, in Letters of Gold, in the Sun, in Silver Copies in the Stars, in Bloody Characters, in the Living Creatures which was in more Bloody ones afterwards Copied in the Death of his Son' (Ch. 41, ll. 193–7). Throughout the work the soul is God's potential mate and finally his Amazonian bride. What is the voice inside Traherne that constantly calls him back, in this work as in others, to the themes of longing, desire, communication, reciprocity, communion and union?

Commentaries of Heaven

Commentaries of Heaven, identified in 1981 and announced in the *TLS* in 1982,[103] with its 400 double-column pages of Traherne's tiny writing, 94 entries and over 4,000 lines of verse, is thought to be a 'late work', possibly still being written in the year before his death.[104] It is astonishingly ambitious, intended to be a huge encyclopedia of Traherne's thought; and its wide range covers most of his themes and shows how they relate to each other, even though the work only goes as far as the letter 'B'. It is a difficult manuscript to read, with words often disappearing in the dark pinch of binding so that one has to peer and guess at the end of many lines, but it is a fascinating manuscript too. The eclectic nature of its themes means that one is always waiting to be surprised.

In *Commentaries* we see Traherne writing about specific doctrines and liturgical practices – baptism, atonement, the Trinity – less tangentially and more deliberately than he does anywhere else, making this work of particular significance to those readers interested in placing Traherne theologically. The encyclopedia also reveals something of the philosophical and scientific shape of his mind as particular areas of interest are developed: 'Act', 'Action', 'Activity I', 'Activity II', following closely one after another, reveal the pressing nature of his exploration of Act; whereas in entries such as 'Ant' and 'Atom' we see his interest in the new sciences, as we do in 'Astronomie' in which he

103 Elliot Rose, 'A New Traherne Manuscript', *TLS* (19 March 1982), p. 324.

104 Traherne refers to the death of Christ as having happened '1640 years ago' so, assuming that Traherne believed that Christ was 33 at the time of the crucifixion, the date of the manuscript would be 1673. This date would also correspond with the publication dates of other works Traherne has cited in the manuscript (e.g. Gale's *Court of the Gentiles*, 1670). In *COH*, 'Antichrist', he notes that he has written 'a whole tract ... to be published' on the theme of *Roman Forgeries*; he was preparing *Roman Forgeries* during 1673. For further details see Richard Jordan, 'The New Traherne Manuscript "Commentaries of Heaven"', *Quadrant*, 27 (August 1983), pp. 73–6, and Julia Smith in *Profitable Wonders*, pp. 46–7.

considers Galileo's observations of 1610. An earlier version of one of
his sentences reads: 'The first things considered in Astronomie is ye
Number of ye Spheres', following the medieval system of Ptolomy. He
crosses out 'is' in the manuscript and changes it to 'of old, was', casting
off the medieval for the modern, and we seem to catch his pen poised in
a moment of intellectual evolution, then repositioned to accommodate
modern astronomy. In *Commentaries*, as elsewhere, he is a man of his
day crossing over, sometimes adventurously and sometimes reluctantly,
from one world-view to another. Some of his thoughts, like the cen-
trality of man in the universe, remain resolutely and unapologetically
anchored in former ages; yet his lengthy entry 'Antichrist', fierce in its
anti-papism (and those similarly disposed entries immediately following), ties the work to his other polemical writing in *Roman Forgeries*
and in *A Sober View*, which concerned themselves with the future
political and theological shape of the nation. In *Commentaries of
Heaven* we see Traherne at once looking backwards and forwards,
sometimes treading carefully, sometimes striding confidently, always
attempting to answer what he feels will be the pressing questions of his
readers.

His need to define can drive him to long arid passages of scholastic
classification complete with technical Latin terminology, but there are
also sentences of dazzling simplicity, fresh and engaging, that light up
the text and drive the reader forward. The titles of articles range widely,
from 'Abhorrence' and 'Abuse' through 'Adoration', 'Adultery', 'Affection', 'Appetite', 'Atheist', 'Atom', through many more to 'Baseness'
and 'Bastard'. The prose is dense, and while much has been made of
Traherne's prolixity as a deliberate part of his method,[105] it takes no
small effort to stay with him for the whole of the *Commentaries*, though
his best passages are astonishingly confident, clear and profound. The
wildly eclectic entries are discrete but related units, the theme of one
often being reiterated in the next though the titles appear at first to be
related only by alphabetical proximity. For instance, the anti-papist
entry 'Antichrist' is immediately followed by 'Antiquity', whose sub-
heading reads: 'That Antiquity in general condemmeth Popery'; similarly 'Baptism', which ends with the Christian imperative to bear fruit,
leads directly into 'Barrennes' where the fruitless tree is deplored. Such
inter-article links occur frequently in the work. Most of his entries end

105 See Martz, *The Paradise Within*, 1964; Carl Selkin, 'Traherne's Cataloguing Style', *English Literary Renaissance*, 6 (1976), pp. 92–103.

with a poem, sometimes one stanza, sometimes a few pages in length. The work was written with the stated intention of being useful for instructing fellow priests and for the 'satisfaction of atheists',[106] and Traherne's asides, such as 'This is the Answer that is to be returned to all sorts of Phanatiques that cavil at the Words in the English Liturgie' ('Baptism', fol. 193r–195r) or 'This is Dr Jackson's cure or rather Antidote against Atheism' (fol. 163r), show that the work was constructed to some degree as a response to the theologically troubled times in which he was living. Expecting theology to be a controversial subject, he hits doctrinal and liturgical matters head on, hoping to equip his reader with ready answers when they come under attack. There is a passion in this work for the furtherance of the Christian faith, but in placing clear theological markers his love of the Church of England in particular is plain. In the poem following 'Article', Traherne describes each of the Thirty-Nine Articles as 'a little joint' of the whole body. In matters of doctrine, all the Articles must be united since relation and proportion are what give symmetry to the whole. So assembled, Traherne says, they strike the viewer dumb as God is seen in perspective, alive as if in bodily form in the Thirty-Nine Articles. *Commentaries* offers a wealth of insight, linking as no other work quite does his poetic and polemical writing.

Commentaries of Heaven's encyclopedic form differs from previously known meditations, treatise or polemic. However, many entries can be traced back to the *Commonplace Book* and *Early Notebook*, which seem to have been compiled in part as preparation for this more ambitious work. The story of the discovery of the manuscript, one of the most dramatic of all the Traherne manuscripts, is one of accident and serendipity. The scorched manuscript was rescued from a burning tip, and despite its dance with death it is one of the most intact of the manuscripts; several seventeenth-century pins used to 'staple' additional material into the book are still intact. The poems, edited by Douglas Chambers, have been published alone, Allan Pritchard

106 The title page reads: 'COMMENTARIES OF HEAVEN wherin The Mysteries of Felicitie are opened and ALL THINGS Discovered to be Objects of Happiness. Evry Being Created & Increased being Alphabetically Represented in the Light of GLORY wherein also for the Satisfaction of Atheists, & the Consolation of Christians, as well as the stance and Encouragement of Divines: the Transcendent Verities of the Holy Scriptures, & the Highest Objects of the Christian faith are in a Clear Mirror Exhibited to the Ey of Reason; in their Realitie and Glory.'

published some prose extracts, as did Anne Ridler and Julia Smith; but this important manuscript has recently been published entire, edited by Jan Ross.[107]

Fragments and notebooks

The Ceremonial Law

The Ceremonial Law, discovered in 1997 at the Folger Library in Washington DC by Julia Smith and Laetitia Yeandle,[108] though not insignificant with its 1,800 lines of rhyming couplets is an unpublished and unfinished poem written in a notebook large enough to contain a poem three times its length. In it Traherne considers the Old Testament books of Genesis and Exodus in short narrative sections, with subtitles such as 'Noah's Rainbow', 'Moses' Call', 'The Rock', 'Manna', etc., retelling the stories as allegories or types to inspire and instruct the reader of his day. There is a down-to-earthness about this typological poem that makes it seem more the work of a teacher than of a mystic. Not only is it less ecstatic than, for instance, the Dobell poems, or *Centuries*, it is also rooted in a strong narrative uncharacteristic of much of his other work. Its concerns are not remote or philosophical. The stories deal with elemental human experiences: thirst, hunger, fear, fire, water, danger, deliverance. By deprivation, by journeying 'through this Wide Abyss Of Desert Horors',[109] the Israelites learn to prize the joys they possess in Elim and to taste the sweetness of manna. So too, the reader is urged to travel into the desert of uncreated nothing in order to see the sweetness of the created world:

---

107 The poems can be found in D. Chambers, ed., *Commentaries of Heaven: The Poems*, Institut fur Anglistik und Amerikanistik, University of Salzburg, Austria, 1989; extracts in Allan Pritchard, 'Traherne's *Commentaries of Heaven* (with Selections from the Manuscript)', *University of Toronto Quarterly*, 53 (1983–84), pp. 1–35; and in Julia Smith, ed., 'Some Extracts from *Commentaries of Heaven*', *PNR*, 18(6) (July/August 1992), pp. 14–20. The complete work can be found in Jan Ross, ed., *The Works of Thomas Traherne*, Vols 2 and 3, Woodbridge, UK: Boydell and Brewer, 2007.

108 See Julia Smith and Laetitia Yeandle, 'Felicity disguisd in fiery Words: Genesis and Exodus in a newly discovered poem by Thomas Traherne', *TLS* (7 November 1997), p. 17.

109 'Elim', ll. 120–1.

Lets sojourn in the Desert Wilderness
Of long and uncreated nothing, guess
What may the Dismall Chaos be, and view
The vacant Ages, while he nought did doe.
Those Empty Barren Places will appear
At last as if they all at once were here
The Silence Darkness and Deformitie
In which we nothing plainly nothing see
Will make the Univers enlightening to them
Even like unto the new Jerusalem.
And while we wisely seek for Heaven there,
Twill clearly make us find our Heaven here.[110]

Traherne interprets the types at several levels. In common with other seventeenth-century readings of scripture, the Old Testament stories and figures are seen as types of the New Testament, but Traherne also reads the contemporary church and sometimes himself into the stories, becoming, for instance, Moses whose shoes must be removed in front of the burning bush and whose transfigured face terrifies before it pleases. And so the types are not remote; his readers may enter into the stories as he does and find themselves alive to scripture. For less imaginative or less sophisticated readers, the moral of each story is clearly indicated.

Curiously, for those readers expecting a poem springing from Genesis to abound in Traherne's customary praise of creation and of original innocence, there is not a pre-lapsarian moment to be seen. The poem begins with 'Adam's Fall'. It carries on with the Old Testament account until 'The Inside' where, just after Moses descends from Mount Sinai, the poem breaks mid-line with the tantalizingly enigmatic 'Men promise to themselves Som great Delight, / Could they but once enjoy the Glorious Sight / Of God on Earth . . .'.[111] The poem never reaches the Promised Land. Its recurring motif is that of journey; from the moment the poem begins the people are displaced persons, outcasts, sojourners, strangers looking for home. The memory of Paradise and the hope of the Promised Land may be its gilded frame, but the poem's narrative sequences unfold largely in a wasteland.

---

110 [Manna] II, ll. 69–80.
111 'The Inside', ll. 9–11.

Church's Year-Book

The *Church's Year-Book*, sometimes called 'The Book of Private Devotions', is untitled by Traherne and has been perused by only a handful of Traherne scholars. It is a treasure trove not just because of the wonderful images it conveys, such as feast days as the 'Marketdays of Heaven' when we clean the dirt from under our nails, don our dusty best and celebrate, but also because it contains a wealth of clues to Traherne's use of and familiarity with the *Book of Common Prayer* and his borrowing from fellow theologians. In it Traherne records prayers and meditations for festivals of the church year from Easter to All Saints' Day. Mysteriously, the pages for Trinity Sunday have been cut out of the book; a second part of the book that would have covered the feasts from Advent to the Annunciation is yet to be discovered.

One imagines Traherne composing the *Church's Year-Book* with a selection of relevant books and commonplaces open before him – the prayers of Jeremy Taylor or George Herbert's 'To all Angels and Saints' leaping out, demanding to be included. One entry alone, on the Resurrection, includes meditations from Edward Sparke, a prayer by Daniel Featley, extracts from four sermons of Lancelot Andrewes, a Latin hymn translated, and a brief passage from a sermon by John Donne. This frequent and varied borrowing is typical of the work as a whole. Added to this there are two other less dominant hands writing the manuscript as well as Traherne's; the *Church's Year-Book* is the fruit of multiple minds in terms of both its authorship and its content.

Traherne sees the Anglican Church as adhering to the teachings of 'Primitive Times' and 'Holy Antiquity', phrases common in both the *Church's Year-Book* and *Roman Forgeries*; he commemorates the saints as received practice in the 'Christian, Catholick & Apostolick' church (*CYB*, fol. 2v). 'Why should we not spend som time upon Holy Days?' he asks. They are 'The Days of Heaven seen upon Earth . . . Appointed Seasons, wherin GOD keepeth Open House' (*CYB*, fol. 100). Abolished in 1645 but never totally suppressed, the *Book of Common Prayer* re-emerged as the embodiment of a church that saw itself as both reformed and catholic; in the *Church's Year-Book*, Traherne's approach to the *Book of Common Prayer* and his borrowing from the popular prayer book commentaries of the period that were likewise both anti-puritan and anti-papist show him to be an apologist for this essentially Anglican tradition.

The Ficino Notebook

This small notebook, held at the British Library, contains extracts from the *Commentaries* on Plato that the Renaissance humanist Marsilo Ficino had translated into Latin: a long Latin life of Socrates, brief notes from Theophilus Gale's *Court of the Gentiles*, part II, and Ficino's 'Argumentum' to his translation of Hermes Trismegistus, as well as other notes. Traherne's comments on Socrates in *Centuries*, his citations of Plato in *Centuries* and in *Christian Ethicks* are all linked to the Ficino translations. It seems he made use of this notebook till the end of his life.

To any but serious scholars equipped with Latin and a love of pains-taking detail, this notebook will remain uninviting. What may be of more general interest is the manner of Traherne's note-taking, his omissions and alterations. For he altered freely the passages he copied, deleting what he deemed of no use and rearranging what he had chosen to suit his purposes. For instance, in one Socratic passage he deleted the part that spiritualized beauty, making it an application of the mind, and included the body only as an image of intellectual beauty. As Catherine Owen notes, 'in this omission we may trace Traherne's own conviction of the intrinsic value of the physical body, and indeed of the whole material world'.[112] Much has been made of Traherne's debt to Pico, Ficino and Renaissance humanism, but although he borrows their words when it suits him, Traherne is never entirely led by their philosophy of man. When what they say about the high place of man in the universe agrees with his high view of man, taken from the early church fathers and the doctrine of the incarnation, he applauds them; when it disagrees he omits or alters their words.

Early Notebook

Traherne's *Early Notebook* is a 396-page manuscript in Latin and English containing his undergraduate notes on ethics, history and geometry, some doodles, brief experimentation with ciphers and codes, a bawdy poem hidden in shorthand, extensive notes from Francis Bacon on, among other things, science and magic, a summary in Latin of

112 Catherine Owen, 'The Thought and Art of Thomas Traherne', University of London Master's thesis (1957), p. 29.

Justin's history, scholastic ethics, poetry of Francis Quarles and a meditation by William Austin, as well as notes from a number of other
books. Traherne's notes on Bacon are perhaps the most fascinating
part of the *Early Notebook*; arguments he records here appear in
Inducements to Retiredness, Christian Ethicks and *Commentaries of
Heaven*. Not least among them is Bacon's metaphor of the divine
compass that directs the ship of the Church, his arguments 'Against
al Quakers, Enthusiasts, &c' (*EN*, p. 103) and his latitudinarian plea
for peace between Protestant parts of the Church. Very little of the
notebook is original to Traherne, and its importance lies mainly in
the glimpses it gives of Traherne's intellectual development. Also
called 'Philip Traherne's notebook', the book originally belonged to
Traherne's older brother: a note on page iii states: 'Philip Traherne is
the true owner of this booke Amen Anno Domini 1655'. However,
Philip's notes come to an abrupt end at page 5 and thereafter the notes
in the book are Thomas's. He seems to have used it as an undergraduate
notebook and then as a more general commonplace book – the later
entries are most likely the work of a young adult Traherne. After
Thomas's death Philip, having inherited his brother's books, used the
notebook again. It then passed on to Rashleigh Duke (1841) and thence
to Percy Dobell (1935), son of Bertram Dobell, the first publisher of
Traherne's poetry.[113] In 1951 Dobell sold the *Early Notebook*, together
with three other Traherne manuscripts, to the Bodleian Library where
it is now held.

The Commonplace Book

This notebook contains two quite separate parts. The second is a fair
copy of the poems described above as the Dobell manuscript, after the
first publisher of Traherne's poetry Bertram Dobell. The first part is a
commonplace of extracts from various authors gathered by Traherne,
it is thought, during the last four years of his life. Many clerical commonplace notebooks of the period were written in Latin with named
sources – Traherne's is primarily in English and his sources frequently
go unnamed. His main sources are Theophilus Gale's *Court of the
Gentiles* and Hermes Trismegistus' *Divine Pymander*. Gale, his contem-

---

113 See notes on pages ii and iii of the *Early Notebook*. For greater detail see
Marks, 'Thomas Traherne's Early Studies', *PBSA*, 62 (1968), pp. 511–36.

porary at Oxford, is a fellow theologian whose ideas appear in many of his works. Hermes, an ancient philosopher[114] favoured by Traherne for his ability to write in a way that for Traherne blended pre-Christian, Hebraic teachings with Christian humanism, appears throughout Traherne's work and perhaps most eloquently in *The Kingdom of God*. *The Commonplace Book* is written in two hands, that of Traherne and an amanuensis, and the interplay of these two in the construction of the manuscript is fascinating. Where the amanuensis copies faithfully and carefully, Traherne abstracts and condenses, altering the passages as he copies to suit his eventual purposes, even inserting comments of his own. A few of Traherne's instructions to the amanuensis remain in the margins. In places Traherne begins a passage that the amanuensis completes; sometimes the reverse happens. Traherne goes back and checks the copying of the amanuensis, occasionally inserting what has been accidentally omitted. Clearly the two worked together closely as Traherne gathered inspiration for *The Kingdom of God* and for what was to become the last completed work of his lifetime, *Christian Ethicks*.[115]

Traherne and conflict

The seven years of Civil War in England (1642–49) were the years of Traherne's childhood – years that witnessed bitter and bloody battles when his city of Hereford was fought over, and acts of wanton cruelty were committed by both sides in the conflict. It is no wonder that in adult life Traherne welcomed the stability that the Restoration provided. The *Select Meditations* are replete with considerations and asides showing his enthusiasm for the restoration of the king and of an established order. His love of kingship is partly a love of pageantry and of symbol, but it is also about the real and profound need Traherne sensed in himself and in his nation for an enduring peace. 'O lord', he writes with real relief, 'when our citties and Teritories are united by Laws in the fear of thy Name: and are at one accord in Calling upon Thee;

---

114 The name Trismegistus means 'thrice great' and there is some debate among scholars as to whether Hermes Trismegistus is in fact a single author or a collection of writings gathered under this title.
115 For a more detailed description of *The Commonplace Book* see Carol Marks, 'Traherne's *Commonplace Book*', *PBSA*, 60 (1966) pp. 458–65.

when they Move by Consent like an united Army How Ravishing is
their Beauty, How Sweet their Order! It is O my God as if the Nation
had but one Soul.'[116]

It is clear from Traherne's verbal assaults, mentioned earlier, on both
the Roman Catholic Church and the 'Independents', that Traherne was
at home in neither of these forms of Christianity. However, the nature
of his commitment to the re-established Church of England (or the
English Church, as he called it) and the depth of his involvement in the
debates that surrounded the developing theology of the re-established
church are just beginning to be understood.

Traherne had been educated at a time when it was illegal to use the
Book of Common Prayer, yet he came to love it. As a post-Protectorate
adult he had to choose between a 'gathered church' and an apostolic
church, with all this now meant in terms of episcopal versus presby-
terian structure. Traherne was educated in a Puritan college. He was
approved by the Puritans,[117] and placed in the living of Credenhill by the
testimonials of several ministers whose Puritan beliefs were such that
they refused to subscribe to the Act of Uniformity when it appeared in
August 1662 and were expelled from their livings. The Act of Uniformity required clergymen to affirm the *Book of Common Prayer* and
to be episcopally ordained before St Bartholomew's Day 1662. Puritan
ministers currently in livings were permitted to remain in their parishes
if they complied with these regulations. Smith and Lowe, Voyle and
Primrose, who had signed Traherne's certificates, were among those
many ministers whose refusal to comply ended their parish ministries.
And yet Traherne himself remained, not only being ordained, but
seeking episcopal ordination in 1660, well in advance of needing to
do so.[118]

He had conscious choices to make, not only about the prayer book
but also about bishops and vestments and the carefully ordered liturgies
of feast days and saints' commemorations. As Donald Allchin notes,
he had to *become* what we now call Anglican. Traherne is described
by a contemporary as one who 'became much in love with the beautiful

116 *SM*, I, 85.
117 Lambeth Palace Library MS. 998 records the patron of Credenhill in
1662: the Puritan Amabella Countess Dowager of Kent, and names the Puritan
ministers who approved Traherne as: William Voyle, William Lowe, Sam Smith,
George Primrose, Robert Breton, Benjamin Baxter, Joseph Cholmley.
118 The see of Hereford was vacant in 1660, when Traherne was ordained by
Robert Skinner, Bishop of Oxford.

order and *Primitive* Devotions of this our excellent Church',[119] as if he underwent a real process of change from Puritan to conforming priest. This could be an outsider's gloss on Traherne's theological changes; Traherne could have been merely protecting his career, but his writings do not suggest that this is so. Here he seems to have found a happy home, yet he never forgot the conflict that surrounded almost every expression of that faith, written and liturgical. Much of the detailed debate in *A Sober View* and *Roman Forgeries* concern the emerging and conflicting doctrinal discussions that were forming the English Church against the backgrounds of Geneva and Rome. Where had the Church of England come from and what shape was it to have? About these issues Traherne was passionate, as he was in his defence of the church against such dissenting groups as Anabaptists, Socinians and Quakers. Amid the expressions of gratitude for and celebration of the church's feasts and festivals we find in the *Church's Year-Book*, there is also a note of defence. Here, as ever, Traherne seems aware of an audience that demands an answer – the very observance of festivals, even of a weekly eucharist, was a cause of contention. Where in scripture are we required to celebrate the Lord's supper so frequently? What can be the relevance of saints' days? What right has the church to establish such celebrations as Easter or Christmas, both of which were dated to correspond with pagan festivals? In the *Church's Year-Book*, as elsewhere, the voices of those with a rigid interpretation of 'sola scriptura' perch, like a persistent parrot, on Traherne's shoulder.

Where *Select Meditations* confesses his profound relief and joy at the re-establishment of the English Church and his horror of those who oppose it,[120] *A Sober View* assesses the orthodoxy of fellow theologians against the doctrines of the Church of England. And in *Roman Forgeries* and the *Church's Year-Book* we see an almost obsessive interest in the continuity of the restoration church with the early apostolic church. In all of these works he sees the re-established church as an inheritor of the earlier church's ritual and order. His directing his reader to scripture and reason, to the Thirty-Nine Articles, the comfortable words, and various prayers from the liturgy are just several of many such anchors throughout his works. Authority derives neither from

119 Preface to *A Serious and Pathetical Comtemplation*, London: George Hickes, 1699.
120 *SM*, I, 85.

Rome nor from the use of scripture alone, he insists, but from that blend of reason and conscience within, and scripture, tradition and state without.

> Let Reason Scripture Church State Conscience joyn
> Church Scripture State about and for me shine
> Reason and Conscience in my Soul within.
>   (*COH*, 'Authoritie')

The feasts and festivals, patterns of governance, habits, viewpoints, customs and practices that we now call Anglican would not have been so called by him. The term did not become common parlance until much later. Nevertheless an Anglican is what he was becoming, and what Anglicans after him have become in part because of him. He is, as Allchin writes, a man 'assimilating a tradition in such a way as to be assimilated by it'.[121]

Central to his passion for a national church was this concern with authority. His love of the English Church was real, but it was not a private love of religion alone; it was also a love of social order and the establishment of national peace and security as well as a love of historic doctrine and practice.[122] The bloodshed and battles were over. The people could live in peace. It was as if for him, at least at the time of the Restoration, the nation at last had one soul.

Yet it was in this settled peace that for many intellectual life became unsettled. Straddling as it did the medieval world-view of preceding years and the modern world of Harvey and Hevelius, the seventeenth century saw an unprecedented emergence of sciences, natural, political and social – a kind of collapse and expansion at the same time that rattled the very foundations of thought. This was especially true for those churchmen whose mindset remained medieval, but whether the church embraced or rejected the new discoveries, those discoveries remain intellectually significant to this day. The issues we still discuss about the place of reason, the nature of authority, the character of the universe, are questions rooted in this seventeenth-century period of rapid intellectual change.

Traherne was not of the reactionary churchman mould. For him all scientific discovery was a revelation of divine truth. Intellectual changes

121 Allchin, *Profitable Wonders*, p. 25.
122 See Smith's Introduction to *SM*.

were afoot; one could sense a building wave and even that it might crash against the bulwarks of one's certainties with imponderable force, but for many in the seventeenth century the spiritual and the scientific were still intricately intertwined. It would have been in no sense strange to look into a microscope and see eternity.[123] Traherne revelled in the new infinities revealed by the microscope (1660) and the telescope (1590). This love of discovery, the sciences in particular, is hinted at many times in his poetry and appears again in *Centuries of Meditations*. But never has it been more obvious than now, in the recently discovered *Kingdom of God*. Traherne devotes ten folio pages to the atom – its properties, immutability, incorruptibility, volatility, strength, power and excellence. He also draws on Harvey and the circulation of the blood, the nature of light, the rules of incidence and the laws of motion, the operations of the sun, the annual and diurnal motions of the moon, and contemporary theories about the possibility of life existing on it. Further chapters take the reader into considerations of philosophers and scientists: Copernicus, Grotius, Descartes (whose *Discourse on Method* was published in the year of Traherne's birth), Gassendus, Hevelius, Dr Charleton, Dr Willis, the learned Gale (a contemporary of Traherne's at Oxford), Richardson, Bacon and 'the Incomparable Mr Robert Boyl', to name a few. Add to these his own experiments with candles and mirrors inspired by his study of light, and the numerous references to watches, springs, clocks and machines found in *The Kingdom of God*, and one sees an intriguing picture of Traherne emerging. Here is a man deeply engaged in the discoveries and discussions, experiments and theories of his day. There is no whiff of the whimsical here; he may be an amateur scientist, and a dabbler in many other fields, but he is an experienced priest, an able theologian and a serious thinker. His poetry, which takes a back seat in *The Kingdom of God*, does not disappear but states with strong conviction:

> Our Dreaming understandings must awake
> And in RIGHT REASON satisfy'd must take
> Their Sovereign Delights . . .
> This brings Men home, and feeds them not with lies:
> Teacheth our duties, and his Laws, to prize:

123 Look, for instance, at the writings of the scientist Robert Boyle, such as *Seraphick Love* (1659) and *The High Veneration Man's Intellect owes to God* (1684–85), that are laced with theology.

And makes Men know in their Inferior State,
The Joyfull Life of Heaven to Imitate.
It leads us to a Real Blessedness,
That we may dayly neer at hand possess.[124]

Buzzing with the power and potential of human research and reason, there is an intimacy that is not always cosiness in his apprehension of the world. Traherne's world was alarming as well as beautiful, frightening in its infinity, full of want and hazard and sometimes solitariness (here, in his unflinching examinations of minute detail, he is not unlike the modern writer Annie Dillard). He writes of a grace-inhabited world just at the time when its tiniest and most distant features were being discovered and explored at a more staggering rate than ever before. The science and religion divide that we have experienced over several hundred years was not yet a yawning chasm, though Traherne sensed that it would become so. It may not be surprising that at this critical time in the development of English and European culture, and in the development of the Anglican tradition, he often draws on the security of antiquity. Charting his way in arguments of Reformation and Counter-Reformation, he turns to the fathers that predated these discussions.

Changes within the church felt equally staggering in their significance and speed. Calvinism and Roman Catholicism exerted separate forces, conformity and noncomformity raged within. There is an apparent irony in Traherne's ardent defence of the national church and condemnation of 'hereticks' alongside his documented friendships with nonconformist sympathizers and those trying to comprehend all within the church such as Sir Edward Harley, Thomas Good and Orlando Bridgeman. His efforts to comprehend may have answered a sincere desire to preserve a single national church based on an irenic disposition towards unity. Or it may be that his involvement with the move to comprehend was a strategic necessity. Comprehension, it is argued, could have been a political tool for keeping dissenters within the fold and thus retaining power by providing the broad mandate requisite for the wielding of power.[125] Seen in this light there is no necessary disparity

---

124 'Invisibles are not diminished by' (*KOG*, Ch. 23, ll. 272–4, 284–9).

125 For an interesting exposition of this view of comprehension see Richard Ashcroft, 'Latitudinarianism and Toleration; Historical Myth Versus Political History,' in Richard Kroll and Perez Zagorin, eds, *Philosophy, Science, and Religion in England, 1640–1700*, Cambridge: Cambridge University Press, 1992, pp. 151–77.

between the condemnation of 'hereticks' and the desire to comprehend all; condemnation and comprehension could be the opposite ends of a single mallet designed to defend the interests of a unified church.

This business of defining the church led Traherne into controversies of a depth we may not have expected from the nature-loving 'Poet of Felicity'. As far as we know, Traherne left no diaries, letters or even a written will, but he did leave us two accounts of personal confrontations, in *Commentaries of Heaven* and *Roman Forgeries*.

Notice the satisfaction with which, in *Commentaries of Heaven*, he describes having the upper hand in his argument with a certain John Tombes, pastor of a local dissenting church in Leominster:

> The Opinion of the Anabaptists seems the most innocent, & . . . yet by a strange . . . fate, it is the seed plot of Heresies, & the grand Nursery of Schismes & Disorders. No man is an Anabaptist long but he sucks in some other horrible Opinion soon after . . .
>
> I have my self conferred with Mr Tombs the great Ringleader of that Sect in this last Age, & have reason to believ he was condemned of his Conscience. For being a deep & judicious man, he could not but see, that his Opinion was utterly ruined, if the Jews were under the same Covenant with us, & therefore he held that the Jews were under a Covenant of Works, & we under a Covenant of Grace, & this he made it his Business to teach in his Sermons at this Amsterdam, his Heretical Church in Leominster in Herefordshire where having the advantage twice to meet him, I both times asked him the same Questions, & both times received the same Answer, that the Jews were under the Covenant of Works. But both times asking him what use or place could be for Sacrifices in a Covenant of Works he was both times as Blank, & mute as a Fish. For Sacrifices were Types of a Mediator & a Savior: their Blood was a shadow of the Blood of Christ. (*COH*, 'Baptism')

'Blank and mute as a fish'. So much for Mr Tombes of Leominster. In the introduction to *Roman Forgeries* a prominent Roman Catholic, a person with a taste for disputation not unlike Traherne's, is similarly dispatched:

> One Evening, as I came out of the Bodleian Library, which is the Glory of Oxford, and this Nation . . . I was saluted by a Person who told me there was a Gentleman his Cosen, in the Quadrangle, a man

that had spent many thousand pounds in promoting Popery, and that he had a desire to speak with me. . . . He was a notable man, of an Eloquent Tongue, and competent Reading. . . . I asked him what he would say, if I could clearly prove, that the Church of Rome was guilty of forging . . . *Councils* that never were, forging Letters in the name of the first Bishops and Martyrs made 5, 6, 700 years after they were dead, to the utter disguising and defacing of *Antiquity*? . . . *Tush these are nothing but lyes*, quoth he. Sir, answered I . . . You met me this Evening at the Library door; if you please to meet me there to morrow morning at eight of the Clock, I will take you in . . . and there I will shew in *your own Authors*, and . . . prove the frauds and forgeries. . . . He would not come; but made this strange reply; *What if they be Forgeries? What hurt is that to the Church of Rome?* No! (cryed I amazed) . . . Is it nothing in Rome to be guilty of counterfeiting . . . *Records of Antiquity*? I have done with you! whereupon I turned from him . . . And with this I thought it meet to acquaint the Reader. (*RF*, introduction)

'. . . And with this I thought it meet to acquaint the Reader.' This account and the record of his encounter with John Tombes is the kind of bragging you might expect to overhear in a conversation between friends: 'Well, she said . . . And I told her . . . She knew I was right' – the kind of thing that might be delicious to recount to a sympathetic friend, but you might not, on reflection, like the whole world to hear. Yet Traherne was prepared to publish these accounts. This may be mere bravado. Or it may be intended to encourage fellow clergy who might themselves be caught up in controversy. However we are to understand these moments of autobiography, they clearly show a man with a taste for the cut and thrust of debate.

Traherne's ventures into controversy should perhaps be no surprise. After all, *Roman Forgeries* was both an attack and a defence. The tone of *Roman Forgeries* is so confrontational that most early Traherne scholars had difficulty placing it in the canon. In the final chapter he suggests that the Roman Church, a 'Mother of Lyes', 'espoused' to the Devil, has produced an 'adulterate brood' and so is 'defiled with so great an Off-spring of notorious *Impostures*'. 'Stink', 'filth', 'defilement', though typical of its day, is hardly the language of modern ecumenism. Some lovers of Traherne have wondered what drove him to write such a book as *Roman Forgeries* and how the same mind that produced such beautiful meditations could also produce such vitriol.

Yet one of the things I have found in studying the newer discoveries is that they draw me back again to *Roman Forgeries*. Far from being the 'odd man out', *Roman Forgeries* is one in a line of controversial texts written by Traherne which, though they deal with different controversies, all have a distinctly similar tone. The tone of voice in *A Sober View* when he writes:

> That God from all Eternity simply and without Caus hateth any, and that there are multitude of Reprobates so hated, is as Damnable poyson as can that way be put into the mouth of a Christian.
>
> I never Knew any Person in Despair in my Life, but this opinion was the Ground of his Despair. Nor can any man do the devil greater Service than by teaching this Doctrine. The first thing the Devil persuaded our first Parents in Paradice was that God did not love them Enough: (*SV*, XXVIII, ll. 143–9)

is not dissimilar even from his best-beloved *Centuries*, where he rails against the vanities of his age those 'barbarous opinions and Monstrous Apprehensions, which we Nick name Civility and the Mode' which 'put Grubs and Worms in Mens Heads: that . . . eat our all their Happiness.' Traherne was hot in the pursuit and purveyance of truth, he got angry about things, and he was not ashamed to thrash an opponent. If we have difficulty marrying this controversial Traherne with the tone of the Traherne we have known, perhaps we have not thoroughly known Traherne in the first place.

What is clear is that Traherne was a debater and a wrestler for truth. He wrestled with particular individuals, with ideas, movements, heresies and, as reading the *Select Meditations* shows, with himself as well. Part of this was due to his thirst for truth. It also had to do with the time in which he lived, with its inheritance of Puritan introspection and religious iconoclasm, in which controversial writing of this kind was common parlance. Traherne was deeply concerned about the security and stability of both church and state. Here we see something much more mature, more layered, more important than a mere love of argument. Mightily engaged as they are in ascertaining doctrinal accuracy and correct church authority and practice, his arguments are also about the preservation and prosperity of the people to whom he had dedicated his life. His passion for the spiritual state of his nation runs, like a red thread, through all his controversial works. They are not isolated, idiosyncratic aberrations from a joyful norm. All the controversial texts share Traherne's profound concern with church doctrine and with church authority.

Friendly with Bridgeman, Harley and Good, noted above, Traherne seems to have thrown in his lot with those seeking to comprehend disparate parties within the church, and yet his forceful confrontations show us that there were lines of toleration he would not cross. When he falls out with the Quakers it is, as we have seen, because of their denial of baptism, the first of all sacraments by which we enter the sacramental life of the church. Traherne's repeated vociferous attack on the Socinians (Unitarians) is really a defence of the doctrines both of the Trinity and the incarnation. Jesus is God, he insists; nothing less will do. The sacraments and creedal doctrines are not negotiable, Traherne insists. If his controversial writings seem harsh to us that may be because in them he is defending things very dear to his heart. He is in a sense setting the boundaries within which happiness can flourish – erecting the walls of Eden. That he was making these walls secure is yet another stroke of his genius for happiness. Even more rooted in the realities and necessities of his time than we may have credited him with before, in securing the foundations for his own time, he secures them for ours.

The following lines from *The Ceremonial Law* describe the Ten Commandments as a kind of severe mercy:

What may we think it but a pledge of Love,
A Brief Epitome of all above;
Felicitie disguisd in fiery Words,
Each one of which an Heavenly Light affords,
Directing Mortals how they might enjoy
The highest Objects in the fairest Way.
            (*TCL*, 'The 10 Commandments')

Traherne's controversies are just this: 'felicitie disguisd in fiery words'. The roots of his felicity are deep in the rocky soil of human struggle, feeding the most magnificent and enduring of trees.

Like Hooker and Andrewes, who shared Traherne's concern with the formation of the church of his time, one question then and now is the same. Do we define the church by its visible and perceived limits, by those who belong outside it, or do we define it positively 'as the place where the Spirit of Truth blows who is to be distinguished at once from the "private spirit" and the "spirit of the world" '?[126] Traherne's controversialist writings, such as *A Sober View* and *Roman Forgeries* and those parts of *Commentaries of Heaven* that guide the reader to 'answers' for problematic challengers, do the former whereas his most masterful works, among which we might list the *Centuries* and *The Kingdom of God*, seek to do the second.

Traherne and the holy life

Much has been written about Traherne and happiness. His admonitions to enjoy the world are famous; his belief in a good creation, in the innocence of childhood, in the pursuit of felicity, to the study of which he claimed to have 'devoted' himself 'wholly', are what we most know and love about his writing. Such confessions as:

> When I came into the country, and being seated among silent trees, and meads and hills, had all my time in mine own hands, I resolved to spend it all, whatever it cost me, in search of happiness ... (C, III, 46)

and

> I came into this world only that I might be happy. And whatsoever it cost me, I will be happy. A happiness there is, and it is my desire to enjoy it. (C, IV, 7)

are the flagships of the 'poet of Felicity' reading of Traherne. 'Nothing but felicity is worthy of our labour' (C, III, 56), he insists. This single-mindedness, born out of his longing for happiness and a frustration that despite all he learned about the world in his studies at university 'There was never a tutor that did professly teach Felicity' (C, III, 37), runs so deep in Traherne that it becomes a vocation. He becomes that tutor. Felicity becomes his great theme. Chapter 2 of this book takes a closer look at felicity in Traherne.

However, one of the problems with the poet of Felicity, for theologians, is that his writings have seemed to have forgotten important matters of sin and salvation and of the Christian call to a life of

126 Nicholas Lossky, *Lancelot Andrewes the Preacher*, Oxford: Oxford University Press, 1991, p. 274.

self-sacrifice. If happiness is so important to Traherne, where does that leave holiness? Traherne wrote that these two were the same thing. After Aristotle and Aquinas, Traherne argues that the happy life is the virtuous one. Felicity is more than temporary happiness; it is *beatitudo* and *eudaimonia*, the blessed life, the life of virtue, 'for no man could be wise that knew excellent things without doing them' (C, IV, 31). Traherne's most highly developed study of virtue is his *Christian Ethicks*, the only work other than the controversial *Roman Forgeries* that he had prepared for publication before his death. In it, as we have seen, he gives a magisterial account of the virtues, their beauties and uses, and how they relate to each other, in hope that his reader will be so attracted by virtue that vice will be of little interest by comparison.

There were other guides to the holy life in circulation when Traherne was writing his. By far the most widely read of these was Richard Allestree's *The Whole Duty of Man* (1658), a manual on Christian ethics designed to give the reader clear, unadorned instructions for holy living. Allestree's work appeals to the common man; Traherne's treatment of virtue seeks a more sophisticated audience. As noted above, Traherne cites *The Whole Duty* in the opening sections of *Christian Ethicks* and distances his work from Allestree's. Where Allestree writes of the individual's duty in a world that is dirty, Traherne explores the faces of goodness in a world that is blessed. While we may see in Traherne less of duty, we find more of vision, and we are drawn by the beauty of virtue.[127]

In choosing to write *Christian Ethicks* as a study of the beauty of the virtues in turn rather than as a prescription on the duty or conduct of his readers, Traherne not only steers his reader away from an ethic of individual morality, such as we see both in Allestree, he also resists the secularization of ethics that was occurring in the writings of fellow seventeenth-century ethicists Hugo Grotius and Thomas Hobbes. Whereas Hobbes, for instance, saw peace as a form of self-preservation, Traherne saw it as a platform for unity. When the various cities move by consent and are united in order, the cities are beautified and the church dignified. 'How ravishing is their beauty, how sweet their order,'

127 For an analysis of the similarities as well as the differences between Traherne and Allestree see Kevin Laam, 'Thomas Traherne, Richard Allestree and the Ethics of Appropriation', in Jacob Blevins, ed., *Re-Reading Traherne: A Collection of New Critical Essays*, Arizona Renaissance Studies, 2007, pp. 62–96.

he wrote; it is 'as if the Nation had but one Soul' (*SM*, I, 85). He is concerned not so much with the preservation of the individual self as with the flourishing of community.

Here we may find a challenge to our modern understanding of virtue that would see morality as largely a matter of personal choices on critical issues. What ought one to do in a given tricky situation or faced with a particularly complicated moral question? The ethical response would seem to be to evaluate alternative rational solutions, preferably from a neutral point of view, and come to a disinterested conclusion, one that is unencumbered by a past and applicable to any relevant present. However, to attempt an ethical answer that is about neutral decision-making is to forget that most people make decisions not in a vacuum but according to their prior moral commitments; they choose what they choose because of the kind of character they have formed. So much so that people often say, when reflecting on crisis decisions they have made, that they only 'did what they had to do' or that they 'couldn't help it', they 'had no choice' but to act in a certain way. Emphasizing moments of decision, to the neglect of the moral life in which the decisions are made, divorces action from agent, and agent from his or her story. As Sam Wells points out, by attempting a solution that inhabits an eternal unstoried present, we arrive at what can only be temporary.

More recent theological studies suggest that to make ethics a matter of solving conundrums is to rob it of its real strength, which lies instead in the everyday decisions we make. These happen in such an ordinary way that we hardly even consider them to be ethical decisions at all, but rather reflexes. You treat another as you would wish to be treated because it seems right to do so. You sacrifice something for the sake of another. You pick up a piece of litter. You defend the rights of the weak. All of these decisions are in fact underpinned by an ethic that seeks to care for the earth, and for each other. They are each in their way expressions of a virtuous life. Modern virtue ethics would argue that virtue ought to be less of a tough decision and more of a habit of life. Virtuous habituation, the habit of virtue by which virtue becomes second nature to the individual, takes us straight back to Aristotle. For Traherne this transformation, while personal, is not private, but occurs, is taught and practised, within the community of faith. Traherne's *Christian Ethicks*, often criticized for its treatment of virtue to the exclusion of vice, in fact slips into dialogue effortlessly with the work of modern virtue ethicists such as Alasdair MacIntyre, Stanley

Hauerwas and Sam Wells,[128] who hold to a largely Aristotelian model of virtue. For Aristotle and for Aquinas after him, morality begins with the acquisition of virtuous habits; for Traherne it begins with the unlearning of 'custom' and the relearning of the habit of virtue. Becoming a child again, as Christ taught, is for Traherne 'deeper far than is generally believed' (C, III, 5). For all his platonic imagery and his much-noted indebtedness to neo-Platonism, Traherne's moral philosophy is situated squarely in the Aristotelian/Thomist tradition. As Paul Cefalu has recently noted, 'With respect to questions of human psychology and cognition, moral philosophy, and the nature of God, Traherne is a new-scholastic who makes use of Platonic imagery and concepts, not a Platonist who sometimes invokes scholastic terminology.'[129]

Traherne's ethic of virtue is also an ethic of activity. For him happiness is not a theory, it is about doing: 'there is an active happiness, which consisteth in blessed operations,' he writes; 'philosophers are not those that speak but do great things' (C, IV, 12). Not only is this ethic of activity seen positively in his discussion of act in *Centuries*, in *Commentaries of Heaven* and in *Christian Ethicks*, it is also seen negatively in, for example, his dealing with the virtue of contentment. 'Contentment is a sleepy thing!' proclaims the first line of his poem on the subject; and it is a virtue largely sidelined in *Christian Ethicks*, despite his admission that there is a value in 'true contentment' that is not mere resignation or enforced happiness. His displacement of contentment in favour of aspiration, desire and the spiritual quest makes it clear that for Traherne happiness is as much in the process of finding as in the pleasure of enjoying. The usefulness of contentment is limited and it comes too near Stoicism to be a famous virtue to Traherne.

If holiness in Traherne is not primarily about self-denial and the performance of duty, as in the case of more popular seventeenth-century handbooks on holiness such as Allestree's, in what does it consist? Although *Christian Ethicks* is addressed to the individual, it urges a

128 For a greater exploration of virtue ethics from a theological perspective see Alasdair MacIntyre, *After Virtue: A Study in Moral Theology*, London: Duckworth, 1984; Stanley Hauerwas and Charles Pinches, *Christians Among the Virtues*, Notre Dame: University of Notre Dame Press, 1997; Stanley Hauerwas, *Character and the Christian Life: A Study in Theological Ethics*, San Antonio: Trinity University Press, 1975; Sam Wells, *Improvisation: The Drama of Christian Ethics*, London: SPCK, 2004.
129 Paul Cefalu, 'Thomistic Metaphysics and Ethics in the Poetry and Prose of Thomas Traherne,' *Literature and Theology*, 16 (2002), pp. 248–69.

holy life that is lived in connection with others and is conceived as a process; it is more concerned with what man may become than with what one man should do. The fact that Traherne has created in it a sweeping account of the virtues, as opposed to a handbook for dutifully living a 'good' life, reflects his central belief that holiness is not just about personal holiness, but about the holiness of life in general. Living the virtuous life is not only about doing one's duty to God and our neighbour, but also about beginning the blessed life, the life of heaven now. We are creatures called to holy living in a world that is called to become the kingdom of God. There is an essential unity about this in Traherne. Where other devotional writers of the period juxtapose the earthly and the heavenly, Traherne proposes a heaven that may begin now and an earth that is full of God's glory. His theology hearkens back to the 'Primitive Devotions' of 'Holy antiquitie'. In many places in *The Kingdom of God*, Traherne refers to John Chrysostom, as he does in *Centuries*. When he cites Irenaeus, Augustine, Hilaire, Theodore, Ambrose, Chrysostom, Gregory the Great and Bernard in *Commentaries of Heaven* and elsewhere he does so not just, although tangentially and in company with his contemporaries, as a means of attacking Rome,[130] but also because the fathers nourished his view of creation and incarnation – a sense of the holiness of the world. This is where holiness is found in Traherne, in the life of virtue that sees the first steps of the life of heaven taken here in this extraordinary world.

Neither holiness nor happiness then, in Traherne, should be considered private matters. Expressed in personal terms though they may be, his considerations lead to this: that happiness and holiness go hand in hand, that the truly happy life, the life of *beatitudo*, is also the life lived to God, in God, for God and through God. As such it is a life that necessarily includes the well-being and happiness of others. The holy life, though it may think differently from the secular life, is therefore not 'set apart' from the world, which has been divinely gifted anyway; and no life that is dedicated to individual happiness alone can achieve its end.

'Love is the true means by which the world is enjoyed: Our Love to others, and others' Love to us', he writes in *Centuries*; 'The sun and stars please me in ministering to you. They please me in ministering to a thousand others as well as you' (C, II, 62, 69). This principle of

130 See *COH*, 'Antiquitie', fol. 106, 107v; see also *COH*, 'Antichrist'. Among the ancient fathers he cites Irenaeus against Rome in *Roman Forgeries*.

reciprocity and relationality is seen by Traherne in the heart of God who is three related persons – the Father, the Son and the Holy Spirit – extending love to the creation: 'God by Love wholly ministereth to others, and yet wholly ministereth to himself, Love having this wonder in it also, that among innumerable millions, it maketh every one the sole and single end of all things . . .' (C, II, 55). What the doctrine of the Trinity says to Traherne is that loving relationship is at the heart of divinity; if we are to be divine, we too must relate in love to each other, to God, to the world. In the media there is at present much talk of happiness and how, despite our modern material and medical gains, we have largely, as a society, lost it. Traherne would say that we may find it again not by the pursuit of personal satisfaction, but by participating in the dynamic of relationship initiated by God. At the heart of his thinking is a God who is, in the doctrine of the Trinity, both personal and communal and a God who, in the doctrine of the incarnation, comes to us, lives as one of us and seeks to be in relationship with us. These two doctrines of the incarnation and the Trinity are cornerstones of all of Traherne's well-known theories of happiness and the enjoyment of the world, as well as of his high view of man. After Athanasius and the Greek Orthodox tradition, Traherne takes the view that God incarnate among us raises all of humanity to be the place where God may dwell; God's chosen home is not only heaven, but also human skin and this small globe of earth.

I

Creatures and Powers

What kind of creatures are we? In what kind of world? These questions preoccupied Traherne from his youth. And his endeavours to understand what it meant to be human and to appreciate his place in the created world started him on a lifelong study of nature and human nature that led to startling perceptions of the human soul and of the universe. Traherne's inquisitive interest in the created world, fed by the burgeoning sciences of his day, was not just of the bug-collecting kind. He was fascinated equally in the telescope and the microscope, pulled by the stretch of both infinities that kept his mind elastic and his thoughts thrilling. An accurate appreciation of creation is, for him, the beginning of happiness. As he wrote in the introduction to *Christian Ethicks*: 'Above all, pray to be sensible of the excellency of the Creation, for upon the due sense of its excellency the life of felicity wholly dependeth.' Traherne's study of creation is nowhere more extensive than in *The Kingdom of God*. There he considers its tiniest details, the great sweeping applications of its underlying principles, and the newest scientific discoveries and theories, all as means of divine disclosure. In a fusion of images in *The Kingdom of God*, Traherne at once figures creation as that body that God has assumed to make himself as visible as it is possible he should be, and a love letter from God to humankind, his beloved.

It is because he believes that the divine is disclosed in the material world that the world takes on a kind of holiness. Creation is itself holy. Here Traherne echoes the Eastern Christian tradition that sees the whole of creation as penetrated with the energy of God. In his 'essence' God remains transcendent and unknowable, but his 'energy' is everywhere present in the material world, in God's operation and action. As Basil the Great explains, 'No one has ever seen the essence of God, but we believe in the essence because we experience the

energy.'[131] This approach is not exclusively a feature of Orthodox or
Catholic spirituality, however. Belden Lane draws our attention to the
writings of Martin Luther in which God, though not seen face to face,
is 'yet encountered with a striking immediacy in the *larvae Dei* – the
created marvels of God's hand, the bread and wine at Mass, even the
twisted mystery of one's own self as created being' (*Landscapes of
the Sacred*, p. 39). As Luther himself put it, 'All created ordinances are
masks or allegories wherewith God depicts his theology; they are
meant, as it were, to contain Christ.'[132] Calvin too was imbued with this
sense of the holy in creation, referring to the natural world as the
theatrum gloriae dei,[133] a theatre of God's glory. In Anglicanism, these
ideas became part of a sacramental theology that included creation.
Brian Horne suggests that Anglicans have given more attention to the
doctrine of creation than any other church in the West, largely, he
believes, because of the writings of Richard Hooker. For Hooker,
whom Traherne called 'the judicious Hooker, that glorious beam of
the English Church, and the admired star of all his nation',[134] the whole
natural order praised and revealed God:

> All other things that are of God have God in them and he them in
> himself likewise . . . God hath his influence into the very essence of
> all things, without which influence of Deity supporting them their
> utter annihilation would not choose but follow. All things therefore
> are partakers of God, they are his offspring, his influence is in
> them . . .[135]

This understanding of creation appeared in the seventeenth-century
writings of Lancelot Andrewes and George Herbert as well as Traherne,
and it rose to the surface again 200 years later in the Oxford Movement.
As Horne notes: 'When John Keble came to edit Hooker's works in the
1830's, he believed that he had found the basis of a sacramental

131 Basil the Great quoted in Kallistos Ware, *The Orthodox Way*, Oxford:
Mowbray, 1979, p. 27.
132 Martin Luther, *Werke, Kritische Gesamtausgabe*, XL.1.463.9, quoted in
J. Inge, *A Christian Theology of Place*, London: Ashgate, 2003, p. 62.
133 John Calvin, *Institutio Christianae Religionis*, I.xiv.20 and II.vi.1.
134 *KOG*, Ch. 22, ll. 1–2.
135 Brian Horne, 'The Sacramental Use of Material Things', in G. Rowell and
M. Dudley, *The Oil of Gladness Anointing in the Christian Tradition*, London:
SPCK, 1993, p. 10.

theology that was not only part of the spiritual heritage of the Church of England, but one that was firmly and truly grounded in the traditions of the early church.'

Horne claims William Temple's *Nature, Man and God* (1934) as the most comprehensive exposition of Anglican sacramental theology. Stephen Sykes too draws on Temple to inform his view that Christianity is incarnational:

> the Son of God appears among humankind as a man. He takes the physics and chemistry of our mortality and makes them his own, body, mind and spirit. In becoming man, God becomes matter (Pierre Teilhard de Chardin). In other words the chosen way of divine self-revelation is in the materiality of human fleshliness, God's presence in which he consecrates not merely humankind but the very stuff of created order.[136]

Traherne's understanding of the holiness of the world is very much of this ilk. Sykes tangentially notes Teilhard de Chardin, which is interesting since Traherne in some ways anticipated the arrival of this twentieth-century Jesuit palaeontologist[137] who, like Traherne, saw the continuing creative power of God present in the universe, what William Wolf calls 'the play of Eternal Wisdom ... in all life'.[138] According to this 'Cosmic Christ' model, Christ is the unifying force of creation, the Alpha and Omega, the head and ruler, the link between all that is divine and human, the eternally creating Word of God.

There are unmistakable resonances here with Traherne, who also senses the ceaseless activity of God in the world, is intrigued by the idea of the world as God's body, and clearly sees Christ as the active centre of all creation. For, as Traherne insists, it is in the cross of Christ that 'we enter into the heart of the universe' (C, I, 56). 'There we may see a Man loving all the world, and a God dying for mankind ... There

136 Address given by Stephen Sykes at a conference, 'The Holy Place: Mission and Conversation', Keele University, 25–26 June 1996.

137 See Graham Dowell, *Enjoying the World: The Rediscovery of Thomas Traherne*, London: Mowbray, 1990, pp. 113f.; and Alison Kershaw, 'The Poetic of the Cosmic Christ in Thomas Traherne's The Kingdom of God', unpublished PhD thesis, University of Western Australia, 2005.

138 'The Spirituality of Thomas Traherne', William J. Wolf, ed., *Anglican Spirituality*, Wilton, CT: Morehouse-Barlow, 1982, p. 16.

we may see the most distant things in Eternity united: all mysteries at once couched together and explained' (C, I, 59).

The strength of the argument that would see the world as God's body is that it enhances the notion of God's personhood. If we deny God a body, how do we understand God as a person? A corporeal God also protects us from the problem of dualism, whereas the incorporeality of God sets up a soul–body dualism in which persons are rightly understood as souls that happen to inhabit bodies. Grace Jantzen has written a fascinating study exploring this notion of the world as God's body that would seek to move us away from just such dualism.[139] But there are problems too in seeing the universe in any sense as God's body since doing so inscribes suffering and evil into Godself, into God's essence. If we say that God suffers too, problems of agency arise. To counter this, Timothy Gorringe notes the importance of God's presence *to* rather than *in* the creation.[140] He suggests that embodiment is a choice God makes. God chooses this form of reality and gifts us with senses so that God through us can explore and celebrate the mystery of the creation.

Traherne himself seems to have been caught between models here. In *The Kingdom of God* he uses imagery of the world as God's body, then in *Commentaries of Heaven* he contradicts this, calling the notion of the world as God's body a mistake.[141] The world is an organ of God, Traherne concludes: God is in the world and speaks to us intimately through the world, but is personally present in Christ. God's spirit breathes through creation; in this sense is all creation inhabited by God. And it is from this enthusiasm he has for a gifted creation that Traherne has been misaccused of pantheism; in fact he is nearer to panentheism. His world, as that of Gerald Manley Hopkins, 'is charged with the Grandeur of God'. Traherne affirms the enduring goodness of creation, believing that when God looked on what God had made and pronounced it good, that Genesis statement was a description of its essence, not its temporary appearance. But all creation is not God as Christ is God. Fascinated as he may be with the essential goodness of creation,

139 Grace Jantzen, *God's World, God's Body*, London: Darton, Longman and Todd, 1984.

140 Timothy Gorringe, *The Education of Desire*, London: SCM Press, 2001, p. 8.

141 'Some hav thought the World to be the Body of GOD, & GOD to be the Soul of the World; & that this WORLD was the Body which GOD Assumed to make himself visible in, to our fleshly Eys ... Plato savors something of this Mistake' (*COH*, 'Assumption', fol. 150r).

it is Christ who is, for him, very God of very God, of one being with the Father, begotten not made.

And yet, for Traherne the creation remains a significant realm of divine disclosure, and our position as enjoyers of that creation is a unique and precious one. If Godself is disclosed in the creation, then our possession of that creation makes us in some sense participators in the life of God. And it is in this context that Traherne's well-known writings on enjoying the world and possessing the world are to be read. 'Your enjoyment of the world is never right, til every morning you awake in heaven: see yourself in your father's palace . . . You never enjoy the World aright, till the Sea it self floweth in your veins . . . till you perceive yourself to be the sole heir of the whole world.' Some readers have seen a kind of greed in Traherne's admonitions to enjoy the world, and found his insistence that the whole world is ours as if ours alone, frankly implausible. Especially when Traherne adds to his above assertions: 'Men are in it [the world] who are evry one sole heirs as well as you.' I think there are two replies to this. The first is Teilhard de Chardin's poetic explanation: 'What I call my body is not part of the universe which I possess totally, but the whole universe which I possess partially.'

The second may be found in Mark McIntosh's assertion that a full possession of the world includes the possession of the needs and desires of others and a sharing in their welfare and good. In his recent work *Discernment and Truth*, McIntosh notes Traherne's remarkable ability to sense the giftedness of creation: Traherne 'senses in all things the beauty and bounty of their divine source and seems to recognize in all of them the calling of the divine Creator to fellowship . . . for Traherne this involves not a relinquishing or abandoning of all things in favor of God, but rather the marvellous freedom to embrace all things as themselves, each and every one uniquely.'[142]

McIntosh goes on: 'What he finds himself drawn toward is not a greater self-abnegation but a growing reception of God's bounty, not the extinguishing of his natural desire but the enlarging of it immeasureably.'[143] Rather than seeing the world as full of items that one must possess or control, Traherne sees each thing in its relation to another, as part of a vast mosaic. When you see things with a grasping eye you see only one fragment in the mosaic; when you see them

142 Mark McIntosh, *Discernment and Truth: The Spirituality and Theology of Knowledge*, New York: Herder and Herder, 2004, p. 238.
143 McIntosh, *Discernment and Truth*, p. 242.

relationally, with God's eyes, you begin to see the shape of the whole. Each thing in relation to another, each thing useful in its place, everything yours and everything that is yours, yours for the sake of everyone else.

Traherne's high view of the giftedness of creation means that he also has a high view of humankind since he sees humankind as the pinnacle of that creation. 'God never shewed Himself more a God than when he appeared man' (C, I, 90), Traherne writes. Where the doctrine of the incarnation speaks to Traherne of God's immanence, the science of infinity speaks to him of God's transcendence. Both aspects of God were apparent to Traherne in the creation. But for Traherne the incarnation had particular implications – it meant that the whole of creation is called to be the place of God's indwelling. 'From Dust I rise' ('The Salutation', l. 25), he writes, 'How like an Angel came I down!' ('Wonder', l. 1). At once heavenly and earthly, we may become the house of God. This is the end of Traherne's doctrine of the incarnation. It is a kind of *theosis*, as the Eastern Orthodox Church would call it, God becoming human so that the human may become divine. As Donald Allchin writes, 'Without the doctrine of our deification by grace the doctrine of the incarnation in the end loses its meaning and finality. For how can God enter into man unless man is made from the beginning to enter into God?'[144] The twin Christian doctrines of the incarnation and the Trinity are the cornerstones of all Traherne's thinking about God and humankind. God is creator. The creation is good. God is relational, as are we in his image. What keeps the world spinning is the dynamic of these relationships – want and satisfaction, longing and having, the desire of God for his creatures and the creation for its original in terms both intimate and infinite. God is writ large in the world if we have eyes to see it.

Sir Walter Raleigh conceived it thus:

> By his own word, and by this visible world, is God perceived of men, which is also the understood language of the Almighty, Vouchsafed to all his creatures, whose Hieroglyphical Characters are the unnumbered stars, the sun and moon written on those large volumes of the firmament: written also on the earth and the seas, by the letters of all those living creatures and plants which inhabit and reside therein.[145]

144 Allchin, *Participation in God*, p. 6.

145 I am indebted to the artist Tom Denny for this quotation. Denny's work in the Traherne window commissioned for Hereford Cathedral reiterates most vividly this theme of a coded creation.

Traherne's imaging of creation as a letter to the beloved is even more laden with love. What he is trying to convey is simply 'God's nearness to humankind, and of our unrealized potential for God'.[146] This divine disclosure and longing was only accentuated by the discovery of the microscope, which made the world, already stretching outwards to the infinity of space, suddenly 'both ways infinite'.

What kind of world do we live in? A world that is endlessly fascinating and ever new, a world that is essentially good, a world with purpose and meaning, a world that is alive, gifted and graced.

In this world we are creatures mixed of earth and heaven. Traherne does not disparage the body or set it below the soul in typical seventeenth-century hierarchical fashion.[147] For him the potential is not far from the actual. God has become man: 'a bridge across the gulf has been built, a bridge that precedes Calvary, as the existence of the sun precedes the moment of dawn.' And yet, we are dependent on the grace of God our creator. 'What e're I have from God alone I have / and Hee takes pleasure in the gifts he gave', Traherne quotes from Quarles in one of his notebooks.[148]

What kind of creature are we? Capable of the highest good, imbued with infinity, designed for eternity, a fit bride for the noblest king. Custom bound, wanting, ambitious, insatiable, relational, wrangling, curious, desirous, failing, fallen, forgiven, beloved.

The extracts

1 The pleasure of God is everywhere

2 On the Atom

3 Ant

4 What if there were infinite numbers of worlds?

5 All Things

6 Assimilation

146 Allchin, *Participation in God*, p. 63.

147 See Vaughan, for instance, the body as a temporary house for the soul a 'loose/And empty house . . . a ruin'd peece', in 'Buriall', and many of the other seventeenth-century metaphysical poets.

148 Bodleian MS. Lat. misc. f. 45 (p. 204). See also C, II, 90; C, III, 82: 'no man breathed more air than first he suck'd in', and *Meditations on the Six Days of Creation*, p. 91.

I

The Pleasure of God is everywhere

The Glory and perfection of Gods
Kingdom discovered by the Material
Cause. That all things Actual, possible
and Impossible are Subject to the
power and Dominion of GOD.

It is Impossible to See the Kingdom, but we must believ, and admire the King. . . . The first Honor of this Kingdom is that it is Gods . . . It relates unto God in no Mean Capacitie. As the Effect to the Cause, the Image to the person, the Son to the Father, the Stream to the fountain. This Image is no Ordinary, but a Great and Living picture: The Light of his Countenance being sealed upon it: It relates unto him, As a Kingdom to the King. A Kings Highness is in the Kingdom. As a Bride to the Bridegroom: which is the Glory and Delight of her Husband: As a Temple to the Deitie: For God doth Inhabit it. It is the House of GOD, where in he dwelleth, and is Adored. He dwelleth in his Kingdom, not as in other Temples, where he is the object of the Adorers Thoughts and Affections only. But as the Skill of an Architect dwelles in his

Work, and the Face of a Spectator in the Mirror he beholds. As the Virtu of the Sun dwels in the Trees and Herbs it inspireth, and a Fountain in the stream, so does the Fullness of the Godhead lodg in his Kingdom. His Omnipresence in its Extent His Eternity in its Duration. His Essence in its Operation. . . . His Greatness in its Magnificence . . . For the Eys of the Lord are upon it Night and Day for ever and ever. It is worthy to be Seen and deserves his Contemplation.

. . . Paradice And Heaven are but parts of his Kingdom. The Lord Executeth his pleasure in all places of his Dominion, in the Heaven of Heavens, and in the Earth and in the Hearts of the Children of Men. In the deep Abyss, in Eternitie, in Endless Spaces: All things possible and Impossible are Subject to him, as well as Actual and Existent. . . .

All Actuals and Possibles being before God, things Actual must needs be perfect, becaus God Acteth by his Essence, and all his Works are according to his Nature. He is Infinit in Essence and his Operation is infinit by a clear Consequence. His understanding is Infinit, and so is his Will. He is infinit in desire, and his pleasure infinit. *Quicquid deus agit, infinite agit.* Whatsoever God does he does it infinitly. When he desires, he Infinitly desires; when he loves, he infinitly Loves, when he Esteems, he infinitly Esteems. And there is a Reason why his Esteeme is infinite. When he enjoyes, he infinitly Enjoyes, when he is pleased, his pleasure is illimited, and there is an infinit Cause in the Object of his pleasure. As his desire is not without reason, so neither is its Measure.

. . . GOD is true in his Judgment, and becaus he does infinitly, he so Esteems God is true in his desire, and becaus there is an Infinit Worth in his Object, his Desire is Infinit. God is true in his Joy, and becaus there is an Infinit Beauty in his object, his Joy is Infinit. . . . Our Happiness is Infinit, becaus the pleasures and Joys of God are Infinit. It is the Pleasure of Almighty Power to exert it self, and its Infinit pleasure to be infinitly Exerted.

. . . The Act of God is Eternal, an Infinit Fountain of all Good things, filling Eternitie with Living Streams . . . The Works of God are Wisdom and Goodness Embodied as it were in Effects. Almighty power, and Infinit pleasure invested in their operations, Glory and Blessedness shining in the Fruitions of their Joys and Treasures. Living streams of Gold and Silver run along in evry channel, a Deluge of Excellencies in their Life and Perfection enriching, and if not Exceeding yet filling and making his Omnipresence an illimited Ocean of Delight and Pleasure, as free and Easy as if nothing did fill up the Space of Its Existence. It surmounteth and Enjoyeth all. Tis the Air wherin we breath, the Region of Delights, and the place of Heaven. If it be better that the World should be limited, it is so: but his Kingdom is Endless: for his omnipresence reacheth on and extendeth for ever, and the Vacuitie that is, is a delightfull Spectacle. Yet in truth there is no Vacuitie. The pleasure of God evry where, tho there be nothing else.

The Kingdom of God, Ch. 17

2

On the Atom

No Imagination can fathom that Depth of Power, by which out of Nothing som thing is made. It is Easier to remove the Earth, then to Create a Sand, to carry up the Seas into the Air, and bring down the Skies, then realize an Atom with the Gift of its Existence. Angels if they were permitted might perhaps do this, but nothing less then GOD can bring an Atom out of Nothing. In Gods Condescention to creat a Mote, we See the Greatness of his Eternal Lov. That he Should make Such a Bright and Glorious World, is a Magnificent Work, and seemeth worthy of God. But that being Infinit in Glory, he Should Stoop So low, as to creat a Sand, can be nothing less then infinit Favor. Infinit Goodness Expressed in a Sand. . . .

When in all Its Operations I behold an Atom and see it representing my GOD unto me: When I behold a Mirror of his Essence, in it and a Temple of his presence, a Token of his Lov, and an offspring of his Will, an attendant upon his Throne, an object of his Joy, a Spectacle of his Ey, a Work of his Hand, a Subject of his pleasure, and a Means of his Glory! Me thinks his Holiness that Suffers him not to make any thing less Excellent then is possible, becomes Visible in a Manner, and Shines most Divinely. When I further behold it in all Ages at once serving me in all its Motions, Transmutations, Peregrinations, Changes, Services, Ends, and Uses, and discern the Benefit of all its Works in the Sun, in the Moon, in the Air, in the Earth, in the Sea, in the Stars, in the Beams of Light, in the Influences of Heaven, in Men, in Beasts, in fowls, in fishes, in Trees, in Jewels, in Fruits, in Flowers, in all the Elements, and Creatures wherever it hath been is, or will be Working, from the Day of its Creation to this Moment, and from this Moment to the End of the World; I am ravished at the Fullness of my Joy, and his Goodness therin. For he hath Endued my Soul with a Light Intelligible, which is able to Shine into all Ages, and given me a Key of Knowledg, wherwith I may open the Gates of Heaven, and enter in to the Fruition of all his Treasures. This litle Atom, great in Value, and in the Glory of its uses, was made Immortal and immutable within, yet Subject to changes, that in many Forms and Appearances in all Generations, it might Minister before GOD, Angels, and Men, for The Manifestation of his Wisdom and power, in Services done for their Joy; his Glory, and my Happiness.

The Kingdom of God, Ch. 19

3

Ant

An Ant is a great Miracle in a little room: a feeble Creature made to be an Ornament of the Magnificent Univers: & no less a Monument of Eternal Lov, than Almighty Power. Its Lims & Members are as Miraculous as those of a Lion or Tygre. It hath a soul within it which rules its Members as great as an Elephants. . . . an Ant in its Spiritual Capacity is a symbol of a Wise laborious Provident Industrious man & well resembles an orderly Peacefull Christian. For which cause Solomon sendeth the Sluggard to the Ant; & so may we the Coward for it is a Creature by all appearance of an Haughty Courage & High Stomach. For he assaults all things & never rests when entangled or endangered. . . . [Traherne recounts a tale he heard from a 'Knight and Traveller' who had witnessed ants filling a dish of water with their own corpses so that others might live.] They came about the Dish, & at last put forward into the Water, till so many were drowned that they made a Bridge with their Bodies for their fellows, over which they went to & fro till they had carried away the sugar. This another Knight his Brother, & all the familie testified. Which, if true, it shews these little Generous Creatures to be very resolute in sacrificing their Lives for the Benefit of their country, & very magnanimous in despising their privat satisfaction in comparison of the Advantage of all the Societie as well as faithfull in their Trust, & of very great & publick Spirits.

Commentaries of Heaven, 'Ant'

4

What if there were infinite numbers of worlds?

Chapter 22

Of the unknown and hidden
Secrets in the Moon and
Stars.

The judicious Hooker, that Glorious Beam of the English Church, and the admired Star of all his Nation, wading into the spring and fountain of Laws, and digging neer unto the root of things, hath some Sage and important Maxims which he casteth up like Sparkling Jewels. Speaking of the first and Eternal Law, which is the fountain of all Laws, he saith, The Being of God is a Kind of Law to his Working; for that Perfection which God is, giveth Perfection to that he doth. Wherupon he observeth, that that, and nothing els is done by God, which to leave undone were not so Good: that there was never sin committed, wherin a less Good was not preferred before a greater: and that the Works of Nature do always aim at that which cannot be bettered. These Seeds being Scattered so near the root of Perfection, these Principles so closely laid in the foundation, these Ingredients giving a Tincture to the very Well-Head of all Demonstration, must needs be of General Concernment in all the streams, as fitly applicable to all Particulars. The uses then and the Services of the Stars may be treasured by these.

Becaus the Wits of the Age are Atheisticaly disposed and pretend the Moon and Stars to be Inhabited, to the utter overthrow of Religion, as they design it; And many Terse Ingenuities hav of late furthered the opinion, Because the Genius of the Time is hammering at Such a thing; and the Sagacitie of humane Nature Restless, in aspiring to the Knowledg of God in his Ways; And becaus som great thing is promised by Nature it self, and by Instinct Expected in the hidden uses and Capacities of those Mighty orbes; and there is a Shadow of Reason at least in their Arguments. It Shall not be amiss, to shew cleerly that if their Discourses, were true no Detriment can accrue to Religion therby.

. . . The Earth is too poor a Cottage, too small a centre, to be the Single and Solitary object of his care and Love. For him that is Omnipresent and Eternal, to confine his Contentments to one litle Spot, and leav all the Rest Empty and Desolate is unworthie of his Majestie, and not very answerable to his Infinit Greatness. Neither is it suitable to his Wisdom, that Worlds of such Infinit Magnificence, Bulk, Number, Distance, and Varietie; should be Created; only for to be, and serv like Sparks of Weak, and Glittering Light, for such a litle Ball, a Point, a Mite as the Earth is, being Capable of so many more uses, if him self pleaseth. Since therfore men are Visible Angels, and there is somthing Mysterious in those Creatures, that are made up of Souls, and Bodies, that all visible and Invisible things are united in them; And they are most desirable to God, Angels, and Men: What if the Stars should be all Inhabited, what would follow? May we conclude thence, that there is no GOD? no Religion? No Blessedness? verily it is more Apparent, that there is a God, a Religion, a Blessedness thereby. What if beyond the Heavens there were Infinit Numbers of Worlds at vast unspeakable distances. And all Those worlds full of Glorious Kingdoms? and all those Kingdoms full of the most Noble and Glorious Creatures. And all those Creatures walking in the Light of Eternitie, full of Joy, evry Moment celebrating the Praises of their Creator. And as full of Love towards each other. Would this Abolish Heaven? Verily in my Conceit, it Enricheth it. For it is more answerable to Goodness, Wisdom, and Felicitie; and demonstrates visibly, that there is a GOD, and that Divines hav not in vain Affirmed GOD to be all Act, since his power is Exerted in filling his Omnipresence with infinit Treasures. I am to delight in all, and all in me.

The Kingdom of God, Ch. 22

5

All Things

Intrinsick Arguments

I found the Desires of the Soul to be Insatiable and its powers Endless, and Knew by nature that they were not made in vain. I felt my Spirit Desolat for want of Objects to employ my Activity Knowledg Alacritie Love Abilitie Esteem and Gratitude upon. I saw I could prize things beyond the Heavens, pierce into the centre, expatiat over all Ages, be present in paradice, at our Saviors Cross and at the Day of Judgement, look into Eternitie and long for interminable and Transcendent

Treasures; That God also did Actualy appear in the Ages, that his
Councels were profound, his Attributes Divine, his Ways most Beautifull, and his Works most Glorious. That his Laws commanded me to
love Him, to love my neighbor as my self, and to lov all that was Good
in all his Creatures, and the Nature of Love was not unknown. And
these were present and concomitant Arguments, lying in me and in the
nature of things making them Delightful. . . .

All Things

1

Heaven! is not that an Endless Sphere
Where all thy Treasures and thy Joys appear?
If that be Heaven, it is Evrywhere.

2

The Earth's a Prison, and a Paradice;
Unto the Holy tis of Endless Price:
A Dungeon to them that live in Vice.

3

It is a Hell, and Heaven since the Fall,
Unto the Vile it is a Pill of Gall,
A very Heaven to the Angelicall.

4

A Globe of Dirt, and yet a Globe of Gold
To Earthy Minds tis Earthy base and old;
Tis new to those that in clear Light behold.

5

The Earth is Heavens Center. For the Skies
Surround it, while it in the middle lies
And Heaven evry where salutes our Eys.

6

All Things were Adams, and all things are ours
Our Suns as bright as his, our fruits and flowers
As Sweet and Good: Nought's Blasted but our Powers.

7

The World's the Yelk[1] of all Eternitie,
Our Saviors Cross doth in the Centre lie,
The Hearts the Speck which Jesus Blood did die.

8

All Earthly Things seem to be Transitory,
Oh Time is Bald behind, before is Hoary
But Ages, Heaven and Earth are full of Glory.

9

Heaven surely is a State and not a Place
To be in Heaven's to be full of Grace
Heaven is wherere we see Gods face.

10

To see the Wealth and Goodness of our God,
The Glory of his Kingdom all abroad,
The Endless Beauty of his Great Abode,

11

The Open Volumes of Eternitie
The Mysteries of all Felicitie
The Works and Wonders of the Deitie

12

And all prepard for me! To see the Sweet
And Heavenly State in which we are, to meet
The footsteps of his Lov in evry Street,

13

To see all Holy Men and Angels greet
Us with Delight, the Heavens beneath our feet
And Crowns of Glory on our Head, is Sweet.

Commentaries of Heaven, 'All Things'

1 Yolk.

6

Assimilation

An Eagle in the Eg, a Litle Bee
Which we at first in a small Magot see,
An Oke in a Small Acorn, or a Man
In Semine: or as the World began,
An Univers that in a Chaos lies
Distinguishd after into Earth and Skies;
All these are but a litle note, which shews
How much my Soul to GOD its Maker owes.
The Soul in its first Birth is less then these
Yet passeth them by infinite Degrees
At last, and is a Sovereign Abyss
Of future Glory Pleasure Joy and Bliss.
Tis Capable of GOD. This I Admire
For this Adore, this sets my Soul on fire.
This I revere, at this Amazd I stand
In this I read my Glorious Makers Hand.
In this He's like Himself: in this he made
Those Things Eternal which Decay and fade,
An Adaequate Effect and Object too,
A proper End of all he meant to do.
A Sole Supreme among all Sole Supremes
GOD is a GOD compleat in all Extremes.
An All sufficient Ocean of Bliss,
The first Eternal Miracle: In this
He's All in all. In evry one he's all,
And evry one's his End, even the most small.
GOD is so Alsufficient he intends
Wholy at once ten thousand thousand Ends,
And evry one of these alone doth note,
Is present with it, and doth it promote,
As if he had no other to regard
As if all other were for that prepard.
Nay he doth further one by Making more
And makes that One far more his End then twas before.

Thus is he wholy present in a Sand
And thus the Sun doth in tenthousand Mirrors stand.

Commentaries of Heaven

7

Happiness in the possession of a glorious Soul

Two things there are concurring to make the Contemplation of the Soul delightfull; its own Worth, and our Interest.[1] for as we naturaly desire to see Things excellent, and most violently long for things infinitly so; we likewise ardently covet to have them ours, and with a Cruel Jealousy long to have them in our own Possession. We could wish our Interest as infinit as their Excellency. And tho these two Desires are inclinations generaly Supprest, either through fear, or some tacite Neglect yet when we remove the impediment that covers them, and look into the Secret of our Essence freely, we cannot chuse but feel them, bec. they are parts of our very selvs never to be extinguished, for however they are buried under Ashes here, they are immortal and will burn for ever.

These two Inclinations as they are high and soaring, so are they Essential to an Happy Creature. For Nothing can be Blessed, that is incapable of it, nothing is capable of Bliss but that which loveth Treasure, and nothing can love Treasure that delighteth not in Propriety.[2] For where there is no Love of Propriety, nor desire of Treasure, there can be no Sence of Felicitie nor Joy in Enjoyment. Indeed there can be no Enjoyment. For this Cause God so implanted these two Desires that they are the Occasion of all our Joys even in Heaven, or of all our Torments in Hell. for the Delight of Heaven ariseth from the Satisfaction of these two, and the Misery of Hell from their frustration. There we rejoyce, becaus all we desire we have: in hell we lament, becaus that is ours, which we hate and abjure.

These two Inclinations hath God endeavored to satisfy most perfectly: he implanted them that they might be satisfied. For being Willing to Communicat him self in his Creatures Blessedness, he made us Capable of being Blessed, and employed his Almighty Power, in making all Objects the most Excellent and the most ours, that was imaginable or

Possible. And wheras all Objects are naturaly within us (in an Objective Manner) that are enjoyed by us; to the intent they may most deeply and intimately be ours; no Objects are more within us, or more ours (keeping within the Compass of Things Created, Visible or Invisible) or more Excellent then the Interior Properties and Endowments of the Soul. Which are in us not as objects only, but as Essential parts of our very Being. For God hath communicated him self to us, by doing all things for us in the most Excellent manner. By his Wisdom and Power he hath provided that those things that are most Excellent should be most within us.

Since therfore the Soul, is so great a Lover of it Self, and so mightily delightest in its own Beauty, how Happy is it that it is so Glorious! how much owest thou unto God Almighty, that by his wisdom and power he hath made those things that are most excellent, most Essentialy, thine, and seated them within! I am amazed when I consider the Perfections of My Soul: of which as it is in other Riches an Evil Use may be made, but a good one too. A man may gaze in a solitary maner upon his own Perfections, and so dote upon them, as to grow Proud therby; which was the fall of Angels. But I will so consider them as to be enflamd with Divine Love in the Meditation, and which is a Strange Effect of ones own Excellency, to be filled with Abhorrence of my self, bec. I hav defiled so excellent a creature. For that God hath put such Amiable and Noble Features within my Soul, and composed it of so many great and wonderfull parts, is the Highest Obligation wherof Nature is capable. But that I have defiled them, the greatest Caus of self abhorrence and Revenge. For the greater my Shame is, the greater is my Humiliation: the greater my Excellency was, the greater my shame is, and the greater my repentance.

The End why God implanted these two Inclinations of which I speak, was his own Glory. For no Glory is like that of a Donor. He desires to be Delightfull, and to be enjoyed: he is infinitly Good and communicative, not to the Hurt, but Pleasure of Spectators. Evil communicats it self to the Hurt of others, Goodness to the Delight. That therfore we might be capable of all Enjoyments, in communion with him, he made us like him self. Who infinitly desires the most Excellent things: And becaus he infinitly desires them, infinitly enjoyeth them. At once he delighteth in their Beauty and Presence. And by both they are his Riches. For nothing can be a Treasure that is not possest, his Nature therfore desires Application, as well as Excellency. Nor indeed can any thing be Excellent that is not applied. For how can it be excellent that is neither pleasant nor usefull. It is Potentialy a Treasure while it is capable of being so, but not actualy till it is enjoyed. So that Interest addes Lustre to the value, and Enjoyment makes the Treasure. Unles you will say that Goodness makes it a Treasure by which it is capable and meet to be enjoyed.

Enjoyment springeth from two Desires. That therfore we might be made capable of Enjoyment and we naturaly desire an Interior Beauty in the Thing it self, and a Happy Pleasure in its relation to us. And becaus the Measure of our felicitie dependeth upon the Measure of that Desire God in Wisdom employd his Power to make it Endless. that our felicity might be so. for if the Inclination be great wherby we are carried to all his Treasures, the Enjoyment will be great in like maner, as the sence of Miserie will be, when all Hope of enjoyment is removed. For the Pleasure of Satisfaction riseth naturaly from the Strength of Longing. And therfore did God make our Desires severe and insatiable, bec. he meant our Eternal Satisfaction, that in the Depth of our Acknowledgement he might be infinitly exalted, and while by reason of our Complacency[3] he is delighted in, might be eternaly glorified.

Seeds of Eternity

1 Share or entitlement.
2 Ownership.
3 Tranquil pleasure.

8

A disguised prince

How Happy hast Thou made me O God in making me to Lov! A Divine and spirituall Lover is a wonderfull Great and unknown Creature. A strang Being here upon Earth. An Image of the Diety in the wilderness. A Disguised prince walking InCognito among forrein people. unknown, unseen, Incredible. Exceeding Great yet very little, Exceeding Rich yet very poor, Exceeding High yet very Low, Exceeding Beautifull yet Invisible, Exceeding Divine, yet not valued. Exceeding Great for it is a Living Sphere of fire wider then the world: yet very Little, for it is Shut up in Mans Body. Exceeding Rich, for it Illustrates all Things, includes and possesses them, yet very poor, perhaps Living in a cave with out house or lands. Exceeding High, for both in reach and Nature it is Higher then the Heavens, yet very Low for it walketh upon the Earth, and very Humble. It swayeth a Scepter over God and Man; yet is very weak for any Body may Destroy it, or at Least the person in whom it Dwelleth. It is Exceeding Beautifull, for it Enflameth all Things, yet is Invisible, for it Cannot be seen. It is an Endless Blessing Tho Not understood. All covet it, All admire it, all Delight in it. It is Rich and pleasant. Every one Desireth it for it is Sweet to be Beloved. It is a Strange Dæmon for it is the Spring of all our affections, the Secret Mine of all our pleasures, the Rule of our Affayrs. The most Great and near and Tender Interest, of which all are Jealous; no man must Touch it.

Select Meditations, II, 64

9

A Magnanimous Soul is alwaies awake

Chapter 28

Of Magnanimity, or Greatness of Soul. Its Nature.
Its Foundation in the vast Capacity of the
Understanding. Its Desire. Its Objects are
infinite and eternal. Its Enquiries are most
profound and earnest. It disdaineth all feeble
Honours, Pleasures and Treasures. A Magnanimous
Man is the only Great and undaunted Creature.

Magnanimity and Contentment are very near allyed, like Brothers and Sisters they spring from the same Parents, but are of several Features. Fortitude and Patience are Kindred too to this incomparable Vertue. Moralists distinguish Magnanimity and Modesty, by making the one the desire of greater, the other of less and inferiour Honours. But in my apprehension there is more in Magnanimity. It includes all that belongs to *a Great Soul*: A high and mighty Courage, an invincible Patience, an immoveable Grandeur which is above the reach of Injuries, a contempt of all little and feeble Enjoyments, and a certain kind of Majesty that is conversant only with Great things; a high and lofty frame of Spirit, allayed with the sweetness of Courtesie and Respect; a deep and stable Resolution founded on Humility without any baseness; an infinite Hope; and a vast Desire; a Divine, profound, uncontrolable sence of ones own Capacity, a generous Confidence, and a great inclination to Heroical deeds; all these conspire to compleat it, with a severe and mighty expectation of Bliss incomprehensible. It soars up to Heaven, and looks down upon all the dominion of Fortune with pity and disdain. Its aims and designs are transcendent to all the Concerns of this little World. Its Objects and its Ends are worthy of a Soul that is like GOD in Nature; and nothing less than the Kingdom of GOD, his Life and Image; nothing beneath the Friendship and Communion with him, can be its satisfaction. The Terrours, Allurements and Censures of men are the dust of its feet: their Avarice and Ambition are but feebleness before it. Their Riches and Contentions, and Interests and Honours, but insignificant and empty trifles. All the World is but a little Bubble; Infinity and Eternity the only great and soveraign things wherewith it converseth. A Magnanimous Soul is alwaies awake.

Christian Ethicks, Ch. 28

10

The Beauty of the Soul, the Goodness of the Body

For Man is taken with all kind of Beauty, but that which is Extraordinary and Miraculous fixeth his Soul: and while he drinks it in, transforms it into Delight. how much more then should he be pleased in that Beauty which is his own! Verily as our Savior hath said it is more Blessed to give then to receive,[1] so is it more Glorious to be a Beauty to, then to see the Beauty of, all the world. Which makes the glory of the Soul the greatest of Joys, for it loves to *communicat* it self in the Image of the Deitie: Tis a foundation upon which we build an Altar of Eternal Praises, and a Temple wherin we dwell. Shall we note and adore the Glory of GOD, and despise the Beauty of his Bride? Shall we hear so great a Thing affirmed in the Scripture as this, the Soul is the Temple of God[2] and shall we not enquire whether it be capable of being so? Shall it be made to inherit all Things and shall we not know it? Shall it be a Vessel of Glory, Equal to the Angels, bought with a

Price, redeemed with the Blood of Jesus Christ, a Partaker of the Divine Nature, an Heir of Eternal Glory, the Sovereign Object of Gods Lov and shall we not ponder how meet it is for these things? Nay shall it be filled with all the fulness of GOD, and yet be desolate, and unacquainted with its own Glory? All Zeal, Conscience, Vertu Religion, Clemency Meekness Contentment Joy Gratitude Courage Honor Care and Industrie arise, with Wisdom Humilitie and Pietie, from this Knowledge, in the enjoyment of which GOD hath seated our Blessedness and Glory. And those Capital Letters upon the Temple Gate of Delphos, which are the Grand Oracle of all the World ΓΝΟΘΙ ΣΕΑΥΤΟΝ[3] were with so much Election Desert and Counsel affixed there, as if they were the only Oracle worthy of the Care of all Nations, speaking to Ages and Kingdoms that upon their coming thither were entertained with Advice, becaus in the Knowledg of one self, the Knowledg of God, and all things appeareth, the End for which we were created, Gods Bounty and Love, the Beauty of his Celestial Kingdom, the Valu of our Saviors Passion, the Means by which we are to attain our End, the Excellency Relation and use of all Objects in Heaven and Earth the grounds of our faith, and the mysteries of felicity are founded in it. GOD is seen to be our Father, and all the things in his Eternity, our Joys and Treasures.

Humanity being thus excellent, and thus esteemed by all, Heathens and Christians, fathers and Philosophers; we shall not think either time, or Labor lost, in the Persuit of it. Bec. that light which we bring into the hidden Recesses of it, will fill even Caves with Glory, and make the darkest prisons shine with Celestial Brightness. we will visit the remotest Corners, and deepest Abysses of the same for the face of an Angel appeareth in evry meanest Particle that can concern it. In doing this, bec. the Body is but the Case of the Soul, we shall as such pass over it in the beginning, tho perhaps afterward we shall repell that opinion as a vulgar Error, that maketh it the impediment and prison of the mind, and looking on it as a glorious Instrument and Companion of the soul, utter things more advantagious concerning it.

In the Body the matter composing it, or the Contexture and form of that matter is considerable. It is generaly agreed that the 4. Elements Earth Air fire and Water are united in its existence, and by their various mixture compose all the several Humors and parts therin, Salt, Nitre Blood, Spirits, flegme Choler melancholy, sweet, Alust, acid, bitter, sharp, and oyly Ingredients having several offices in the same. And thus much we say concerning the matter of it, which is so copious and various in so small a Room, that with great Probability it may be supposed, that there is nothing material in heaven or Earth, or under the Earth or in the Sea, even to the Deepest minerals, or remotest Influences, or highest Stars, wherof some portion is not present in the Body of man, that litle World within it self, made to rule and possess the Greater. Alum, Rosin, stone, the seeds and Principles of Iron Gold and silver, with whatsoever els in Trees or Herbs or fruits or flowers or fowls or Beasts or fishes concurring to illustrate and adorn as well as serv that Excellent Creature, to shew as it were the Glory of that Being which is the Darling and Delight of the whole World.

Seeds of Eternity

1 Acts 20.35.
2 1 Corinthians 3.16; 6.19.
3 Know thyself.

II

The Person

1

Ye Sacred Lims,
A richer Blazon I will lay
On you, then first I found:
That like Celestial Kings,
Ye might with Ornaments of Joy
Be always Crownd.
A Deep Vermilion on a Red,
On that a Scarlet I will lay,
With Gold Ile Crown your Head,
Which like the Sun shall Ray.
With Robes of Glory and Delight
Ile make you Bright.
Mistake me not, I do not mean to bring
New Robes, but to Display the Thing:
Nor Paint, nor Cloath, nor Crown, nor add a Ray,
But Glorify by taking all away.

2

The Naked Things
Are most Sublime, and Brightest shew,
When they alone are seen:
Mens Hands then Angels Wings
Are truer Wealth even here below:
For those but seem.
Their Worth they then do best reveal,
When we all Metaphores remove,
For Metaphores conceal,
And only Vapours prove.
They best are Blazond when we see
The Anatomie,
Survey the Skin, cut up the Flesh, the Veins
Unfold: The Glory there remains.
The Muscles, Fibres, Arteries and Bones
Are better far then Crowns and precious Stones.

3

Shall I not then
Delight in these most Sacred Treasures
Which my Great Father gave,
Far more then other Men
Delight in Gold? Since these are Pleasures,
That make us Brave!
Far Braver then the Pearl and Gold
That glitter on a Ladies Neck!
The Rubies we behold,
The Diamonds that Deck
The Hands of Queens, compard unto
The Hands we view;
The Softer Lillies, and the Roses are
Less Ornaments to those that Wear
The same, then are the Hands, and Lips, and Eys
Of those who those fals Ornaments so prize.

4

Let Veritie
Be thy Delight: let me Esteem
True Wealth far more then Toys:
Let Sacred Riches be,
While falser Treasures only seem,
My real Joys.
For Golden Chains and Bracelets are
But Gilded Manicles, wherby
Old Satan doth ensnare,
Allure, Bewitch the Ey.
Thy Gifts O God alone Ile prize,
My Tongue, my Eys,
My cheeks, my Lips, my Ears, my Hands, my Feet,
Their Harmony is far more Sweet;
Their Beauty true. And these in all my Ways
Shall Themes becom, and Organs of thy Praise.

12

Wonder

1

How like an Angel came I down!
How Bright are all Things here!
When first among his Works I did appear
O how their GLORY me did Crown?
The World resembled his *Eternitie*,
In which my Soul did Walk;
And evry Thing that I did see,
Did with me talk.

2

The Skies in their Magnificence,
The Lively, Lovely Air;
Oh how Divine, how soft, how Sweet, how fair!
The Stars did entertain my Sence,
And all the Works of GOD so Bright and pure,
So Rich and Great did seem,
As if they ever must endure,
In my Esteem.

3

A Native Health and Innocence
Within my Bones did grow,
And while my GOD did all his Glories shew,
I felt a Vigour in my Sence
That was all SPIRIT. I within did flow
With Seas of Life, like Wine;
I nothing in the World did know,
But 'twas Divine.

4

Harsh ragged Objects were conceald,
Oppressions Tears and Cries,
Sins, Griefs, Complaints, Dissentions, Weeping Eys,
Were hid: and only Things reveald,
Which Heav'nly Spirits, and the Angels prize.
The State of Innocence
And Bliss, not Trades and Poverties,
Did fill my Sence.

5

The Streets were pavd with Golden Stones,
The Boys and Girles were mine,
Oh how did all their Lovly faces shine!
The Sons of Men were Holy Ones.
Joy, Beauty, Welfare did appear to me,
And evry Thing which here I found,
While like an Angel I did see,
Adornd the Ground.

6

Rich Diamond and Pearl and Gold
In evry Place was seen;
Rare Splendors, Yellow, Blew, Red, White and Green,
Mine Eys did evrywhere behold,
Great Wonders clothd with Glory did appear,
Amazement was my Bliss.
That and my Wealth was evry where:
No Joy to this!

7

Cursd and Devisd Proprieties,[1]
With Envy, Avarice
And Fraud, those Feinds that Spoyl even Paradice,
Fled from the Splendor of mine Eys.
And so did Hedges, Ditches, Limits, Bounds,
I dreamd not ought of those,
But wanderd over all mens Grounds,
And found Repose.

8

Proprieties themselvs were mine,
And Hedges Ornaments;
Walls, Boxes, Coffers, and their rich Contents
Did not Divide my Joys, but shine.
Clothes, Ribbans, Jewels, Laces, I esteemd
My Joys by others worn;
For me they all to wear them seemd
When I was born.

1 Rights or laws of ownership.

13

Activity I

Traherne introduces the poem in such a way as to draw his authorship of the poem into question: the soul must 'move in the most violent & irresistible Maner, which I have seen nearly exprest in this following

Poem' (fol. 35v); yet alterations in the manuscript suggest authorial changes rather than copying errors.

> As hungry men lov feasts, as Greedy Gold
>   Mens Thoughts persue,
> As High Preferments win both yong & old
> As Eys of flesh a Lovely Beauty view
> So Souls their Joys & their Delights persue.
>
> Nor can we ceas! no more then Thirst from Wine,
>   Or Sence from Pleasure
> Or fiery flames can ceas to burn or shine
> Or Naked Beggars ceas to covet Treasure
> No more can Appetite, to close with Pleasure.
>
> The Soul of Man so Strangely's made for Bliss
>   That it to love
> The very fountain of His Being is.
> The force of all his Soul a Weight doth prove,
> Good is the Centre, & the Weight is Love.
>
> The SUN must burn & cannot chuse but shine;
>   Remove its Rays,
> Remove its All. It doth itself refine,
> Promote, Delight, Exalt, & Clothe with Prais,
> It Crowns it self by shedding forth its Rays.
>
> Its Beings Light; its Essence is to Shine.
>   It needs must burn;
> Its Nature prompts to that, it cant decline.
> Or Shine it must, or into Darkness turn:
> Or quite Extinguish or els ever burn.
>
> Just so is Man. He needs must burning shine,
>   His Life is Love
> To live that Life His Soul was made Divine;
> Who cannot chuse but like the Sun above,
> Be burning still, & som thing needs must love.

Commentaries of Heaven

14

Insatiableness

II

This busy, vast, enquiring Soul
　　Brooks no Controul,
　　No Limits will endure,
　　Nor any Rest: It will all see,
Not Time alone, but ev'n Eternity.
　　What is it? Endless sure.

'Tis mean Ambition to desire
　　A single World:
　　To many I aspire,
Tho one upon another hurl'd:
Nor will they all, if they be all confin'd,
　　Delight my Mind.

This busy, vast, enquiring Soul
　　Brooks no Controul:
　　'Tis hugely curious too.
Each one of all those Worlds must be
Enricht with infinit Variety
　　And Worth; or 'twill not do.

'Tis nor Delight nor perfect Pleasure
　　To have a Purse
That hath a Bottom of its Treasure,
Since I must thence endless Expense disburse.
Sure there's a GOD (for els there's no Delight)
　　One Infinit.

15

Christ's Assumption of Human Nature

The Assumption of our Bodies

The Assumption of the Bodies of the first at the Resurrection, is a verity founded on the Will & Power of GOD, & revealed to us by Way of Prophesie. It is a Mysterie consonant to Reason, because it is infinitly requisite to the Harmony of the World: for the Want of that one Note would spoil all the Melodie. Without the Immortalitie of Humane Bodies (the reason of whose Creation is to be seen in another place) the Beauty & Perfection of the Univers would be lost. For unless Humane Bodies were of Eternal Use the Creation of the World would be in vain. This World was made to serv our Bodies: Our Bodies therefore must be made for some Superior End, which they cannot Attain, without Imortality.

CHRIST's Assumption of our Humane Nature

The last & highest Assumption that is known in the World, is the Assumption of our Humane Nature into the Eternal GODHEAD by Jesus Christ, of which we intend to speak particularly because it is the Supreme & most Important. The Possibility & the Certainty of this Assumption, the Maner of it, the Cause & Effects of it, the End for which it is, with other Observations about it, we are now to declare. . . .

The Maner of it

Being GOD from all Eternity, in the fullness of Time he took upon him the form of a Servant, & was made in the likeness of Man; being, as Athanasius saith, GOD of the Substance of the Father, begotten before the Worlds, & MAN of the substance of his Mother born in the World: Perfect GOD & perfect Man, of a Reasonable Soul & Human flesh subsisting: Equal to the Father as touching his GODHEAD, & inferior to the Father as touching his Manhood: Who although he be GOD & Man, yet he is not Two but One CHRIST. One not by the Conversion of the GODHEAD into flesh, but by taking of the

Manhood into GOD: one altogether, not by confusion of Substance, but by unitie of Person. For as the reasonable Soul & Flesh are one Man, so GOD & MAN is one CHRIST.

This Orthodox ancient & learned father hath in this Creed, embraced by the Catholick Church, declared himself to be an Acute Philosopher. Well distinguishing between the Soul & Body, & clearly discerning that one person is oftentimes made up of two Natures: not by the Confusion of two Substances, for either remaineth in it self Intire, but by a Personal Union; that is, by an Union of such a kind, that two intire & perfect Natures concur together to make up one Compleat and Reasonable Individual, there being a Communication of the Properties of either to the Compleat Individual so existing. Neither is the Soul Corrupted when it Assumes the Body, nor is the Assumption made by the Conversion of the Soul into the Bodie, (for then there could be no Communication of Properties,) but either remaining in its own Being, both are, tho by Nature distinct & perfect, joined together by an Unity of Person . . .

Its Causes

. . . I admire at the Impudence & Pride of the Socinian[1] that can pretend to believ the Scripture, & yet discredit this Glorious Mysterie. He denies the Truth of our Saviors Satisfaction to Divine Justice on the Cross: not because our Savior did not offer up himself a Sacrifice for Sin, & lay down his Life a Ransom for many. But because it cannot enter into his fine & Politick Noddle how GOD should become a Man, or how there should be three Persons in the same Divine & Eternal Essence. His Reason is so Sickly that he cannot digest it, but Sound & Perfect Reason asserteth faith, & evidently sheweth it. vid. Satisfaction Trinitie, etc.

Correllaries

How highly is our Savior to be Adored in whose Humanitie the fullness of the GODHEAD dwelleth; whose Love was such that being Rich, he became poor for our Sakes: & forsook the Glory of his Throne & his Blessedness to be made a Curse for us! The End was that GOD might appear on Earth, that GOD might be seen with our Bodily Eys, that GOD might Suffer on the Cross, & Die for our Sins; & make

Satisfaction to the Eternal Justice of his Eternal Father for the Sons of Men. And therefore it is said He took not on him the Nature of Angels, but the Seed of Abraham, for no Power less than infinit could satisfy a Justice infinitly offended. The Great End of this Assumption was that he might be made Sin for us. (that God might be made Sin for Man!) That we might be made the Righteousness of GOD in him.

O Height & Depth & Length & Bredth of Divine Love! For He of GOD was made unto us Wisdom Sanctification Righteousness & Redemption.

O the High & Glorious Estate of Man! So beloved an Isaac, as to be exchanged by such a Ram! O Lamb of GOD that takest away the Sins of the World, thy name be Glorified forevermore!

Commentaries of Heaven, 'Assumption'

1 Unitarian. Denied the doctrine of the Trinity and the divinity of Christ.

16

Another Adam

I am made in the Similitude of God, and all the Treasures in Heaven and Earth are to becom mine *as they are his*. Till I know this I am nothing. Adam was the Head of Mankind, and evry Son of Man is another Adam. Whom all the Works of God Serv, whom all the Ways of God Delight, whom all the Laws of God Exalt; whom all the Counsels of God do Beautifie, and whom all the Joys in Heaven attend: All Eternitie Surrounding his Soul with Satisfactions and Treasures.

Inducements to Retiredness, V

17

Such is the Nature of Man

For such is the Nature of Man, that being a lover of himself, and Conscious of his own Emptiness, he Eagerly pursues a Happiness somwhere; and cannot rest without a Clear and apparent Treasure. If he hath not possession in another World, he will Scarcely be persuaded to let goe his possessions here. He will Cleav to his Enjoyments upon Earth, till he be sure of the Joys of Heaven. Neither doth he rest satisfied, unless he be surrounded with Joys in this present Life, and see The Lov of God, apparently shining in all his Ways: a present felicity being Earnestly desired, and grasped by evry one. In order therfore to his satisfaction, it is meet to open his Eys, and removing that Blindness, that hinders him from seeing God's Kingdom, to discover the Treasure that is hid in the field of the Gospel, and to Shew those Heavenly things that are abov us and beneath us, before us, and behind us, within us and round about us. For there is another Life, and another food; another Liberty, and another Bondage; another Honor, and another Shame; another Want and another Abundance; other Riches, Pleasures, friends, Relations, Concernes, Employments and Affayrs, which blind and Carnal Men are unacquainted with. Another Throne, and another Kingdom even in this World, tho not of this World; another Conversation and another World even here to be Enjoyed. For we are in God's Kingdom even now, and *to him that loved us, and Washed us in his own Blood, and made us Kings and Priests unto God,* we may Sing Honor, Glory, and Dominion for Ever and Ever. Amen.[1] Nothing is Wanting but an Ey from above.

The Kingdom of God, Ch. 3

1 Revelation 1.5b–6.

18

Infinite Bounty hides itself in its own Infinity

God is infinit: and his Goodness is his Essence. The Reason of all our Joy, Obedience, Faith and Love, the Reason of Gods proceedings in all his Ways, His Invitations, and Causes Caresses, his promises and Threatnings, his Labors and Endeavors, by Prophets and Apostles; the reason of all their care to win us to the Knowledg and Lov of the Truth, the true Reason of all our Ambition, Curiositie, Desire, and Insatiable Avarice, the reason of all our Affection and Labor hang on these two Transcendent things, first that Gods Goodness is Infinit; and Secondly, His Infinit Goodness is ours. Like unto which are these two, His King-

dom is Illimited in Extent and Glory; And it is the peculiar possession
of evry Soul. Its valu and our Interest in it are the Sole reason of all
Obedience, nay of all Law as well as Duty and Desire. It is the Secret
Right and private Estate of evry person. Evry ones Interest[1] is infinit in
it. We feel our Right by a tacite Instinct, and our want[2] of it by open
Experience. Hence arise all those Grudges of Nature, which are no
other then Secret Repinings at its open Wrong. The Soul feels it self
deprived, and bereaved of a Kingdom infinit in Excellency and (tho it
Knows not how, nor why) is always tending towards it, and is sore
Afflicted. Discontentments and Complaints are in the Bosom, becaus it
perceivs all things are not, as they should be, its own peculiar Enjoyments. it Knows not whom to accuse, nor what to rectifie, nor how to
remedie the Cause of its Displeasure. Methinks I should be Infinitly
Beloved, saith the Conscience in it self; And that the God of Lov should
Manifest himself in Goodness; that I should be caressed and Exalted
and honored, and magnified, and made Supremely Blessed and that his
Wisdom should provide Him a glorious Kingdom, and his Goodness
make it mine by his Bounty. My Spirit tells me there should be infinit
objects of Delight and pleasure. and that the Divine Essence should
prepare most Bright and Blessed Realities within and beneath and
beside it self and make all mine, and magnifie it self in me, and me in
it self, and do all for me, and before me. We know not where the Fault
lies, but are apt to charge God Foolishly. For GOD hath prepared all
these; tho we perceiv it not. The Fault is in our selvs. We are unrighteous
and pervers, Blind, and Corrupt, Disorderly and Rebellious. We see not
the Glory of his Kingdom, we valu not the Excellency of his Lov, we
behav Our selvs frowardly and Scorn to prize those things, which he
freely giveth, or to delight in the Greatest and Best Enjoyments; becaus
they are effects of a Bounty and Goodness that shineth forever. Becaus
we are prevented[3] with his Blessings; We discern not their Necessity;
nor understand their Excellency. We unjustly Prefer things rare, and
Scarce, things Litle, and vain, that are not given us, before all the Great
and Glorious Blessings of God and Nature, that are truly bestowed on
us. His Infinit Bounty hideth it self in its own Infinity. it is lost in its
freedom to us; Had we not the Sun we should esteem it: were the sea
unmade we should desire it. The sight of our Eys and the Health of
our Bodies, would be more sweet and desirable if they were absent
from us. It is a strange thing that a Blind man should see the valu of
his Eys, better then one that has them. becaus men are Lazy or Distracted, and so Seldom Study the Works of GOD, and the powers of

the Soul, becaus they so litle acquaint themselvs with his Attributes and perfections, and So rarely Meditat upon his Holy Laws, and Ways, instead of Receiving his Gifts and Bounties quietly, with Knowledg and Gratitude, They Cavil at their Greatness, and scorn their Presence. and disturb the Stream of his Goodness, and defend their unbelief by many Arguments. It is unconceivable into what a Depth of Miserie we are faln. We are alienated from the Life of God through the Ignorance that is in us, and so horridly Ignorant that Gross thick Darkness Covereth the people, And there is a Vail over the Face of all Nations. Those things that are most Clear and near, being unknown; and those that are infinitly Easy thought impossible. Those that are Infinitly Safe, are thought dangerous; those that are infinitly Convenient, are thought absurd: those that are Natural, we account Strange, and against Nature, and those that are truly Best are feared as the Worst in all nature. God who is Infinit and Eternal in Glory is seldom considered. He that is Everlasting is a Wonder. It is a Strange thing that he who is all Act, should Wholy Exert his power: that he that is Infinit Lov, should giv Infinit Riches, or he have an Infinit or Eternal Kingdom, that is Infinitly Blessed and Glorious. We Measure GOD by our selvs, and becaus we are finit, would limit the Deitie in his Operations. We deny that Allmighty power can do Infinit things, and by our unbelief it is com to pass, that we quarrel at the Greatness of our Happiness. The Principles of Reason, the properties and perfections of our Souls, the Inclinations of Nature, and the Highest Interests of Humanity are all involved in our Fall, and buried in its ruines. Our Hopes are nipt in the Bud for fear of presumption, our Desires Crusht in the Growth with pretended Pietie. A Modesty prejudicial to nature is affected by us, we gag our Dissatisfactions and suppress their Clamors, we renounce our Libertie, and giv up our selvs to an implicit Bondage, we see not the root of our Discontents and yet in the midst of all this Corruption we are as Confident and Dogmatical, as if we had all the Light of the Holy Angels.

The Kingdom of God, Ch. 16

1 Share or stake.
2 Lack.
3 Preceded.

19

Allurement

Awake my Soul, and soar upon the Wing
Of Sacred Contemplation; for the King
Of Glory wooes; he's pleased to allure
Poor feeble Dust! Altho thou art impure,
He condescends, vouchsafing to come down
That with his Glory he might Ashes crown.
Canst thou attend to any other charmes?
Or chuse out better and Diviner Armes
To lodg in! Or can any smiles but his
Attract or melt or pleas thee with true Bliss!
O Glory! O Delight beyond compare!
O Ravishments of Joy! What great and rare
And Heavenly Tidings doth his Gospel Bring!
The Lord of Hosts, the GOD of Armes, the King
Of Blessedness, in all the Majesty
And Powr and Beauty which the Angels see,
Salutes and Kisses a poor Worm! His Love
From Everlasting shind and was above
All Comprehension Great Transcendent pure.
The King of Glory doth my Soul allure.
Not like a Syren to Deceitfull Joys
Whose Charm, whose Beauty, whose Embrace destroys,
But like a GOD surrounded with the Glory
Of Times and Ages in their longest Story.
Whole Hosts of Seraphims frequent his Courts,
Armies of Saints attend upon his Throne,
Assemblies, Congregations and Resorts
Of Angels do before the Holy One
Bow down and Worship; Cherubims adore,
His Glory for his rich and Sacred Store.
Realms Ilands Continents Queens Empires Kings
In glorious Troops upon my GOD attend
And evry Creature his high praises sings
Yet he is pleasd to make my Soul his friend,
Nay more, his Bride! Can any comprehend

The Sweetness of his Love, the extasie
Of my Estate! His Lov doth magnify
A Leper, and a very Beggar prize
Exalting Lazarus above the Skies.
The Sun comes like a Bridegroom forth, to shew
The shining of his Love to me below
And evry Star from far doth by a Glance
Of twinkling Light imply my Happy Chance.
The Moons a Messenger that steals by Night
In to my Bedchamber, Her face is Bright
Becaus she from the King of Glory came,
Tho in her self shee's Dark. Her Beams enflame
My Soul with Lov. His Lov did melt the Seas,
The wide and liquid Seas my Soul to pleas.
Els they would all be frozen up in Ice.
The very Earth is made a Paradice
And clad in Sweet and Royal Liveries
Of Curious flowrs: It emulates the Skies
And by its Riches shews from whence she Came,
The silver Strings and Streams my Soul inflame.
While passing by they lick and kiss my feet
Milk Hony Gold Arabian Spices, sweet
Perfumes Wines Oyles all these he from abov
Doth send as Sacred Tokens of his Love.
My very Body was his Gift, His Laws
His ancient Ways his Counsels plead his Cause.
The lives of fishes and the Blood of Beasts
His Goodness sacrificeth, and such Feasts
Provides, that Sea and Land and Air conspire
To pour out their Wealth, while I admire
The Glory of his Lov, whose Bounty is
The Root and Fountain of my endless Bliss.
It stops not here, it overflows all Shores,
And while my ravished soul his Lov adores
It makes all Men and Angels my Delights
And satisfieth all my Appetites.
Apostles Prophets Patriarchs Martyrs are
His great Ambassadors: they all declare
And testify his Lov. His Word, his Melting Word
Ten thousand Joys and Raptures doth afford.

No kind and tender Mother doth allure
Her Child so Winningly, No virgin sure
So lovs her Lov, nor ever was there seen,
A Proud, but tamd, enflamd, heart-wounded Queen
Subdud by Love, whose Lov did tyrannize
So much ore her, as his Above the Skies
Doth him enflame. His Essence is all Love
His Lov is infinit it is above
All Measure and Excess, No Pride doth feed
A lov enragd, that doth all Bounds exceed
In an High minded Soul, that doth endeavor
Long time to check that flagrant growing Feaver;
No Love revenging its too long restraint,
With greater violence, can even paint
The Life of his. He woed me by his Son.
I can no more. What hath his Goodness don!
His Spirit is a Secret Agent too,
The Holy Ghost him self comes down to woo
He speaks for GOD and whispers in the mind,
Kissing the Ear that to his Mouth's inclind.
The Rhetorick of all the Worlds employd
To Woo for him; and if thou art not cloyd,
My Soul, with Kindnesses, His Crown and Throne
And Endless Kingdom all conspire in one,
His Soul, thy Soul, and all his Friends say Come:
GOD is alone thy Glory and thy Home.

Commentaries of Heaven, 'Allurement'

2

Happiness and Holiness

We in first world countries have it all. Our standard of living has never been higher, our life expectancy keeps increasing, we are educated, liberated, inoculated, insured, inured, leisured, mobile, ostensibly democratic. So why are we not completely happy? For it seems that we are also unsettled, displaced, rootless, abandoning, overfed, over-stimulated, anxious, complacent, addicted, hectic, exhausted, some-times neurotic, ravaged by the strains of incessant mobility, innovation and choice.

Not always. We do enjoy satisfactions and pleasures, the benefits of relationships, the ease of luxuries. There is much in our ordinary lives that is good; even if it rides atop the unasked questions about meaning and worth – our own or anyone else's. Yet profound happiness we often find elusive. Some of us wait for happiness to come. Some of us fail to recognize everyday happiness when we are in it. Some of us imagine happiness not to be our entitlement, but something rare or accidental for which we should not seek.

For over 200 years happiness, or at least the pursuit of it, has been considered a basic human right in the United States, second only to life and liberty, according to the framers of the Declaration of Independence who enshrined it in the phrase: 'Life, Liberty and the pursuit of Happiness'. Still, we are not sure where to find it. Martin Seligman's study *Authentic Happiness* (2003) founded the new 'discipline' of positive psychology (Jeremy Bentham meets evolutionary neuroscience). In the wake of this new thinking, a resurgence of interest in happiness, and a hope that it may be a teachable science, has spawned much media interest and several recent studies[149] that pay homage to Bentham's adage

---

149 Richard Layard, *Happiness: Lessons from a New Science*, London: Penguin, 2005; Richard Schoch, *The Secrets of Happiness: Three Thousand Years of Searching for the Good Life*, London: Profile, 2006; Darrin McMahon, *The*

'the greatest happiness for the greatest number' and try to make a distinction between lasting joys and transient pleasures. All of this suggests that happiness is a subject worth studying. At least one public school in England is going so far as introducing classes on happiness, with a psychologist from Cambridge University piloting the scheme.[150]

If, as it seems, we must 'study felicity', there can be no better teacher than Traherne. Having been disappointed that his classical education missed out felicity entirely, he resolved to take up the study himself: 'When I came into the Country, and being seated among silent Trees, had all my Time in mine own hands, I resolved to Spend it all, whatever it cost me, in Search of Happiness', wrote Traherne in his 'autobiographical' third Century. Felicity, blessedness, happiness, joy – this was his life's work.

Perhaps the most fundamental question, though, is not where to find happiness, but why happiness matters in the first place. It matters, Traherne would say, at the smallest or broadest levels because joy is the first principle of creation. The God who has and is all sufficiency desires a creation with which to share the overflow of life. There is too much joy; it springs into creation. Traherne would see all creatures as part of this divine expression of joy – the desire to be with and for another.

Here we enter the hinterlands of Ecstasy in its loose and its more precise sense (Greek *ek stasis*, going out of oneself), and happy those hinterlands may be. But I do not think ecstasy is primarily what happiness is about in Traherne. Ecstasy is out of the ordinary; happiness, thankfully, is more mundane. For every ecstatic moment there may be hundreds of hours of ordinary happiness that we very often take for granted. I will never forget reading the entries in the diary of a young widow. Day after day the entries were mundane: a trip to the library with her young son John; her husband taking the boy to the toy shop and 'spoiling' him with a longed-for model truck; accounts of bills paid, appointments kept, occasions remembered; the chance meeting of an old friend in a restaurant; the pride of having such a fine son and a caring husband. Then there came a break of blank pages that covered the unwritable days when her husband lay dying of sudden heart failure. One day, after his death, the heartbreaking scrawl: 'Must try, for John's

---

Pursuit of Happiness: A History from the Greeks to the Present, London: Allen Lane, 2006; Paul Martin, *Making Happy People*, London: Fourth Estate, 2006.

150 Wellington College in Crowthorne, Berkshire; I am indebted to the Revd Richard Birt for drawing my attention to this fact.

sake, to stop crying.' More blank pages. Then simply, 'I so wish life could be hum-drum again.' Her diary was never resumed.

Ecstatic as some of Traherne's most famous utterances are, it is ordinary happiness that he most seeks and the way to that happiness that he seeks to show his reader. The subtitle of *Christian Ethicks* (as we have seen, the only work after *Roman Forgeries* that he had fully prepared for publication before he died) is 'The Way to Blessedness'. In it he promises to lead his reader 'to true Felicity' by the explication of virtue. 'Blessedness', 'Felicity'; another name for this happiness/holiness is joy. Rather than being primarily a feeling, Christian joy is the mark of a holy life. It is a fruit of the Spirit. It is a way of seeing and being in the world that accepts the limitations of human frailty and is open to the gift of grace.

Traherne's *Centuries* opens with another promise – to fill the volume with 'Profitable Wonders', those things that will exalt the beauty of truth, drawing his reader by the allure of the sensed but unknown: 'Do you not feel your self Drawn with the Expectation and Desire of som Great Thing?' he asks. Nowhere in his study of felicity is happiness of the private, self-help variety. It is everywhere about engaging with another. We are drawn *to* and *by* the attraction of something altogether outside ourselves. Happiness is about the flow of life, being part of that flow and aware of one's choices and freedoms within it. It is about participating in the life of God.

In all of this, though, there are different kinds of and ways to felicity. I am using the term felicity here in place of happiness because it was Traherne's own preferred word, and also because it suggests blessedness, that state more than transient happiness, that has to do with participation in God. All happiness in Traherne is so tinged. There may be other ways of considering felicity in Traherne; I have chosen three: enjoying the world – deliberate felicity; holiness of life – accidental felicity; and divine holiness – essential felicity.

Traherne's admonition to 'enjoy the world' appears many times in *Centuries* and elsewhere in his writings. His meditations on enjoying the world, which are some of his best loved, encourage his readers to see themselves as heirs of creation and beloved of God. Creation is made for you, he says, it is your duty and your joy to be the enjoyer of it. I call this 'deliberate felicity' because it calls Traherne's reader to make a choice to see the world in a certain way. It is asking us, in a life provided with basic necessities, to choose happiness, and to see the tremendous wealth that is given us in ordinary things.

The second kind of or way to felicity is that to which Traherne seeks to lead his reader in writings such as *Christian Ethicks*. This is the life of virtue, the holy life, the blessed life. I call this 'accidental felicity' because although blessedness is the end to which he aims, he does so indirectly here. Virtue is the choice, virtue is the action, happiness is the eventual result or in classical terms 'accident'. It is in this sense that he may write in the *Centuries* that 'Happiness and holiness were the same thing'; it is the things which 'are in them selves Holy that make us Happy' (*SM*, II, 54). More than incidental, though not the sole aim, the felicity of the holy life is in some sense an accident. It is what happens when we are not expecting it, when we are busy learning or applying the virtue of patience or of courage or of humility or of justice.

The third felicity about which Traherne writes is the 'essential felicity' of God. This finds perhaps its clearest expression in *The Kingdom of God*, where we see a God who is the fountain of all blessedness. 'Being is his happiness' (*KOG*, Ch. 13, l. 11), and it is in the nature of Godself that we most clearly see the marriage of happiness and holiness.

This God who is all blessedness invites us to a blessed life, the life of *eudaimonia*. Here Traherne's model is Aquinas, and to a lesser extent Aristotle.[151] God's essence is love and the blessedness of God's life is manifest in the loving friendship that exists in the heart of God whose love between the persons of the Trinity flows and refills in a circle of communion and union. But there is another side to this nature that is love, the face of passion, and here is where Traherne touches less on the happiness and more on the holiness of God. Many times in Traherne's writing God's holiness is directly linked with the passionate nature of his love. The Lambeth fragment *Love* is perhaps the finest example of this, and Chapter 12 of *Christian Ethicks*, 'Of Holiness: Its Nature, Violence, and Pleasure', gives some indication of the tone he takes in addressing the holiness of God. Whereas human holiness traffics in the practicalities of life, divine holiness is awesome and austere. Zeal and fire, jealousy and desire are the signs of this holiness. The happiness of God may be *eudaimonia*, but the holiness of God is restless and burning; yearning and zealous, jealous and ardent, all are part of the perfection of divine desire. And yet the two, happiness and

---

151 The problem with Aristotle, according to Traherne, is that although he produced the model of virtuous habituation that Traherne uses, he never seemed to indicate the final end of that happiness. What was it for? This, Traherne says, Aristotle left in ruins.

holiness, can never be severed. Delight comes from satisfaction and there is not satisfaction without preceding desire. This is Traherne's everlasting circle: delight and desire, happiness and holiness, in God as much as in we God's creatures; 'all Delight springs from the satisfaction of violent Desire: when the desire is forgotten, the delight is abated . . . The sence of our want must be quick upon us to make the sence of our enjoyment perfect' (*CE*, Ch. 26).

Ironically it is God's refusal to exercise violence on us, violent as God's own desire may be, that allows us the freedom to become holy. 'That God should not be able to deserve our Love, unless he himself made us to love him by violence, is the Greatest Dishonour to him in the World', asserts Traherne (*CE*, Ch. 12). The same ardent love that is the mark of God's holiness is also the brake on God's act. And so Traherne's chapter on holiness ends with a divine conundrum – God adventuring the possibility of sin so that the possibility of true righteousness and holiness might also exist: 'Infinite Love to the Best of all Possible Things made the worst of all things that could be possible'. Ultimately divine holiness, the very perfection of his act and the ardency of his love, makes human imperfection possible. And God the holy becomes God the risk-taker as humankind the lowly becomes humankind the potentially good. So we may see holiness and happiness alike not as something remote and fixed, a kind of exalted state, but as immediate and dynamic – a part of the process and perfection of love.

At the heart of Traherne's theology is a wanting God, and we are to want in his image. 'You must Want like a GOD, that you may be Satisfied like GOD' (*C*, I, 44), writes Traherne. The first problem that this raises for many Christians is that it seems to fly in the face of the scriptural admonition to deny oneself and take up the cross. The second and perhaps more profound problem is that it challenges the long-held philosophical conviction that any god worth his salt neither needs nor lowers himself to desire anything. We are comfortable talking about God's will, his purposes or designs, but not God's desires. We want God to be reliable, unchanging and all-sufficient; Traherne's picture of God challenges this notion of divine 'impassibility'. In fact an impassible God is closer to Aristotle's 'Unmoved Mover' than to the God revealed in the biblical witness who seeks and yearns, who is betrayed and spurned, who nevertheless forgives again and who sometimes turns to wrath. We are left with a dilemma. On the one hand if we posit an 'impassible' God we run the risk of making God too remote; on the other, positing a passionate God runs the risk of remaking God in our image. Helen Oppenheimer deals with these questions succinctly in her recent study *Making Good*. She warns: ' "Impassibility" needs most subtle explanation if it is not to render God's love inaccessible' (page 38) and she suggests a rendering of 'impassibility' as 'unshaken' rather than 'unmoved', which leaves room for desire in the heart of God.

For Traherne the word 'want' carried with it notions of insufficiency that have virtually disappeared from the modern sense of the word. 'To want' meant 'to lack' as much as it meant 'to desire'.[152] For him to say that God wanted was even more challenging than it sounds today. God wanted, he says, 'from all Eternity' and at the same time he had from all eternity in himself, all he could want. 'He Wanted the Communication of His Divine Essence, and Persons to Enjoy it. He Wanted Worlds, He wanted Spectators, He wanted Joys, He wanted Treasures. He wanted, yet he wanted not, for he had them' (C, I, 41). In God, who is the fullness of all blessedness, want is an exercise of divine capacity. In us, it is an exercise in humility. Hence humility has an important role to play in Traherne's theory of happiness; knowing our wants is not about drawing up a mental shopping list, but about knowing our lacks as well as we know our desires. Finding our wants both ways answered, desire satisfied and renewed, humility in our lacks and hope in our longings: this is what happiness is about in Traherne. This is what Traherne means when he writes: 'I must lead you of this, into another World, to learn your Wants. For till you find them you will never be Happy. Wants themselves being sacred Occasions and Means of Felicitie' (C, I, 43).

The extracts

1 I came into this world only that I might be happy
2 Felicity
3 On retiring away from the world
4 The Study of Felicitie
5 Walking
6 Prizing, Wanting, Enjoying

152 For greater exploration of this theme see D. Inge, *Wanting Like a God: Desire and Freedom in the Work of Thomas Traherne*, SCM Press, forthcoming 2008.

I

I came into this world only that I might be happy

7

... Is it not the shame and reproach of Nature, that men should spend
so much time in studying Trades, and be so ready skild in the Nature
of clothes, of Grounds, of Gold and Silver, &c. and think it much to
spend a little time, in the study of God, Themselvs, and Happiness?
What hav men to do in this World, but to make them selvs Happy?
Shall it ever be praisd, and despised? Verily Happiness being the Soveraign and Supreme of our Concerns, should hav the most peculiar
portion of our Time: and other things what she can spare. It more
concernes me to be Divine, then to hav a Purs of Gold. And therfore
as Solomon said, We must dig for her as for Gold and Silver; and that
is the way to understand the fear of the Lord, and to find the Knowledg
of God. It is a strange thing that Men will be such Enemies to them
selvs: Wisdom is the Principal Thing yet all neglect her · wherfore Get
Wisdom, and with all thy Getting get understanding. Exalt her and she
shall promote thee, she shall bring thee to Honor when thou dost
embrace her. She shall giv to thy Head an Ornament of Grace, a Crown
of Glory shall she deliver to Thee.[1] Had you certain Tidings of a Mine
of Gold, would the Care of your Ordinary Affairs detain you, could
you hav it for the Digging? Nothing more ruins the world, then a
Conceit, that a little Knowledge is sufficient. Which is a mere lazy
Dream, to cover our Sloth or Enmity against GOD. Can you go to a
Mine of Gold, and not to Wisdom; (to dig for it;) without being guilty,

either of a Base Despondency and Distrust of Wisdom, that she will not bring you to such Glorious Treasures as is promised; or els of a vile and Lazy Humor that makes you despise them, becaus of that little, but long labor, you apprehend between? Nothing keeps men out of the Temple of Honor, but that the Temple of Vertue stands between. But this was His Principle that loved Happiness, and is your friend. I came into this World only that I might be Happy. And whatsoever it cost me I will be Happy. A Happiness there is, and it is my desire to enjoy it.

8

Philosophers are not only those that Contemplat happiness, but Practise virtue. He is a Philosopher that subdues his vices, Lives by Reason, Orders his Desires, Rules his Passions, and submits not to his sences, nor is guided by the Customs of this World. He despiseth those Riches which Men esteem, he despiseth those Honors which men esteem, he forsaketh those Pleasures which Men Esteem. And having proposed to him self a Superior End, then is commonly discerned, bears all Discouragements, breaks thorow all Difficulties and lives unto it: That having seen the Secrets, and the Secret Beauties of the Highest reason, orders his Conversation, and lives by Rule: tho in this Age, it be held never so strange that He should do so. Only He is Divine becaus he does this upon Noble Principles, Becaus GOD is, becaus Heaven is, because Jesus Christ hath Redeemd him, and becaus he Lovs Him: not only becaus vertue is Amiable, and felicity Delightfull; but for that also.

9

Once more we will distinguish of Christians. There are Christians, that place and desire all their Happiness in another Life, and there is another sort of Christians that desire Happiness in this. The one can defer their Enjoyment of Wisdom till the World to com: And dispence with the Increas and Perfection of Knowledg for a little time: the other are instant and impatient of Delay; and would fain see that Happiness here, which they shall enjoy herafter. Not the vain Happiness of this World, falsly called Happiness, truly vain: but the real Joy and Glory of the Blessed: which Consisteth in the Enjoyment of the Whole World in Communion with God, not this only, but the Invisible and Eternal: which they earnestly covet to Enjoy immediatly: for which reason they daily pray Thy Kingdom come; and travail towards it by learning Wisdom as fast as they can. Whether the first sort be Christians indeed, look you to that. They hav much to say for themselvs. Yet certainly they that put off felicity with long delays, are to be much suspected, for it is against the Nature of Lov and desire to defer. Nor can any reason be given, why they should desire it at last, and not now. If they say Becaus God hath Commanded them, that is fals: for He offereth it now. Now they are commanded to have their Conversation[2] in Heaven, now they may be full of Joy and full of Glory. Ye are not streightned in me, but in your own Bowels. Those Christians that can defer their felicity may be contented with their Ignorance.

10

He that will not Exchange his Riches now, will not forsake them herafter. He must, but will hardly be persuaded to do it willingly. He will leav them, but not forsake them · for which caus two Dishonors cleav unto him; and if at Death, eternaly. First, he coms off the Stage unwillingly, which is very unhandsom: and secondly He prefers his Riches abov his Happiness. Riches are but servants to Happiness, when they are Impediments they ceas to be Riches. As long as they are Conduciv to Felicity they are desirable; but when they are incompitable Abominable. For what End are Riches endeavored, Why do we desire them but that we may be more Happy? When we see the Persuit of them destructiv to Felicity, to desire them is of all things in Nature the most absurd and the most foolish. I ever thought that Nothing was desirable for it self but Happiness, and that whatever els we desire, it is of valu only in relation, and Order to it.

13

One great Discouragement to Felicity, or rather to great Souls in the persuit of Felicity, is the Solitariness of the Way that leadeth to her Temple. A man that studies Happiness must sit alone like a Sparrow upon the Hous Top, and like a Pelican in the Wilderness. And the reason is becaus all men prais Happiness and despise it; very few shall a Man find in the way of Wisdom: And few indeed that having given up their Names to Wisdom and felicity, that will persevere in seeking it. Either He must go on alone, or go back for company. People are tickled with the Name of it, and som are persuaded to Enterprize a little, but quickly draw back when they see the trouble, yea cool of them selvs without any Trouble. Those Mysteries which while men are Ignorant of, they would giv all the Gold in the World for, I hav seen when Known to be despised. Not as if the Nature of Happiness were such that it did need a vail: but the Nature of Man is such, that it is

Odious and ingratefull. For those things which are most Glorious when most Naked, are by Men when most Nakedly reveald most Despised. So that GOD is fain for His very Names sake, lest His Beauties should be scorned to conceal her Beauties: and for the sake of Men, which naturaly are more prone to prie into secret and forbidden things then into Open and common. Felicity is amiable under a Vail, but most Amiable when most Naked. It hath its times, and seasons for both. There is som Pleasure in breaking the Shell: and many Delights in our Addresses, previous to the Sweets in the Possession of her. It is som Part of Felicity that we must seek her.

Centuries of Meditations, IV

1 Proverbs 4.5–9; 16.16.
2 Behaviour, manner of life; Philippians 3.20.

2

Felicity

Prompted to seek my Bliss abov the Skies,
　　How often did I lift mine Eys
　　　　Beyond the Spheres!
Dame Nature told me there was endless Space
Within my Soul; I spy'd its very face:
　　　Sure it not for nought appears.
　　What is there which a Man may see
　　　　Beyond the Spheres?
　　　　FELICITY.

There in the Mind of God, that Sphere of Lov,
　　(In nature, hight, extent, abov
　　　　All other Spheres,)
A Man may see Himself, the World, the Bride
Of God *His Church*, which as they there are ey'd
　　　Strangely exalted each appears:
　　His Mind is higher than the Space
　　　　Above the Spheres,
　　　　Surmounts all Place.

No empty Space; it is all full of Sight,
    All Soul and Life, an Ey most bright,
        All Light and Lov;
Which doth at once all things possess and giv,
Heven and Earth, with All that therin liv;
      It rests at quiet, and doth mov;
    Eternal is, yet Time includes;
        A Scene abov
        All Interludes.

3

On retiring away from the world

Retirement is therfore Necessary to him, that Studieth Happiness, becaus it is the Gate that leadeth therunto. For in Retirement alone can a Man approach to that which is Infinit and Eternal. Infinity and Eternity are only to bee seen by the Inward Ey. By Expanding the Understanding and by the Introversion of the Soul, do we approach unto those: namely by observing and Noting what is within. For Man is such a Wonderfull Creature that Infinity and Eternity is [hid?] within Him. And if these are within Him, all the Things they contain, are within Him likewise. For it is as Easy, for a Cabinet to be in a Palace and yet those Treasures with which it is replenished to be out of that Palace; as for the Eternity of God to be in the Soul of Man, while the Things contained in Eternity are out of that Soul, in which Eternity is contained.

Becaus Eternity is contained in the Soul, a Man in finding Him self findeth Eternity; and becaus in finding Him self he findeth Eternity, in finding Him self he findeth All Things. For All Things are contained in Eternitie. Since therfore in Retirement alone a Man findeth Him self, in Retirement alone he findeth All Things. Nor can there be any Rest, till he findeth All Things his Delights and Treasures.

Inducements to Retiredness, I

4

The Study of Felicitie

36

Having been at the University, and received there the Taste and Tincture of another Education, I saw that there were Things in this World of which I never Dreamed, Glorious Secrets, and Glorious Persons past Imagination. There I saw that Logick, Ethicks, Physicks, Metaphysicks, Geometry, Astronomy, Poesie, Medicine, Grammer, Musick, Rhetorick, all kind of Arts Trades and Mechanicismes that Adorned the World pertained to felicity. At least there I saw those Things, which afterwards I knew to pertain unto it: And was Delighted in it. There I saw into the Nature of the Sea, the Heavens, the Sun, the Moon and Stars, the Elements, Minerals and Vegetables. All which appeared like the Kings Daughter, All Glorious within,[1] and those Things which my Nurses and Parents should hav talkt of, there were taught unto Me.

37

Nevertheless som things were Defectiv too. There was never a Tutor that did professely Teach Felicity: tho that be the Mistress of all other Sciences. Nor did any of us Study these things but as *Aliena*, which we ought to hav Studied as our own Enjoyments. We Studied to inform our Knowledg, but knew not for what End we so Studied. And for lack of aiming at a Certain End, we Erred in the Maner. How beit there we received all those Seeds of Knowledg that were afterwards improved; and our Souls were Awakened to a Discerning of their faculties, and Exercise of their Powers.

39

The Best of all Possible Ends is the Glory of GOD, but Happiness was that I thirsted after. And yet I did not erre · for the Glory of God is to make us Happy. Which can never be don but by giving us most Excellent Natures and Satisfying those Natures: by Creating all Treasures of infinit Valu, and giving them to us in an infinit maner, to wit both in the Best that to Omnipotence was possible. This led me to Enquire, Whither All Things were Excellent and of Perfect Valu, and whither they were mine in Propriety?

52

When I came into the Country, and saw that I had all time in my own hands, having devoted it wholy to the Study of Felicitie, I knew not where to begin or End; nor what Objects to chuse, upon which most profitably I might fix my Contemplation. I saw my self like som Traveller, that had Destined his Life to journeys, and was resolvd to spend his Days in visiting Strange Places: who might wander in vain, unless his Undertakings were guided by som certain Rule; and that innumerable Millions of Objects were presented before me, unto any of which I might take my journey · fain I would hav visited them all, but that was impossible. What then should I do? Even imitat a Traveller, who becaus He cannot visit all Coasts, Wildernesses, Sandy Deserts, Seas, Hills, Springs and Mountains, chuseth the most Populous and flourishing Cities, where he might see the fairest Prospects, Wonders, and Rarities, and be entertained with greatest Courtesie: and where indeed he might most Benefit himself with Knowledg Profit and Delight: leaving the rest, even the naked and Empty Places unseen. For which caus I made it my Prayer to GOD Almighty, that He, whose Eys are open upon all Things, would guid me to the fairest and Divinest.

53

And what Rule do you think I walked by? Truly a Strange one, but the Best in the Whole World. I was Guided by an Implicit Faith in Gods Goodness: and therefore led to the Study of the most Obvious and Common Things. For thus I thought within my self: GOD being, as we generaly believ, infinit in Goodness, it is most Consonant and Agreeable with His Nature, that the Best Things should be most Common · for nothing is more Naturall to infinit Goodness, then to make the Best Things most frequent; and only Things Worthless, Scarce. Then I began to Enquire what Things were most Common: Air, Light, Heaven and Earth, Water, the Sun, Trees, Men and Women, Cities Temples &c. These I found Common and Obvious to all: Rubies Pearls Diamonds Gold and Silver, these I found scarce, and to the most Denied. Then began I to consider and compare the value of them, which I measured by their Serviceableness, and by the Excellencies which would be found in them, should they be taken away. And in Conclusion I saw clearly, that there was a Real Valuableness in all the Common things; in the Scarce, a feigned.

55

That any thing may be found to be an infinit Treasure, its Place must be found in Eternity, and in Gods Esteem. For as there is a Time, so there is a Place for all Things. Evry thing in its Place is Admirable Deep and Glorious: out of its Place like a Wandering Bird, is Desolat and Good for Nothing. How therfore it relateth to God and all Creatures must be seen before it can be Enjoyed. And this I found by many Instances. The Sun is Good, only as it relateth to the Stars, to the Seas, to your Ey, to the feilds, &c. As it relateth to the Stars it raiseth their Influences; as to the Seas it melteth them and maketh the Waters flow; as to your Ey, it bringeth in the Beauty of the World; as to the feilds; it clotheth them with Fruits and flowers. Did it not relate to others it would not be Good. Divest it of these Operations, and Divide it from these Objects it is Useless and Good for nothing. And therfore Worthless, because Worthles and Useless go together. A Piece of Gold cannot be Valued, unless we Know how it relates to Clothes, to Wine, to Victuals, to the Esteem of Men, and to the Owner. Som little Piece in a Kingly Monument severd from the rest hath no Beauty at all. It enjoys its valu in its Place, by the Ornament it gives to, and receivs from all the Parts. By this I discerned, that even a little Knowledg could not be had in the Mysterie of Felicity, without a great deal. And that that was the reason why so many were ignorant of its nature, and why so few did attain it; for by the Labor required to much Knowledg they were discouraged, and for lack of much did not see any Glorious motives to allure them.

56

Therfore of Necessity they must at first believ that Felicity is a Glorious tho an unknown Thing. And certainly it was the infinit Wisdom of God, that did implant by Instinct so strong a Desire of felicity in the Soul, that we might be excited to labor after it, tho we know it not, the very force wherwith we covet it supplying the place of Understanding. That there is a Felicyty we all know by the Desires after, that there is a most Glorious felicity we know by the Strength and vehemence of those Desires: And that nothing but Felicity is worthy of our Labor, becaus all other things are the Means only which conduce unto it. I was very much animated by the Desires of Philosophers, which I saw in Heathen Books aspiring after it. But the misery is *It was unknown.* An altar was erected to it like that in Athens with this inscription TO THE UNKNOWN GOD.

59

The Image of God implanted in us, guided me to the maner wherin we were to Enjoy · for since we were made in the similitud of God, we were made to Enjoy after his Similitude. Now to Enjoy the Treasures of God in the Similitud of God, is the most perfect Blessedness God could Devise. For the Treasures of GOD are the most Perfect Treasures and the Maner of God is the most perfect Maner. To Enjoy therfore the Treasures of God after the similitud of God is to Enjoy the most perfect Treasures in the most Perfect Maner. Upon which I was infinitly satisfied in God, and knew there was a Dietie, becaus I was Satisfied. For Exerting Himself wholy in atchieving thus an infinit felicity He was infinitly Delightfull Great and Glorious, and my Desires so August and Insatiable that nothing less then a Deity could satisfy them.

60

This Spectacle once seen, will never be forgotten. It is a Great Part of the Beatifick Vision. A Sight of Happiness is Happiness. It transforms the Soul and makes it Heavenly, it powerfully calls us to Communion with God, and weans us from the Customs of this World. It puts a Lustre upon GOD and all his Creatures, and makes us to see them in a Divine and Eternal Light. I no sooner discerned this but I was (as Plato saith, *In summâ Rationis Arce Quies habitat*) seated in a Throne of Repose and Perfect Rest. All Things were well in their Proper Places, I alone was out of frame and had need to be Mended · for all things were Gods Treasures in their Proper places, and I was to be restored to Gods Image. Wherupon you will not believ how I was withdrawn from all Endeavors of altering and Mending Outward Things. They lay so well methoughts, they could not be Mended: but I must be Mended to Enjoy them.

Centuries of Meditations, III

1 Psalm 45.13.

5

Walking

To *walk* abroad is, not with Eys,
But Thoughts, the Fields to see and prize;
    Els may the silent Feet,
        Like Logs of Wood,
Mov up and down, and see no Good,
    Nor Joy nor Glory meet.

Ev'n Carts and Wheels their place do change,
But cannot see; tho very strange
    The Glory that is by:
        Dead Puppets may
Mov in the bright and glorious Day,
    Yet not behold the Sky.

And are not Men than they more blind,
Who having Eys yet never find
    The Bliss in which they mov:
        Like Statues dead
They up and down are carried,
    Yet neither see nor lov.

To *walk* is by a Thought to go;
To mov in Spirit to and fro;
    To mind the Good we see;
        To taste the Sweet;
Observing all the things we meet
    How choice and rich they be.

To note the Beauty of the Day,
And golden Fields of Corn survey;
    Admire the pretty Flow'rs
        With their sweet Smell;
To prais their Maker, and to tell
    The Marks of His Great Pow'rs.

To fly abroad like active Bees,
Among the Hedges and the Trees,
   To cull the Dew that lies
      On evry Blade,
From evry Blossom; till we lade
   Our *Minds*, as they their *Thighs*.

Observ those rich and glorious things,
The Rivers, Meadows, Woods, and Springs,
   The fructifying Sun;
      To note from far
The Rising of each Twinkling Star
   For us his Race to run.

A little Child these well perceivs,
Who, tumbling among Grass and Leaves,
   May Rich as Kings be thought,
      But there's a Sight
Which perfect Manhood may delight,
   To which we shall be brought.

While in those pleasant Paths we talk
'Tis *that* tow'rds which at last we walk;
   But we may by degrees
      Wisely proceed
Pleasures of Lov and Prais to heed,
   From viewing Herbs and Trees.

6

Prizing, Wanting, Enjoying

13

To be Holy is so Zealously to Desire, so vastly to Esteem, and so Earnestly to Endeavour it, that we would not for millions of Gold and Silver, Decline, nor fail, nor Mistake in a Tittle. For then we Pleas God when we are most like Him. We are like Him when our Minds are in Frame. Our Minds are in Frame when our Thoughts are like his. And our Thoughts are then like his when we hav such Conceptions of all objects as God hath, and Prize all Things according to their value. For

God doth Prize all Things rightly. Which is a Key that Opens into the very Thoughts of his Bosom. It seemeth Arrogance to pretend to the Knowledg of his Secret Thoughts. But how shall we hav the Mind of God, unless we Know his Thoughts? Or how shall we be led by his Divine Spirit, till we hav his Mind? His Thoughts are Hidden: but he hath revealed unto us the Hidden Things of Darkness.[1] By his Works and by his Attributs we know His Thoughts. And by Thinking the same are Divine and Blessed.

14

When Things are ours in their Proper Places, nothing is needfull but Prizing, to Enjoy them. God therfore hath made it infinitly Easy to Enjoy, by making evry Thing ours, and us able so Easily to Prize them. Evry thing is ours that serves us in its Place. The Sun servs us as much as is Possible, and more then we could imagine. The Clouds and Stars Minister unto us, the World surrounds us with Beauty, the Air refresheth us the Sea revives the Earth and us. The Earth it self is Better then Gold because it produceth fruits and flowers. And therfore in the Beginning, was it made Manifest to be mine, becaus Adam alone was made to Enjoy it. By making One, and not a Multitud, God evidently Shewed One alone to be the End of the World, and evry one its Enjoyer: for evry one may Enjoy it as much as He.

15

Such Endless Depths lie in the Divinity, and the Wisdom of God, that as He maketh one, so He maketh evry one the End of the World: the Supernumerary Persons being Enrichers of his Inheritance. Adam and the World are both mine. And the Posterity of Adam enrich it Infinitly. Souls are Gods Jewels.[2] Evry one of which is worth many Worlds. They are his Riches becaus his Image · and mine for that reason. So that I alone am the End of the World. Angels and Men being all mine. And if others are so, they are made to Enjoy it for my further Advancement. God only being the Giver, and I the Receiver. So that Seneca Philosophized rightly, when he said, *Deus me dedit solum loti Mundo, et totum Mundum mihi soli*. God gave me alone to all the World, and all the World to me alone.

18

The WORLD is not this little Cottage of Heaven and Earth. Tho this be fair, it is too small a Gift. When God made the WORLD, He made the Heavens and the Heavens of Heavens,[3] and the Angels and the Celestial Powers. These also are Parts of the World: so are all those infinit and Eternal Treasures that are to abide for ever, after the Day of Judgement. Neither are these, some here, and some there, but all evry where, and at once to be Enjoyed. The WORLD is unknown, till the Value and Glory of it is seen: till the Beauty and the Serviceableness of its Parts is Considered. When you enter into it, it is an illimited feild of Varietie and Beauty: where you may lose your self in the Multitude of Wonders and Delights. But it is an Happy Loss to lose one self in Admiration at ones own Felicity: and to find GOD in exchange for oneself. Which we then do when we see Him in His Gifts, and Adore his Glory.

19

You never Know your self, till you Know more then your Body. The Image of God was not seated in the features of your face, but in the Lineaments of your Soul. In the Knowledg of your Powers, Inclinations and Principles, the Knowledg of your self cheifly consisteth. Which are so Great that even to the most Learned of men their Greatness is Incredible; and so Divine, that they are infinit in Value. Alass the WORLD is but a little Centre in Comparison of you. Suppose it Millions of Miles from the Earth to the Heavens, and Millions of Millions above the Stars, both here and over the heads of our Antipodes: it is surrounded with infinit and Eternal Space: And like a Gentlemans house to one that is Travelling; It is a long time before you com unto it, you passe it in an Instant, and leave it for ever. The Omnipresence and Eternity of God are your Fellows and Companions. And all that is in them ought to be made your familiar Treasures. Your Understanding comprehends the World like the Dust of a Ballance, measures Heaven with a Span and esteems a thousand yeers but as one Day. So that Great Endless Eternal Delights are only fit to be its Enjoyments.

20

The Laws of GOD, which are the Commentaries of his Works, shew them to be yours: becaus They teach you to lov God with all your Soul, and with all your Might.[4] Whom if you lov with all the Endless Powers

of your Soul, you will lov Him in Him self, in His Attributs, in His
Counsels, in all his Works, in all His Ways: and in evry Kind of Thing
wherin He appeareth, you will Prize Him, you will Honor Him, you
will Delight in Him, you will ever desire to be with him and to pleas
Him. For to lov Him includeth all this. You will feed with Pleasure
upon evry Thing that is His. So that the World shall be a Grand Jewel
of Delight unto you: a very Paradice; and the Gate of Heaven. It is
indeed the Beautifull Frontispiece of Eternitie · the Temple of God, the
Palace of his children. The Laws of God Discover all that is therin to
be Created for your sake. For they command you to lov all that is
Good, and when you see well, you enjoy what you lov. They apply the
Endless Powers of your Soul to all their Objects: And by ten thousand
Methods make evry Thing to serv you. They command you to lov all
Angels and Men, They command all Angels and Men to lov you. When
you lov them, they are your Treasures; when They lov you, to your
great advantage you are theirs. All things serv you for serving them
whom you lov, and of whom you are Beloved. The Enterance of His
Words giveth Light to the Simple.[5] You are Magnified among Angels
and Men: Enriched by them, and Happy in them.

21

By the very Right of your Sences you Enjoy the World. Is not the Beauty
of the Hemisphere present to your Ey? Doth not the Glory of the Sun
pay Tribut to your Sight. Is not the Vision of the WORLD an Amiable
Thing? Do not the Stars shed Influences to Perfect the Air? Is not that
a marvellous Body to Breath in? To visit the Lungs: repair the Spirits:
revive the Sences: Cool the Blood: fill the Empty Spaces between the
Earth and Heavens; and yet giv Liberty to all Objects? Prize these first:
and you shall Enjoy the Residue. Glory, Dominion, Power, Wisdom,
Honor, Angels, Souls, Kingdoms, Ages. *Be faithfull in a little, and you
shall be Master over much.*[6] If you be not faithful in esteeming these,
who shall put into your Hands the true Treasures. If you be Negligent
in Prizing these, you will be Negligent in Prizing all. There is a Diseas
in Him who Despiseth present mercies, which till it be cured, he can
never be Happy. He esteemeth nothing that he hath, but is ever Gaping
after more: which when he hath He despiseth in like manner.
Insatiableness is Good, but not Ingratitud.

22

It is of the Nobility of Mans Soul that He is Insatiable · for he hath a Benefactor so Prone to Give, that He delighteth in us for Asking. Do not your Inclinations tell you that the WORLD is yours? Do you not covet all? Do you not long to hav it; to Enjoy it; to Overcom it? To what End do Men gather Riches, but to Multiplie more? Do they not like Pyrrhus the King of Epire, adde hous to hous and Lands to Lands, that they may get it all? It is storied of that Prince, that having conceived a Purpose to invade Italy, he sent for Cineas, a Philosopher and the Kings friend: to whom he communicated his Designe, and desired his Counsel. Cineas asked him to what Purpose he invaded Italie? He said, To Conquer it. And what will you do when you hav Conquerd it? Go into France said the King, and Conquer that. And what will you do when you have Conquerd France? Conquer Germany. And what then? said the Philosopher. Conquer Spain. I perceive said Cineas, you mean to conquer all the World. What will you do when you have conquerd all? Why then said the King we will return, and Enjoy our selvs at Quiet in our own Land. So you may now said the Philosopher without all this adoe. Yet could he not Divert him till he was ruind by the Romans. Thus men get one Hundred Pound a year that they may get another; and having two covet Eight, and there is no End of all their Labor; becaus the Desire of their Soul is Insatiable. Like Alexander the Great they must hav all: and when they hav got it all be quiet. And may they not do all this before they begin? Nay it would be well, if they could be Quiet. But if after all, they shall be like the stars, that are seated on high, but hav no Rest, what gain they more, but Labor for their Trouble? It was wittily fained that that Yong man sate down and Cried for more Worlds. So insatiable is Man that Millions will not Pleas him. They are no more then so many Tennis-Balls, in Comparison of the Greatness and Highness of his Soul.

23

The Noble Inclination wherby Man thirsteth after Riches and Dominion, is his Highest Virtu, when rightly Guided: and Carries him as in a Triumphant Chariot, to his Soveraign Happiness. Men are made Miserable only by abusing it. Taking a fals way to Satisfy it, they Persue the Wind: Nay labor in the very fire, and after all reap but Vanitie. Wheras, as Gods Lov, which is the fountaion of all, did cost us Nothing: so were all other Things prepared by it, to satisfy our Inclinations in the Best of Manners, freely, without any cost of ours. Being therfore all Satisfactions are near at hand, by going further we do but leav them: And Wearying our selvs in a long way round about, like a Blind man, forsake them. They are immediatly near to the very Gates of our Sences. It becometh the Bounty of God to prepare them freely: to make them Glorious, and their Enjoyment Easy. For becaus His Lov is free so are his Treasures. He therfore that will Despise them becaus he hath them is Marvellously Irrational. The Way to Possess them is to Esteem them. And the true Way of Reigning over them, is to break the WORLD all into Parts, to examine them asunder; And if we find them so Excellent that Better could not Possibly be made, and so made that they could not be more ours, to rejoyce in all with Pleasure answerable to the Merit of their Goodness. We being then Kings over the Whole World, when we restore the Pieces to their Proper Places, being Perfectly Pleased with the whole Composure. This shall giv you a thorow grounded Contentment, far beyond what troublesom Wars, or Conquests can acquire.

25

Your Enjoyment of the World is never right, till you so Esteem it, that evry thing in it, is more your Treasure, then a Kings Exchequer full of Gold and Silver. And that Exchequer yours also in its Place and Service. Can you take too much Joy in your fathers Works? He is Himself in evry Thing. Som Things are little on the outside, and Rough and Common, but I remember the Time, when the Dust of the Streets were as precious as Gold to my Infant Eys, and now they are more precious to the Ey of Reason.

27

You never Enjoy the World aright, till you see how a Sand Exhibiteth the Wisdom and Power of God: And Prize in evry Thing the Service which they do you, by Manifesting His Glory and Goodness to your Soul, far more then the Visible Beauty on their Surface, or the Material Services, they can do your Body. Wine by its Moysture quencheth my Thirst, whether I consider it or no: but to see it flowing from his Lov who gav it unto Man, Quencheth the Thirst even of the Holy Angels. To consider it, is to Drink it Spritualy. To Rejoice in its Diffusion is to be of a Publick Mind. And to take Pleasure in all the Benefits it doth to all is Heavenly · for so they do in Heaven. To do so, is to be Divine and Good and to imitat our Infinit and Eternal Father.

28

Your Enjoyment of the World is never right, till evry Morning you awake in Heaven: see your self in your fathers Palace: and look upon the Skies and the Earth and the Air, as Celestial Joys: having such a Reverend Esteem of all, as if you were among the Angels. The Bride of a Monarch, in her Husbands Chamber, hath no such Causes of Delight as you.

29

You never Enjoy the World aright, till the Sea it self floweth in your Veins, till you are Clothed with the Heavens, and Crowned with the Stars: and perceiv your self to be the Sole Heir of the whole World: and more then so, becaus Men are in it who are evry one Sole Heirs, as well as you. Till you can Sing and Rejoyce and Delight in GOD, as Misers do in Gold, and Kings in Scepters, you never Enjoy the World.

30

Till your Spirit filleth the whole World, and the Stars are your Jewels, till you are as Familiar with the Ways of God in all Ages as with your Walk and Table: till you are intimatly Acquainted with that Shady Nothing out of which the World was made: till you lov Men so as to Desire their Happiness, with a Thirst equal to the zeal of your own: till you Delight in GOD for being Good to all: you never Enjoy the World. Till you more feel it then your Privat Estate, and are more present in the Hemisphere, Considering the Glories and the Beauties there, then in your own Hous. Till you remember how lately you were made, and how wonderfull it was when you came into it: and more rejoyce in the Palace of your Glory, then if it had been made but to Day Morning.

31

Yet further, you never Enjoy the World aright, till you so lov the Beauty of Enjoying it, that you are Covetous and Earnest to Persuade others to Enjoy it. And so perfectly hate the Abominable Corruption of Men in Despising it, that you had rather suffer the flames of Hell then willingly be Guilty of their Error. There is so much Blindness, and Ingratitud, and Damned folly in it. The World is a Mirror of infinit Beauty, yet no Man sees it. It is a Temple of Majesty yet no Man regards it. It is a Region of Light and Peace, did not Men Disquiet it. It is the Paradice of God. It is more to Man since he is faln, then it was before. It is the Place of Angels, and the Gate of Heaven. When Jacob waked out of His Dream, he said, *God is here and I wist it not. How Dreadfull is this Place! This is none other, then the Hous of God, and the Gate of Heaven.*[7]

32

Can any Ingratitud be more Damned then that which is fed by Benefits? Or folly Greater then that which bereaveth us of infinit Treasures? They Despise them meerly becaus they hav them: And invent Ways to make them selvs Miserable in the Presence of Riches. They Study a thousand New fangled Treasures, which God never made: and then Griev and Repine that they be not Happy. They Dote on their own Works, and Neglect Gods. Which are full of Majesty Riches and Wisdom. And having fled away from them becaus they are Solid Divine and True, Greedily persuing Tinsild vanities, they walk on in Darkness, and will not understand. They do the Works of Darkness, and Delight in the Riches of the Prince of Darkness, and follow them till they com into Eternal Darkness. According to that of the Psalmist *All the foundations* of the Earth are out of course.[8]

36

The Common Error which makes it Difficult to believ all the World to be wholy ours, is to be shund as a Rock of Shipwrack: or a Dangerous Quicksands. For the Poyson which they Drank hath infatuated their fancies and now they Know not, neither will they understand, they walk on in Darkness. *All the foundations of the Earth are out of Cours.* It is Safety not to be with them. And a Great Part of Happiness to be freed from their Seducing and Enslaving Errors. That while Others liv in a Golgotha or Prison, we should be in Eden, is a very Great Mystery. And a Mercy it is that we should be Rejoycing in the Temple of Heaven, while they are Toyling and Lamenting in Hell, for the World is both a Paradice and a Prison to different Persons.

39

Your Enjoyment is never right, till you esteem evry Soul so Great a Treasure as our Savior doth: and that the Laws of God are sweeter then the Hony and Hony Comb[9] becaus they command you to lov them all in such Perfect Maner. For how are they Gods Treasures? Are they not the Riches of His Lov? Is it not his Goodness that maketh Him Glorious to them? Can the Sun or Stars serv Him any other Way, then by serving them? And how will you be the Son of God, but by having a Great Soul like unto your Fathers. *The Laws of God command you to live in His Image · and to do so, is to live in Heaven.* God commandeth you to lov all like Him, becaus He would hav you to be his Son, all them to be your Riches, you to be Glorious before them, and all the Creatures in serving them to be your Treasures, while you are his Delight, like him in Beauty, and the Darling of his Bosom.

40

Socrates was wont to say, *They are most Happy and neerest the Gods that needed Nothing.* And coming once up into the Exchange at Athens, where they that Traded Asked Him, What will you Buy: what do you lack? After he had Gravely Walkt up into the Middle, spreading forth his Hands and turning about, *Good Gods,* saith he, *who would hav thought there were so many Things in the World which I do not want!* And so left the Place under the Reproach of Nature. He was wont to say, *That Happiness consisted not in Having Many, but in Needing the Fewest Things: for the Gods Needed Nothing at all, and they were most like them that least Needed.* We Needed Heaven and Earth, our Sences, Such Souls and Such Bodies, with infinit Riches in the Image of God to be Enjoyed: Which God of his Mercy having freely prepared, they are most Happy that so live in the Enjoyment of those, as to need no Accidental Trivial Thing. No Splendors, Pomps and Vanities. Socrates perhaps being an Heathen, knew not that all Things proceeded from God to Man, and by Man returned to God: but we that know it: must need All Things as God doth that we may receiv them with Joy, and liv in His Image.

41

As Pictures are made Curious by Lights and Shades, which without Shades, could not be: so is Felicitie composed of Wants and Supplies, without which Mixture there could be no Felicity. Were there no Needs, Wants would be Wanting themselves: And Supplies Superfluous. Want being the Parent of Celestial Treasure. It is very Strange; Want it self is a Treasure in Heaven: And so Great an one, that without it there could be no Treasure. GOD did infinitly for us, when He made us to Want like GODS, that like GODS, we might be satisfied. The Heathen DIETIES wanted nothing, and were therfore unhappy; For they had no Being. But the LORD GOD of Israel the Living and True GOD, was from all Eternity, and from all Eternity Wanted like a

GOD. He Wanted the Communication of His Divine Essence, and Persons to Enjoy it. He Wanted Worlds, He wanted Spectators, He wanted Joys, He wanted Treasures. He wanted, yet he wanted not, for he had them.

42

This is very strange that GOD should Want · for in Him is the Fulness of all Blessedness: He overfloweth Eternaly. His Wants are as Glorious as Infinit. Perfectiv needs that are in His Nature, and ever Blessed, becaus always Satisfied. He is from Eternity full of Want: Or els He would not be full of Treasure. Infinit Want is the very Ground and Caus of infinit Treasure. It is Incredible, yet very Plain: Want is the Fountain of all His Fulness. Want in GOD is a Treasure to us. For had there been no Need He would not hav Created the World, nor Made us, nor Manifested his Wisdom, nor Exercised his Power, nor Beautified Eternity, nor prepared the Joys of Heaven. But He Wanted Angels and Men, Images, Companions. And these He had from all Eternitie.

43

Infinit Wants Satisfied Produce infinit Joys; And, in the Possession of those Joys, are infinit Joys themselves. *The Desire Satisfied is a Tree of Life.*[10] Desire imports som thing absent: and a Need of what is Absent. GOD was never without this Tree of Life. He did Desire infinitly · yet He was never without the Fruits of this Tree, which are the Joys it produced. I must lead you out of this, into another World, to learn your Wants. For till you find them you will never be Happy. Wants themselvs being sacred Occasions and Means of Felicitie.

44

You must Want like a GOD, that you may be Satisfied like GOD. Were you not made in His *Image*? He is infinitly Glorious, becaus all His Wants and Supplies are at the same time in his Nature from Eternity. He had, and from Eternity He was without all His Treasures. From Eternity He needed them, and from Eternity He enjoyed them. For all Eternity is at once in Him · both the Empty Durations before the World was made, and the full ones after. His Wants are as Lively as His Enjoyments: And always present with Him. For His Life is Perfect, and He feels them both. His Wants put a Lustre upon His Enjoyments, and make them infinit. His Enjoyments being infinit Crown his Wants, and make them Beautifull even to GOD Himself. His Wants and Enjoyments being always present, are Delightfull to each other, stable Immut-able Perfectiv of each other, and Delightfull to Him. Who being Eternal and Immutable, Enjoyeth all His Wants and Treasures together. His Wants never Afflict Him, His Treasures never Disturb Him. His Wants always Delight Him, His Treasures never Cloy Him. The Sence of His Wants is always as Great, as if his Treasures were removed: and as lively upon Him. The Sence of His Wants, as it Enlargeth His Life, so it infuseth a Valu, and continual Sweetness into the Treasures He Enjoyeth.

45

This is a Lesson long enough: which you may be all your Life in Learning, and to all Eternity in Practising. *Be Sensible*[11] *of your Wants, that you may be sensible of your Treasures.* He is most like GOD that is sensible of evry Thing. Did you not from all Eternity Want som one to give you a Being? Did you not Want one to give you a Glorious Being? Did you not from all Eternity Want som one to giv you infinit Treasures? And som one to give you Spectators, Companions, Enjoy-ers? Did you not Want a Dietie, to make them Sweet and Honorable by His infinit Wisdom? What you wanted from all Eternity, be sensible of to all Eternity. Let your Wants be present from Everlasting. Is not this a Strange Life to which I call you? Wherin you are to be present with Things that were before the World was made? And at once present even like GOD with infinit Wants and infinit Treasures? Be present with your Want of a Diety, and you shall be present with the Dietie. You shall Adore and Admire Him, Enjoy and Prize Him; Believ in Him, and Delight in Him: See Him to be the Fountain of all your Joys · and the Head of all your Treasures.

46

It was His Wisdom made you Need the Sun. It was His Goodness made you need the Sea. Be Sensible of what you need, or Enjoy neither. Consider how much you need them. For thence they Derive their Value. Suppose the Sun were Extinguished: or the Sea were Drie. There would be no Light, no Beauty, no Warmth, no Fruits, no Flowers, no Pleasant Gardens, Feasts, or Prospects. No Wine no Oyl no Bread, no Life, no Motion. Would you not give all the Gold and Silver in the Indies for such a Treasure? Prize it now you have it, at that Rate, and you shall be a Grateful Creature: Nay you shall be a Divine and Heavenly Person. For they in Heaven do Prize Blessings when they hav them. They in

Earth when they hav them Prize them not, They in Hell Prize them,
when they hav them not.

Centuries of Meditations, I

1   Romans 11.34; 1 Corinthians 2.10, 16.
2   Malachi 3.17.
3   1 Kings 8.27.
4   Matthew 22.37.
5   Psalm 19.7.
6   Luke 19.17.
7   Genesis 28.17.
8   Psalm 82.5.
9   Psalm 19.10.
10 Proverbs 13.12.
11 Cognizant, fully aware.

7

Desire

1

For giving me Desire,
An Eager Thirst, a burning Ardent fire,
A virgin Infant Flame,
A Love with which into the World I came,
An Inward Hidden Heavenly Love,
Which in my Soul did Work and move,
And ever ever me Enflame,
With restlesse longing Heavenly Avarice,
That never could be satisfied,
That did incessantly a Paradice
Unknown suggest, and som thing undescried
Discern, and bear me to it; be
Thy Name for ever praisd by me.

2

My Parchd and Witherd Bones
Burnt up did seem: My Soul was full of Groans:
My Thoughts Extensions were:
Like Paces Reaches Steps they did appear:

They somwhat hotly did persue,
Knew that they had not all their due;
    Nor ever quiet were:
But made my flesh like Hungry Thirsty Ground,
  My Heart a deep profound Abyss,
And evry Joy and Pleasure but a Wound,
So long as I my Blessedness did miss.
    O Happiness! A Famine burns,
    And all my Life to Anguish turns!

3

    Where are the Silent Streams,
The Living Waters, and the Glorious Beams,
    The Sweet Reviving Bowers,
The Shady Groves, the Sweet and Curious Flowers,
  The Springs and Trees, the Heavenly Days,
  The Flowry Meads, the Glorious Rayes,
    The Gold and Silver Towers?
Alass, all these are poor and Empty Things,
  Trees Waters Days and Shining Beams
Fruits, Flowers, Bowers, Shady Groves and Springs,
No Joy will yeeld, no more then Silent Streams.
    These are but Dead Material Toys,
    And cannot make my Heavenly Joys.

4

    O Love! ye Amities,
And Friendships, that appear abov the Skies!
    Ye Feasts, and Living Pleasures!
Ye Senses, Honors, and Imperial Treasures!
  Ye Bridal Joys! Ye High Delights;
  That satisfy all Appetites!
    Ye Sweet Affections, and
Ye high Respects! What ever Joys there be
  In Triumphs, Whatsoever stand
In Amicable Sweet Societie
Whatever Pleasures are at his right Hand
  Ye must, before I am Divine,
  In full Proprietie[1] be mine.

5

This Soaring Sacred Thirst,
Ambassador of Bliss, approached first,
Making a Place in me,
That made me apt to Prize, and Taste, and See,
For not the Objects, but the Sence
Of Things, doth Bliss to Souls dispence,
And make it Lord like Thee.
Sence, feeling, Taste, Complacency[2] and Sight,
These are the true and real Joys,
The Living Flowing Inward Melting, Bright
And Heavenly Pleasures; all the rest are Toys:
All which are founded in Desire,
As Light in Flame, and Heat in fire.

1 Ownership.
2 Tranquil pleasure.

8

The Flow of Happiness

To Enjoy God is to take Complacency,[1] and delight in him, for being what he is, and doing what he does, Loving what he Loves, requiring what he requires: It is to rest in him, as the compleat and Satisfactory Object of all our Desires. . . .

To Enjoy God in his Essence is to take Infinit Complacency in him for being what he is: What can the Soul of Man desire more then that God should be Infinit and Eternal Lov? Lov which is the fountain of all Benefits, Honors, and Pleasures, Lov which is the Glory and Happiness of its Object, Lov which is the Tender, and compassionat Principle, its Objects Bliss and Security. Lov which is the End of all Endeavors, and the Soul of Enjoyments Lov which is the Wary and circumspect affection, studying all ways how it may pleas, and oblige its Object, Lov which Crowns its Object with Delights and Pleasures, and the more it is, is the more pleasing: Lov is infinit and Eternal in God, Nay tis God! for God is Lov, and he that dwelleth in Lov, dwelleth in God, and God in him.[2] The very essence of God is Lov unto all, and Lov unto me. O Sing, Sing O My soul with David Sing! . . .

To Enjoy God in his Counsels, is to see all his Deliberations Mature, and Eternal; all his Determinations Eligible, and Perfect; all his thoughts most pure and precious; all his Decrees most Wise and Holy, and Good and Blessed. The Glory of his Love So Brightly shining in all his Councels, that his Wisdom and Goodness do not more Appear in his Works, then in those wherunto the Soul is ready to break out with David. How precious also are thy Thoughts unto me O God. How Great is the Sum of them! If I should count them, they are more in Number then the Sand, when I awake, I am still with thee![3] . . .

To Enjoy him in all his Works is to Enjoy him in Heaven and Earth, in Angels and Men, in the Sun, and Moon, and Stars, in all Kingdoms and Ages, in the Elements and minerals, vegetables, and Animals, in the seas and Rivers and Springs, and fountains, in Hills, and Valleys, in the Clouds and Meteors, in evry thing Visible and Invisible being present with him in all Worlds, seeing and Esteeming all the Beauty and Goodness of all his Creatures. For this is the fruit of all his Labors, to make himself an Infinit Benefactor, and evry one of all his Saints the End of all Things. The Sons of Men think they do much when they make some one Object Happy in the possession of a few Lands, and a little Gold and Silver: But he is Illimited in Bounty and giveth all things. . . .

We Enjoy him in our own Souls, when we consider the Greatness and Dignity of our Inward Man and consider the Happiness of being made in his Image, rest Satisfied in our Existence, and Celebrat his Praises with Infinit Thanksgivings, evry one Saying with S. Paul, Blessed be God that I am, that I am; for as I see my Self coming out of his Hands, I am Infinitly Satisfied, all my Wishes are Accomplished: for God is Infinitly Blessed, and Glorious, and it is Enough to be like him. . . .

And therfore upon the Whole, we Shall Lov him, as he loved us, and delight as much in his felicitie, as he doth in ours: And loving him ten thousand times more, then we lov our selvs, we Shall more delight to See his Wisdom, Goodness and power his, then if it were Seated in our Selvs; his Praises will be our Joys, and all Worlds infinitly more delight for being his, then for being ours. We Shall be more Blessed in him then in our selvs, and more rejoyce in his Glory, then if it were possible to be transferred upon us. And which is very Marvellous, Self Lov will tempt us to all this. For the more we lov our Selvs, the more capable We are of being Obliged, and the more we are obliged, the more we shall delight in his Happiness and Glory, that hath obliged us: So that being Infinitly obliged, we Shall infinitly delight in his Happiness and Glory: and See our Happiness wholy without us, wholy within us, coming to us, and proceeding from us, overflowing Eternaly with Joys and Thanksgiving.

The Kingdom of God, Ch. 39

1 Tranquil pleasure.
2 1 John 4.16.
3 Psalm 139.17–18.

9

The Circulation

I

As fair Ideas from the Skie,
    Or Images of Things,
Unto a Spotless Mirror flie,
    On unperceived Wings;
And lodging there affect the Sence,
    As if at first they came from thence;
While being there, they richly Beautifie
The Place they fill, and yet communicat
Themselvs, reflecting to the Seers Ey,
    Just such is our Estate.
No Prais can we return again,
    No Glory in our selvs possess,
But what derived from without we gain,
From all the Mysteries of Blessedness.

2

No Man breaths out more vital Air,
    Then he before suckt in.
Those Joys and Praises must repair
    To us, which tis a Sin
To bury, in a Senceless Tomb.
An Earthly Wight[1] must be the Heir
Of all those Joys, the Holy Angels Prize,

He must a King, before a Priest becom,
And Gifts receiv, or² ever Sacrifice.
  Tis Blindness Makes us Dumb.
Had we but those Celestial Eys,
  Wherby we could behold the Sum
Of all his Bounties, *we should overflow*
With Praises, did we but their Causes Know.

3

All Things to Circulations owe
  Themselvs; by which alone
They do exist: They cannot shew
  A Sigh, a Word, a Groan,
A Colour, or a Glimps of Light,
  The Sparcle of a Precious Stone,
A virtue, or a Smell; a lovly Sight,
A Fruit, a Beam, an Influence, a Tear;
But they anothers Livery must Wear:
  And borrow Matter first,
  Before they can communicat.
  Whatever's empty is accurst:
And this doth shew that we must some Estate
Possess, or never can communicate.

4

A Spunge drinks in that Water, which
  Is afterwards *exprest.*
A Liberal hand must first be rich:
  Who blesseth must be Blest.
The Thirsty Earth drinks in the Rain,
  The Trees suck Moysture at their Roots,
Before the one can Lavish Herbs again,
Before the other can afford us Fruits.
No Tenant can rais Corn, or pay his Rent,
  Nor can even hav a Lord,
  That has no Land. No Spring can vent,
  No vessel any Wine afford
Wherin no Liquor's put. No Empty Purs,
Can Pounds or Talents of it self disburs.

5

Flame that Ejects its Golden Beams,
Sups up the Grosser Air;
To Seas, that pour out their Streams
In Springs, those Streams repair;
Receivd Ideas make even Dreams.
No Fancy painteth foule or fair

But by the Ministry of Inward Light,
That in the Spirits Cherisheth its Sight.

The Moon returneth Light, and som men say
The very Sun no Ray
Nor Influence could hav, did it
No forrein Aids, no food admit.

The Earth no Exhalations would afford,
Were not its Spirits by the Sun restord.

6

All things do first receiv, that giv.
Only tis GOD above,
That from, and in himself doth live,
Whose All sufficient Love
Without Original can flow
And all the Joys and Glories shew

Which Mortal Man can take Delight to know.
He is the Primitive Eternal Spring
The Endless Ocean of each Glorious Thing.

The Soul a Vessel is
A Spacious Bosom to Contain
All the fair Treasures of his Bliss

Which run like Rivers from, into the Main,
And all it doth receiv returns again.

1 Living being.
2 E're.

10

Humility makes us capable of Happiness

Humility makes men capable of all Felicity. . . .

All the cost of our Redemption, all the hatred of our Stupidity and Perverseness, all the hope of Heaven, all our Penitence and Grief, all our Fear and Expectation, all our Love and all our Joy are contained in Humility: there they are expressed, there they are exercised: There they are enlarged, and beautified in like manner: There they grow deep, and serious, and infinite: there they become vigorous and strong; there they are made substantial and eternal. All the Powers of the Soul are employed, extended and made perfect in this depth of Abysses. It is the basis and foundation of all Vertue and Gratitude whatsoever. It is in some sort the very fountain of Life and Felicity it self. For as nothing is great but in comparison of somewhat less; so nothing is sweet but what is New and Eternal. All Life consists in Motion and Change. The pleasure of Acquiring is oftentimes as great, and perhaps alwaies greater than that of Enjoying. The long possession of that which we have alwaies had, takes away the sence, and maketh us dull: Old and Common things are less esteemed, unless we rub up our Memories with some helps, to renew them and our sences together. Gifts are alwaies sweeter in the coming, than in the abiding with us. And if what I observe in the course of nature be of any force, there is no possibility of enjoyment, at least no perfection in fruition, without some relation to the first Acquisition. Old things are apt to grow stale, and their value to be neglected, by their continuance with us. I have noted it often in the joy that young Heirs have, when they first come to their Estates, and the great felicity which Lovers promise to themselves, and taste also when they meet together in the Marriage-bed. The pleasures of all which pass off by degrees, not solely by reason of our dulness and stupidity, but far more from a secret in the nature of things. For all Delight springs from the satisfaction of violent Desire: when the desire is forgotten, the delight is abated. . . .

Humility by leading us to the bottom of our Condition, sets our Original before our eyes, considers that eternal abyss of Idleness and Vacuity out of which we were taken, that miracle by which we were made of Nothing. How destitute we should have been in our selves had not GOD created the World, had he not been pleased to communicate himself and his Glory to us. How weak and unable we were to devise or desire any Felicity, yet how infinitely necessary the preparation of it after we were created. How great our desires and expectations were, how sore and urgent our wants and necessities: how much we needed infinite Wisdom, and almighty Power to fill Immensity with the omnipresence of their Glory, and to fill their omnipresence with Effects and Treasures: How gracious and good GOD was to do all this for us, without our asking: and how justly *Davids* rapture may be taken up by the Soul, *The King shall joy in thy strength, O Lord, and in thy Salvation how greatly shall he rejoyce! Thou preventest him with the blessings of Goodness, thou settest a Crown of pure Gold on his head! His glory is great in thy Salvation, Honour and Majesty hast thou laid upon him. For thou hast made him most Blessed for ever; thou hast made him exceeding glad with thy Countenance!*[1] We might have been made, and put, in the condition of Toads; who are now created in the Image of GOD, have dominion over all his Works, and are made capable of all Eternity.

Christian Ethicks, Ch. 26

1 Psalm 21.1–6.

I I

'Tis better starve, than eat such empty Fruit

VIII

And if the Glory and Esteem I have,
Be nothing else than what my Silver gave;
    If for no other ground
    I am with Love or Praises crown'd,
'Tis such a shame, such vile, such base Repute
'Tis better starve, than eat such empty Fruit.

Christian Ethicks, Ch. 28, 'Of Magnanimity'

12

Aristotle's Happiness

Felicity is rightly defined, to be *the Perfect fruition of a Perfect Soul, acting in perfect Life by Perfect Virtue*. For the Attainment of which Perfection, we must, in the Way to Felicity, endure all Afflictions that can befall us. For tho they are not Parts of Felicity themselves, yet we may acknowledge them great Advantages for the Exercise of Virtue, and reckon our Calamities among our *Joys*, when we bear and overcome them in a virtuous Manner, because they add to our *Honor*, and contribute much to our Perfection, both here, and hereafter.

For this purpose we are to remember, that our present Estate is not that of Reward, but Labour: It is an Estate of Trial, not of Fruition: A Condition wherein we are to Toyl, and Sweat, and travail hard, for the promised Wages; an Appointed Seed Time, for a future Harvest; a real Warfare, in order to a Glorious Victory: In which we must expect some Blows, and delight in the Hazzards and Encounters we meet with, because they will be crowned with a Glorious and joyful Triumph; and attended with ornaments and trophies far surpassing the bare Tranquillity of idle peace.

When we can cheerfully look on an Army of Misfortunes, without Amazement we may then freely and Delightfully contemplate the Nature of the Highest Felicity.

Aristotle never heard of our Ascension into Heaven, nor of sitting down in the Throne of GOD, yet by a lucky Hit (if I may so say) fell in point blanck upon the Nature of Blessedness. For a perfect fruition by perfect virtue, is all that can be thought of . . .

Perfect life is the full exertion of perfect power. It implies two things, Perfection of Vigour, and perfection of intelligence, an activity of life, reaching through all Immensity, to all Objects whatsoever; and a freedome from all Dulness in apprehending: An exquisite Tenderness of perception in feeling the least Object, and a *Sphere of activity* that runs parallel with the Omnipresence of the Godhead. For if any Soul lives so imperfectly, as to see and know but some Objects, or to love them remisly, and less then they deserve, its Life is imperfect, because either it is remisse, or, if never so fervent, confined.

Christian Ethicks, Ch. 2

13

Of holiness: Its nature, violence, and pleasure

Holiness (if it be strictly defined) is that Vertue in GOD, by which he Loveth the most Perfect Things, and infinitely delighteth in them. For by Vertue of this Affection he shunneth and hateth all that is profane, pursuing and delighting in all that is Holy . . .

For infinite Goodness must needs desire with an infinite violence, that all Goodness should be compleat and Perfect: and that Desire, which makes to the Perfection of all Goodness, must infinitely avoid every slur and Miscarriage as unclean: and infinitely aim at every Grace and Beauty, that tends to make the Object infinitely perfect, which it would enjoy. It cannot desire less then infinite Perfection, nor less then hate all Imperfection, in an infinite Manner. . . .

It infinitely hates all that is Bad, and as infinitely desires to Correct the same.

. . . to exert Almighty Power in a remiss and lazy manner is infinitely Base and Dishonourable, and therefore unclean because so Odious and Distastful. *Lukewarmness* is Profane, as well as *Malice*. And it hath pleased GOD to brand it with a worse and more fatal Censure. No folly or iniquity can dwell with him; Omission is both. To be hated is to be rejected; but to be beloved Lukewarmly is to be embraced with polluted and filthy Armes. And for this Cause, the fire of his Jealousie burns most *devouringly* about the Altar. He will be sanctified in all them that draw nigh unto him, and but to touch his Ark irregularly, is to be consumed.

. . . Perfection is his Essence, and he could not be himself upon any Abatement. It is a great Wonder! But the smallest Thing in the world may spare somewhat of it self rather than that which is infinite. Upon the least substraction, that which is infinite is made finite, and the Loss is infinite. We cannot be at all Beloved by Almighty GOD unless we are infinitely Beloved.

Christian Ethicks, Ch. 12

14

God's happiness and ours are one

53

Those Things are most Excellent that are most Agreeable with the Nature of God. Tho the Nature of God being Goodness and Lov, those Things are most agreeable to his nature wherein Goodness is Satisfied and Lov Delighted. Those Thing[s] are most Excellent that are most Expedient for the Happiness of his creatures: becaus Goodness and Lov Delighteth in makeing His creatures Happy.

54

Becaus Goodness is Satisfied and Love Delighted in the Happiness of His creatures, Those Thing[s] are in them selves Holy that make us Happy. And those alone hath he Commanded by his Laws. There being a concurrance of all Interest to make us Obedient.

55

Since Gods Goodness and our Happiness are Individually one, Gods Goodness is our Happieness. And those things most Holy that are Agreeable unto both, Him and us.

56

Those Things are most Holy which are most Agreeable with Gods Glory. Whose Glory is that he is Infinit Lov.

57

Those Things are most Holy that are the Greatest Similitude of his Eternall Nature. Since therfore God is Lov he commandeth Lov: which being the first Begotten of his Goodness, the most Conduciv to our Happiness, the Similitude of His Essence, and the onely thing conformable to His Glory, is the most Holy, absolute Best and most necessary, so that no Laws could possibly be made but those which are the Laws of Lov. The Best Laws being most Inevitable.

58

Who would not keep those Laws, to which we are obliged by Infinit obligations, which are them Selves the Greatest and which command Things most Agreeable to God and us? who would Not Sing and Rejoyce in their unity? who would not Exult and be Ravished with joy to See Gods Goodness and our Happieness so Individually united! His Glory love and Blessedness conspire to make us Blessed.

59

Becaus His Image is most Holy, He made His Image in which alone all the rest of His works are Sanctified, by which alone He is Glorified, to which alone His Laws are Natural, and for the sake of which He created All Things; which is then Holy when like Him it Loveth all, and Delighteth to be Beloved.

60

The Blessedness of God consisteth in this, that He is Infinite Lov. For by lov He enjoyeth all His works, by Lov He delighteth in all our Happieness, by love He is the Treasure of all His Hosts: in being Lov He is most Beautifull, and ever Meet to be Delighted in. For being Lov he is praised by His Holy Angels and by all his Hosts in the Heaven of Heavens.

61

By being Lov alone, was it possible that He should be wise. For the greatest wisdom is to be the End of all, of which He is the Author; to Glorifie Himselfe and enrich others; to enjoy the Treasures which He gives away; to satisfie Himselfe and exalt us; to Knit our Happieness all in one; to enrich Himselfe by Giving His Treasures; to possess all in such a manner, as to be the joy of all. And all this He Atcheiveth, or is by Lov alone.

Select Meditations, II

15

But after all to be Beloved is the Greatest Happieness

But after all to be Beloved is the Greatest Happieness. All This Glory
and all these Treasures, being but the Appendencies, and the ornaments
of that person that is our Bride or Friend, prepared all for the Sake of
Lov, to commend and Sweeten it more unto us. But How Great must
His Lov be, who not onely created the Heavens and the earth for one,
but becaus a Lover is the sweetest thing, and Himselfe the most Glori-
ous Lover, created the most Glorious Image of Himselfe to giv us and
made many Millions of Angels Cherubims and Men to Honor and
Attend that Image, that Like a God He might be Lov unto us! Nay
How Glorious and full of Wisdom is that work, that maketh every
one of Those Attendants So Glorious a Sovereign that being after his
Similitude the supreme of all, He Should Still be an Attendant to that
Single Image who was our First Friend, and yet Himselfe the principal
Lover and all the Residue His Attendants! every one being So the Sun
in Heaven among the plannets! Yet is all this Atcheived by Lov, for
God is Lov. And all this shews his Lov unto my Soul. Yea it Shews
indeed that for which I intirely Lov Him, that He is Infinite Lov to
every Soul!

Select Meditations, II, 40

3

Sin and Salvation

A recurring challenge for modern theologians and literary critics approaching Traherne has been the problem of sin. How does one marry a high doctrine of creation such as Traherne's, with its emphasis on the presence of God in creation and its focus on the innocence of childhood, to a doctrine of redemption with its understanding of the totality of the fall and the need for sacrifice? Traherne's insistence on the goodness of the world and the capacity of the soul led some mid twentieth-century literary critics of Traherne such as Keith Salter and Carol Marks to accusations of Pelagianism. Other critics saw in him intimations of pantheism and a general lack of christology. Alison Sherrington notes the absence of christological imagery in Traherne's poetry, claiming that his poetry seeks to explore a mystical union with God via the created world rather than via Christ. In the poetry there is 'a mystical union with the world, which seems to take his [Christ's] place as the Mediator between God and man';[153] Traherne may be a Romantic, even a nature mystic, but there is little in him that is essentially Christian, she concludes. Robin Attfield suggests that Traherne comes close to pantheism;[154] others that Christ is missing in his work, that in fact his mysticism precludes Christ.[155]

153 Alison Sherrington, *Mystical Symbolism in the Poetry of Thomas Traherne*, St Lucia, Queensland: University of Queensland Press, 1970, p. 132.

154 Robin Attfield, 'Thomas Traherne and the Location of Intrinsic Value,' *Religious Traditions*, 6 (1983), pp. 66–7.

155 Pat Pinsent, 'The Image of Christ in the Writings of Two Seventeenth-Century English Country Parsons: George Herbert and Thomas Traherne', in S. Porter, M. Hayes and D. Tombs (eds), *Images of Christ: Ancient and Modern*, Sheffield, UK: Sheffield Academic Press, 1997, pp. 227–38; Franz Wohrer, *Thomas Traherne: The Growth of a Mystic's Mind: A Study of the Evolution and the Phenomenology of Traherne's Mystical Consciousness*, Salzburg Studies in English Literature, University of Salzburg, 1982. See also, Peter Maitland, 'Thomas Traherne's Path to Felicity: The Missing Christ', MA Carleton Unversity (Canada), 1994.

While some of the best-known poetry may lend itself to such interpretations, no reader of the whole of Traherne's newly expanded
corpus could come to such conclusions. Not only is Traherne's personal
testimony of struggle with sin evident in *Select Meditations*, but
recent manuscripts, as we will see, robustly defend the person of Christ
and the place of the cross, and explore the means of redemption. In
light of these newer discoveries, the poetry takes on a different hue.
Clements' somewhat isolated claim that in the poetry 'whilst the language of Christ as Redeemer is sparse, the sense of Christ redeeming
all things by his regenerative presence is implicit throughout'[156] can now
be justified.

Here we touch on some of the same territory covered in the first
chapter, since we encounter head on Traherne's notion, derived from
Hooker and Sanderson and rooted in the church fathers before them, of
a God come down to earth and a world taken up into divinity. Following
the teachings of the early church fathers and the first four councils, in
particular Gregory of Nyssa, Gregory Nazianzen, St John Chrysostom
and Irenaeus, Traherne explores a theology in which the salvation of the
person, of a nation, and of the whole created world are linked.

The 'absent Christ' critics of Traherne forget that for Traherne it is
Christ's regenerating power present in creation that makes the creation
sing. This ancient belief that God continues to create and recreate, the
doctrine of a continuous creation, not unknown in the Eastern church,
resurfaced in Traherne's day in the writings of fellow seventeenth-
century theologians. In a recent thesis on Traherne, Alison Kershaw
notes the difference between those seventeenth-century theologians
such as Nicholas Lockyer and others, who saw Christ's work as
redemption of a world at war with itself, and those like Isaac Barrow
who saw Christ alongside creation from the beginning as creator, sus-
tainer, redeemer. Where Lockyer's world is 'the slaughter house that
belongest to hell', God's kitchen where 'hearts that are made fat are
killed on earth, and rosted in hell,'[157] Isaac Barrow's world is reformed

156 A. L. Clements, *The Mystical Poetry of Thomas Traherne*, Cambridge,
MA: Harvard University Press, 1969.

157 Nicholas Lockyer, *England Faithfully watcht with, In Her Wounds: Or,
Christ as a Father sitting up with his Children in their swooning state; Which is
the summe of severall Lectures painfully preached upon Colossians I*, London:
1645, p. 86, cited in Alison Kershaw, 'The Poetic of the Cosmic Christ in Thomas
Traherne's The Kingdom of God', unpublished PhD thesis, University of Western
Australia, 2005, p. 100.

and renewed by he who 'of old did truly and properly give being to all things'.[158]

The key scriptural passage from which the discussion emerges is Paul's Christ hymn in Colossians 1.15–20.

> He is the image of the invisible God, the firstborn of all creation; for in him all things in heaven and on earth were created, things visible and invisible, whether thrones or dominions or rulers or powers – all things have been created through him and for him. He himself is before all things, and in him all things hold together. He is the head of the body, the church; he is the beginning, the firstborn from the dead, so that he might have the pre-eminence. For in him all the fullness of God was pleased to dwell, and through him God was pleased to reconcile to himself all things, whether on earth or in heaven, by making peace through the blood of his cross.

The rise and fall of thrones, dominions, rulers and powers was no idle talk in Traherne's day; the experience of civil war, the Commonwealth and Restoration informed this discussion of pre-eminence and headship in ways we can only imagine. It is no wonder that there was a wide divergence of theories about how God might be reconciling all things to himself and making peace through blood. In one model Christ is an 'intruder' on creation, a saviour who descends, pays a price and makes peace. In such a model Christ purchases his pre-eminence as the first-born of all creation by his suffering and death. 'Christ hath purchased this preheminence, and he payd the father the uttermost farthing . . . and therefore he ought to have it'.[159] In another model Christ is present in the world from the beginning, since all things were created by him and for him, and in him all things consist.

Traherne's incorporation of Paul's Christ hymn in Chapter 25 of *The Kingdom of God* shows Christ come not as a stranger but as the intention and fullness of all things. For in him all things consist. These phrases 'All things' and 'All in all' are explored at length in several entries in *Commentaries of Heaven*, but they occur frequently through-out Traherne's work as a whole and are especially frequent in *The*

158 Isaac Barrow, 'His Onely Son', *The Works of Isaac Barrow, D.D., Vol. I*, London: 1700, p. 281, quoted in Kershaw, p. 101.

159 Tobias Crispe, 'Christ's Preheminence: Collos. I Ver. 18 That in all things hee might have the preheminence', *Christ Alone Exalted in fourteene Sermons preached in, and neare London*, London: 1643, p. 140, quoted in Kershaw, p. 99.

Kingdom of God which, like *Commentaries of Heaven*, seeks to consider all things, the whole of creation, time and eternity, in relation to God. For Traherne all things connect, the earthly and the heavenly, temporal and eternal, begotten and made, past, present and future; and all things, even things fallen, have in them the capacity to participate in the life of God. St Paul's claim that 'He that descended is the same also that ascended up far above all heavens, that he might fill all things' (Ephesians 4.10) reflects not a human wish, but a divine intent. God wills to fill all things by his descended Christ. 'Redemption is the name for this will, this action, this concrete Man who is God with us and for us'.[160]

The work of redemption begins then long before the cross. It precedes Calvary in Traherne's equation, just as light pre-exists the moment of dawn. It is foreshadowed in the ceremonies of Old Testament Law and begun in Christ at his incarnation. It is perhaps because redemption begins here that Traherne's defence of the incarnation is particularly fierce. Against the Socinian heresy burgeoning in his day Traherne rails because it denies the divinity of Christ and his place as a person in the Trinity. The problem, however, with this understanding of redemption is that it seems to undermine the uniqueness of Christ's sacrifice on the cross. If Christ's regenerating power is present in creation from the beginning, what is the point of all that suffering?

Traherne must have known himself that while the cosmic Christ model of redemption fits neatly with an affirmative view of creation it does not adequately answer questions of sacrifice, atonement and payment for sin, because in more recently discovered and/or unpublished works we see him working with other redemption narratives. He follows the model of Christ as substitute, a sacrifice made in our place and on our behalf. In Traherne's article 'Atonement' in *Commentaries of Heaven*, for instance, his repeated themes are the necessity of sacrifice, the necessity of the sacrifice being pure and spotless, the payment for sin, the fall of Adam, and the satisfaction of divine justice. The typology of his long epic poem *The Ceremonial Law* also prefigures sacrifice. He goes so far with this image as to set the Father against the Son in *The Kingdom of God*, where the Son, like the bridegroom who cleaves to his wife, forsakes the Father for the love of his bride. At other points we see Christ the victor in the cosmic battle, and Christ

160 Joseph Sittler, 'Called to Unity', *The Ecumenical Review*, 14 (1961–62), pp. 184–6, quoted in Kershaw, p. 108.

the mediator as well as Christ the regenerating power.[161] We may see that although the cosmic Christ model is Traherne's dominant model it is not his only one.

What are we to make of the fall in Traherne? The most thorough study of this subject is Patrick Grant's *Transformation of Sin*, which sees Traherne following not the Augustinian model of total corruption but the model of Irenaeus, the early church father for whom sin was the result of wrong moral choices. In his understanding of the Atonement in *Centuries*, Traherne identifies Christ with Adam; the cross is not primarily about the defeat of Adam and the corruption of the whole race, but about Christ as the new Adam and the creation of a new innocence. Traherne calls the cross 'that Tree of Life in the Midst of the Paradice of God!' (*C*, I, 55). Certainly Christ comes to regain what Adam lost, but the emphasis is on renewal rather than defeat. More important, notes Grant, 'is the attempt Traherne makes to stress the closeness between Adam and Christ so that, just as in Irenaeus, the Atonement is a mark of optimism that signifies the dignity of man's nature as well as restores his fallenness'.[162] On the cross, writes Traherne, 'we may see Mans sin and infinit value' (*C*, I, 59). 'What an infinite Dignity Man is exalted for whom God counted none Worthy to suffer but His own son' (*C*, II, 33). Like Irenaeus, for Traherne in *Centuries* the condition of man once salvation is won is a return to innocence.

However, in *Commentaries of Heaven*, atonement is about man accepting the fact that he has displeased God and God's displeasure being pacified; God's aversion and man's defilement must both be removed before they can be 'at one'. Atonement 'is the Agreement between God Almighty pacified, & Man converted, wherby the Penitent Sinner is again received into favor. So that the Aversion of GOD & the Defilement of Man, are both removed before Atonement can be made.' It is 'the Propiciation or Satisfaction which is made to Divine Justice. For man; or the Sacrifice which is offered & accepted in his Steed'.[163]

---

161 For further explanation of these models see R. C. Moberly, *Atonement and Personality*, 1901; Leonard Hodgson, *The Doctrine of the Atonement*, London: Nisbet, 1951; F. W. Dillistone, *The Christian Understanding of Atonement*, London: Nisbet, 1968; J. Moltmann, *The Crucified God*, London: SCM Press, 1974; Frances Young, *Sacrifice and the Death of Christ*, London: SPCK, 1975.

162 Patrick Grant, *The Transformation of Sin: Studies in Donne, Herbert, Vaughan and Traherne*, Amherst, MA: University of Massachusetts Press, 1974, p. 189.

163 *COH*, 'Atonement', fol. 173r.

Similarly, in 'Adam's Fall' in *The Ceremonial Law*, from the first animal killed to cover Adam's nakedness to the sacrificial lambs offered on the altar to the sacrifice of Christ, it is blood that saves.

> This Blood first spilt doth cleans the World, & is
> An Embleme of the Way to Sinners Bliss.
> He that was made a bloody Sacrifice
> For Man, & as his Ransom for him dies,
> From Him the Robes of Righteousness we take,
> Which only clothes, & doth us Glorious make.
> See O my soul, thy GOD hath mindfull been
> Of Thee, before thyself on Earth was seen.

For Traherne, as we have seen, redemption starts with the incarnation. God has entered not only into humankind but into the whole of creation, changing for ever the position of humanity and the world. He is the cohesion of the universe, making a cosmos of chaos. As Lightfoot's commentary on Colossians suggests, even laws like gravity are 'an expression of his mind'.[164] But Christ is also the sacrifice and the substitute, the propitiation for our sins. Although he used them both, Traherne never fully resolved the tension between these two models of incarnational and sacrificial redemption.

More recently, kenotic theology has linked these two models, exploring the incarnation itself as a sacrifice. The idea of *kenosis* – the self-emptying of Christ – is, of course, nothing new. Springing from Philippians 2.1–11, in which Christ empties himself in the incarnation, taking on the form of a servant and is made in the likeness of man, and intimated in Gregory of Nyssa (*Oratio Catechetica Magna*, XXIV), these ideas, long held by the Eastern Orthodox Church, surfaced again in Anglicanism in the teaching of the Oxford Movement and later liberal catholics: Charles Gore, for whom the incarnation was the substructure of the atonement, and in the teaching of William Temple for whom kenotic theology was not just about a moment in time but a revelation of sacrifice at the heart of God. As Douglas Dales notes in *Glory*, his recent study of Archbishop Michael Ramsey, Ramsey interpreted Philippians 2.5–11, in which Christ 'humbles himself', as indicating the deeply sacrificial nature of the incarnation: 'self-

164 J. B. Lightfoot, *Saint Paul's Epistles to the Colossians and to Philemon*, Grand Rapids, MI: Zondervan, 1957, p. 154.

abandonment does not belong to the earthly life alone,' wrote Ramsey, 'for it is the experience in history of the self-giving of the eternal God.'[165] Here, as for Traherne, salvation begins long before Calvary, but the uniqueness of Christ's sacrifice is maintained. There is a point to Christ's suffering. Patrick Grant calls the cross 'a mark of optimism that signifies the dignity of man's nature' and that is part of Traherne's story, but for him the cross is also a deep revelation of God's nature and love. As Ramsey insists, 'Only the crucifixion is the deepest visible point of the divine self-giving, which entered history at Bethlehem and which begins in heaven itself.'[166]

It is in this sense that Traherne's call to become divine must be heard. To be in Christ is to be humbled even unto death, emptied of self-obsession and filled with life communicative, held in love and related to other persons. If we are to become divine it is in this sense of total self-giving as well as self-love. Although Traherne would most likely not have heard of kenotic theology as such, his dominant and subsequent models of redemption are perhaps best described to the modern reader along these lines.

All of this is in one sense theoretical. It leaves unanswered practical questions of how redemption may be worked out in the life of the Christian. One place to start may be in Traherne's exploration, in *Christian Ethicks* and elsewhere, of the four estates in which we live – the estates of 'innocency', 'misery', 'grace' and 'glory'. These four estates were a common seventeenth-century trope, and in using them Traherne is in the company of many others who saw the soul in pilgrimage.[167] At first reading the four estates seem to set a clear dialectical progression for the seeking soul. Well-known Traherne critic A. L. Clements reads the Dobell poems similarly as a 'creation, fall, redemption' narrative: poems from 'The Salutation' through to 'The Preparative'

165 *The Gospel and the Catholic Church*, p. 25, quoted in Douglas Dales, *Glory Descending: Michael Ramsey and His Writings*, Norwich: Canterbury Press, 2005, pp. 36–7.

166 *The Gospel and the Catholic Church*, p. 25, quoted in Dales, *Glory*, p. 37.

167 See Thomas Jackson, *A Treatise on the Primaeval Estate of the First Man* (posthumous, 1844); John Bartlet, *The Practical Christian* (1670); Samuel Crooke, *The Guide unto True Blessednesse* (1625). These, of course, were preceded by Augustine's *Enchiridion*, tracing the soul's progress towards salvation. For a fuller explication of Traherne's four estates see Michael Suarez, 'Against Satan, sin, and death: Thomas Traherne and the "inward work" of Conversion', in John Hawley, ed., *Reform and Counterreform Dialectics of the Word in Western Christianity since Luther*, Berlin: Mouton de Gruyter, 1994, pp. 77–103.

representing the creation; those from 'The Instruction' to 'Speed' representing the fall; and from 'The Design' to 'Goodnesse' representing redemption. But Clements also notes that there is not an altogether clear progression: Traherne doubles back and repeats. Similarly in his discussion of the four estates, Michael Suarez points out that to see the estates as a progression in which each subsequent estate negates its predecessor is to misread Traherne. The estate of glory has from the earliest church fathers to the present day been seen as a fulfilment rather than a negation of the estate of grace. For Traherne the 'end' is both the destination or endtime and the *telos*, or divinely ordered purpose. The estate of 'innocency' cannot be negated since its principal feature, felicity, is the yardstick by which 'misery' is measured; further still, the estate of 'glory' contains within it a return to original innocence. 'I must become a child again,' Traherne insists; salvation is in some sense a return. As Suarez notes, 'for Traherne, the several estates of salvation history have a fluid character and a mutual presence';[168] 'Innocence' and 'grace' both offer intimations of 'glory' and there is an ever-present terrible possiblity of returning to 'misery', even to apostacy, from 'grace', to which danger Traherne's own confessions of apathy and sinfulness witness. So strong is this tendency to drift between 'misery' and 'grace' that in some of his writings Traherne obliterates the distinction between the two, lumping them both under one umbrella – the 'estate of Trial'. The estate of Trial is 'mixed of misery and grace', he writes. To aspire towards God is no one-time event, but the continual work of the soul. More cheerfully, shards of glory may be spotted now in the lower estates that make up our daily life. For Traherne, then, the early estates are not something bitter to leave behind, but an opportunity for immediate glimpses of glory as well as for soul formation. It is 'better to be placed in a State of Trial, then immediately placed in the Throne of Glory', he writes in *The Kingdom of God*, because it is in this state of Trial that we may beautify ourselves as brides. Everywhere you look in Traherne, salvation is process rather than moment; and despite the necessary casting off of false notions, it is primarily a progress towards rather than a leaving behind. This reflects something of Traherne's notion of continual creation, incarnation and divine passion. For Traherne's God does not simply create and depart, but creates and recreates continuously. Unlike some of his contemporaries, Traherne's reading of the four estates leads

168 Suarez, 'Against Satan', p. 92.

not to a neat system of compartments but into his bride/soul narrative, and from there to Traherne's larger theme of love. We are in the state of trial (that is, misery and grace combined), so that we may be made the perfect partner for divine love.

The extracts

1 Traherne's experience of the Fall

2 The Apostacy

3 The Approach

4 Baptism

5 Atonement

6 Mercy, redemption, incarnation, works and grace

7 The Gospel Mysteries

8 O Jesu God, whose own Dear Blood

9 Manna

10 Meditations on the Cross

11 A Broken and a contrite Heart

12 More Easily ceas to liv, then Love

13 On Love

14 The soul is perfected by trials

15 Lost and found

16 All Harsh and Sour Virtues came in by Sin

17 A Wise man on Earth might hav his Conversation in Heaven

1

Traherne's experience of the Fall

7

The first Light which shined in my Infancy in its Primitive and Innocent Clarity was totaly Ecclypsed: insomuch that I was fain to learn all again. If you ask me how it was Ecclypsed? Truly by the Customs and maners of Men, which like Contrary Winds blew it out: by an innumerable company of other Objects, rude vulgar and Worthless Things that like so many loads of Earth and Dung did over whelm and Bury it: by the Impetuous Torrent of Wrong Desires in all others whom I saw or knew that carried me away and alienated me from it: by a Whole Sea of other Matters and Concernments that Covered and Drowned it: finaly by the Evil Influence of a Bad Education that did not foster and cherish it. All Mens thoughts and Words were about other Matters; They all prized New Things which I did not dream of. I was a stranger and unacquainted with them; I was little and reverenced their Authority; I was weak, and easily guided by their Example: Ambitious also, and Desirous to approve my self unto them. And finding no one Syllable in any mans Mouth of those Things, by Degrees they vanished, My Thoughts, (as indeed what is more fleeting then a Thought) were blotted out. And at last all the Celestial Great and Stable Treasures to which I was born, as wholy forgotten, as if they had never been.

8

Had any man spoken of it, it had been the most easy Thing in the World, to hav taught me, and to hav made me believ, that Heaven and Earth was GODs Hous, and that He gav it me. That the Sun was mine and that Men were mine, and that Cities and Kingdoms were mine also: that Earth was better then Gold, and that Water was, every Drop of it, a Precious Jewel. And that these were Great and Living Treasures: and that all Riches whatsoever els was Dross in Comparison. From whence I clearly find how Docible our Nature is, in natural Things, were it rightly entreated. And that our Misery proceedeth ten thousand times more from the outward Bondage of Opinion and Custom, then from any inward corruption or Depravation of Nature: And that it is not our Parents Loyns, so much as our Parents lives, that Enthrals and Blinds us. Yet is all our Corruption Derived from Adam: inasmuch as all the Evil Examples and inclinations of the World arise from His Sin. But I speak it in the presence of GOD and of our Lord Jesus Christ, in my Pure Primitive Virgin Light, while my Apprehensions were natural, and unmixed, I can not remember, but that I was ten thousand times more prone to Good and Excellent Things, then evil. But I was quickly tainted and fell by others.

9

It was a Difficult matter to persuade me that the Tinsild Ware upon a Hobby hors was a fine thing. They did impose upon me, and Obtrude their Gifts that made me believ a Ribban or a Feather Curious. I could not see where the Curiousness or fineness: And to Teach me that A Purs of Gold was of any valu seemed impossible, the Art by which it becomes so, and the reasons for which it is accounted so were so Deep and Hidden to my Inexperience. So that Nature is still nearest to Natural Things · and farthest off from preternatural, and to esteem that the Reproach of Nature, is an Error in them only who are unacquainted with it. Natural Things are Glorious, and to know them Glorious: But to call things preternatural, Natural, Monstrous. Yet all they do it, who esteem Gold Silver Houses Lands Clothes &c. the Riches of Nature, which are indeed the Riches of Invention. Nature knows no such Riches · but Art and Error makes them. Not the God of Nature, but Sin only was the Parent of them. The Riches of Nature are our Souls and Bodies, with all their Faculties Sences and Endowments. And it had been the Easiest thing in the whole World, that all felicity consisted in the Enjoyment of all the World, that it was prepared for me before I was born, and that Nothing was more Divine and Beautifull.

11

By this let Nurses, and those Parents that desire Holy Children learn to make them Possessors of Heaven and Earth betimes: to remove silly Objects from before them, to Magnify nothing but what is Great indeed, and to talk of God to them and of His Works and Ways before they can either Speak or go. For Nothing is so Easy as to teach the Truth becaus the Nature of the Thing confirms the Doctrine. As when we say The Sun is Glorious, A Man is a Beautifull Creature, Soveraign over Beasts and Fowls and Fishes, The Stars Minister unto us, The World was made for you, &c. But to say This Hous is yours, and these Lands are another Mans and this Bauble is a Jewel and this Gugaw a fine Thing, this Rattle makes Musick &c. is deadly Barbarous and uncouth to a little Child; and makes him suspect all you say, becaus the Nature of the Thing contradicts your Words. Yet doth that Blot out all Noble and Divine Ideas, Dissettle his foundation, render him uncertain in all Things, and Divide him from GOD. To teach him those Objects are little vanities, and that tho GOD made them, by the Ministery of Man, yet Better and more Glorious Things are more to be Esteemed, is Natural and Easy.

12

By this you may see who are the Rude and Barbarous Indians. For verily there is no Salvage Nation under the Cope of Heaven, that is more absurdly Barbarous than the Christian World. They that go Naked and Drink Water and liv upon Roots are like Adam, or Angels in Comparison of us. But they indeed that call Beads and Glass Buttons Jewels, and Dress them selvs with feather, and buy pieces of Brass and broken hafts of Knives of our Merchants are som what like us. But We pass them in Barbarous Opinions, and Monstrous Apprehensions: which we Nick Name Civility, and the Mode, amongst us. I am sure those Barbarous People that go naked, com nearer to Adam God and Angels: in the Simplicity of their Wealth, tho not in Knowledg.

13

You would not think how these Barbarous Inventions spoyle your Knowledg. They put Grubs and Worms in Mens Heads: that are Enemies to all Pure and True Apprehensions, and eat out all their Happines. They make it impossible for them, in whom they reign, to believ there is any Excellency in the Works of GOD, or to taste any Sweetness in the Nobility of Nature, or to Prize any Common, tho never so Great a Blessing. They alienat men from the Life of GOD, and at last make them to live without GOD in the World. To liv the Life of GOD is to live to all the Works of GOD, and to enjoy them in His Image, from which they are wholy Diverted that follow fashions. Their fancies are corrupted with other Gingles.

14

Being Swallowed up therfore in the Miserable Gulph of idle talk and worthless vanities, thenceforth I lived among Shadows, like a Prodigal Son feeding upon Husks with Swine.[1] A Comfortless Wilderness full of Thorns and Troubles the World was, or wors: a Waste Place covered with Idleness and Play, and Shops and Markets and Taverns. As for Churches they were things I did not understand. And Scholes were a Burden: so that there was nothing in the World worth the having, or Enjoying, but my Game and Sport, which also was a Dream and being passed wholy forgotten. So that I had utterly forgotten all Goodness Bounty Comfort and Glory: which things are the very Brightness of the Glory of GOD: for lack of which therfore He was unknown.

Centuries of Meditations, III

1 Luke 15.11–32.

2

The Apostacy

One Star
Is better far
Than many Precious Stones:
One Sun, which is abov in Glory seen,
Is worth ten thousand Golden Thrones:
A juicy Herb, or Spire of Grass,
In useful Virtu, native Green,
An Em'rald doth surpass;
Hath in't more Valu, tho less seen.

No Wars,
Nor mortal Jars,
Nor bloody Feuds, nor Coin,
Nor Griefs which they occasion, saw I then;
Nor wicked Thievs which this purloin:
I had no Thoughts that were impure;
Esteeming both Women and Men
God's Work, I was secure,
And reckon'd Peace my choicest Gem.

As *Eve*
I did believ
My self in *Eden* set,
Affecting neither Gold, nor Ermin'd Crowns,
Nor ought els that I need forget;
No Mud did foul my limpid Streams,
No Mist eclypst my Sun with frowns;
Set off with hev'nly Beams,
My Joys were Meadows, Fields, and Towns.

Those things
Which *Cherubins*
Did not at first behold
Among God's Works, which *Adam* did not see;
As Robes, and Stones enchas'd in Gold,

Rich Cabinets, and such like fine
Inventions; could not ravish me:
    I thought not Bowls of Wine
Needful for my Felicity.

All Bliss
Consists in this,
To do as *Adam* did;
And not to know those superficial Joys
    Which were from him in *Eden* hid:
    Those little new-invented Things,
    Fine Lace and Silks, such Childish Toys
      As Ribbans are and Rings,
Or worldly Pelf[1] that Us destroys.

For God,
Both Great and Good,
The Seeds of Melancholy
Creäted not: but only foolish Men,
    Grown mad with customary Folly
    Which doth increase their Wants, so dote
    As when they elder grow they then
      Such Baubles chiefly note;
More Fools at Twenty Years than Ten.

But I,
I knew not why,
Did learn among them too
At length; and when I once with blemisht Eys
    Began their Pence and Toys to view,
    Drown'd in their Customs, I became
    A Stranger to the Shining Skies,
      Lost as a dying Flame;
And Hobby-horses brought to prize.

The Sun
And Moon forgon,
As if unmade, appear
No more to me; to God and Heven dead
    I was, as tho they never were:

Upon som useless gaudy Book,
When what I knew of God was fled,
    The Child being taught to look,
His Soul was quickly murthered.

        O fine!
      O most divine!
    O brave! they cry'd; and shew'd
Som Tinsel thing whose Glittering did amaze,
    And to their Cries its beauty ow'd;
    Thus I on Riches, by degrees,
    Of a new Stamp did learn to gaze;
        While all the World for these
I lost: my Joy turn'd to a Blaze.

1 Derogatory or jocular term for money, wealth.

3

The Approach

1

That Childish Thoughts such Joys inspire,
Doth make my Wonder and his Glory Higher;
    His Bounty, and my Wealth more Great,
It shews his Kingdom and his Work Compleat:
    In which there is not any Thing
Not meet to be the Joy of Cherubim.

2

He in our Childhood with us walks,
And with our Thoughts Mysteriously he talks;
    He often visiteth our Minds,
But cold Acceptance in us ever finds:
    We send him often grievd away;
Els would he shew us all his Kingdoms Joy.

3

O Lord I wonder at thy Love,
Which did my Infancy so Early move:
    But more at that which did forbear,
And move so long, tho Sleighted many a yeer:
    But most of all, at last that Thou
Thyself shouldst me convert I scarce know how.

4

Thy Gracious Motions oft in vain
Assaulted me: My Heart did Hard remain
    Long time: I sent my God away,
Grievd much that he could not impart his Joy.
    I careless was, nor did regard
The End for which he all these Thoughts prepard.

5

But now with New and Open Eys,
I see beneath as if above the Skies;
    And as I Backward look again,
See all his Thoughts and mine most Clear and Plain.
    He did Approach, he me did Woo
I wonder that my God this thing would doe.

6

From Nothing taken first I was,
What Wondrous Things his Glory brought to pass!
    Now in this World I him behold,
And me enveloped in more then Gold;
    In deep Abysses of Delights,
In present Hidden Precious Benefits.

7

Those Thoughts his Goodness long before
Prepard as Precious and Celestial Store,
    With curious Art in me inlaid,
That Childhood might it self alone be said,
    My Tutor, Teacher, Guid to be,
Instructed then even by the Deitie.

4

Baptism

Its Author

There are three that bear Record in Heaven, the Father, the Word, &
the Holy Ghost; & these Three are one. The whole Trinity was seen in
our Saviors Baptism, & by their Authoritie we are baptized, in the
Name of the Father, Son & Holy Ghost.

Its Outward use

There are three that bear Witness in Earth, the Spirit & the Water &
the Blood, & these Three agree in one. The Spirit is named first here,
that was named last before Because in Order of Nature he proceedeth
from the Father by the Son to the Sons of Men; & so is last in the Holy
Trinity, but in order of Nature first among the three here, which tho
they are not one in Nature, agree in one, because the Spirit of Faith &
Miracles, the Water in Baptism, & the Blood of Martyrs testifie the
same thing. For as the Testimonie of Jesus is the Spirit of Prophesie, as
he was manifest in the flesh, justified in the Spirit, & seen of Angels:
so he promised to send the Comforter, who should testifie of him: &
ordained Baptism & continues to uphold it by the power of his Spirit
that it might be a visible sign apparently testifying to al the World, the
truth of his being here upon Earth, abiding as a Monument of Antiquity
for that purpose among us.

Its End

Its inward use is to be measured by its End, which is not to Sanctify
us; but to signify to us the Mysterious Maner of our Sanctification &
to exhibit the Nature of our Spiritual Washing to the Ey of Beholders.
A man is converted, regenerated, illuminated, newborn and Sanctified,
when he is changed within, when he repents & believs, when he dies
unto the World & lives unto God, when he sees him & knows him, &
loves him & delights in him, & begins lovingly to make it his Business
to please him: not when he is sprinkled in the Water without doing

these. Nevertheless he is said to be buried with Christ by Baptism into his Death, to be regenerated therin, & made a child of God, a Member of Christ, & an Heir of the Kingdom of Heaven: Even as all the Jews were promiscuously said, to drink of that Rock that followed them, & that Rock was Christ; or as the Bread is said to be our Saviors Body or the Wine his Blood: all which expressions must be understood in a Sacramental Maner. The most Wicked varlet on Earth when he receivs the Sacrament of the Lords Supper, eats the Body & drinks the Blood of Christ in a Sacramental Maner. And so is every one Regenerated, that is Baptized, in a Sacramental Maner. This is the Answer that is to be returned to all sorts of Phanatiques that cavil at the Words in the English Liturgie.

Its inward use

Its inward use is Monitory & Obligatory. First it is Instructive, for in our own we ought to remember our Saviors Baptism wherin he was declared to be the Son of God by a voice from Heaven: wherin the Holy Ghost came down upon him in the form of a Dove, nay & the Heavens were opened too, as it were to receiv him. Our Baptism intimates that Our Eternal Father loves us, that we are the Sons of GOD, that we are to be Temples of the Holy Ghost & Heirs of Heaven, all which he ought to believ that is Baptized. Since the Heavens are open to receiv him it is his Duty to live a holy Life, to be Meek & full of Lov, since the Dove is come upon him, to die to the World, to renounce all its Pomp, & Vanities, to forsake all its Pleasures & despise its Lusts & Riches, to abhor Satan with all Anger Envy Malice and Rebellion which are the Works of the Devil, to liv unto God in Contemplation & Lov, & to hav his conversation in Heaven. And upon this Condition God assures him, that his Sins are pardoned, & the Pardon is Sealed in Baptism. It is Obligatory to him, which is the second use of it; for in this Sacrament he solemnly vows all these things: & it is his Seal towards God by which his vow is ratified: And he is thereupon declared, & received for a child of GOD in the Church: & admitted by this Gate to the Fruition of all its Publick & Celestial Privileges, which if he be not wanting to himself, if he break not the vow, he may enjoy forever.

Observations

Baptism came into the church in the Place of Circumcision: which was a Seal of the Covenant of Grace made to Abraham & his Children. And therfore on the one side our children may be Baptized, and it is Impietie to forbid them, so on the other side we must not ascribe more to Baptism than the Apostle did to Circumcision. It is a Clearer Sacrament, but does not give the Person Baptized the least Libertie or Security in Sin.

For he is not a Jew which is one outwardly neither is that Circumcision which is outward of the flesh: but he is a Jew which is one inwardly & Circumcision is that of the Heart, in the Spirit & not in the Letter, whose practise is not of Men but of GOD. Romans 2:28–29. Even so, he is not Christian which is one outwardly, neither is that regeneration of Baptism which is outward in the flesh; but he is a Christian, which is one inwardly, Baptism is that of the Heart, in the Spirit.

As Circumcision was among the Jews, so is Baptism among the Christian, Gods sign & mark upon his people, the sheep of his pasture.

Against the Quakers, that proudly renounce outward Baptism, upon pretence it is needless because they are Baptized with the Holy Ghost, we observ, that all they that had the Holy Ghost in Primitive times were baptized. Many were Baptized before, & many after they received the Holy Ghost, but not one without being Baptized, was admitted into the Visible Member-ship of Christ & the Church. As you may see at large in the Acts of the Apostles.

As for the Anabaptists, that abhor the Baptizing of Infants, that of our Savior is fitly applyed to them, *Suffer little children to com unto me, & forbid them not, for of such is the Kingdom of Heaven.* He received them, layed his Hands on them, & blessed them, before they actualy repented or believed: which he would not have done had they been uncapable of his favor & Blessing. Faith & Repentance is as necessary to his favor, as it is to Baptism.

He would not have thus received & Blessed an impenitent Sinner, & an Actual Unbeliever, grown up to the years of Discretion which plainly shews he makes a Distinction between Men & Infants, & deals with both according to their Capacitie.

The Anabaptists deny the Being of a National Church. Wheras our Savior deals with nations in their National Capacitie, threatens Cities that reject his Disciples, as well as particular persons, & commands his Apostles to go & teach, (not single men, but) all Nations, baptizing them in the Name of the Father, & of the Son, & of the H. Ghost. And if there be a National Church, it is one of the Greatest Impieties in the World to destroy it.

The Opinion of the Anabaptists seems the most innocent, & is one of the most thorney & difficult opinions in the World: yet by a strange & (almost) unsearchable fate, it is the seed plot of Heresies, & the grand Nursery of Schismes & Disorders. No man is an Anabaptist long but he sucks in some other horrible Opinion soon after.

The great Reason why Anabaptism opens a Gate to all other Errors & Heresies is this. It destroyeth the foundation: for by making the Jews to be under one Covenant & the Christians under another, they utterly enervate the Old Testament, & bereave themselves of the Rule by which they should judge of the Publick Estate & Condition of Kingdoms: Concerning which we have precepts & presidents in the Old Testament, but none in the New.

That the Jews were under the Covenant of Grace is evident, because the Gospel was preached to Abraham, because none of them could be saved by the Covenant of Works, because they were redeemed by Christ and justified by Faith as well as we. And that a National Church is lawfull under the Gospel is clear, because it is prophesied that Kings should be her Nursing Fathers & Queens her Nursing Mothers, & that all the Kingdoms of the World shall be the Kingdom of the Lord & of his Christ: which cometh to pass when all Kings & Kingdoms submit to our Saviors Laws, & make Profession of the Christian Religion.

I have my self conferred with Mr Tombs the great Ringleader of that Sect in this last Age, & have reason to believ he was condemned of his Conscience. For being a deep & judicious man, he could not but see, that his Opinion was utterly ruined, if the Jews were under the same Covenant with us, & therefore he held that the Jews were under a Covenant of Works, & we under a Covenant of Grace, & this he made it his Business to teach in his Sermons at this Amsterdam, his Heretical Church in Leominster in Herefordshire where having the advantage twice to meet him, I both times asked him the same Questions, & both times received the same Answer, that the Jews were under the Covenant of Works. But both times asking him what use or place could be for Sacrifices in a Covenant of Works he was both times as Blank, & mute as a Fish. For Sacrifices are Types of a Mediator & a Savior: their

Blood was a shadow of the Blood of Christ, who was in very deed the Lamb of God slain from the Beginning of the World.

That which compelleth him to sin against his conscience in this matter for the Support of his Opinion, is the Nature of the Covenant made with the Jews. For if the Covenant which GOD made with Abraham included him & his Seed, & all the Seed of Abraham were Members in Covenant with God by virtu of that Covenant, the very same Covenant being made with Christians must of Necessity include them & their seed: And all the Children of Christians will be Members in Covenant. Which he abhors as Poyson: for them they must be admitted by visible Rites into Church fellowship. & be declared by the Ordinance appointed for that End, Heirs according to the Promise.

The covenant made with Abraham is expressly noted to have been 430 yeers before the Law was given, & is made by the Apostle Different from the Law nay & opposite to it, which the Law could not destroy. Gal. 3. And is in that Chap. called the Gospel.

True Reason is as Sacred & Divine as the Holy Scripture: being the Word of GOD in the Essence of the Soul: & of such Authoritie, that the Scriptures themselves could have no Authority without it. For let GOD say, or command what he will, if Reason did not require, that Creatures should believ & obey their Creator, there would be no Force in his Word at all. They therefore that so boldly & familiarly despise Reason, overthrow the Foundation of all Religion. And of this the Anabaptists are apparently Guilty.

All they that are Baptized ought to remember & keep their vows. A Heathen cannot, but an Infant Baptized may become an Apostate.

Commentaries of Heaven

5

Atonement

In 'Atonement' the repeated themes are the necessity of sacrifice, the necessity of the sacrifice being a pure and spotless, divine being, the payment for sin, the fall of Adam, satisfaction of divine justice. These are repeated over and over again in this article as a direct defence of Trinitarian theology and atonement theology against the Socinians.

The Etymology of the Word

Atonement is an English Word which seemeth to be compounded of At & One, for to Atone is to set at one those persons that were divided. Whereupon we are to consider the Division between God & man the Cause of the Division, & the Maner of the Atonement for Atonement is a Word applicable to any Means of Reconciliation whatsoever, if accepted in the full Latitude & Extent of its Signification; but in the Sacred & co[nsta]nt use of it, tis now restrained to signifie the Means of our Peace with God, who is offended with us, & ought to be pacified.

Its Signification

The Word may signifie either the Act of Reconciliation it self, or the Means required before the Act of Reconciliation be perfected. The Natural force of it immediately regards the Act, but in common use it is referred to the Means, by which the Atonement is made. Thus the Atonement which Aaron was to make under the Old Law, for the Souls of the people, was previous to that Reconciliation itself intended therby. An Atonement was to be made for the Altar, that it might be esteemed Holy, upon which the Sin-offering of Atonement was to be offered: and the People rich & poor were to offer half a shekel evry one to the Lord, to make an Atonement for Souls, & the Money so given is called the Atonement Money of the Children of Israel. Not as if either the Thing itself nor the Act of offering it were indeed the Atonement; But the Cause of the Atonement or the Means wherby that was atchieved bears the name of the Effect which therby was atchieved.

Its Nature

An Atonement as it signifieth properly the Union between GOD & Man, is the Consequent of Mans Acceptableness that had been Displeasing, & of the Pacification of GODS Mind, that had been displeased. It is the Agreement between God Almighty pacified, & Man converted, wherby the Penitent Sinner is again received into favor. So that the Aversion of GOD & the Defilement of Man, are both removed before Atonement can be made. But as it signifieth the Meritorious Cause of the Atonement, which is finaly compleated between GOD &

the offended, an Atonement is the Propiciation or Satisfaction which is made to Divine Justice. For man; or the Sacrifice which is offered & accepted in his Steed.

Its Kinds

The Atonement made for Sin, is either Typical or Real. All the Sacrifices of the Old Law whereby Atonement was made were meer Shadows, & purely figurative, & accepted of the Jews in token only of GODS Acceptance of a greater Sacrifice.

Commentaries of Heaven, 'Atonement'

6

Mercy, redemption, incarnation, works and grace

Chapter 14
Of Mercy, The Indelible Stain and Guilt of Sin.
Of the Kingdom which GOD recovered by Mercy,
The transcendent Nature of that Duty,
with its Effects and Benefits.

Such is the infinite Justice of God, and the Severity of his Displeasure at Sin, his Holiness so Pure, and his Nature so irreconcilable, his Hatred so real and infinite against it, that when a Sin is committed, his Soul is alienated from the Author of the Crime, and his infinite Displeasure will ever see the Obliquity, and ever loath the Deformity therein.

The Person of a man is concerned, in (and always represented in the Glass of) his Action. Union between him and his Deeds is Marvellous. Tis so close, that his Soul it self is hated or Beloved in his Actions. As long as it appeareth in that deed which is Odious and Deformed, he can never be Beloved.

How slight soever our Thoughts of Sin are, the least Sin is of infinite Demerit, because it breaketh the Union between God and the Soul, bereaveth him of his Desire, blasteth his Image, corrupteth the Nature of the Soul, is committed against infinite Goodness and Majesty, being as the Scripture speaketh *Exceeding sinful*, because it is committed against infinite Obligations and Rewards, displeasing to all the Glorious Angels, abominable to all the Wise and Holy, utterly against all the Rules of Reason, and infinitely Opposite to the Holiness of God, who is of purer Eys then to behold the least Iniquity. So that unless there be some way found out to deliver the Soul from the Guilt of Sin, to blot out the Act and to purifie it from the Stain, there can be no Reconciliation between GOD and a Sinner. That an offence so infinite should be Eternally punished, is the most reasonable thing in the World. . . .

In the midst of this Black and Horrid Condition, the Mercy of GOD appeared like a Morning Star,[1] and the Redeeming Love of GOD was that alone which was able by its Discovery to dispell the Mystes of Darkness that were round about him.

As all things were before turned into Evil, by the force of Sin, and conspired to sink him lower into the Bottomless Pit; so all the Evils of his present condition were, by this infinite Mercy, turned to his Advantage, and his Condition in many Respects far better than before.

It is fit to see how Sin enfeebled his Soul, and made him unable to serve GOD; that we might the better understand the Manner of his Recovery, and how his Spiritual Life and Power is restored, in the new strength which he received in his Saviour.

The Account of it is this: By his *self Love* he was prone to desire all that was Profitable and Delightful to him: While therefore GOD infinitely Loved him, being apparently the fountain of all his Happiness, he could not chuse, (as long as he considered it) but Love GOD and Delight in him, it was natural and Easie to celebrate his Praises. But when he was hated of GOD, tho he could not chuse but acknowledge that hatred *Just*; yet his Self Love made him to look upon GOD in a Malevolent manner, as his Greatest Enemy and his Eternal Tormentor. All that was in GOD was a Terror to him. His power, his Eternity, his Justice, his Holiness, his Goodness, his Wisdome, his Unalterable Blessedness, all was a grief and Terror to his Soul, as long as the Hatred of GOD continued against him it made him desperate to think it would continue forever, and reduced him to the miserable slavery of hating GOD even to all Eternity.

But when the Love of GOD towards Man appeared, the Joy wherewith he was surprized, was, in all Likelyhood, so far beyond his Expectation, and his Redemption so far above the Powers of Nature, that his very Guilt and Despair enflamed him with Love. GOD appeared now so Welcome to him, and so Lovely above all that was before, that it was impossible for him to look upon GOD, and not to Love him with Greater Emazement and Ardor then ever. Self Love, that Before compelled him to hate GOD, carried him now most violently to the Love of GOD; and the Truth is, the Love of GOD in the Eye of the Understanding, is the influence of the Holy Ghost proceeding from the Father by the Son into the Soul of the Spectator. For GOD is Love, and we therefore Love him, because he first Loved us.[2] A faln man is Still a reasonable Creature, and having more reason to Love GOD then he had before, is by the pure Nature of his Essence infinitely more prone to Love GOD, and delight in him, and praise him for ever, because he is so mercifully and so Strangely restored. Thus are we in Christ restored to the Exercise of that Power which we lost by Sin: But without him we can do Nothing.[3]

When all the Kingdom of GOD was at an End by the fall of man, and all the Labor of the Creation lost, by the Perversness of him for whom the whole World was made; GOD by his Mercy recovered it, and raised it out of the Rubbish of its Ruines, more Glorious than before. Which is the chief reason for the sake for which we introduce the Mercy of GOD, as our best pattern. For when a man has injured us, by Nature there is an End of all the Lovely Exercises of Peace and Amity. If natural Justice should be strictly observed; but then the Season of Grace arrives, and the Excellencie of Mercy shews it self in the Lustre of its Wisdome, and so our Empire is continued, our loss retrived: For by shewing Mercy we often recover the Love of an Enemy, and restore a Criminal to the Joy of our friendship. We lengthen out our Goodness and Heighten its measure; we make it victorious, and cloath it with Glory above the Course of Nature. And all this we are enabled to do by the Coming of *Jesus Christ*, who hath restored us to the Hope of Salvation, and taught us a Way to increase our own Goodness by other mens Evils, to turn the vices of others into our own Vertues, and to Live a Miraculous Life of Worth and Excellency in the midst of Enemies, Dealing with men better than they deserve, adorning our selves with Trophies by the Advantages of their vileness, making our selves more Honourable by the Ignominy they cast upon us, more Lovely and Desirable by the Hatred which they bear towards us.

The foundations upon which we Exercise this Vertue, are wholy Supernatural. To be kind to the innocent is but Justice and Goodness, but to be Kind to the Malevolent is Grace and Mercy. And this we must do, *because our Father which is in Heaven Causeth his Sun to rise on the Just and the unjust and his Rain to descend on the Righteous and the Wicked.*[4] Because Mercy is the Head Spring of all our Felicities, therefore should we shew Mercy, as we have obtained Mercy. As the Blood was sprinkled upon the Tabernacle and all its Utensils; so is the Blood of Christ upon the Heathens, and the Earth, and all our Enjoyments. They are Daily Monitors of Mercy to us, because they are purchased by the Blood of Christ. For of him it is, that the Heavens declare the Glory of GOD, and the firmament sheweth his Handy work to us sinners at this day. The Salvation of Sinners being the only End for the sake of which we can be permitted now to enjoy them.

The Incarnation of our Lord Jesus Christ is an incredible mystery to them, that do not consider the Love of GOD towards Men, in the Creation of the World. But they that measure it by his Laws and works, and see it in the value of their own Souls, would think it very Strange, if that Love which appeareth so infinite in all other things, should be defective only in its Ways of Providence. They easily believe, it may express it self in the Incarnation. Especially Since all Ages are Beautified with the Effects and Demonstrations of this verity, that *GOD so Loved the World, that he gave his only begotten Son, that whosoever believeth in him should not perish but have Everlasting Life.*[5] For Love is apt to transform it self into all shapes, that the necessity of its Object requires; and as prone to suffer as rejoyce with it, as apt to suffer for it, as with it. Many fathers have died for their Children, many for their Country, but the Love of GOD exceedeth them all. To be beloved in our Guilt is exceeding Wonderful: but this also is in the Nature of Love; it may be provoked with the Guilt, or moved with Compassion at the misery of a Sinner.

Where the Love is extreamly violent, and the weak Estate of the Object fit for Compassion, it is more inclined to Pity than Revenge: Tho where the Object is strong, and endued with all advantages, it is more offended at the Outrage of its Rebellion. . . .

The Degrees and measures of that Mercy which was shewn to Man in his Redemption, are very considerable. When he was Weak and unable to help himself, when he was Guilty, when he was an Enemy, when he was Leprous and deformed, when he was Miserable and Dead, before he desired, or Thought of such a Thing, God freely gave his Son to die for his Salvation, and condescended to propose a reconciliation. Which should teach us, tho higher then the Cherubims, and more pure then the Light, tho our Enemies are never so base, and injurious, and ingrateful, nay Obstinate and Rebellious, to seek a reconciliation by the most Laborious and Expensive Endeavors, to manifest all our Care and kindness toward them, pursuing their Amendment and Recovery.

For the same Mind ought to be in us that was in Christ Jesus: who being in the form of GOD thought it no Robbery to be Equal with GOD, yet took upon him the Form of a Servant, and being found in fashion as a man, humbled himself to the Death, of the Cross: Wherefore GOD also hath highly exalted him, and given him a Name above every Name that at the Name of Jesus every Knee might bow.[6] The very reason why we so infinitely adore him, being the incomparable Height and Perfection of his Mercy, expressed in his Humiliation and Abasement for us. If we would enter into his Glory, we must walk in the Way which he hath trod before us, for that only will lead us into it.

Christian Ethicks, Ch. 14

1 Lamentations 3.23.
2 1 John 4.19.
3 John 15.5.
4 Matthew 5.45.
5 John 3.16.
6 Philippians 2.5–10.

7

The Gospel Mysteries

The Introduction

Two thousand yeers before my Savior came,
In Hieroglyphick Laws I see His Name.
My GOD prepard, before my self was born,
Great Joys wherewith I might my Life adorn.
He first ordaind that I a Life should liv
Of Sweet Delights; which His fair Hand did giv;
From whence since I by Sin revolted am,
He since ordaind his son to be a Man.
Whom that I might more certainly descrie,
With ancient figures He did Beautifie:
And made those Types the pleasant Posies be
Of His great Lov, & Kindness unto me.
Wherein I might with Joy & Sacred Pleasure,
His Goodness read, & see my Glorious Treasure

Would it not Ravish one that He should com,
To such Delights even from a Beggars Womb!
That from a hous where nothing could be seen,
He should be raisd to such a vast Esteem?
In Lands remote I see myself made High,
And Wonder at the State which there I spie.
My Soveraign LORD I in a long Design,
See ruling Kingdoms by His Might Divine.
And Things Disposing, that my Soul might be
So long before Enricht with Majestie.
Being made by Ways that Wisely do conspire,
Prevent,[1] fulfill, Exceed my Whole Desire,
A Princelike Heir of glorious Works, that pleas
My Soul, far more then Kingly Palaces.
I there behold a Tabernacle reard,
Wherin my GOD Himself for me appeard.
That He should com & in the World be seen,
That He should woe, & treat His Heavenly Queen
On Earth, that she His GLORY, here might see,
And be Espoused to the DIETY.
It is a Signe, we Equal Objects are
Even with the Angels of His Lov & Care
If not far more. For GOD with Men doth talk
In Wildernesses, & with Sinners Walk.
That I should see my self with fleshly Eys,
Concernd in such a World of Mysteries;
That such a people should two thousand yeers,
Their prayers pay, their Songs, their vows, their Tears,
In such a sort, & for me Minister;
That He by them might me to Joys prefer;
That they should serv in such Magnificence,
And with such Pomp, in splendid State dispence
Their Publick Worship; that in Ages they
Might to my Glory me more straight convey;
And serv for me! That I might so becom
A King more Great, a Prince, a Priest, a Son;
It so Transports me, & my Soul doth Bless
I know not how my Glory to Express:
My Glorying Heart so much is pleasd with this,
That Words suffice not to describe my Bliss!

Adams Fall

The KING of Glory, who on High doth Dwell,
Who doth even all the Seraphims excell,
Reigns over Angels, & is there Admired,
By all His Hosts, where Nothing is Desired:
He came when Adam fell & from the Grave,
A Sinfull Creature by His Lov did save.
In Curious Types He did Express His Care,
And shewd the Means His Wisdom did prepare.
One sind, another died: A Beast was slain;
An Innocent was kild, a foe doth reign.
GOD sees the Nakedness that Man was in,
Covers his shame, & clothes him with the Skin.
This Blood first spilt doth cleans the World, & is
An Embleme of the Way to Sinners Bliss.
He that was made a bloody Sacrifice
For Man, & as his Ransom for him dies,
From Him the Robes of Righteousness we take,
Which only clothes, & doth us Glorious make.
See O my soul, thy GOD hath mindfull been
Of Thee, before thy self on Earth was seen.
And purposing to bring Thee in, among
His Creatures here, that Thou mightest sing the Song
Of Joys, He makes all present Things thy Treasures
And fils all Ages for thy Soul with pleasures.
The Curious City, & the Spacious Skies,
The Glorious Sun that entertains thine Eys,
The Temple, & the Kingdom which he gave
Are Glorious Things, Great, Sweet, Divine & Brave.
But Thou must enter into Ages too
And these His Chambers deckt with Treasures view
And all things by the Ey of Wisdom see
For Thee prepared by the Dietie.

Abels Lamb

How Early do I see a Sacrifice!
Confirming me, by Abel slain, it Dies!
The Lamb of GOD, that takes away our Sin,
Is slain, even when the World doth first begin.
An Innocent, that from all Blemish free,
Owning no Sin, might aptly Die for me.
A Usefull Creature that is fit for meat:
To note that we our Sacrifice must Eat.
A Creature meet to clothe us with its Wool,
And Skin: How Apposite; How plain, how full.
No Wolf nor Vulture whom its fangs do arm,
And fit for Mischief; doing Creatures harm;
Is fit for this but one that meek in Mind,
The only proper Sacrifice we find.
Els Bears & Tygres might hav fitter been
For Death, that in the Wilderness are seen.
A firey, furious, Dangerous, Ravenous Beast
Is fittest to make Death a Bloody feast.
But GOD & Lov all these for Man Despise,
His Altar wils no Guilty Sacrifice.
Tis Strange, what He loves best our GOD doth make,
His only Sacrifice for Sinners Sake.
        This Rite so Deeply was imprest in men,
That when they GOD hav all forgot, even then
They this retained: & Sacrifices still
The most remote & Barbarous Nations kill.
Hence did the Heathens all of old derive
Their Offerings, they Abels Lamb revive.
Is it not Sweet in many distant Lands
To see the footsteps of Divine Commands;
To see Blind Pagans to record their fate,
And shew the Parents which they imitate.
In bloody Gore they all Embrew their Hands,
And do, what none among them understands,
Confess themselves Transgressors, Offerings bring
By others Death approach the Heavenly King.
Wherever Scattered they from Babel were,

This Relick ever with them doth appear.
And they that els the Godhead had not Known,
By it being taught a Dying SAVIOR own.

The Ceremonial Law

1 Go before.

8

O Jesu God, whose own Dear Blood

1

O JESU GOD, whose own Dear Blood
Was Shed to do a Sinner Good!
    A Bleeding Deitie!
Vaild over in Humanitie!
And Crucified for me!
A God so rent and torn, and Scourgd and Naild!
    O how thy Goodness hath prevaild!
O what a Benefit it makes me See
The Goodness, and the Lov of God to me!

2

And did the Great Creator move
The Heavens with an Equal Love!
    Did he Intend my Bliss,
With an Affection like to this?
O what a deep Abyss!
The very Glory of the King of Kings
    Is the first fountain of those Springs
That feed my Soul! His GODHEAD Ministers,
And such a Worm abov himself preferres!

3

O Say not So! His Lovs too Great,
His Essence too, is too Compleat,
    To be so Injurd! He,
(All Worth and all Felicitie,)
    Must Ever abov thee

Prefer himself, and be! It is most fit
　　My Friend that I Should this Admit.
For while he does prefer himself, I see
My self preferd in all felicitie.

4

　　The King of Glory Peace and Bliss
　　My Greater Self my better is.
　　　　He did all things for me.
　　His Goodness is the Deitie,
　　　　And my Felicitie!
He died for me! Ah Say no more! His Lov
　　Will too Severe and piercing prove!
It is Intollerable and may Kill
With Sweetness. Let it Softly then distill.

The Kingdom of God, Ch. 11

9

Manna

IV

But theres a Deeper Mystery than this
That leads us further in the Way to Bliss
Tho Manna that to us from Heaven came
Contains, or is a Type of Jesus Name.
This sinfull World we mortals must confess
To be the Horrid howling Wilderness.
Ourselvs like Jews Obdurat foes to GOD,
For Sin Ejected his Divine abode.
Our souls devoid of Spiritual Strength
And all without a Savior at the length
To be destroyd, or cast into that Hell
Where Damned Devils, now faln Angels dwell:
Hungry and pining all with fierce desire
To covet Bliss, unable to Aspire
Wishing to feed on those Celestial Joys
The loss of which all Strength in us destroys.

But faint & feeble while or failing Eys
In Languishments of Thirst do Tantalize.
We see his Bliss but cannot take Delight
Nor Love nor prize nor sate our Appetite
We cannot prais being faln, as before,
Nor in his Lov delight, nor him adore.
Till Jesus comes who doth our Strength renew,
On whom we feed, while we his Lov do view.
From Heaven the Bread of Life in him comes down
And all the Grass in all the Meades doth Crown.
All flesh is Grass:[1] Like Dew his Sweat & blood
Is sprinkled upon all & turns to food.
He being once received again we can
Adore & love as when the World began
Nay more, more Lov, more strength his Love inspires
This is the Bread of Life my soule admires.

                                      The Ceremonial Law

1 Isaiah 40.6; 1 Peter 1.24.

10

Meditations on the Cross

55

. . . our Saviors Cross is the Throne of Delights. That Centre of Eternity, *That Tree of Life* in the midst of the Paradice of GOD!

56

There are we Entertained with the Wonder of all Ages. There we enter into the Heart of the Univers. There we Behold the Admiration of Angels. There we find the Price and Elixar of our Joys. As on evry side of the Earth all Heavy things tend to the Centre; so all Nations ought on evry Side to flow in unto it. It is not by going with the feet, but by Journeys of the Soul, that we Travail thither. By withdrawing our Thoughts from Wandering in the Streets of this World, to the Contemplation and Serious Meditation of his Bloody Sufferings. Where the Carcase is thither will the Eagles be Gathered together. Our Eys must be towards it, our Hearts set upon it, our Affections Drawn and our Thoughts and Minds united to it. When I am lifted up saith the Son of man I will draw all Men unto me. As fishes are Drawn out of the Water, as Jeremie was Drawn out of the Dungeon, as S. Peters Sheet was Drawn up into heaven; so shall we be Drawn by that Sight from Ignorance and Sin and Earthly vanities, idle Sports Companions Feasts and Pleasures, to the Joyfull Contemplation of that Eternal Object. But by what Cords? The Cords of a Man, and the Cords of Lov.[1]

57

As Eagles are Drawn by the Sent of a Carcais, As Children are Drawn together by the Sight of a Lion, As People flock to a Coronation, and as a Man is Drawn to his Beloved Object, so ought we. As the Sick are Drawn by the Credit of a Physician, as the Poor are Drawn by the Liberality of a King, as the Devout are Drawn by the fame of the Holy, and as the Curious are Drawn by the Nois of a Miracle so ought we. As the stones were Drawn to the Building of Thebes by the Melodie of Amphion, as the Hungry are Drawn with the Desire of a Feast, and the Pitifull Drawn to a Wofull Spectacle so ought we. What Visible Chains or Cords draw these? What Invisible Links allure? They follow all, or flock together of their own accord. And shall not we much more? Who would not be Drawn to the Gate of Heaven, were it open to receiv him? Yet nothing compels Him, but that which forceth the Angels · Commoditie[2] and Desire. For these are Things which the Angels desire to look into. And of Men it is Written, They shall look on Him whom they hav Peirced.[3] Verily the Israelites did not more Clearly see the Brazen Serpent upon the Pole in the Wilderness, then we may our Savior upon the Cross.[4] The Serpent was seen with their Eys, the Slayer of the Serpent is seen with our Souls. They had less need to see the one, then we to see the other.

58

The Cross is the Abyss of Wonders, the Centre of Desires, the Schole of Virtues, the Hous of Wisdom, the Throne of Lov, the Theatre of Joys and the Place of Sorrows; It is the Root of Happiness, and the Gate of Heaven.

59

Of all the Things in Heaven and Earth it is the most Peculiar. It is the most Exalted of all Objects. It is an Ensign lifted up for all Nations, to it shall the Gentiles seek,[5] His Rest shall be Glorious: the Dispersed of Judah shall be gathered together to it, from the four Corners of the

Earth. If Lov be the Weight of the Soul, and its Object the Centre · All Eys and Hearts may convert and turn unto this Object: cleave unto this Centre, and by it enter into Rest. There we might see all Nations Assembled with their Eys and Hearts upon it. There we may see Gods Goodness Wisdom and Power: yea his Mercy and Anger displayed. There we may see Mans Sin and infinit value. His Hope and Fear, his Misery and Happiness. There we might see the Rock of Ages, and the Joys of Heaven. There we may see a Man Loving all the World, and a GOD Dying for Mankind. There we may see all Types and Ceremonies, figures and Prophesies. And all Kingdoms Adoring a Malefactor: An Innocent Malefactor, yet the Greatest in the World. There we may see the most Distant Things in Eternity united: all Mysteries at once couched together and Explained. The only reason why this Glorious Object is so Publickly Admired by Churches and Kingdoms, and so little thought of by Particular men, is becaus it is truly the most Glorious. It is the Root of Comforts, and the Fountain of Joys. It is the only Supreme and Soveraign Spectacle in all Worlds. It is a Well of Life beneath in which we may see the face of Heaven abov: and the only Mirror, wherin all things appear in their Proper Colors · that is sprinkled in the Blood of our Lord and Savior.

60

The Cross of Christ is the Jacobs ladder[6] by which we Ascend into the Highest Heavens. There we see Joyfull Patriarchs, Expecting Saints, and Prophets Ministering, Apostles Publishing and Doctors Teaching. All Nations concentering, and Angels Praising. That Cross is a Tree set on fire with invisible flame, that Illuminateth all the World. The Flame is Lov. The Lov in His Bosom who died on it. In the light of which we see how to possess all the Things in Heaven and Earth after His Similitud. For He that Suffered on it, was the Son of GOD as you are: tho He seemed a Mortal Man. He had Acquaintance and Relations as you hav, but He was a Lover of Men and Angels. Was He not the Son of GOD and Heir of the Whole World? To this poor Bleeding Naked Man did all the Corn and Wine and Oyl, and Gold and Silver in the World minister in an Invisible Maner, even as he was exposed Lying and Dying upon the Cross.

61

Here you learn all Patience, Meekness, Self Denial, Courage, Prudence, Zeal, Lov, Charity, Contempt of the World, Joy, Penitence, Contrition, Modestie, Fidelity, Constancy, Perseverance, Holiness, Contentation[7] and Thanksgiving. With whatsoever els is requisit for a Man, a Christian or a King. This Man Bleeding here was Tutor to King Charles the Martyr: and Great Master to S. Paul the Convert who learned of Him Activity, and Zeal unto all Nations. Well therfore may we take up with this Prospect, and from hence behold all the Things in Heaven and Earth. Here we learn to imitat Jesus in his Lov unto all.

Centuries of Meditations, I

1 Hosea 11.4.
2 Suitability, usefulness, convenience.
3 Zechariah 12.10; John 19.37.
4 Numbers 21.6–9; John 3.14.
5 Isaiah 11.10.
6 Genesis 28.10–16.
7 Payment in satisfaction, expiation of sin.

11

A Broken and a contrite Heart

A Broken and a contrite Heart[1] is made up of knowledge Sorrow and Lov: knowledge of our primitiv felicitie in Eden, Sorrow for our fall, Lov to God so Gratious and Redeeming. know ledg of our Happiness in being Redeemed, Sorrow for sin against our Redeemer, Lov to God yet Continuing favorable and Gracious. Knowledg of the Joys prepared for us, Sorrow for our unworthyness in living beneath them, Lov to God for his Goodness Magnified and Exalted over us. one Broken Sigh, or Contrite Groan is more Acceptable to God, then Thousands of Rams, and ten Thousand Rivers of oyl, and maketh more pleasant musick in his Eares, then all the fained musick of the Spheres. Which because it is so He Botleth up our Tears. for they Abide in the places wherever because they are pearls, Dissolved pearl, Tho not vanishing; which he reserveth in Store for the Holy Angels. Neither is this Metaphorical, He really Bottleth all our Teares.[2] For they Abide in the places where they fall, and in those Moments wherein they were Shed, are Treasured up for all Beholders. Are not all the parts of all Eternitie present at once to God; are not all their contents present in them, Is not all Eternity present [to] our understanding: if not in us! How then shall it otherwise be, but that Gods Eternitie is a Bottle like the Heavens Wherein the Tears of Penitents Glitter like the Stars; Scattered at a Distance, yet all before us! O my God since I know my selfe the Joy of Angels in Repenting, the very knowledge of that Shall encreas my Tears, Sweeten my Sorrow, Alleviat yet Augment and compleat my Repentance. Were it not for the Sun no vapors would arise, Light immitted rarifies and prepares them. Light Emitted makes them Transpire.[3] Light Reflected Elivates in Counion. Light immitted, Emitted, and reflected as they all ascend refines and carries them. Without Light there would be no vapors; without which vapors recondensing into clouds, there would be no Rain, no fruits, no flowers. clouds of Penitence may seem to overwhelme and oppress the Face, but not appear till first raised by the Sun of Righteousness Shining on the Earth which is Mans Heart. Light immitted is Glory Seen, which melts and Softens, Light Emitted is Lov returned, which Transpires as Sighs and bears us upwards, light reflected is the means of Grace Shining [on] the Soul, and cooperating with the Spirit, which works within us With Sighs and Groans unutterable. without which sighs There can be no clouds Tears fruits or flowers. Since Therefore Repentance is a work of the Light, and Sin can never be Hated but in the open day, since those clouds on the face of Happienes Beautifie the Heavens, fructifie the Earth, and make it flourish, Since the world is the better for some Rainy Days, and Sinners Tears are Dissolved pearl that Shine for-ever, I will not be without some of those, but Esteeme Repentance Disguised Happieness. And wonder at God for making every Thing a part of Eternal Blessedness.

Select Meditations, I, 93

1 Psalm 51.17.
2 Psalm 56.8.
3 Immitted: inserted, introduced. Emitted: given off, discharged.

12

More Easily ceas to liv, then Love

It seemeth as if God the Father Loved us better then his Son. For God
so Loved the World, that he gav his only begotten Son that whosoever
believeth on him should not perish; but hav Everlasting Life.[1] It seemeth
that the Son of God loved us better then his Father, for when Enmity
and Variance fell out between us, he forsooke his Father, and did cleav
unto us like a Bridegroom that forsaketh Father and Mother to cleav
to his Wife.[2] This is that we Know not how to Judg of. Even in the
Depth of our Guilt, he so loved us, as to becom Bone of our Bone, and
Flesh of our flesh. To lov us in our Beauty, was nothing if compared.
Many an earthly Bridegroom loveth his Wife so. But after we fell into
the Odious Deformity and Leprosie of Sin to be Contracted to us with
out Need, Shews that his Lov was desperat, and more violent then
Burning Flame. He forsook not his Father, even while he forsook him.
And tho for our sakes being Rich, he became poor,[3] yet even while he was
poor, he Enjoyed his Riches. As when he cam down from Heaven upon
Earth, he was in Heaven. When he left the Throne of Glory to die upon
the Cross, he was Reigning in the Throne of Glory. His Father was
pleased, while he was displeased, and made him the object of his Anger,
and gave him up unto Death, yet for this very caus also highly Exalted
him and gav him a Name abov evry Name, that at the Name of Jesus,
Evry Knee should bow of things in Heaven, and things in Earth, and
things under the Earth.[4] His Lov was Wounded, and his Soul divided
upon our Transgression. He hated us as Sinners, And there our Savior
rather forsook him, then us, and undertook for us. He loved us as his
Creatures, and there our Savior and he were united, his only beloved Son
was well-pleasing unto him, in Redeeming us: and yet in Redeeming us
Endured the Wrath of his Eternal Father. That there should be Secrets
enow in the Nature of Lov, to Justify these things is Strange, and tis very
pleasant to see them answering the Miracles and prophesies that confirm
our Faith. For Gods Kingdom is his Bride, all his Happiness being seated,
in Beautifying, Enriching, and Saving it. Evry Soul is so perfect, that it is
his Bride in like Manner. GOD is the Bridegroom, and the whole
Kingdom her Dower. Many Waters cannot quench Lov.[5] Even offences
Somtimes, and those of the Highest Nature are not able to Extinguish
it. The more we Lov, the more we are Exasperated with an Adulterate

Wife. Yet som Men so lov so intirely, that they can forgiv and labor by all Means to make her penitent and upon her returning purity Liv happily, with her. Lov at once pressing to Contrary Effects, to Kill, and Adore her. So deeply is it Engraven in the Nature of som, and Encorporated in their Soul, that they can more Easily ceas to liv, then Love.

The Kingdom of God, Ch. 14

1 John 3.16.
2 Genesis 2.23–24.
3 2 Corinthians 8.9.
4 Philippians 2.5–10.
5 Song of Songs 8.7.

13

On Love

If a Man give all the Substance of his House for Lov, it could utterly be Contemned. GOD abov all things desires Lov, our Naked Lov, above thousands of Worlds of Gold, and silver. It is so high and Inestimable, that it is impossible to be bought, no Price can reach it. It is generous and free, and incapable of being base. It cannot be salable, or Mercenary in its effusions. It is an Argument of being no less, then Infinitly precious, that it cannot be Equald, nor Attaind by Crowns or Kingdoms. Had we been to buy the Lov of GOD, tho we had been able to make Worlds, and offer them for it, we must hav gone without it; for it is Contrary to the Nature of Lov to be bought and Sold. It must be a free Esteem of the Person that loves a Sincere and voluntary Choyce, a desire of him, and a Complacency in him that is beloved; or Lov is far Enough from appearing towards him: yet here behold Infinit Lov most freely given, that had no Beginning. . . .

From everlasting he was Infinit, and Eternal Lov, and determined to Creat the Best of Things: Determining to Creat the Best, he created Lov: Creating Lov he Created the Image of himself; And in that, the Best of all possible things; for Nothing is above the Image of GOD, but God himself. Lov is the fellow of Almighty GOD, and fit to be with him for evermore. It is pure and Good, and Kind, and Glorious, and full of respect and fear, and Circumspection; an Amiable and

Joyfull Thing, and fit to be Enjoyed: so like, that being described, one would think it He. It is Invisible, yet seeth all things; Indivisible, yet comprehendeth all; Great without Bulk, an Infinit Sphere without Dimensions, a Centre Comprehending the very Heavens, apparently here, yet Secretly present in other Places. It moves in it self, without changing place; Admitteth all things, Excludeth nothing; shineth upon all without sending forth Beams; Is High without pride, Low without Baseness, Potent without a Body, Beautifull without a Face; Knows no Distance, but is Immediatly neer unto all its objects; Lives Eternaly, yet is never old; Sees Eternity, and Delights in it; filles Immensity in a Mysterious Manner, Moves at Liberty within it self, being wholy Quiet; Goes thorow all, is in all; can feel like GOD in another person: can liv in its Object: Tis the fountain, Soul, and End of things. . . .

It is the Light of Heaven, the Way to Happiness, the Crown of Rewards, the fullfilling of Laws, an All possessing Treasure: O what Wonder hath He Wrought in Creating Lov!

The Kingdom of God, Ch. 32

14

The soul is perfected by trials

As summer fruits owe their Maturitie to the Verdure of the Spring and to the tender Buds, and Early Blossoms that appeared in the Beginning: so doth she [the soul] all her Amiableness and Glory to the virtues, wherwith She comes Cloathed from the Estate of Trial. It is far better to be raised to a Kingdom by Noble Means; more Glorious to be fitted for it by a brave Education; and commended to it by a Royall Exposure to Gallant Exploits, from whence a Man may return laden with Honors, and Trophies, and becom his Peoples Joy, and the Glory of his Throne; then to be taken from a Dung hill, and (without Desert) immediatly Clapt in the Throne. So is it better to be Glorified with Hazzards, and thence to return laden with virtues to the Throne of Heaven, then to be seated in it, without any Preparation in a lazy Manner, Passive unprofitable. The Virgin is an Amazon, a Beautifull Soldier that hath many Enemies to Conquer; her own Appetites, and Weaknesses, as well as all her Temptations. She is so Transcendent a Creature, that no one Name will Containe her: A Virgin, a Bride, a Wife, a Mother, a Daughter, a Soldier, a Priest, a Subject, a King, a Servant, a Son, a friend, an Image, a Temple, a Throne, a Vine, a Garden, a fountain, a Sun, a Star, a City, a Sea, a Crown, a Jewel, a Realm, a Dominion, a Principalitie, a Power, a virtue, an Angel, an Haven, a Heaven, a Deitie: And in all these Capacities hath Strength enough to resist her weaknesses, being armed, and inspired with Many Advantages; A Knowledg of Eternitie; a Lov of God; a Desire of Heaven; a Sight of Obligations; a Hope of Rewards; a fear of evil; a Delight in Good; a Lov of Happiness, and a Sense of his Eternal favor; a Knowledg to whom She relates, and how much She is beloved: which tho they are not enough to compell, and Necessitate her Care, are Strong enough to incline, and Engage her care, and her care alone sufficient to make her Enemies, and make her faithfull. For no Power in all Worlds is able, without her own consent, to corrupt her will. All things Work together for her Good,[1] and nothing but her Self is able to hurt her. Weak Enemies, oppositions, and Dangers overcome, are Eternaly Crowned with Infinit Recompences. The very care is Delightfull by which she is Secured, and the Bliss Eternal.

The Kingdom of God, Ch. 42

1 Romans 8.28.

15

Lost and found

5

By being endued with power to keep his laws I am advanced to his Throne; and to do that which above all Things in Heaven and Earth He desireth: and therein I am made His Bride to Delight Him. For haveing made the world that I should enjoy it, and in it Him, He cheifly desireth that I should doe that, which is the End for which He made the world, and me His Image. Nor is the Creation of many worlds So pleasing unto Him, as that I Should keep his laws in the world He hath made, and live in His Similitude.

6

By falling into Sin I revolted from His Love and Defaced His Glory. Neither could I by any other means be Redeemd from Hell but by the Incarnation of His Son, by whose Death I am restored to Glory.

7

Being restored to glory, I may again live in the Similitude of God: and as all his works are made more rich by the Death of His Son, Soe are all works more Ardently Desired, being the end now as well of my Redemption, as of my first creation. Whereby he is made more precious to me, and I to Him. So that at this day the Heavens and the earth are not onely like Adams Eden but the Stage and Theatre of my Saviours passion. And He for undergoing Such Things for me a Greater Treasure Then all beside.

8

Haveing restored me so to enjoy his Glory, if I do it not, my Sin is Greater then it was before: and Therefore have I need to take Greater Care then Adam in Eden.

9

The Sons of men being made Greater Treasures then Heaven and earth are more to be beloved: and his Bounty in giving them more to be esteemed, Howbeit they have made it Difficult, by withdrawing their love from Him and me, and by Swerving from His Image.

10

His Compassion Nevertheless to me and them, should move me to imitate his tender pitty. Now pitty Embalms Love, and makes it more vigorous, Especially to such Divin and Noble creatures.

11

By corrupting them selves and turning after vanity they have Blinded the world and me in like manner. Thick Darkness covereth the Nations, and Gross Darkness the people.[1] which is cheifly contracted by their Inventing and following other Treasures, for by magnifiing Riches of their own Devising, they have Covered the Treasures of Innocent Eden, forgotten the Delights of God, Buried in oblivion them selves and the world; Eclipsed the clear and open Joys of True Felicity.

12

Nevertheless even vanities them selves may be made Enjoyments, when by courage and wisdom we over come them.

13

Victory and Triumph are now Added to our former Delights. Benefits arising even from Sin it Selfe. but Such is the power of prevayling Custom, and Such the Darkness which those clouds and Snares have induced upon the Earth, that none, or but very few can clearly see them.

14

In being a Son of God like Jesus Christ, in forgiving Sinners, and living contrary to their Inferior customs, I shall recover Glory more Great then before: Those very Things that increas the Difficulty, Increas my Happiness when they are over com. So that a way of conquering be layd open, All Things shall work togeather for Good to Him that is faithfull.[2] For He Shall not only be mor approved by How much the Greater his oppositions are: but by How much the Rubbish is, in this world of chaffe, be soe much the more Orient in the Eys of God like a Singular Jewel. Nor is this Meditation quickly to be over. For by how much the more Desolate the world is left by Revolting Sinners, by how much the Greater the Number is of owls and Dragons that Defile it with their manners, by How much the more is an inEstimable man in the Midst of Dragons; that being wise and Holy walketh with God in the Enjoyments of His works. Their thoughts are fled, they have left it Desolate and made the world a wildernes by neglecting to Consider the wisdom and power of Him that made it. And therefore doth his soul more Earnestly Desire one to Contemplat the Glory and Goodness that he hath placed in it.

15

God hath use now for an Holy man, which maketh Him more precious then the Golden wedge of Ophir, use for him Greater then what Angels are Admitted to, more Sublime then any Employment that Adam had in Eden, namely the calling of those wonderfull ones to their Ancient possessions, to the Enjoyment of God, to their Inheritance of the world, to the Recovery of their Blessedness, and to the Similitude of God in the possession of Greater Things then Adam Enjoyd. Hell from beneath, and the joy of their returne, Highly Magnifie and Advance their office.

Select Meditations, II

1 Isaiah 60.2.
2 Romans 8.28.

16

All Harsh and Sour Virtues came in by Sin

All *Harsh* and *Sour* Virtues came in by Sin: and we are to look upon them, not as Vertues intended by God and Nature, but occasioned afterwards, because their Use and Existence is accidental.[1]. . .

When we fell into Sin, we let Death and Misery into the World, contracted shame and guilt upon our selves, defiled our Nature with Deformities and Diseases, and made many Things upon that Occasion, necessary to our Happiness, that before were not so: And whereas they have a Mixture of *Bitterness* and *Advantage* in them, we may thank our selves for the *Bitterness*, and GOD for the *Advantage*: For as we by Sin forfeited our *Happiness*, so a new Obedience, consisting in the practice of proper Vertues, was necessary to recover it. Vertues, whose Names and Natures were of another kind, and never heard of before: All which we must look upon, not as Food, but Physick, and considering them under the notion of Remedies, not admire that there should be something in them Distasteful to Sence, tho they are now, when their Occasions are known, infinitely agreeable to Reason.

They are but an *Æquivocal* Offspring of the Fall: Sin could never beget such beautiful Children, as Meekness, Repentance, Patience, Alms-Deeds, Self Denyal, Submission and Resignation to the Divine Will, Fortitude, Contentment in all Estates, &c.

While there was no Sin, there was no need of *Penitence*; while there was no *Pain* or Misery, no *Patience*; Without wrongs and Injuries there is no use of *Meekness*; nor place for *Alms-Deeds*, where there is no *Poverty*: no Courage, where are no Enemies. In *Eden* there was no ignorance, nor any Supernatural Verities to be confirmed by Miracles; Apostles therefore and Prophets, Ministers and Doctors were superfluous there, and so were Tythes and Temples, Schools of Learning,

Masters and Tutors, together with the unsavoury Duty incumbent on Parents to chastise their Children. For as all would have been instructed by the Light of Nature, so had all been Innocent, and Just, and Regular: Whereupon no Magistrate had been needful to put any to Shame, no Courts of Judicature, nor Lawyers in the World. No Buying and Selling, and thereupon no commutative Justice, because the Blessed Earth had naturally been fertile, and abounded with rich and Glorious Provisions: Nakedness had been the Splendor and Ornament of Men, as it will be in Heaven: the Glorious Universe had been their common House and Temple, their Bodies fited for all Seasons, no Alien or Stranger, no Want, Distress, or War, but all Peace, and Plenty, and Prosperity; all Pleasure, and all Fellow Citizens throughout the World. Masters and Servants had been unknown, had we continued in that Estate, all had enjoyed the Liberty of Kings, and there had been no Dominion, but that of Husbands and Fathers, a Dominion as full of sweetness, as so gentle and free a Relation importeth. I can see no Use that there had been of *Trades* and Occupations, onely the pleasant Diversion that *Adam* had in dressing the Garden, and the consequents of that: I am sure there had been no Funeral *Pomps*, no *Sickness*, *Physick*, or *Physician*. There had been no *Faith* in the *Incarnation* of the Son of God, because no occasion for that Incarnation; no Ceremonial *Law of Moses*, no *Baptism*, nor *Lords Supper*; because there were no supernatural Mysteries to be Typified, but the clear Light of a Diviner Reason, and a free Communion with God in the Right discharge of those Vertues, Divine and Moral, which naturally belong to the Estate of Innocency. All which Original and Primitive Vertues ought now to continue, as it were the Face of Religion beneath that *Mask* or *Vizor* of Ordinances and new Duties, which Sin and Corruption hath put upon it; Tho we have forgotten the Vertues of our first Estate, and are apt now to terrifie our selves with that *Disguise*, wherewith we have concealed their Beauty, by regarding only the Vertues, that were occasioned by Sin and Misery.

It is a great Error to mistake the *Vizor* for the *Face*, and no less to stick in the outward *Kind* and Appearance of things; mistaking the Alterations and Additions that are made upon the Fall of Man, for the whole Business of Religion. And yet this new Constellation of Vertues, that appeareth aboveboard, is almost the only thing talked of and understood in the World. Whence it is that the other Duties, which are the *Soul* of Piety, being unknown, and the *Reason* of these together with their Original and Occasion, unseen; Religion appears like a sour and ungratefull Thing to the World, impertinent to bliss, and void of

Reason; Whereupon GOD is suspected and hated, Enmity against GOD and *Atheism* being brought into, and entertained in the World. . . .

Let it be your Care to dive to the Bottom of true Religion, and not suffer your Eyes to be Dazled with its Superficial Appearance. Rest not in the *Helps* and *Remedies* that it bringeth, but search for the Hidden Manna, the substantial Food underneath, the Satisfaction of all Wishes and Desires, the true and Cœlestial Pleasures, the Causes of Love, and Praise, and Thanksgiving founded in the Manifestations of Gods Eternal favour, especially in the Ends, for the sake of which all Helps and Remedies are prepared. For it is exceeding true, that *his Laws are Sweeter then the Hony and the Hony Comb, and far more precious then thousands of Gold and Silver.*[2]

Christian Ethicks, Ch. 1.

1 Subsidiary rather than happening by chance.
2 Psalm 19.10.

17

A Wise man on Earth might hav his Conversation in Heaven

. . . I knew not what more to Desire, but that as I was seated in a World of Delights & Treasures I should be carefull to prize them, which was in the Root & seed all that my Religion required. I saw that I was a Son of God, his Image & friend, made to live in Communion with him, & called to sit and to reign in his Throne as the Scriptures testified: And that he who loved me thus much in mine Innocency, might possibly redeem me being faln into Sin: & that my Redemption by the Death of his Son, was not more Wonderfull then Glorious, seeing I was restored by it to the fruition & Enjoyment of all his Treasures. That as my Sin was infinitly Black in Transgressing the Law of a GOD so Gracious, his mercy was no less infinit in passing by the Crime of a Delinquent so highly obliged, but infinitly to be admired & far more infinitly Glorious. That his Love was true, & that all mankind was corrupted, being dead in Sins & Trespasses, That the means of Grace were most truly Beautifull necessary & precious. For that all men had need to be enlightened and restored. That the persons of men being so highly exalted in the Bosom of God, were as highly to be reverenced honored & beloved. That all other things were well, & I only out of Frame & that therfore my Business was to correct & amend my self: a Business very difficult, but reduced into litle Room finaly that *All Things* work together for Good to them that love God,[1] & twas impossible to be further miserable than we swerved from the Paths of Wisdom & Holiness: that in his presence there was fulness of Joy, & that a Wise man on Earth might hav his Conversation[2] in Heaven.

Commentaries of Heaven, 'All Things'

1 Romans 8.28.
2 Manner of life.

4

Christian Liberty

Where 'enjoying the world', 'felicity' and the promise of salvation sparkle on the surface of Traherne's writing, human freedom, agency and act are the deep pools beneath. In his encyclopedic *Commentaries of Heaven*, Traherne gives 13 pages (26 columns in total) to the consideration of 'Act': divine act, kinds of actions, the necessity of act, the ceaselessness of activity, in articles and poems that spill one into the next – 'Act', 'Action', 'Activity' – each seeming to breed another. Several chapters in *Christian Ethicks* explore the nature of liberty, while in *Centuries* the importance of freedom is alluded to in statements such as 'all creation waits on our liberty'. Questions of human freedom are intimately connected with his larger arguments on the capacity of the soul, the dignity of man and his place in the universe. In *Commentaries of Heaven* he writes: 'A soul in Act is all that ere can be . . . Image and Mirror of [God]self it is, His lovly Bride the Substance of His bliss' (*COH*, 'Act', III). Without the power to choose and to act we can never be fit for heaven; we can never, in the story of redemption in which God seeks the soul as lover, be a suitable bride. It is not surprising then that in various ways in many of his works he asks the question: how free are we?

Nowhere is this question explored in more detail than in *A Sober View of Dr Twisse*, in which the Calvinist/Arminian debate goes under the microscope of his mind, its main and secondary arguments dissected and examined at length. Whereas later Calvinism asserted that God had predestined or chosen some (the elect) for salvation, Arminians (after the Dutch theologian Jacobus Arminius) believed in the universality of redemption, insisting that Christ died for all (ironically, a claim to which Calvin too would have assented) and that, according to free will, man had the capacity to access or spurn God's grace. The debate, read today largely as a philosophical discussion of human freedom, agency and act, was in its own day also a debate about national identity, the future shape of the church and of the nation. For Traherne and his contemporaries, of course, philosophy, theology and politics were not discrete categories; the modern call we sometimes hear to keep religion out of politics and politics out of religion and both of them out of philosophy would have sounded deeply suspect, in fact impossible.

Both Puritans and their opponents used Calvin: Thomas Cartwright and John Whitgift, for example, from opposite poles quote Calvin against each other in the sixteenth century. 'Calvinism' can be an ambiguous term. Do we mean by it the teachings of Calvin or the later more extreme distillations of his thought that he would have eschewed? For Calvin himself absolute predestination was not the major organizing principle that it became for later Calvinists. Where Calvinism under Elizabeth I and James I was part of the theological mainstream in England (there were at least 39 editions of the Geneva Bible published in England between 1579 and 1615, all of which had a predestinarian catechism bound with them; during the 1590s the archbishops of York and Canterbury endorsed absolute predestination; Calvinist teachings abounded in the universities; at the grassroots level, it was common to refer to oneself in a will as 'an elect saint'), in the hands of men like William Prynne and William Perkins Calvinism became casuitical, encouraging intense self-scrutiny and speculations about true and counterfeit faith. As the historian Patrick Collinson puts it, 'it both fed into and fed upon that devout anxiety about eternal destinies . . . to become an enervating obsession'.[169] Then, too, it was an international movement, with writings by no means going in one direction only, from Geneva outwards. English Calvinists exerted their own influence on the Continent. By the time Traherne was ten years old the writings of William Perkins had been translated into Czech, French, Spanish, Dutch and German.[170] By the time Traherne was an adult Calvinism had evolved into something Calvin himself might not have recognized.

169 Patrick Collinson, 'England and International Calvinism', in *From Cranmer to Sancroft*, London: Hambledon Continuum, 2006, p. 95. The casuitical nature of later Calvinist discussion can be seen in titles such as William Perkins' *A case of conscience, the greatest that ever was: How a man may know whether he be the child of God or no* (1592), or *A Golden Chain* (1591), which includes a diagram or table of the causes of salvation and damnation.

170 For a fuller and recent account of international Calvinism see Collinson, *From Cranmer to Sancroft*. See also R. T. Kendall, *Calvin and English Calvinism to 1649*, Carlisle: Paternoster, 1997; Basil Hall, 'Calvin against the Calvinists', in G. Duffield, ed., *John Calvin*, Appleford: Courtenay Press, 1966, pp. 19–37.

Throughout the sixteenth and seventeenth centuries Calvinist/Arminian questions were a matter of political life and death. Criticism of Protestant orthodoxies might be construed as a lack of patriotism, or sympathy for foreign Catholic powers. Careers, livelihoods, even lives themselves stood in the balance. The language that surrounds these freedom debates is some of the most vociferous of the seventeenth century. And in this Traherne is no exception.

Debate was fierce in print and in pulpits, in some cases within the same pulpit. One example of this is the famous 'Temple Debate' in which Richard Hooker, Master of the Temple, shared the pulpit of the Temple Church with Walter Travers (assistant to the Master). While Hooker propounded in the mornings a theology rooted in the fathers of the Primitive Church, reasoned experience and scripture, Travers in the afternoon hammered home a radical form of Calvinism. According to the seventeenth-century historian Thomas Fuller, 'the pulpit rang pure Canterbury in the morning and pure Geneva in the afternoon'. And the preachers were cousins. It is no wonder that individual thinkers sometimes warred within themselves when it came to this question.

Traherne himself seems torn, on the one hand admitting in *A Sober View* that as part of the Thirty-Nine Articles the doctrine of predestination is admissible, while also siding with Henry Hammond, 'one of the Most Orthodox Divines that ever this Nation Produced, Equaly Eminent in Prudence and Modesty, while he is Singularly learned and Judicious abov measure' (*SV*, VI, ll. 3–5) and his work *A Pacifick Discourse* in which Hammond argues in favour of universal redemption. Hammond's tenets are 'perfectly consonant to the Doctrine of the Church of England, which being rightly understood is the most Wholsom and Excellent in the World' (*SV*, IV, ll. 37–9), insists Traherne. All people are redeemed and God deals with them as free agents desiring voluntary obedience. Yet he also claims that the modest Calvinist Richard Sanderson has the edge on Hammond because Sanderson conforms more perfectly to the Church of England's teachings 'for he that denieth the Article of Election, loppeth away one great Branch from the Doctrine of the Ch. of England: as he that denieth the Gift of Liberty doth violate a great part of Experience and Reason' (*SV*, VII, ll. 19–22). As Traherne admits, 'all verity fitteth in the Golden Mean: and to erre on either Extreme is Equally Dangerous' (*SV*, VI, ll. 44–5). Traherne is never comfortable, however, with the term 'reprobate' and he falls back again and again on universalist scriptures, such as 'Whosoever believeth on him shall be saved' (*SV*, XXV) and 'God is good to all and his mercies are over all his works' (*SV*, XXVIII). It is interesting to note that although the title of his Calvinist/Arminian work, *A Sober View of Dr Twisse*, would lead one to expect a disquisition of staunch Calvinism, Traherne in fact takes leave of Calvinist Twisse early on in the work, devoting a disproportionate number of sections to the more moderate views of Sanderson and Hammond. The important dialogue of the work is, in fact, not absolute predestination, but this 'amicable and lovely contention' between universalism and moderate Calvinism.

Calvinism remained the dominant religious model in England throughout the first two decades of the seventeenth century. So extreme were some of its tenets that more moderate thinkers were driven into the arms of Rome. One such was the Cambridge scholar Benjamin Carier, son of a Protestant preacher, whose study of the ancient church fathers and of church history led him to conclude that the largely Calvinist Church of England had made both priests and sacraments redundant and that it would not be long before they made the king so too. He wrote a warning to the king: 'I beseech Your Majestie lett not Calvin's "church of the predestined" deceave you.' Calvinism was unfit 'to keepe subjects in obedience to their sovereigns' for soon 'they will openly maintayne that God hath as well predestinated men to be trayters as to be kinges.'[171] The move away from extreme Calvinism begun during King James' reign grew stronger under Charles II, whose pro-Catholic leanings became too strong for some of his supporters. Traherne's patron Sir Orlando Bridgeman, for example, was one who, faced with the choice between king and conscience, chose the latter and fell from royal favour. Traherne was with Bridgeman in this fall; he dedicated *Roman Forgeries*, his first published work, to Bridgeman, thus aligning himself publicly with his ousted patron. This, coupled with his stated acceptance of some form of predestination in *A Sober View*, suggests that Traherne could never entirely leave behind the Calvinist doctrines of his Puritan days, despite his frequent attempts to qualify and moderate the more extreme interpretations of Calvinism. Despite his attraction to universalist texts and his insistence that God's love extended to all, it is almost as if, in predestination, he assented mentally to a doctrine that his heart would not embrace. He consents to the doctrine of his church, but a heartsong of mercy and grace throbs through the lines of his writings.

In the midst of this philosophical, political and theological turmoil,

171 Benjamin Carier, *A Treatise written by Mr doctour Carier*, Liege: 1640.

what are we to make of Arminianism? Was it simply a backlash corrective to Calvinist excesses or was it an attempt, as its critics believed, to
return the nation to popery?

John Donne, in November 1629, preached against men who

> will abridge and contract the large mercies of God in Christ . . . men
> that are loth that God should speak so loud as to say 'He would have
> all men saved', and loth that Christ should spread his armies or shed
> his blood in such a compasse as might fall upon all men that think
> no sin can hurt them because they are elect and that every sin makes
> every other man a reprobate. But with the Lord there is *copiosa
> redemptio*, plentifull redemption, and an overflowing cup of mercy.[172]

You can hear a distinct fatigue with the Calvinist obsession to determine
who is in and who is out, and a deep longing for generosity and
mercy in matters eternal. Whereas the university presses were almost
exclusively Calvinist before 1624, Arminian works gradually began to
appear so that by 1635, as Nicholas Tyacke notes, the publishing
situation in England was transformed. At least nine books printed in
this year were favourable to Arminian doctrine, the most notable being
Samuel Hoard's *God's Love to Mankind* (1633), which became one of
the primary texts for Traherne's *A Sober View of Dr Twisse*.[173]

There were philosophical implications too, in the debate: questions
concerning fate and destiny that cut to the heart of how one understood
one's human situation. In *Centuries*, Traherne seems to side with
human freedom. 'O infinite liberality of God the Father! O admirable
and supreme Felicity of Man! To whom it is given to have what he
desires, and to be what he wisheth,' writes Traherne, quoting the renaissance humanist Pico della Mirandola (C, IV, 77). Pico goes too far,
admits Traherne, but the human person does carry within the power
for change. He has power to choose whatever he wishes – he may
choose to become one spirit with God; 'by choosing a man may be
turned and converted into Love' (C, IV, 80). The reforming force of
Calvinism had been to seize authority from the medieval church and

172 *Sermons*, IX, 119.
173 The texts to which Traherne refers in *A Sober View* are Samuel Hoard's
*Gods love to mankind. Manifested by dis-prooving his absolute decree for their
damnation* (1633, 1656, 1658); William Twisse's posthumous *The riches of Gods
love*, which answers Hoard (1653); and Henry Hammond's *Pacific Discourse*
(1660), containing long extracts from a letter by Sanderson.

to restore unto God God's rightful place as initiator and determiner. Hence the importance of God's eternal decrees: God ordered, God chose, according to divine foreknowledge. But the more extreme Calvinism became, the more Arminianism seemed a viable corrective to those extremes. Arminianism placed some of the initiative with the individual; more importantly it insisted that grace was available to all. William Laud, perhaps the best-known Arminian voice in England, elevated the role of the sacraments to effectively supplant the grace of predestination. God, through the sacraments, retained his place as initiator, and humans retained their God-given power to choose, to accept or reject what God offered to all.

For Laud, as for many others, extreme Calvinism threatened not just human freedom but the efficaciousness of Christ's sacrifice. As Thomas Jackson, one of Traherne's sources, wrote, those in the Church of England who taught that Christ died for none but the elect restricted the sufficiency of Christ's sacrifice to 'some sorts of men', when in fact Christ 'redeemed not only every one of us in particular, but all mankind'.[174] Like Jackson, Traherne is uncomfortable with doctrines that seem to limit God's love and grace. In *A Sober View* Traherne seems less passionate about determining who is saved and who is damned than he is with determining how beneficial or detrimental the doctrine of predestination may be to persons in their relationship with God. As we have seen, the doctrine of predestination was an attempt to wrest power from the medieval church and give it back to God. *God* acted, chose, determined, initiated, decreed. Traherne can see the necessity for this, but he can also see the danger in the doctrine of predestination: that some people will come to believe that God chooses to hate some and prefer others. This implication of the doctrine never sits well with him. He cannot escape the fundamental belief that God is love, delighting in its object's happiness. 'The first thing the Devil persuaded our first Parents in Paradise was that God did not love them Enough,' he insists.

God's longing for us, our freedom and choice, those refrains of felicity so familiar to us from *Centuries* and the poetry are, after all, here too, like a current that pulls him back again and again to the shore of God's goodness. Underneath the technical language and the intense attention to fine points of doctrine, giving meaning to his passion for a national church, there is the familiar base note of the intimate and personal, a God who loves and seeks to be loved by us. Even at his

174 Jackson, *Works*, VIII, 217–18.

most theologically technical, and publicly disputational, Traherne is not far from this refrain.

I call this chapter 'Christian Liberty' rather than liberty. Not the radical liberty of Renaissance humanism as it is sometimes read from Pico's *Oratio*, but the freedom of obedience. Not freedom from, that looks over its shoulder in flight, but freedom unto, freedom to do, to act, to be and to become in accordance with God's generous design. Here, in exploring Christian freedom, we approach Traherne's pneumatology: salvation from becomes salvation for. Good Friday moves on to Easter and to Pentecost. We are made for union with God: in all his intricate and passionate discussion of Calvinism, Traherne never forgets this vision; it is what keeps him from falling into any extreme. Like Richard Hooker, he sees God's power and wisdom in all things, in the created world and in humankind made in God's image. C. S. Lewis wrote of Hooker:

> Every great system offers us a model of the universe; Hooker's model has unsurpassed grace and majesty . . . Few model universes are more filled – one might say, drenched – with the Deity than his. 'All things that are of God,' and only sin is not, 'have God in them and they in himself likewise, and yet their substance and his are wholly different.' God is unspeakably transcendent; but also unspeakably immanent.[175]

Such is Traherne's model; it is a model in which finely drawn lines of eternally 'elect' and 'reprobate' do not sit easily.

Traherne's high view of humanity and his understanding of the dynamic of desire that is central to the relationship between God and the individual leads him to a high view of agency. It is true that Traherne is much concerned with the individual – what you can do, what you can become, how amazing the human soul is. But all of these meditations are drawn back to the shore by the tidal pull of relationality in his work. We are for and to each other for ever. The social critique in Traherne is implicit throughout his work; it is there in the admonitions to enjoy the world (everything serves you and it serves your neighbour and it serves you in serving him and him in serving you) and in his insatiable quest for felicity (which is found in the communion of souls), as it is in the occasional morsels that motivate to specific charitable and sacrificial actions. In an ideology that asks us to read every desire

175 C. S. Lewis, *English Literature in the Sixteenth Century, excluding drama*, Oxford, 1954, p. 460.

less as a need to possess and more as a call to appreciate the depth of our interconnectedness with each other and with all of creation, delineated discussions of equality, justice and equitable wealth dispersal seem otiose. The sparseness of his admonitions on matters of social wrongs indicates not a neglect of the subject but a wish to avoid stating the blindingly obvious. Freedom in Traherne is always much more about freedom for and freedom to rather than freedom from.

The Calvinist/Arminian question is one that has not gone away. Although the political heat may have gone out of the argument, the philosophical conundrum remains. Recent studies such as Millard Erickson's *What Does God Know and When Does He Know It?*, or Linda Zagzebski's 'Recent Work on Divine Foreknowledge and Free Will' in *The Oxford Handbook of Free Will*, are just a few among the many new works that revisit the Calvinist questions of divine foreknowledge and human freedom with an urgency some might scarcely expect in our individualistic age. Has our generational unease with authority revealed yawning theological gaps that cause us to seek a new certainty? Like our own age, the thinkers of the seventeenth century had gained certain freedoms and lost precious certainties. There was a need for new theological, social and political maps. Traherne, along with so many of his fellow theologians, was in the thick of these debates.

How free are we? Traherne's passion for his national church keeps him technically within the bounds of moderate predestinarian doctrine, but within that framework his recurring impetus is always towards human freedom and human choice. He constantly urges his readers to become, to unlearn, to be reborn, to choose, to enjoy, to love, to live. For him freedom is not about the lack of superficial restraint, but about the correct poise of the soul. It is not about an unharnessed horse or an unfettered will, but about having a mind unclouded by custom, vanity, pride, about clarity of vision and buoyancy of spirit. This is what makes his radical version of freedom utterly unstoppable. It is founded in bounty and funded from deep pools of love. We are totally free, Traherne would argue, within the law of Love which, as he writes in *The Kingdom of God*, is 'at once a freedom from all law, and the severest law in the World, but a willing and delightfull law of the most constraining, and Indispensable Necessitie.'[176]

---

176 *KOG*, Ch. 11, ll. 17–19.

The extracts

I

Jacob have I loved, Esau have I hated

It is my Wonder therfore how it should be possible for men to pinch so hard upon one Text,[1] and to squeeze Blood and Desperation and Terror out of it, and Odiousnesse and Injustice and Tyranny with whatsoever els is evil, while there is no Expression in the Bible like it; making a thousand other places vail to this one, and doing violence to them all rather then unto this. While indeed they do violence to this and then all subvert God's Kingdom, deface his Glory, Destroy and abolish the Nature of things, I may say, all things. For Law, Reward, Punishment, Gospel, Christ, Redemption, Sin, Justice, God, Heaven, and Happiness, are all Changed, and touched and shaken (as much as man can shake) by this Exposition: while the Place may safely and clearly be understood in the Light of Truth, which you here have seen. Therfore I say remember, which way ever you interpret it: Whether of Hatred and Wrath laying Waste Esau at last for his Sins; or a less degree of Love in passing over Esau, when Jacob was illuminated and irresistibly called, both which are agreeable, and both true, and both perhaps intended and meant in the place: be sure I say to believ firmly that Esau was once an Object of God's Love, and that evry man Primitively and Originaly is so. For that Doctrine which some suck from this Text, That God from all Eternity simply and without Caus hateth any, and that there are Multitudes of Reprobates so hated, is as Damnable poyson as can that way be put into the mouth of a Christian.

I never Knew any Person in Despair in my Life, but this Opinion was the Ground of his Despair. Nor can any man do the Devil greater Service then by teaching this Doctrine. The first thing the Devil persuaded our first Parents in Paradise was that God did not love them Enough: That he envied their Perfection, and kept som thing from them that it was good to know. And ever since he tempteth us to unbelief. And chiefly assaulteth our Faith here. He cannot endure that we should believ that *God is Love*.² He would fain have us believ he loveth us not. And when we believ that, he knoweth what follows Naturaly, the Poyson is taken, the seed is sowen, the Enemy hath don it; and it will grow up in Alienation and Enmity against him. Besides all which this Opinion hindereth the knowledge of God in the World: For *God is Love*: and Love is infinit in Goodness and Bounty; Love delighteth in its object's Happiness; Love is the Fountain of all Joys; Love is Communicative and Distributive of its Treasures; Lov is infinit in its Riches: Love designes the Exaltation of its Creature: Love is Holy, Wise, and Glorious: Love is that Joy and Prais of All. *In his Presence there is fulness of Joy, and at his right hand there are Pleasures forever more*.³ All this by that sour and bitter Doctrine of Gods Eternal Hatred, misrepresenting his Decrees, is obscured and withdrawn, or made in effectual; so that Men, while they ought to Delight in his Highness, and to come with Joy and Melody into his Presence, Celebrating his Praises; being enslaved, and made Servile in their Spirits, through fear and Dread, they first think basely of themselvs and dislike GOD, and then are presently or finally estranged from him.

A Sober View of Dr Twisse, XXVIII

1 Traherne is referring to Malachi 1.3, quoted by St Paul in Romans 9.13, a text that had become a key text of arch-Calvinism.
2 1 John 4.7–8.
3 Psalm 16.11.

2

He Cheerfully committed the World to his Creatures Ingenuitie

But his Goodness was Infinit, and designed to Make them so perfect, that they should be Divine and Heavenly, the most GODLIKE and Celestial Things that were possible. Being therfore himself a free Agent, Glorious and Holy, becaus he Acted by an inward principle, and was good freely, without Necessity, Compulsion or constraint; He adventured to make high Creatures like himself, that might Act freely That they might be Divine and Holy too, the springs and fountains of Excellent Actions, Admirers, Honorers, Adorers, and Praisers, Lords, and Lovers, Friends and Sons, most high and Admirable Persons abov the reach of Fate after the Similitude of the Deitie, and able to pleas the Deitie in Works of Righteousness, and Wisdom like his own: In works of Goodness and Kindness, in Acts Voluntarie Gratitude, that they might be Glorious and Blessed, while he Delighted in them and Enjoyed them for ever. To constrain them, was to dishonor them, and to make them Necessary Agents, was to make them Engines and Mecanical Instruments, Dead, and Passiv moved by another, not the Sons of God, nor in the Divine Image: neither free, nor capable of Glory. For this cause he made them free, and determined to Entrust them with the use of Libertie, that they might pleas him with a liberal and free Behavior Infinitly desiring their Perfection; not at all intending that they should use it ill, but Earnestly serving them in the Regular and pious use of that Infinit power, which was indeed the Extreme Height of his favor, and the very Crown and perfection of all his Gifts, to be Wise, Holy, Glorious, and Eternaly Blessed. For by this Means he adventured the possibilitie of a Sin into his Creatures Hands, which he Infinitly hated; meerly that by Governing themselvs well, and Acting right, they might become Wise, as the Angels of GOD, and be the Authors of Actions, which God doth Infinitly prize, and without which all his other Works would be insignificant. Thus his Infinit Goodness, by the utmost Excess of its perfection, made Evil possible, It self neither doing, nor intending Evil; but designing the Imitation of it self, and the Beauty of the Universe. For it put the Gate of Fate into the Hand of its Creature, and made it able to let in Sin, and Hell and Death, with all Sorts of Miseries, and Deformities into the World; or to Crown the Works of God with Excellent Actions, which God Esteemed more then thousands of Rams, and tens of thousands of Rivers of Oyl;[1] and which (tho this is very incredible) he more Valueth then Heavens full of Gold, or the Earth it self full of all its Treasures. For all Inanimate Creatures, all Mechanical and Necessary Agents, the sea, the Sun, the Heavens, and the Earth were but Dung in comparison of these free Agents, which were made Lords of the residue and are the trees of Righteousness, whose Actions are the fruits of his Vineyard. All obligations are but Dung set to the Root of these Trees. For ye are Gods Husbandry ye are Gods Building.[2] Now evry Man Knows that the fruits are more precious then the Lands, more Sweet and Amiable, more High and Delightfull. Since therfore it is more Blessed to giv then to receiv,[3] how much more are we bound to God, that we are able to return Works of our own unto him, more Delightfull then all his unto us, not to Say Him. For his Works cannot pleas him Till we Enable him by our Ingenuitie and Pietie to delight in us, and crown us with Complacency.[4] No Plantation pleaseth the owner without its fruits. For the Earth which drinketh in the Rain which cometh oft upon it, and bringeth forth Herbs meet for them by whom it is dressed, receiveth Blessing from God, But that which beareth Thorns, and Briers is rejected, and is nigh unto cursing, whose End is to be burned. What profit is there of all the World, if it be barren and unfruitfull?

God therfore with Infinit Care, made Seasonable and Mighty provisions; such and so many as might possibly Consist with the Glory of his Creature, (and not overthrow the Righteousness of his Kingdom) to secure in us the right use of our Libertie. And having made it Morally Impossible, there should be any Sin, or Evil, notwithstanding the Wills he bestowed on them; He Cheerfully committed the World to his Creatures Ingenuitie, hoping and expecting a Return of Glorious Delights and Thanksgivings, in Pietie and Godliness.

The Kingdom of God, Ch. 8

1 Micah 6.7.
2 1 Corinthians 3.9.
3 Acts 20.35.
4 Tranquil pleasure.

3

Whatever invades our Liberty, destroys it

From GODS Love of Righteous Action it proceedeth, that he made ours so compleatly capable of becoming Righteous, and that he adventured a Power into our Hands of offending. It is a strange thing, that the Excess of the Hatred of all Sin should make Sin possible, and that the most perfect Righteousness should be the Accidental Cause of Unrighteousness. But yet it is so, an infinite Love to the Best of all Possible Things made the worst of all things that could be possible . . .

To make Creatures infinitely free and leave them to their Liberty is one of the Best of all Possible Things; and so necessary that no Kingdome of Righteousness could be without it. For in every Kingdome there are subjects capable of Laws, and Rewards, and Punishments. And these must be free Agents. There is no Kingdome of Stones nor of Trees, nor of Stars; only a Kingdome of Men and Angels. Who were they divested of their Liberty would be reduced to the Estate of Stones and Trees; neither capable of Righteous Actions, nor able to Honor, or to Love, or praise: without which Operations all inferior Creatures and meer Natural Agents would be totally Useless. So that all the Glory of the World depends on the Liberty of Men and Angels: and therefore GOD gave it to them, because he delighted in the Perfection of his Creatures: tho he very well knew there would be the Hazzard of their abusing it, (and of Sin in that abuse) when they had received it. The abuse of it he infinitely hated yet could not prevent it, without being Guilty of a Greater Evil. He infinitely hated it, because those Actions of Love and Honor which should spring from the right use of it, were the onely fair off-spring, for the sake of which the whole World was made, and without the right use of their Liberty all Creatures, Angels and Souls would be in vain: he could not Prevent it without being himself Guilty of what in them he abhorred.

For himself to be Guilty, was the worst of Evils, and absolutely impossible. Twas better let them make their Power vain themselves, then do so himself. For the Author of that vanity, be it who it will, is the Author of the Sin. If *they* would make it vain, *He* could not help it, for him to divest them of the use of Liberty after he had given it, was as inconsistent with himself, as it was with their Beauty to abuse it: the Act of giving it by taking it away being made vain. He infinitely hated that the Liberty should be frustrated, which he gave unto men, for their more perfect Glory: he laid all Obligations upon them to use it well, and deterred them (as much as was possible) from abusing it, but would not transfer their fault upon himself, because he fore saw they were about to do it; which he certainly had done, had he made their Power vain *himself*, after he had given it. Either to refuse to give the Power, or Having given it, to interpose and determine it without their Consent, was alike detrimental to the whole Creation. For indeed it is impossible, that he by determining their Wills, should make them the Authors of Righteous Actions, which of all things in the World he most desired. There is as much Difference between a Willing Act of the Soul it self, and an Action forced on the Will, determined by another, as there is between a man that is dragged to the Altar, whether he will or no, and the man that comes with all his Heart with musick and Dancing to offer sacrifice. There is Joy, and Honour, and Love in the one, fear and constraint, and shame in the other. That GOD should not be able to deserve our Love, unless he himself made us to Love him by violence, is the Greatest Dishonour to him in the World: Nor is it any Glory or Reputation for us, who are such sorry Stewards, that we cannot be entrusted with a little Liberty, but we must needs abuse it.

GOD adventured the possibility of sinning into our hands, which he infinitely hated, that he might have the Possibility of Righteous Actions, which he infinitely Loved. . . .

That we might do these in a Righteous Manner he placed us in a mean Estate of Liberty and Tryal, not like that of Liberty in *Heaven* where the Object will determine our Wills by its Amiableness, but in the Liberty of *Eden*, where we had absolute Power to do as we pleased, and might determine our Wills our selves infinitely, desiring and Delighting in the Righteous use of it, hating and avoiding by infinite Cautions and Provisions all the unjust Actions that could spring from it. . . . To be Good, to be Holy, to be Righteous is freely to delight in Excellent Actions, which unless we do of our own Accord no External Power whatsoever can make us, Good, or Holy, or Righteous: because no force of External Power can make us free; whatever it is that invades our Liberty, destroys it.

Christian Ethicks, Ch. 12

4

Extracts from *Roman Forgeries*

Dedication and 'Advertisement to the Reader'

To the Right Honorable Sir Orlando Bridgeman knight and Baronet One of his Majesties Most Honourable Privy Council; the Author Devoteth his best Services and Dedicateth the Use and Benefit of his Ensuing Labors.

[The title *Roman Forgeries* rightly suggests that the work is primarily concerned with questions of authenticity and authorship; for Traherne the point of asking those questions is so that one might determine authority. His gripe is not with Roman Catholic theology; he does not engage in criticism of Roman doctrine, biblical exegesis, religious devotion, practice or discipline except as it pertains to Roman supremacy and papal authority. This is what *Roman Forgeries* is all about – who should be in charge, and why. Antiquity, Unity, Succession, Veracity are all intimately linked in this quest for authentic authority. And so it is to Antiquity that Traherne first turns when he cites the early church father Irenaeus's guidelines for discovering heresy as his model for *Roman Forgeries* in his 'Advertisement to the Reader'.]

Irenaeus, *one of the most Ancient Fathers, Scholar to S. Polycarp*, S. *John*'s Disciple, in his Book against Heresies, giveth us four notable marks of their Authors: First, he sheweth how they Disguise their Opinions; *Errour never shews Itself*, saith he, *lest it should be taken naked; but is artificially adorned in a splendid Mantle, that it may appear truer than Truth it self, to the more unskilful.* 2. That *having Doctrines which the Prophets never preached, nor God taught, nor the Apostles delivered, they pretend unwritten Traditions: Ex non Scriptus legeuter*, as he phraseth it. 3. *They make a Rope of Sand, that they may not seem to want Witnesses, passing over the Order and series of Writings, and as much as in them lies, loosing the Members of the Truth, and dividing them from each other: for they chop and change, and making one thing of another, deceive many.* &. But that which I chiefly intend is the fourth; *They bring forth a vast multitude of Apocryphal and Spurious Writings, which them selves have feigned, to the amazement of Fools; and that those may admire them, that know not*

the Letters (or Records) *of the Truth*. How far the Papists have trodden
the foregoing Paths, it is not my purpose to unfold. Only the last, the
Heretical pravity of *Apocryphal* and *Spurious Books*; how much they
have been guilty of imposing on the World by feigned Records, I leave
to the evidence of ensuing Pages; which I heartily desire may be answerable to the Merit of so great a Cause.

The sin of forgery

Chapter 1

The Sin of *Forgery* is fitter to be ranked with Adultery, Theft, Perjury,
and Murder, than to be committed by *Priests* and *Prelates*: One *Act* of
it is a Crime to be punished by the *Judges*; what then is a whole *Life*
spent in many various and enormous Offences of that nature?

If a *Beggar* forge but a Pass, or a Petition, putting the Hands and
Seals of two *Justices of the Peace* to it, he is whipt, or clapt into the
Pillory, or marked for a Rogue, though he doth it only to Satisfie his
Hunger.

If a Leafe, a Bond, a Will, or a Deed of Gift be razed, or interlined
by Craft, it passeth for a Cheat; but if the whole be counterfeited, the
Crime is the greater.

If an Instrument be forged in the *Kings* Name, or his Seal counterfeited, and put to any *Patent*, without his privity and consent, it is High
Treason.

If any Records of Antiquity be defaced, or wilfully corrupted, relating
to the benefit of men, it is like the Crying Sin of *removing thy Neigh-
bours Landmark*, which *Solomon* censures in the *Proverbs*. But if those
Records appertain to the Right of Nations, the Peace of Mankind, or
the Publick Welfare of the World, the Sin is of more mysterious and
deeper nature.

. . . If the Records so counterfeited concern the Church, either in her
Customs or Laws, her Lands, or the limits of her Jurisdiction, the Order
of her Priests, or any other Spiritual or Ecclesiastical Affair besides
other sins contained in it, there is Superadded the Sin of *Sacriledge*.

The highest degree of Forgery is that of altering the *Holy Scriptures*;
because the Majesty offended being Infinite, as well as the Concernment, the Crime is the more heinous.

The highest, next under that, is to counterfeit *Rules* in the Names
of the *Apostles, Oecumenical Councils*, most glorious *Martyrs*, and

Primitive *Fathers*, that is, to make *Canons*, Letters, Books, and *Decrees* in their Names, of which they were not the Authors.

If the Church of Rome be guilty of this Crime, her *Antiquity* and *Tradition*, the two great Pillars upon which she standeth, are very *rotten*, and will moulder into nothing. (pp. 1–3)

Questions of authenticity and authorship: Isidore, Bishop of Spain

[Having disclosed as irregular the claim that the Bishop of Rome should have supremacy, Traherne sets out to investigate one of the earliest sources that backs that claim – the collection of councils supposedly compiled by Bishop Isidore (560–636) in 790. Traherne devotes much of the first six chapters of the *Roman Forgeries* to exploring the authorship and authenticity of the text attributed to Isidore; here are just a few examples of his work.]

. . . The *Roman Chair* being thus lifted up to the utmost Height it could well desire, care must be taken to secure its Exaltation, After many Secret Councils therefore, and powerful Methods used for its Establishment; for the increase of its Power and Glory, (furthered by the Luxury and Idleness of the Western Churches) . . . there came out a *collection of Councils and Decretal Epistles*, in the Name of *Isidore*, Bishop of *Hispalis*, about the year 790. In which book there are neatly interwoven a great company of forged Evidences, or feigned Records, tending all to the advancement of the Popes Chair, in a very various copious and Elaborate manner. (pp. 28–9)

[James Merlin and Isidore Hispalis (on whose work Merlin drew heavily) were two of the best-known collectors of the councils and Traherne takes great pains over their works. There is some confusion about Isidore, sometimes called Isidore Hispalensis, and later Isidore Mercator. Traherne maintains that once it was proven that Isidore Hispalensis could not have been the author, being long dead before events in the book occurred, another Isidore (Mercator) was invented in his place.]

James Merlin's pains was to publish *Isidore*, with some collections and Additions of his own. He positively affirmeth him to be that Famous *Isidore* of *Hispalis*, a Saint, a Bishop, and a Father of the Church: though as *Blondel* and Dr. *Reynolds* accurately observe,

S. *Isidore* of *Hispalis* was dead 40, 50, 60 years, before some things came to pass that are mentioned in that Book of the Councils.

Blondel in a Book of his, called *Pseudo Isidorus*, or Turrianus Vapulans, *Cap.2.* observes, how the lowest that write of *Isidores* death, fix it on the year 647. as *Vasaeus* in his Chronicle: Others on the year 643. as *Rodericus Toletanus Hist. lib. 2. cap. 18*. Or on the yeer 635. as the *proper Office of the Saints of Spain*: or on the year 636.

. . . Admit *Vasaeus* in the right, that *Isidore* lived till the year 647, yet the Book which is Fathered upon him, can be none of his; for it mentions things which come to pass long after. (from pp. 44–6)

[Still at pains to expose Isidore's work as a forgery, Traherne switches to a later argument between Dr Reynolds' work (Conf. Cap 8 Divis. 3) and Hart in which Reynolds challenges the Roman Catholic Hart about the impossibility of Isidore being the author of the collection attributed to him. As Traherne uses Roman texts to disprove Roman supremacy, so Reynolds also challenges Hart using Hart's own favourite author.]

. . . Dr *Reynolds* in his Conference with *Hart*, having smartly checked him for his *fourscore Bishops* out of one *Isidore*, asked him, *About what year of Christ* Isidore *did die? How doth Genebrard write?* (because Genebrard was *Hart*'s most admired Author.) He answereth, About the year 637. as he proveth out of *Vasaeus*. Asking him, *When the General Council of* Constantinople, *under* Agatho, *was kept?* He answereth, *In the year 681. or 682. or thereabouts. Then* Isidore *was dead above 40 years*, saith Reynolds, *before that General Council. He was*, saith Hart, *but what of that? Of that it doth follow, that the Preface written in* Isidores *name, and set before the Councils, to purchase credit to those Epistles, is a counterfeit, and not* Isidore's: *For in that Preface there is mention made of the General Council of* Constantinople, *held against Bishop* Macarius *and* Stephanus, *in the time of Pope* Agatho, *and the Emperour* Constantine: *which seeing it was held above 40 years after* Isidore *was dead, by* Genebrard's *own confession, by his own confession* Isidore *could not tell the fourscore Bishops of it. And so the 80 Bishops which* Turrian *hath found out in one* Isidore, *are dissolved all into one Conterfeit, abusing both the name of* Isidore, *and fourscore Bishops. Hart* was unable to answer him, and fled from the Point. (pp. 62–3)

[Traherne reaffirms his own commitment to and reverence for the ancient councils of the church.]

The *Councils*, and true Records, we Reverence with all Honour due to Antiquity: And for that very cause, we so much the more abhor that admixture of Dross and Clay, wherewith their Beauty is corrupted. Had we received the Councils sincerely from her, we should have blest the Tradition of the Church of *Rome* for her assistance therein: But now she loveth her self more than her Children, and the Pope (which is the Church Virtual) is so hard a Father, that he soweth Tares instead of Bread, and for Eggs feedeth us with Scorpians; We abhor her practices, and think it needful warily to examine, and consider her Traditions. (p. 89)

[Here as elsewhere Traherne makes it clear to his reader that he has examined these texts himself and has not simply written on the basis of hearsay. In fact, he goes so far as to record exactly whose copies of Isidore's councils he borrowed. His incredulity at the cheek of his opponents to reinvent a second Isidore, the authorship of the first having been disproved, is apparent.]

. . . As Merlin, (who was a Doctor of Divinity of Great Account) so likewise all the following *Collectors* among the Papists, derive their Streams from this *Isidore*, as their Fountain. And for this cause I was the more desirous to see the *Book*, which is very scarce to be found; and the more scarce, I suppose, because if the Fountain be unknown, a greater Majesty will accrue to the Streams. The Booksellers-Shops afforded me none: but at last I met with two of them; the one with the Learned Dr *Barlow*, *Margaret Professor*, and Provost of Queens College in *Oxford*, the other in the *Bodleian* Library: The one was Printed at *Collein*, *An.* 1530. The other at *Paris* beforementioned. Either had all, and both affirmed *Isidore Hispalensis* to be the Author.

Though some afterwards are careful to distinguish *Isidore Hispalensis* from *Isidore Mercator*. The one failing, the other obtruded as the Author of the Work: the latter Collectors unanimously leaving out *Hispalensis*, and calling him only by the Name of *Mercator*. But how the Name of *Isidore Mercator* should come before the Book, the Wisest Man in the World, I suppose, can scarcely *Divine*.

It is said, *that* Eulogius *Bishop of* Corduba *had a Brother, whose Name was* Isidore, *whose condition of Life was Banishment, whose Nation* Spain, *whose Trade was Merchandize: And that this Spanish Merchant flying out of his Country, upon the account of Religion, chose rather to intrust this most precious Treasure, which he had saved from the Lust of Barbarians, to the care of the Germans, than to expose*

it to the Rage of those Wasters and Destroyers wherewith Spain *was
at that time infested, as the Monks of* Mentz; *at least, who, upon is
having sojourned there, took occasion to put his Name before the Book
that was then in their hands, would have the World really believe.* This
is *Blondel*'s conjecture, which he raiseth from the real existence of such
an *Isidore.*

. . . For *morally* speaking, it is impossible, that a Merchant should
be the Author of it; especially at that time, when the Records lay
scattered perhaps in a hundred Libraries, and were all to be sought in
obscure *Manuscripts.* An Ass may be expected to meddle with an Harp,
as soon as a Merchant with the Mysterious Records of the Church.
How came *Lay-men* to be so Judicious? Had any Merchant so great a
Skill as this imports? It is improbable *fourscore Bishops* should know
it, much more that they should urge him to do that, which with their
own Learning and Function fitted them to do far better: Yet *Isidore* in
his Preface writeth this:

'. . . You Eighty Bishops who urged me to begin and perfect this
Work, ought to know, as ought all other Priests of the Lord also,
that we have found more than those 20 chapters of the Nicene
Council . . .'

It is a shame to the Church of *Rome*, that a Lay-man should be the
Fountain of all her Records: and that in very deed, the greater part of
them should be in no Manuscript nor Library in the World, being never
seen nor heard of till *Isidore* brought them out of *Spain*: that no man
can tell what *Isidore* made the Book, which is now the President, and
the sole storehouse of all their Collections, is a little infamous; especially
since they believed of old unanimously that the Bishop *Isidore* of *Hispalensis* was its ancient Author. (from pp. 90–3)

Questions of allegiance

[Traherne reaffirms his assertion that the Church has its origins in
Jerusalem, not Rome. Significantly here allegiance to Rome is a political
as well as a spiritual threat; whoever bears allegiance to chair higher
than the king's throne is not a reliable subject of the King.]

For the Christian Churches received their beginning from *Jerusalem*,
before the Church of *Rome* had any Being.

Consider it well, and you shall find this the removing of a *meer stone* of highest importance, an Encroachment upon the Territory of other Patriarchs, an Usurption of all Spiritual and Secular Power, to the subversion of Emperours, Kings and Councils.

For if all are to obey her, as Jesus Christ did his Eternal Father; if it be granted to the Roman Church, by a Singular Priviledge, to open and shut the Kingdom of Heaven to whom she will; if no King, Emperour or Council, hath power to judge the Pope, while he hath power to judge all; Kings, Emperours and Councils are made subject to him, and nothing can escape the Sublimity of his Cognizance.

Besides this *Treatise of the Primacy, Peter Crab* has 34 new *Canons of the Apostles* more than *Isidore* and *Merlin*: so that Antiquities are daily increasing in the Church of *Rome*, and Records are like Figs, *new* ones come up instead of the old ones. (pp. 108–9)

The excommunication of Africa

[At the sixth Council of Carthage in the sixth century, the whole of the African church was excommunicated because it protested at the right of Rome to have jurisdiction over Africa. Traherne holds this to be further evidence of the absurdity of supreme power being held by Rome. The Protestant claim against papal authority, far from being a recent innovation, is, he would argue, exactly what those early church fathers were also claiming. In refusing to accept supreme authority seated in Rome, the post-Reformation Protestants and the early church fathers of Africa hold hands, over the gap of hundreds of years, acting of one accord.]

He [Nicolinus] pretends that the African Fathers did not refuse the Primacy of *Rome*, but acknowledge its Supremacy, or its *Primacy over them* yet is all this but a copy of his countenance, a common flourish in the Frontspiece of their work: for if they submitted to the Popes *Primacy over them*, why should they be Excommunicated? He knows well enough, when we come close to the matter, that these *Rebellious Protestants*, and those *Catholick Fathers*, were of the same judgement, and acted the same thing. (p. 144)

[Traherne lampoons a claim that is backed by prejudiced witnesses. Janizaries were a Turkish military force in the 1330s made up of Christian youths taken as prisoners of war and retrained as Mohammedans.

Their strength grew until they became unruly and in 1826 were dissolved by the Sultan.

Perkin Warbeck was a pretender to the English throne during the reign of Henry VII. He claimed to be Richard of Shrewsbury, 1st Duke of York, younger son of Edward IV, but was in fact a Fleming born in Tournai in 1447. After several attempts at the throne, he was hanged as a traitor in 1499. This morsel of history had recently been brought to popular notice by the dramatist John Ford who had turned Warbeck's story into a play first performed in 1630. Here Traherne is tapping into both popular culture and political history and tainting the Roman church in shades of the turncoat and the traitor.]

Jesuits are the Popes *Janizaries*, and fit to be so imployed; And the *Vatican* is an admirable Storehouse doubtless for the Greek too, a very Pit of Witnesses for the Popes Supremacy. As if *Perkin Warbeck* should have brought Evidence out of his own Closet to prove himself King of *England*. (pp. 145–6)

From the Appendix

[Traherne claims that it is Rome who first departed from the true church by going to such absurd lengths to secure its supremacy when at the sixth Council of Carthage the whole African church was excommunicated because it protested at the right of Rome to have jurisdiction over Africa.]

The *Roman Church* is in a great strait; but she may thank her self. She threw her self into this *Peril*, by making herself a Schismatick, an Usurper, a Forger. She first breaks the *Rule*; and if the Pope and his Doctors about him be the *Roman Church*, as they certainly must needs be: (for all that depart from them shall be Schismaticks:) if the Head of the Church, and all the Members that cleave unto it, be the *Roman Church*, she first brake the *Rule*, and then forged Ancient Canons in the Name of the Nicene *Council*, to defend her Exorbitancy: she cut her self off from the true church in the Sixth Council of *Carthage*, by a perverse inveterate obstinancy; and to acquit her self afterwards, laid the Curse and Scandal upon others. She pretends, at least, that the most Holy Churches were Excommunicated; that 217 Bishops in a Sacred Council, *Alypius*, S. *Augustine*, *Aurelius*,[1] and all his Collegues, were *puffed up with pride* by the *Instigation of the Devil*, and accursed by a *Dreadful Excommunicator*: for so it is in the *Epistle of Boniface 2*.

to *Eulalius*. And now she hath nothing left to support her Enormity, but that *Greatness* alone, which by these forgeries she hath acquired and maintained. These *Thorns* are never to be pulled out, but the Veins and Sinews will follow after: For in rejecting these (Thorns in her sides) all her *Authority, Infallibility, Antiquity, Tradition, Unity, Succession, Credit* and *Veracity* is gone. (pp. 305–6)

1 Under Aurelius there were a series of councils from 393 to 424. The most celebrated is of May 419 when the Roman claim to jurisdiction over Africa was strongly contested.

5

All Creatures stand in expectation of your Liberty

42

One thing he saw, which is not commonly discerned; and that is, that God made Man a free Agent for his own Advantage; and left him in the hand of his own Counsel, that he might be the more Glorious. It is hard to conceiv how much this tended to his Satisfaction. For all the things in Heaven and Earth being so Beautifull, and made as it were on purpose for his own Enjoyment, he infinitly admired Gods Wisdom in that it salved his and all Mens Exigencies, in which it fully answerd his Desires; for his Desire was that all Men should be happy as well as he. And he admired his Goodness, which had enjoyned no other Duty, than what pertained to the more convenient fruition of the World which he had given: and at the Marvellous Excellency of his Lov, in committing that Duty to the Sons of Men, to be performed freely. For therby he adventured such a Power into the Hands of his Creatures, which Angels and Cherubims wonder at, and which when it is understood all Eternity will admire the Bounty of Giving. For he therby committed to their hands a Power to do that which he infinitly hated · which nothing certainly could mov him to Entrust them with, but some infinit Benefit which might be attained therby. What that was if you desire to Know, it was the Excellency Dignity and Exaltation of his Creature.

46

O the Superlative Bounty of GOD! Where all Power seemeth to ceas, he proceedeth in Goodness: and is wholy infinit Unsearchable and Endless. He seemeth to hav made as many things depend upon Mans Liberty, as his own. When all that could be wrought by the Use of His own Liberty were attained, by Mans Liberty he attained more. This is Incredible, but Experience will make it Plain. By his own Liberty he could but Creat Worlds and giv himself to creatures Make Images and endow them with faculties, or seat them in Glory. But to see them Obedient, or to enjoy the Pleasure of their Amity and Praises, to make them Fountains of Actions like his own, (without which indeed they could not be Glorious:) or to enjoy the Beauty of their free Imitation, this could by no means be, without the Liberty of his Creatures intervening. Nor indeed could the World be Glorious, or they Blessed without this Attainment. For can the World be Glorious unless it be Usefull? And to what Use could the World serv Him, if it served not those, that in this were supremely Glorious, that they could Obey and Admire and Lov and Prais, and Imitat their Creator? Would it not be wholy useless without such Creatures? In Creating Liberty therfore and giving it to his Creatures he Glorified All Things: Himself, his Works, and the Subjects of His Kingdom.

48

By this you may see, that the Works or Actions flowing from your own Liberty are of Greater Concernment to you then all that could possibly happen besides. And that it is more to your Happiness what you are, then what you enjoy. Should God giv him self and all Worlds to you, and you refuse them, it would be to no purpose · should he lov you and magnify you, should he giv his Son to Dy for you and command all Angels and Men to lov you, should he Exalt you in his Throne, and giv you Dominion over all his Works and you neglect them it would be to no purpose. Should he make you in his Image, and employ all his Wisdom and Power to fill Eternity with Treasures, and you despise them it would be in vain. In all these Things you hav to do; and therfore your Actions are great and Magnificent, being of infinit Importance in all Eys. While all Creatures stand in Expectation what will be the result of your Liberty. Your Exterior Works are little in Comparison of these. And God infinitly desires you should demean your self Wisely in these Affairs: that is Rightly. Esteeming and receiving what he gives, with Veneration and Joy and infinit Thanksgiving. Many other Works there are, but this is the Great Work of all Works to be performed. Consider Whether more depends upon Gods Lov to you, or your Lov to Him. From His Lov all the Things in Heaven and Earth flow unto you; but if you lov neither Him nor them, you bereav your self of all, and make them infinitly evil and Hurtfull to you and your self abominable. So that upon your Lov naturaly depends your own Excellency and the Enjoyment of His. It is by your Lov that you enjoy all His Delights, and are Delightfull to Him.

Centuries of Meditations, IV

6

By chusing a Man may be Converted into Lov

77

O Infinit Liberality of God the father! O Admirable and supreme felicity of Man! to whom it is given to hav what he desires and to be what he Wisheth. The Bruits when they are brought forth bring into the world with them what they are to possess continualy. The Spirits that are abov were, either from the beginning or a little after, that which they are about to be to all Eternities. Nascenti Homini omnigena vitæ Germina indidit Pater, God infused the Seeds of evry Kind of Life into Man, Whatever seeds evry one chuseth those spring up with him, and the fruits of those shall he bear and enjoy. If sensual Things are chosen by Him he shall becom a Beast, if Reasonable a Celestial Creature; if Intellectual an Angel and a Son of God; And if being content with the lot of no Creatures, he withdraws Himself into the Centre of His own Unitie, he shall be one Spirit with GOD, and Dwell abov all in the Solitary Darkness of his Eternal Father.

78

This Picus Mirandula[1] spake in an Oration made before a most learned Assembly in a famous university. Any man may perceiv, that He permitteth his fancy to wander a little Wantonly after the maner of a Poet: but most deep and serious things are secretly hidden under his free and luxuriant Language. The Changeable Power he Ascribeth to Man is not to be referred to his Body · for as he wisely saith, Neither doth the Bark make a Plant, but its stupid and nothing-perceiving nature: neither doth the Skin make a Beast, but his bruitish and sensual Nature, Neither doth Seperation from a Body make an Angel but his Spiritual Intelligence. So neither doth his Rinde or Coat or Skin or Body make a Man; to be this or that, but the Interior Stupidness, or Sensuality, or Angelical Intelligence of his Soul, make him accordingly a Plant, a Beast, or an Angel. The Deformity, or Excellency is within.

80

By chusing a Man may be turned and Converted into Lov. Which as it is an Universal Sun filling and shining in the Eternity of GOD, so is it infinitly more Glorious then the Sun is, not only shedding abroad more Amiable and Delightfull Beams, Illuminating and Comforting all Objects: yea Glorifying them in the Supreme and Soveraign Maner, but is of all sensibles the most Quick and Tender; being able to feel like the longlegged Spider, at the utmost End of its Divaricated feet: and to be wholy present in every place where any Beam of it self extends. The Sweetness of its Healing Influences is Inexpressible. And of all Beings such a Being would I chuse to be for ever. One that might inherit all in the most Exquisit Maner, and be the Joy of all in the most Perfect Measure.

Centuries of Meditations, IV

1 Pico della Mirandola.

7

Love will not be compelled

As for GOD his Way is perfect; like curious needle work on either side, compleat and exquisite.

All that we can fear, or except against, is his Omission, in forbearing to compell his Creatures to love, whether they will or no. But in that Liberty which he gave them, his Love is manifested most of all. In giving us a Liberty it is most apparent: for without Liberty there can be no Delight, no Honour, no Ingenuity, or Goodness at all: No action can be Delightful that is not our Pleasure in the Doing. All Delight is free and voluntary by its Essence. Force and Aversion are inconsistent with its nature. Willingness in its operation is the Beauty of the Soul, and its Honour founded in the freedom of its Desire. Whatsoever it does not desire and delight in, tho the matter of the performance be never so excellent, the Manner is spoiled, and totally Blasted. Now can we compel another to desire or delight in any Thing? The Soul in it self hath an Inclination to, or an aversion from every object. The Ingenuity and Worth of the Soul is expressed in the Kindness of its own Intention, in the freedom of its Desire to do what is Excellent, in the delight it taketh to love, its Goodness is founded. Now the GOD infinitely hated Sin, yet he gave us an irrevocable Power to do what we pleased, and adventured the Hazzard of that which he infinitely hated, that being free to do what we would, we might be Honourable and delightful in doing (freely, and of our own Accord) what is Great and Excellent. For without this Liberty there can be no Love, since Love is an active and free affection; that must spring from the Desire and pleasure of the Soul. It is the Pleasure of a Lover to promote the Felicity of his object. Whatsoever Services he is compelled to do, he is either meerly passive in them or Cross unto them, they are all void of the Principal Grace and Beauty that should adorn them, and make them pleasant and satisfactory: men may be Dead, and moved like stones; but in such causes there is no Love, neither do they act of themselves, when they are over-ruled, and forced by another. For this cause hath it pleased God, in order to our Perfection, to make the most Sublime and Sovereign Creatures all *Free*, wherein he hath expressed the greatest Love in the World. As we may see by all the Displeasures and Pains it hath cost him, through our Abuse of so illimited and great a perfection. But where his Love is most Highly and Transcendently expressed, there are we most prone to suspect it, Nature is so Cross and disorderly. There can be no Wisdom without a voluntary Act, for in all Wisdome there is Counsel and design. Where no consultation nor Election precedes, the best operation in all the World is Blind and Casual. Fortune and chance must have no hand in that which wisdom Effecteth: no more then Force and necessity must have in that Goodness, where all the kindness ought to be in the Intention of the Benefactor. There is something in it which I cannot explain. It is easily conceived, but will never (I think) in Words, be expressed. The *Will* has a mighty hand in all the Divinity of perfect Goodness. It is the *Mind* of the Doer that is the principal object of all our Desire and Expectation.

Having for these Causes made his Creatures free, he has forfeited their Choise, and secured their Determination, as far as was possible.

He hath done all that can be devised to make them Love us, and left nothing undone but only that which was absolutely necessary that they might *Love*. They could not Love us, if they were not left to themselves to do it freely. And their *Ability* being provided for, nay an Inclination given to make them willing, he has strictly commanded & enjoyned them to Love, by Nature allured them, & ordered us so, that we might be fit to be Beloved, he hath made it sweet and rational to Love, given them his own Example, and solemnly protested that he will accept of no Love to himself, but what is accompanied with Love to his friends and servants, engaged them to Love, or be Eternally miserable. And if for all this they will not Love, the fault is none of his. All that he has done to let secure their Love to himself, he has done to secure their Love to us: and is as much or more concerned in their Love to us, then in that which himself requireth and Expecteth. Nay he hath made it impossible for them (truly) to Love themselves without doing of it: And if they will neither Love GOD nor themselves, we may well be despised for Company. He infinitely desires their Love, and would take infinite Pleasure in the Operation. There is no Way to make themselves Honourable and Delightful to GOD, but only by Loving us, as his soul requireth. And by all these Inducements and Causes, are we our selves stirred up to Love, freely to exert the Power of Love to others in like manner.

Christian Ethicks, Ch. 19

8

Love is freely Wise yet cannot be otherwise

For perfect Love does not only consult but finish its own Objects Welfare, and in becoming all therunto it is able: And therfore the Love of God is the more perfect, bec. it is infinit and Eternal. It is not the Power, but the Act of Loving. Power to lov is subject to Miscarriages; It is neither Wise nor Holy. But the Act of loving in a most Wise and Holy manner, casteth out all fear. It is Wise and Holy by its Essence. And tho it soundeth strange like a very Paradox, it is freely Wise yet cannot be otherwise. an Act of Lov is of its own Pleasure Gracious, Good, and Blessed, bec. it is an Act of Lov: yet is so most necessarily bec. it is an Act of Love. The very same reason makes it both. An Act of Love is the Power of Loving exerted freely: and when it is exerted, it is by its Essence Good and Gracious to its object. It cannot be without its own Pleasure: It cannot be an Act of Lov without being Good and Gracious. Its Essence dependeth on it self and all the Qualities Essential therunto depend upon its Existence. which it self dependeth upon its Choice and Pleasure. So that all the Necessities under which we conceiv it to lie, depend upon its own Pleasure, and are not Oppressions therunto, but Liberties and pleasures. It is impossible for Love to be without its Object in God, bec. Lov is its object. It is worthy to be the Object of infinit and Eternal Love, by reason of its perfections. For infinit and Eternal Lov doth infinit and Eternal Good, to innumerable Millions of persons, in doing that Good to it self which it naturaly desires. It desires Naturaly, yet with Councel and Determination: And the infinit and Eternal Good which it doth to it self, is accomplished in its own Eternal Existence. It is infinit and Eternal Love, ever Blessed in all its Elections. It is not Eternal becaus of this alone; It never ever began; but bec. of this too, it ever never endeth. It ever endeth; it never endeth: and for this very reason it ever began, bec. it never began. It is Lov and Act freely exerted, but ever so.

Love

9

All Goodness is spoiled by Compulsion

That Vertues might be *ours*, in being wrought by *our selves*; and be Vertues *indeed*, in being wrought with *Difficulty*; that we might be so much the more Laudable and Glorious in our eternal Condition, GOD gave us Liberty, in the beginning, that we might chuse what we would, and placed us in such an Estate; that, having in us only the Seeds and Principles of all Vertue, we might exercise our natural Powers of our own Accord, for the Attainment of that actual Knowledge, Wisdom and Righteousness, wherein the Perfection of our soul consisteth, and by which the Perfection of our Bliss is to be enjoyed. That being Naked by Nature, tho Pure and clean, we might cloath our selves with our own *Habits*, attain the Glory of those Ornaments, in our own Acts, for which we were created; And work our *own* Righteousness, in such a Way as GOD had appointed.

For the Glory which we were to attain, is that Goodness which we are to shew in our own voluntary Care and obedience; and that Goodness is chiefly expressed in the kind and Genuine Exercise of our own Liberty, while we are tender of Displeasing him, to whom we are Obliged, and so Good as to gratifie his Desires, tho we had no restraint upon us.

To make our selves amiable and beautiful, by the Exercise of our own Power, produces another kind of Beauty and Glory, than if we were compelled to be good by all his preventing Power. All Goodness is spoiled by Compulsion. Our own Actions, springing from an interiour Fountain, deep within the Soul, when voluntarily and freely exerted, are more acceptable; and the Will, whence they spring, is more excellent and perfect. This I would have you to note well, for the intrinsick Goodness and Glory of the Soul consists in the Perfection of an excellent Will, and without this it might be a piece of Dirt surrounded with Gold; but no imputed or annexed value could make it a Jewel.

Christian Ethicks, Ch. 4

10

Men should return to God of their own Accord

Thus you see we give many things to Dr Hammond, and restore him that which he would throw away. But above all things we beseech the Reader to remember this. That the Desire of Happiness and the Love of Goodness is so implanted in the Soul that it can never be rooted out. And that as Light is in the Sun an Essential Property; so Natural, that the Sun cannot be, unless it shine; this Inclination is so planted and encorporated in the Soul, that in all Estates it is incorruptible; it is impossible to Eradicate it without the Dissolution of our Being. For could this Love to Happiness be removed, there would be no Misery in Hell, nor Happiness in Heaven, nor obligation to virtu, Nor Concernment nor Desire: Consequently no Government nor Kingdom, nor Reward nor Punishment. For which caus God implanted this Spark of his Immutability in us that we should ever love Good and hate Evil, our Election and Choise being freely carried, yet inevitably, to the End, as it were by the highest Necessity, and never failing to embrace it, when we think upon it, being indifferent only as to the Means; and our principal Duty being to keep our Ey open and our Consideration awake. Hence it cometh to pass that in Heaven they rejoyce in their Happiness, becaus what they love is present with them. In hell they griev and are miserable becaus those Good things which they infinitly lov are absent from them, and those Evils only present which they violently hate. Upon Earth the Sovereign Good is the End of all, to which they are carried whether they will or no. And all Aim to be Eternaly Blessed. So that Eternal Blessednes is evry ones Desire. Evry one desires to be Happy and Easy in their Way. This they do habitualy whatever they are doing: and this Bent is the Spring and fountain of their Actions. But they differ in Particulars. Som are carried directly to their End, and these are Happy. Others are deluded and distracted with pleasures, and taken up with present and Transitory things, that are Good in their kind, at least in their Thoughts and Powerful and near, loving to be idle they care not to examine and compare them with Eternal, and so miscarry. But still this Principle in all Estates is exerting it self, according to the Modificacions Causes and Circumstances wherwith it is attended.

It is not Inconvenient to say that any man may be Happy, that will: it magnifies the Riches of God's free Grace. And when we shall understand how Conducive Mens own Actions are to their Glory, and how much it concerns them in respect of Blessedness that their Actions should be their own: we shall admire God for so attempering his Grace, that they may be ours. For God gaineth Glory by giving Glory. His Glory being to give Glory unto us. And besides his Favor which is Extrinsecal, there is no Glory can befall his Image like that of Living in GODS Similitude of its own Accord.

I do not beleev it at all inconvenient that a Man should return unto God of his own Accord. Nor at all impossible now the Holy Ghost is given with the Son of God, but in it self the most Easy and with all the most Convenient and Pleasant thing in the World. It is so easy, that one would think it is impossible it should be otherwise in Nature and Reason. For Man is a Creature Prone to Lov as the Sun is to Shine, and God is an object infinitly to be Beloved. Happines may be had if it be seriously desired and it cannot chuse but be desired. It is as easy for a Man not to be filled with light when he openeth his Eys in a Summers Day as for a man not to See the Love of God, in the Ages and the World when he looketh on them: and as Easy for a Mirror to be set against the Sun, and the Sun not to be within the Mirror, as for the Soul to see God in the Glory of his Love, and not be enflamed with his love. Of all things that are it is the most Convenient, for it is that which of all things God most desires, his Saints endeavor, His Angels rejoyce in, and his Laws require, even a Voluntary Returne from Flight and

Enmity, to Love and Communion. O that there were such a Heart in Men! And why we should not say, It is convenient to return on their own accord I cannot tell. But it is not convenient to say they do, becaus whether it be so or no we cannot tell. Certainly there are very few that are Known so to hav done, But if any do as the rest perish with Greater Infamy, becaus they do not what is so Easy and so Convenient: the other enter into Heaven with Greater Glory: in as much as they do that which above all things in all Worlds God most desireth.

Tho all might upon Terms so Gracious and Easy and Means so Great and Abundant, so Powerfull and Supernatural, yet few do, very few; of their own accord Embrace Gods Love and Eternal Glory. So few that Neither is the Number sufficient for the Regiment of the Earth, nor the Compleating of Heaven. What if one should be converted in an Age, and 500 or 1000 six Ages after in many Nations over all the World? What Chasms would this breed in Gods Kingdom. What incertainties would it introduce in the world. He hath taken care therfore for the Perpetuity of his Church in all Ages: by resolving that the Welfare of the Univers should not depend wholy upon the Will of Men, and upholding the World for his Elect sake, serveth his Elect for the Worlds sake. He disperseth them severally in evry Age over all Nations, that they might the more Commodiously Season the whole Earth of which many things might worthily be Spoken, concerning which here I shall say nothing.

A Sober View of Dr Twisse, XVI

II

The Recovery

I

To see us but receiv, is such a Sight
As makes his Treasures infinit!
Becaus His Goodness doth possess
In us, His own, and our own Blessedness.
Yea more, His Love doth take Delight
To make our Glory Infinite
Our Blessedness to see

Is even to the Deitie
A Beatifick Vision! He attains
His Ends while we enjoy. In us He reigns.

2

For God enjoyd is all his End.
Himself he then doth Comprehend.
When He is Blessed, Magnified,
Extold, Exalted, Praisd and Glorified
Honord, Esteemd, Belovd, Enjoyd,
Admired, Sanctified, Obeyd,
That is receivd. For He
Doth place his Whole Felicitie
In that, who is despised and defied
Undeified almost if once denied.

3

In all his Works, in all his Ways,
We must his Glory see and Prais;
And since our Pleasure is the End,
We must his Goodness and his Lov attend.
If we despise his Glorious Works,
Such Sin and Mischief in it lurks,
That they are all made vain
And this is even Endless Pain
To him that sees it. Whose Diviner Grief
Is hereupon (Ah me!) without relief.

4

We pleas his Goodness that receiv:
Refusers Him of all bereav.
As Bride grooms Know full well that Build
A Palace for their Bride. It will not yeeld
Any Delight to him at all
If She for whom He made the Hall
Refuse to dwell in it
Or plainly Scorn the Benefit.
Her Act that's Wo'ed, yeelds more delight and Pleasure
If she receivs, Then all that Pile of Treasure.

5

But we have Hands and Lips and Eys
And Hearts and Souls can Sacrifice.
And Souls themselves are made in vain
If we our Evil Stubbornness retain.
Affections, Praises, are the Things
For which he gave us all these Springs,
They are the very fruits
Of all these Trees and Roots
The Fruits and Ends of all his Great Endeavors,
Which he abolisheth whoever Severs.

6

Tis not alone a Lively Sence
A clear and Quick Intelligence
A free, Profound, and full Esteem:
Tho these Elixars all and Ends to[o] seem
But Gratitude, Thanksgiving, Prais,
A Heart returnd for all these Joys,
These are the Things admird,
These are the Things by Him desird.
These are the Nectar and the Quintessence
The Cream and Flower that most affect his Sence.

7

The voluntary Act wherby
These are repaid, is in his Ey
More Precious then the very Skie.
All Gold and Silver is but Empty Dross
Rubies and Saphires are but Loss
The very Sun and Stars and Seas
Far less his Spirit pleas.
One Voluntary Act of Love
Far more Delightfull to his Soul doth prove
And is abov all these as far as Love.

12

The Freedom of the Bride

In respect of the Soul that is Subject to him, much might be said: I Shall Study Brevitie. Had God Created his Image in immediat Glory, the Beauty of Goodness being clearly seen, would immediatly have attracted its Desires, and hav ravished its affections for evermore: so that there had been no Consultation no Debate, no Trial, but a swift, and Rapid Union of Souls unchangeably abiding for ever. Liberty had been Excluded, and necessity only, tho a Gratefull Necessity imposed upon it. Now for the soul to Act by necessity destroys its Glory. The utmost Height wherin it could be placed was the Top of libertie, on either Side the Descent is downwards.

It is the Glory of God, that he is a free, and Eternal Agent. Had any thing been before him to compell him, had he acted by an Inward Principle of Necessitie, without Desire, and Delight, he had been Passiv, and dishonorable. To giv us therfore the Power of Doing all that is Excellent, without the Necessitie of doing it, is the vertical Point, the very Zenith, or utmost Hight of our Exaltation. To decline from which on Either hand, is to debase us. To giv us no Power, or to compell us to use it, is Equaly destructiv to our vertue, and Glory. But you will say, Notwithstanding that Necessitie, there had been a perfect Lov, and Libertie, for as much as Delight and Desire constrain by an Inward Inclination, and God himself being most free, is also the most Necessary Agent in all Worlds. For he so infinitly Delights in all that is Good, that it is Impossible he Should do otherwise, then he doth: because his Delight, and his Will are one. Delight being Nothing but the fervency and efficacy of Desire as it were, and the Ratification of our choise in the fruition of our Object. To this we answer. First it is true, that the Soul in Heaven had been carried to its Supreme felicitie by a free Inclination which would hav beautified the Necessitie, which the presence of its object inflicted, and in that Estate our Lov had been free and willing, tho by the very sweetness of our Bliss, it became Immutable. But there is this Difference between God, and us; God was purely the first Author of his own Choise; His Delight was Infinitly free, and the Necessitie of its Working was not impressed from without; Nothing but its Freedom, and Desire carried him to the Act, wherin he delighted. Wheras the Beauty of an outward object would constrain us with an imposed Necessitie impressing both the Delight and Necessitie at once: which tho it did not bereav us of the Pleasure, would rob us of the Beauty and Glory of the Action: And we being rational Creatures and able to reflect, and Examine Things, Should complain, and be distasted, if we found that Wanting, which is chiefly requisite to our Consummation: who are infinitly pleased, now we see the Pleasure, and the Glory of our Act United! Secondly GOD intended more then this for his Bride; She must hav features, and Graces more Delightfull, Ornaments more Amiable, and Beautifull; so Divine, that the very Memory of them should be sweeter, then all that in a Solitary State of Stiffe, and Passive Glory can be devised. What is it to be faithfull in the Sight and presence of our Lord; And to be Good, while we are Infinitly pleased? Sight and Lov are so individualy united in the Beatifick Vision that it is Life Eternal to know God. The Glory of a free Agent being the Beauty of his Actions, the more Beautifull the Actions are, which he is made capable of performing, with the Greater Glory is he to be crowned when he hath well, and freely performed the Same: Wheras all is Easy, Safe, and Secure, all imposed by a Fatal Efficacie,[1] all inevitable, we are meerly Passiv, tho we like the operation, at least are So Electiv, as to hav but litle Share in it, litle Thanks is due for such an Obedience, litle Worth, or Virtue is in it. God had a mind to enrich our Actions with Infinit Excellency and to make us the Sole, and Absolute Authors of our own operation. Therfore it is Said, that we are his Workmanship, Created in Christ Jesus unto Good Works, which God had before prepared, that we Should Walk in them.[2] For all that moves Beauty and Delight is Advantagious for us. And those Acts which are wrought with the Greatest Difficultie, upon the least Advantage, when they are Excellent, are the most Glorious. We Walk by faith, and not by Sight;[3] and for this very Reason God would have us saved by faith, becaus the Actions wrought by faith are more weak and Tender, but withall more Honorable, and Holy, more full of obedience, and Ingenuitie, freedom, fidelitie, Gratitude, and Worth, then those that are wrought (without these) in the Highest Glory. So to lov God, as to be Willing to Creat all Worlds for him, and Sacrifice all our Desires to him, and give him all the Pleasures, and Honors of all Empires, while we see him, is Nothing: tho we could extend to Infinit Gifts, and Benefits, it would be a small return of Gratitude, and obedience to him, whose Beauty and Goodness are Infinite. But in a Glimmering imperfect Light to honor him whom we see not, and in the midst of Hazzards, Assaults, and Temptations, in his Absence, to be faithfull, Notwithstanding all the Discouragment of

Pain, and Trouble, to be carefull to pleas him, in an Estate wherin we may be inconsiderat, and close our Eys, to keep them open, and Watchfully to serv him, is Somwhat more then cherubims in Glory perform.

But this is not all. His Bride must hav som things peculiar to her Sex, which God himself doth not Enjoy, unless it be in her: Things not agreable to his Essence but most Convenient in her both in her Estate and Person. They had been Deformities in Him, which in her are suavities, and becoming Graces: He is the Bridegroom, and therfore must be Strong, Almighty, and firm; she the Bride, more weak, and Tender, and Delicat: He is to prepare Enjoyments; She to Enjoy them: He to Provide, She to inherit: He to Govern, She to reign under his protection; She to Conceiv the offspring of Delights which he begetteth; She more infinitly to Prize him, and he to delight in that Esteem: He to give, She to receive: He to Bless, and She to Prais: He to support, and She to depend. Neither is She free alone, as he is (with whom nevertheless it is Impossible to Erre;) but frail, and Mutable: being placed in such an Estate, wherin there is Danger, least She may realy become evil. He from all eternity loved her with a Constant Infinit, and Eternal Lov, but She may forbear to Lov Solicitousness in her Lord: And as there are Pleasures peculiar to the Estate of Woers, and perhaps Sweeter then those of Marriage, but wholy different; So was She placed in the Estate of Trial, as a virgin untouched, that She might Experience all the Approaches of So Beautifull a Suiter, and Gratifie his Affection with the Greater Pleasure. God did Study to make his Bride more Acceptable to himself, then Imagination could devise; more Beautiful; and more Delightfull, then the Estate of a Creature would seem to permit. He was sure there could be no Excess in her being Delightfull: All the Works of God were made to attend upon the Marriage, and if She refuseth to lov, they are all prepared to no purpose. It is absolutly in her power, whether she will, or no; O What fear, and Compassion! What Expectation, and Desire! What Agonie, what Weakness and Danger, till the Work be done! But O what unspeakable Joy! What Consolation! What Virtue! What Praise, What Blessedness, and Glory, when all the Danger is over, and the Satisfaction attained, and the Perfection of Holiness happily Secured!

The Kingdom of God, Ch. 42

1 The power of fate.
2 Ephesians 2.10.
3 2 Corinthians 5.7.

5

Advice on Christian Life and Ministry

Being a clergyman in Traherne's day required a certain amount of strategy. Not only did one have to find one's own way in a time of tremendous theological and ecclesiastical upheaval, with all that meant in terms of risk, stability and the pursuit of truth, but one also had to carry a congregation through those changes as their priest, while acting as doctor, lawyer, peacekeeper and arbiter of disputes. The country parson came across every kind of human predicament, failure and loss. Whatever glossy images of humanity he may have started out with would have been swiftly modified to include the muck of life, and one feels it is with real conviction that Traherne writes: 'Innocent no man is in this world. Much Less a congregation' (*SM*, IV, 52). How well was he, or were any of his contemporaries, prepared for such ministry? The fact that there were no theological colleges in Traherne's day was perhaps ameliorated by the equally simple fact that all colleges were in some sense theologically literate. Educated persons of the seventeenth century had some knowledge of scripture and of theology, as they would have of Latin, humanity, rhetoric, philosophy, history and science; all of these were considered necessary training for life. You could hardly get through Oxford or Cambridge without a daily diet of sermons and prayers, a smattering of church fathers and a keen awareness of the politico-theological and philosophical debates of the day, but there was no specific 'training' for ministry. There were hurdles to get through, to be sure; Traherne was 'approved' by a group of Puritan ministers who had themselves been approved. His Puritan credentials were clearly strong enough; then when ecclesiastical rules changed, he sought episcopal ordination and conformed to the Act of Uniformity. Whatever hoops were set up, he seems to have passed through them. But like Herbert, whose pastoral guide *The Country Parson* aided so many ministers, and like many others who wrote in a similar vein, Traherne was aware that more preparation was needed than approval by a clutch of clergy, and more resolve was required to sustain ministry than a simple wish to be useful. 'It is no small matter to dwell in community or in a congregation, and to convers there without complaint, and to persevere faithfully in it until Death. Blessed is He that hath there Lived well, And Ended Happily,' he writes (*SM*, IV, 52).

Despite the lack of formal theological training in Traherne's day, ordinands of his period and beyond would have felt the need for guidance as they prepared for ordination, and many found models of ministry in the wide array of published manuals that emerged. Carrying on into the eighteenth and nineteenth centuries, before the foundation of theological colleges, nigh on a hundred such manuals were published. Anthony Russell reminds us that these volumes quote directly from Herbert's *The Country Parson* with striking frequency. 'Perhaps nothing demonstrates with greater clarity the way in which his small book may be regarded as the root-stock from with Anglican pastoral theology and practice, particularly in rural ministry, has been shaped.'[177]

Unlike Herbert, Traherne did not write a specific handbook of advice on ministry; however, the similarities between Herbert's advice in *The Country Parson* and Traherne's advice scattered throughout his writing are many. Although we cannot be sure Traherne read *The Country Parson*, we do know that he read and revered Herbert,[178] calling him 'the divine poet' (*KOG*). Herbert's 'To All Angels and Saints' is quoted in its entirety in the *Church's Year-Book*; 'Longing' appears in *The Kingdom of God*. Given that *The Country Parson* was such a seminal book of its kind it is unlikely that Traherne would have entirely missed it. Herbert advises the ordinand to read the 'Fathers' and the 'Schoolmen' and 'the later Writers' and to compile a commonplace book for future use. These are all practices Traherne followed. Of preparing for ministry, Herbert writes in *The Country Parson* that one should not think 'that when they have read the Fathers. Or Schoolmen, a minister is made, and the thing done. The greatest and hardest preparation is within' (Chapter 2). Traherne agrees, suggesting that the scriptural models assume retirement from the world as a preparation for ministry. Moses needed 'forty yeers Concealment, for forty yeers Exposure', but

177 Anthony Russell, 'The Country Parson', a lecture given at Salisbury Cathedral, Wednesday 12 May 1993, the 400th anniversary of Herbert's birth.
178 For an interesting article on Herbert as Traherne's mentor see Nabil Matar, 'The Temple and Traherne', *English Language Notes*, 25 (December 1987), pp. 25–33.

Jesus' example is even more distilled: 'whose Proportion of Retirement, was ten years, to one of Exposure' (*ITR*, ll. 338–42).

However, lessons were also to be gleaned from contact with professionals and with institutions. As Herbert wrote, being a pastor, a lawyer and a doctor meant culling knowledge from as many relevant sources as one could find, including, especially, exposure to the workings of the law:

> The Countrey Parson desires to be all to his Parish, and not onely a Pastour, but a Lawyer also, and a Phisician. Therefore hee endures not that any of his Flock should go to Law; but in any Controversie, that they should resort to him as their Judge. To this end, he hath gotten to himself some insight in things ordinarily incident and controverted, by experience, and by reading some initiatory treatises in the Law, with *Daltons* Justice of Peace, and the Abridgements of the Statutes, as also by discourse with men of that profession, whom he hath ever some cases to ask, when he meets with them ... (Chapter 23)

Traherne's work as surrogate dean for the Dean of Hereford's consistory court, a responsibility that, as we have seen, involved him in regular court visits over a sustained period of time, would have given him important insights into the law. For him the works of the courts and of magistrates is also the work of God. 'Seek the Secret Service of God, Examine what they do in his Courts, and thou shalt find that they are doing the Work of Heaven', he writes in *Inducements to Retiredness*, and he urges magistrates to exercise judgement with kindness (*ITR*, ll. 645–6, 662–4).

Attending consistory and other courts also offered clergy or ordinands exposure to rhetorical skills that might stand them in good stead when it came time to debate matters theological and ecclesiastical. Traherne was aware of the need to have a ready answer when questioned vigorously on matters of doctrine and faith. In fact *Commentaries of Heaven* was written at least in part to supply such answers to difficult questions – its title page claims the book is written not just to 'Alphabetically Represent' all things 'In the Light of Glory', but also for 'the satisfaction of Atheists, & the Consolation of Christians, as well as the Assistance & Encouragement of Divines'.

Preparing for and exercising ministry in the church requires a balance, Traherne asserts, of retirement from and engagement with the world: 'we conclude, that our Life is to be Spent, not only in Retirement, nor only abroad. Life is made Harmonious, by a Sweet Mixture of these Extremes, and a Wise Improvement of both' (*ITR*, ll. 612–13).

Traherne's own ministry seems to have followed this pattern of mixed extremes in his transition from country parson to private chaplain. Much has sometimes been made of this change because of the striking contrasts it seems to pose – parochial/cosmopolitan and rural/ urban – although Traherne may not have found the transition so fundamentally shaking. His calling was essentially the same wherever he exercised it. Neither would Herbert have seen Traherne's role changing very much; he writes: 'those that live in Noble Houses are called Chaplains, whose duty and obligation being the same to the Houses they live in as a Parsons to his Parish'. The office of a chaplain is no different from the office of a parson and the chaplain must not decline to challenge his Lord and Lady when need be. Because 'after a man is once a Minister, he cannot agree to come into any house, where he shall not exercise what he is, unlesse he forsake his plough, and look back' (Chapter 2).

Some of the central questions that surrounded seventeenth-century ministry are not so very different from today's questions. Is the parish priest's primary effort to be preaching the word or 'doing' things in the parish, such as visiting, organizing events, being involved in local schools, charities, community efforts? Should local traditions be respected or challenged? How important is visiting the sick? Herbert's *The Country Parson*, as well as calling the pulpit the 'joy and throne' of the parson, also devotes chapters to 'The Parson's charity', 'The Parson in Circuit', 'The Parson comforting' and 'The Parson in Sacraments', whereas works such as Richard Bernard's *The Faithful Shepherd* urge their readers to preaching as the parson's primary concern. The records of Traherne's parish and his own writings suggest that he favoured Herbert's active, hands-on approach.

The question of whether country festivals such as rogation (beating the bounds) and harvest were really Christian or merely a Christian gloss on paganism was a topic for fierce debate in Traherne's day and has arisen again in recent years. Writers such as George Gifford (*The Countrie Divinite*, 1581) would not tolerate country festivals and traditions, whereas a great part of ministry for Herbert is about being out and about with parishioners, and about honouring the local traditions loved by his people. Herbert writes: 'the Country Parson is a lover of old customes, if they be good and harmless: and the rather, because country people are made much addicted to them ... Particularly he loves procession and maintains it.' Herbert's parson condescends 'even to the knowledge of tillage and pastorage ... because people by what they understand, are best led to what they understand not' (Chapter 4). Traherne goes further, claiming that 'The keeping of these Days [Rogation] was no Novel Superstition, but a Venerable Institution of Pious Antiquity, As S. Aug. witnesseth in his Sermon on Ascension Eve: & in another concerning Rogation Sunday' (*CYB*, fol. 22v). For Traherne beating the bounds is important precisely because it shows the victory of Christianity over paganism, rather than supporting neo-pagan practice: it is 'an Act of Triumph & Publick Joy' in which white-robed Christians, as valiant troops, literally march across the parish claiming the very fields for God. Here, as so often, Traherne reiterates his passionate belief that faith is not a private concern. His answer to the country festival sceptics is plain:

> Pitty then it is that out of pretended fear of Superstition, Men should neglect Primitv & Excellent Devotion: or out of fals Groundless fear, Endeavor to Disannul such Heavenly Constitutions; there are som things that carry so much Light & Beauty in them, that they need not be written in a Law, being Asserted by Reason & Taught by Nature. (*CYB*, fol. 23r)

We should not be surprised to see such militant images rising out of Traherne's writing. Raised in a time of war, his formative years were framed in the vocabulary of battle, blood and heroic valour. Even in his much-loved peaceful Restoration, battles were still being fought, though now of an intellectual, theological and political nature; and Traherne, despite his poetic theme of felicity, is acutely aware of the need to be prepared. His advice on ministry is littered with soldierly admonishments, and his asides in *Commentaries of Heaven*, such as 'This is Dr Jackson's cure or rather Antidote against Atheism' (fol. 163r), or 'This is the Answer that is to be returned to all sorts of Phanatiques that cavil at the Words in the English Liturgie' (fol. 193v), clearly suggest that he expected clergy to be caught up in the defence of the English Church against dissent from within and atheism from without.

The parish priest was at the same time, however, responsible for teaching in a parish in which levels of literacy would have varied widely, and catechizing was one of the primary teaching tools available.

Traherne's churchwardens described him as someone skilled in instructing the youth. For inspiration for sermons he looked, as did so many others, to the intelligent and fascinatingly layered sermons of Lancelot Andrewes; but this style, perfectly suited as it was to the court, would not have met the needs of all of Traherne's parish. Herbert suggested the use of stories and sayings as well as catechisms and scripture, and Traherne's love of sayings is reflected in his comment: 'Here [an] Aphorism and there a Song: Here a suplication and there a Thanksgiving. Thus do we bespangle our way to Heaven' (*SM*, IV, 18). But I think Traherne experimented even further in his teaching techniques. Traherne's departure, in *Christian Ethicks*, from the catechetical style such as we see in Richard Allestree's hugely popular *The Whole Duty of Man* suggests a dissatisfaction with pure catechesis. It seems likely that his long poem *The Ceremonial Law* was one attempt to create a teaching tool of a much more imaginative and engaging kind. There he takes individual stories from the Old Testament and sets them to poetry, using the pneumonic device of rhyme, and imagery that will linger in his reader's memory. In a technique that feels really rather modern compared to the dry catechesis of many of his contemporaries, Traherne's reader is invited to explore the story from several angles, often stepping inside the story, almost acting its parts. And in *Select Meditations*, he writes what appears to be a kind of twelve-point catechism of happiness titled: 'Instructions Teaching us how to Liv the life of Happieness' (*SM*, II, 31). They are not about rules to keep or doctrines to remember but about catching a vision of what one can be and how one can live a life of wisdom, happiness and glory in the love of God. Traherne's message to those entering ministry – in fact, to any Christian – is not to neglect the teaching of scripture and to reinvent, when necessary, techniques for making the love of God real to one's audience.

Above all there is the nurturing of one's relationship with parishioners. 'Towards thy neighbor thou must behave thy Selfe with as much candor and sweetness as if He were an unspotted Angel', Traherne insists. The priest should bear 'an Enflamed Lov' for the works of others, thirsting for their happiness, suffering oneself to be injured for their benefit. It is one of the priest's tasks to help the parishioner improve the wrongs and injuries they have done: make amends, change their habits, turn around. In all of this the priest's own loves are at once starved and fed: 'Oh that my heart might be made a Stepping Stone for any ones Ascent into the Kingdom of Heaven' (*SM*, IV, 53).

What Traherne is urging here is something more akin to friendship than to governance. Perhaps he has taken to heart what Herbert wrote about the Parson's many acts of kindness, generosity, and being alongside – 'there is much preaching in this friendliness' (Chapter 35).

In addition, he urges the exercise of four cardinal virtues: courage, prudence, temperance and justice. A daily exercise in prudence for him, and a practice he would advise to others, is the guarding of one's tongue (*SM*, II, 100; III, 2). He asks God to teach him to use his tongue prudently, seasonably and to God's glory, and he bemoans his weakness when it comes to speaking too quickly, especially when tempted to reply to those who are talking vanity. Sometimes, the most prudent action is simply to leave. He writes, 'I will be more silent when they talk of vanitie. And since I cannot accompany their Imaginations and the thoughts of God; I will either overrule their Souls, or Depart the company' (*SM*, III, 2), as one at his wit's end. These glimpses, in all their ragged humanity, of Traherne trying his best to practise the virtues he espouses of courage, prudence, temperance and justice lend an air of real credibility to his advice on ministry, and they deepen our appreciation of his more exuberant assertions like 'To giv is the Greatest Sensuality in the World, and to be Doing Good, the Highest Epicurism' (*ITR*, ll. 352–3) or 'You need nothing but open eyes to be ravished like the cherubim' (*C*, I, 37). In his down-to-earth advice on ministry Traherne shows his reader that for him simple goodness is the work of a lifetime. 'Dare to be good', he writes in *Christian Ethicks* – this is true valour.

Besides these four cardinal virtues there are the four theological virtues – faith, righteousness, holiness and humility – which, Traherne argues, underpin the rest. Righteousness, he says, is justice by another name, whereas holiness is more – it is the zeal by which we render unto things their sacred value, it is about seeing the world through the eyes of God. Humility is the jewel by which all happiness is enjoyed, because until we know our wants (that is, our lacks) we cannot know our treasures.

By his example Traherne advises clergy to be involved in the community of other clergy. Traherne enjoyed the company of fellow clergy and supported them in their work; this was typical of parish clergy of the time. As Patrick Collinson writes, 'It is emphatically not the case that every parish was a desert island and its incumbent Robinson Crusoe in a Geneva gown'.[179] And yet Traherne was no stranger to

179 Collinson, *From Cranmer to Sancroft*, p. 50.

solitude; he knew its demands (he claimed that whoever would follow happiness must sit alone like a pelican in the wilderness) and its value. Retirement from the world was not just applicable to ordinands, but something that one needed to revisit from time to time: 'That life which Armor cannot protect in Taverns. Solitude secureth more then a Castle' (*ITR*, ll. 207–8).

Traherne advocated celibacy for clergy using Christ, who gave himself to all rather than to one, as his example:

> One Great reason, why our Savior, who is rightly stiled THE GREAT EXEMPLAR, remained Single: was becaus in His Solitary and Virgin State, . . . He could more easily apply Him self to many Persons . . . This Rule is not Universal, but it holdeth infallibly in Public Ministers. (*ITR*, ll. 455–62)

Friendships and marriage were ultimately allurements away from the interior life. 'It is better', he writes, 'only to hav an infinit Benevolence toward all the World, a Moderate friendship with the Good and Excellent: an Intire illimited friendship with God alone' (*ITR*, ll. 389–91). Where Herbert urges the parson to be out among the people, visits every afternoon and invites them regularly to his home to dine, Traherne seems to need times of solitude to replenish his spiritual strength.

Traherne's own testimony reveals a man in the thick of ministry, not lost in a world of theoretical felicity, but engaged in the knocks and bumps of parish life with its foibles and personalities. He tried to steer an even course among his parishioners, to be moved to compassion by their sorrows, while remaining unmoved by either their censures or by his own need of approval.

> . . . if they were miserable as the most are, to be filled with great comp[a]ssion, to retain the Sence of the Eternal Diety. To Lov them as the Saviour of the world doth, not to follow their Opinion, not to be Provoked by their censure, not to approve ones selfe to them, not to give them occation of evill Speech, not to be swayed by their example, are Difficult Things, and He that passeth Thorrow all thes Bryers well, and is in e[v]ry moment prudent shall be more beautifull then if he had never sinned nor been a mong them. (*SM*, IV, 52)

This advice means Traherne the parson, despite an inclination towards friendliness, would always remain on the edges of intimacy with his parishioners. But his devotion to Bridgeman suggests that he also knew the cost of loyalty to a friend in a party-political world. His writing reveals the tension of a priest who lives in both these worlds; that he is neither all hard theology nor all folksy wisdom of the down home variety, but a dweller in differing realms is one of his appealing qualities.

Richard Hooker the country parson and Lancelot Andrewes the urbane bishop and court preacher were both models of a kind for Traherne. Most of his ministry was in the parish at Credenhill where, like Hooker, he worked among his people while writing theology. Like Andrewes he knew what it was to find favour with eminent men, move to London, enjoy for a time the company of those not far from the king. Traherne uses the Easter Sermons of Andrewes in his meditations after Easter, and both Hooker and Andrewes on the subject of angels in his Michaelmas meditations. From Andrewes he took a model of prayerfulness, modelling *The Thanksgivings* after Andrewes' *Preces Privatae*; from Hooker he gleaned, among other things, a desire to communicate with laity as well as clergy. Although in his notebooks Traherne wanders in and out of Latin and Greek, most of his writing for publication is in English. Even his controversial responses are not in Latin, as for example are Andrewes' *Responsio* to Cardinal Bellarmine or John Cosin's *Historia* on transubstantiation. Like the majority of those of his generation as disparate as Jeremy Taylor and Richard Baxter, Traherne wrote as much for lay people as for clergy and almost always with an English audience in mind. No stranger to doctrinal controversy, as such dedicated works as *A Sober View* and *Roman Forgeries* clearly indicate, he nevertheless largely shared Hooker's concern to write for a wider audience.

No matter is too small for Traherne's attention. He condescends to give advice about everyday life as much as about prayer or retirement. One gloriously human glimpse we get of Traherne is in his advice on clothing in *Commentaries of Heaven*. Traherne allows for the practicality of clothes, even for those degrees of distinction in eminence that clothing may mark and preserve, but his advice to followers of fashion – they that 'delight in vanitie, & place their Glory in the Pomps of the World, that study fashions, & love to riot in the luxurie of Clothes' – is clear. 'Be not a Bubble', he says; do not spread forth sails too big for your ship.

Here one is reminded of the letters from Lady Brilliana Harley to her son at Oxford, who went up to Oxford a good Puritan boy, sober and discreet in his attire, schooled by his mother in the power of plainness, only to acquire, year by year, more and more fabulous clothing until he would write requiring a hat with a brim bigger than could be found anywhere in London. Bigger was better, lavish was best, and as fashion followed the court, clothing became more and more outlandish. The Harleys were family friends of Traherne's. It is against this trend towards the ridiculous that Traherne advises his reader, sounding not unlike his staunchly Puritan friend Lady Brilliana herself when he writes: 'Clothes are pittifull Suiters; Dost thou esteem any Body the more for his Clothes? ... It is eminent folly to spread forth Sailes to big for thy Ship. Be not a Bubble; be solid like God, & let all thy Worth be within.' This last sentence, though written about mere attire, seems to me among the most memorable of Traherne's many bits of advice on life and ministry. 'Be not a bubble; be solid like God.' Who can say better than that? It sounds like it was written exactly with the twenty-first century in mind. 'Let all thy Worth be within' is as good a starting point as any for those who want to maintain a witness that challenges the materialistic and superficial tendencies of our age.

How should we live? Traherne says to ministers: be among your people. Take time away for soul formation and restoration. He says to all: be attentive to scripture and respectful of the church's teachings. Guard your tongue, continue in prayer, be charitable, give alms, be kind. But before and beneath these things he says: know what you are inside, where your life comes from and where it is headed. Anchored in the love of God, free in your engagements with others, open to grace, determined in faithfulness, be not a bubble; be solid.

The extracts

1 Lines from 'Silence'
2 In Praise of Solitude
3 The balance of retirement and action
4 We are to grow Rich by enjoying what we have
5 The Allurement of Friendship
6 On Celibacy
7 Behaving well towards all things
8 Pastoral advice on the keeping of Rogation

I

Lines from 'Silence'

A quiet Silent Person may possess
All that is Great or High in Blessedness.
The Inward Work is the Supreme: for all
The other were occasiond by the Fall.
A man, that seemeth Idle to the view
Of others, may the Greatest Business do.
Those Acts which Adam in his Innocence
Performed, carry all the Excellence.
These outward Busy Acts he knew not, were
But meaner Matters, of a lower Sphere.
Building of Churches, giving to the Poor,
In Dust and Ashes lying on the floor,
Administring of Justice, Preaching Peace,
Ploughing and Toyling for a forc't Increas,
With visiting the Sick, or Governing
The rude and Ignorant: This was a thing
As then unknown. For neither Ignorance
Nor Poverty, nor Sickness did advance
Their Banner in the World, till Sin came in:
These therfore were occasiond all by Sin.
The first and only Work he had to do,
Was in himself to feel his Bliss, to view
His Sacred Treasures, to admire, rejoyce
Sing Praises with a Sweet and Heavnly voice,

See, Prize, Give Thanks within, and Love
Which is the High and only Work, above
Them all.

2

In Praise of Solitude

That Retirement is so Cheap, is one very Commendable, among its other Qualities. The Hony and Wine which God proclameth is here to be sold without money, and without Price.[1] Here are no Incentives to Gallantry: No Causes Engaging a Man to the Study of Vanities: No use of Costly Attires, Jewels, or Embroyderies. They that court Adulterat favor, must do it in Palaces. Worthless things are to be persued with Sweat and Toyl Glorious and Substantial things are easily acquired. A man may talk face to face with God, even while He is as Naked as Adam. And by the Expence only of His Thoughts, purchase for Himself Eternal favor. The Lov of God, as it is most Glorious is most free. And therfore Cheap becaus it preventeth[2] us. It was from all Eternity, and therfore may be approached at any time. It is Omnipresent, and therfore may be seen in any place. It is ever Infinit, and is therfore evry where, Pleasant to be Enjoyed. Being it self Naked and most Glorious, it desire nothing but Naked Lov: And in that infinitly Delighteth. Frize, a Cottage, a Wooden Dish, are sufficient for Him that is alone: and abundant to him that Delighteth in God, and liveth with the Dietie. But he that is Ambitious of favors, either in Kings Thrones, or in Ladies Bosoms, must persue them with Gold and Court them with Hangings. Things unprofitable are made always Dear; and this ariseth from infinit Lov. Things Excellent are always Common; and this agreeth with infinit Goodness. It is a Paradox in Nature, but a Truth in Heaven Things Cheap are most Precious.

Exaltations and Honors, among Riches and Beauties, hav persued me, as much as they hav fled from other men. I hav tasted the very Cream of Earthly Delights. And hav had many Treasures under my Hand by way of Eminence. Perhaps also without the Bitterness and Inconveniences which follow the Enjoyments of this World. I hav reason to believ that I hav had as many Strict and Close Amities, with Persons of the Greatest Principles and Bravest Worth. But all that I hav learned from them was Solomons Vanity:[3] Their frailty and Narrowness maketh them Worthless. I must

be Beloved of all Mankind, and be the Image of the Dietie, and reign
Enthroned in the Bosom of God; or els for ever be Dissatisfied. Now
in Retirement, we Acquire this, which is the Life of Heaven.

Among those Things which withdraw us from Retirement, I shall
not name Splendid Houses, Crowns and Scepters, Gold and Pompous
Clothes; nor Feasts and Palaces: The outward Carcase which appears
unto Children: But the Ends of them, for which they are Esteemed:
Their inward Sweetness, which is the Soul and Spirit, unseen by the
Vulgar World: A long Influence upon other Souls; a deep Interest in a
Multitude of Affections; Honor and Power acquired therby; Delightfull
Intercourse, and Mutual Enjoyment; Zeal and Admiration; Dominion,
Greatness, Highness and Glory. these are Joys and Pleasures, that may
be Tasted by Angels. yet such is the frailty of our Corrupt Estate, that
we may Surfeit on these. Which we then do, when we are Distracted
by them from the Lov of God, or Disturbed in the Enjoyment.

It is True indeed, that where we can reconcile them, with our union
and Communion with God; they are in themselvs Desireable, as a
Great Part of the End of our Creation. For Man is made a Sociable
Creature, and is never Happy till His Capacities are filled with all their
Objects, and his Inclinations hav attained their proper Ends. But these
Objects are Wide and many, their fountains are Dispersed, and lie
abroad: they cannot therfore but in Retirement be at once Enjoyed.
Truly Acquired, they are Worthy of God. But the Sweetness of them
lies much in their Causes. for it consists in the Contemplation of those
Noble Things, we hav don in the Atchievment: And cannot well but
by recollected Thoughts within, be Enjoyed. To gain a Confluence
of Praises by Surreptitious Means, is to Wear a Crown and Scepter
that is Stoln. The Noble Paths of Honor and Vertue are found in
Retirement.

Do not Men in Retirement prepare Illustrious Scenes for the Theatre?
Do not Bridegrooms retire, when they Adorn themselvs with Glorious
Ornaments? Do not Kings first cloth themselvs in privat, before they
com abroad in Publick? Are not all the Great Transactions of the World
managed in Privat before they appear? Even Solomons Temple was
prepared in the Solitudes. Sermons Preached by Bishops, the Glory of
the most famous Conventions, the Prosperity of Kingdoms, is provided
in Retirement. And all the Miraculous Effects of Government in War
and Peace, are Secretly Hammered at the Council Table. Yea, and as if
that were not Secret Enough, evry man alone in His Closet, and within
Himself first meditateth, what there he proposeth. Retirement is a Life

Wherin Men, like the Pilot at the Helm of a Ship, move the Greatest Weight with the Greatest Ease. We then are Doing the Greatest things when we seem Doing Nothing. The Leagues of Princes are Examined in Retirement: the Laws of Kingdoms are there Conceived: there those Edicts and Proclamations are fitted, that are Publickly promulged, and praised among the People. If in any Thing you would be Excellent, you must be much alone. Historians, Philosophers, Physicians and Divines, acquire the Excellencies of their Degree in Retirement. So do Poets, Lawyers, Councellors, Magistrates and Orators. If Thou wouldst be Excellent in Wisdom and Glory, thou also must spend many Days to Adron thy self with those in Retirement. Those Glorious Things which seem in the Beginning to Allure us from it now appear the greatest Incentives that Necessitat us to it: And tho we should grant, that Dominion and Power are best Enjoyed, in the presence of those who are Living Souls, becaus of the Pleasure of their Lov and Communion: yet is that Honor and Glory we desire, by Retirement attained, becaus there we provide those Materials, and Clothe our selvs with those Ornaments, that are necessary to our Exposure. Where Shall a Man find the Ways of Meekness Humanity and Courage, unless in Privat he meditateth on them; and Digest those Precepts in his own Soul, which perhaps he hath heard before in Publick? Where shall a man meet with the Rules of Prudence; or learn those Arts wherby He should order and Subdue His Passions; or those Motivs, upon which he should Direct his Affections: if he ponder not upon them in his Privat Solitudes? Verily It is as reasonable to go to Sea without Ship Sails or Mariners, as to launch abroad in the world without these. It is a more Arduous Thing, to Govern the World, then to Rule a Kingdom: And as much more profitable to Him that doth it, as the World is Greater then a Princes Dominion. To appear in Glory among the Sons of Men, to be Divine and Honorable, to Inherit Ages, to Possess all the Joys of Heaven and Earth, is a Deeper Secret, then to be attained in a little Time. To be the Joy of Assemblies, and to stand in the Congregations of the Righteous,[4] as one that reapeth their Universal Praises, and is Advanced, as the Darling of God and Nature: is far Greater then to hav gotten Skill in Chymistrie, or to hav been made an Exact Historian, or Grammarian, but to possess all these things after the Divine Image, is most Glorious. To inhabit that Light which is inaccessible, and there to Enjoy them: to liv in Secret, and thence to behold them, is with the Diety to see, and Continualy to feel them.

Were all men innocent, Exposures would be far more safe and Happy then they are, there would be less in them either of Danger or Temptation: But now we hav so many poysons to Correct; so many Injurious and Sour Humors to meliorat, so many Thorns and Briars to handle; so many pervers and Malignant Spirits to deal with: a man would think Retirement a Blessing conceded from Heaven. And embrace Solitude as a little Breathing Space, wherin he may be Exempted from a lesser Hell, or Earthly Purgatory. But becaus this may very much be Corrected by the Chois of Company, we shall not proceed upon such a Deep Advantage. Rather we will shew how much Retirement is to be preferred abov the Best Company I ever yet met with: and upon what Causes we are to prefer it.

Forty yeers Concealment, for forty yeers Exposure, was the Proportion in Moses.[5] But when we Consider the Great Skill that we stand in need of, and the Abundance of Work that we hav to do; our Saviors Example may seem more Eligible: whose Proportion of Retirement, was ten yeers, to one of Exposure. For the Term of His Concealed Life was Thirty full yeers, and that of His Publick less then Three. He Spending ten parts of His Time in Secret towards God, that He might spend one profitably among men. Not but that he was able much Sooner to hav gon abroad: but this He did for our Example.

Inducements to Retiredness, II

1 Isaiah 55.1.
2 Precedes.
3 Ecclesiastes 1.1–3.
4 Psalm 1.5.
5 Acts 7.22–30.

3

The balance of retirement and action

There is such a Necessity of Doing Good to others; that unless a man can make Retirement his Calling, and Spend his Days in preparing Things that shall Benefit the World; he must come abroad; and somtimes be Conversant among men, that after Weariness he might be renewed. for in Order to others we must enjoy our Selves. God in His Wisdom Ordaining this, that he might unite Men together. For had they no need of refreshing themselvs by Vertuous Actions one with another, it might possibly follow that like a Rope of Sand, they would be disunited, and fall to pieces. No man standing in need of others, evry man then might single out himself, and abide alone. Wheras now we are all made in Communion with God, to Enjoy the Benefit and Delight of others. His Divine Bounty so Wisely, and Sweetly Disposing Things, that we might be Blessings to them, and they to us: and in this, He to us all.

Hence we conclude, that our Life is to be Spent, not only in Retirement, nor only abroad. Life is made Harmonious, by a Sweet Mixture of these Extremes, and a Wise Improvement of both. That as God in Him self doth Enjoy all Things, in Order to all, so might we. For to Enjoy all, and yet not in Order to all is Defectiv. We are quickned and awakned by Conversation. One Estate is fed by another. For as no man can live without Breathing; which is a Reciprocation of Drawing in, and Returning Air; so neither can any man live Happily without a Mixture of Business and Retirement. We so therfore ought to retire, that we might gain Strength to manage our Business; and so wisely to enter into the World, that we might be more Great and Vigorous in our Retirement: making either of these Confer unto other. For in Retirement we see the Light in which we Act abroad: Abroad we do the Deeds, that Enrich Retirement with Delight and Glory. Bees flie abroad to make Hony, but eat it at home. Abroad we do those Acts of vertue, whence Pleasure and Honor ever arise.

Inducements to Retiredness, III

4

We are to grow Rich by enjoying what we have

By Retirement therfore we approach unto Truth, becaus there we see the Verity of Bliss, and the Blessedness of Nature, the Value and Glory of Gods Works, the Vanity of those who Delight in their own. And indeed, that to be delivered from the Cumber of Estates and Secular Pleasures, is a true Releas from Servitude and Dangers, that in a Quiet Life and Clear Light, we might see GOD and convers with his Glory. Their Opinion is that themselvs are the only Makers of Riches, and that Gods Works are to be Despised for Trifles, either becaus they be Common or freely given. That Clothes are to be regarded more then

the Body, and Ornaments to be preferd abov the Members. That Scarcity, not Service maketh Jewels; els the Stars would be Esteemed more,
that Men who hav nothing but the Wide World are poor and miserable,
and that a Twenty Shillings piece is a greater Caus of Joy then the Sun:
that nothing is ours, but what we hav under lock and Key, or at least
within a Ring-Hedge; and that He is Great who hath many Revenues.
that no man can be Possessor of other mens Delights, nor be Heavenly
in his own, that all are Confined, that Men are limited and Streightned
by each other, and that nothing before themselvs were born can by any
means be to them a Treasure. All these Opinions are fals in the World.

In Retirement we see the Grandure and Glory of our True Estate.
That Heaven and Earth is first ours, and then that in all Estates, it is
more ours, and more richly so, becaus of the Varietie of the Sons of
men that much Riches is needless and Superfluous to the Enjoyment of
the World, that we are far richer then if Crowns and Scepters should
fall out of the Heaven into our Bosoms. That the Sons of Men, are our
Greatest Treasures as they are God Almighties, that evry man is Heir
of all His Works, and that the Best Way wherin they can be Enjoyed is
the Divine Image. That we are to grow Rich, not by seeking what we
Want, but by Enjoying what we have. That it is Madness to Despise
Blessings becaus they are present. That we are all Kings, becaus we are
all pleased in all the Places of Gods Dominion. That we are in a Better
Estate then we were in Eden and hav more Treasures then Adam had.
That all the Ages are filled with Delights, and that one Soul is a Greater
Treasure then the Whole World, that all Things considered the World
is a Place of Eternal Joys, a Region of Heavenly Light, a Paradice of
Glory, and all Kingdoms evry mans Possessions, that to retire to them
is to enter into Heaven, and that the way is so perfect wherby all things
are ours, that we are to rest satisfied in God with Infinit Joy, and to
Glorifie his Name forevermore.

Inducements to Retiredness, II

5

The Allurement of Friendship

To giv is the Greatest Sensuality in the World, and to be Doing Good,
the Highest Epicurism. He therfore that intendeth a Voluptuous Life,

chuseth the most chois and Excellent Company, that he might Giv and be Doing Good, with the greatest pleasure. But many times like Waspes in Hony combs or unwelcom Flies in pure liquors, other persons fall in, for whom we need to be prepared. That will watch for our Halting; misinterpret our Meaning; misrepresent our Words: offend; take offence; be Churlish; profane, Censure, Exasperate: So that tho with some we hav Secure and Heavenly Libertie; we must of necessity be fortified and Prepared for all: And be as well Armed when we are made Publick, as if all the World were wholy Vicious. Nor is the Kindness and Favor of Friends so pleasant, nor the Conversation of Discreet ones so Delightfull: but that one Sour Herb shall imbitter all: nay Derive Greater Bitterness from the Beauty of that Conversation, which it apparently Hinders: So that were it not for the Benefit which we mean to do, the Pleasure is Greater of Abiding at Home.

But Suppose our Conversation free from Intruders. Our most perfect friends hav som Dissonancies, that Crack the Harmony. Discords towards us, and Defects in themselvs. It is Infinitly Delightfull to pour out ones Soul into anothers Bosom, while we are open and unfold the Mysteries of felicity. Especialy if it be to a person whom we lov, and that Delighteth in them. But after we hav discoursed the Principal Heads once over; there is a Certain Aversness to Talk of them again: and they run out into Vulgar Discours that is Heavy and Unprofitable. Which to a Man that tastes the Joys of Heaven is unwelcom: and always a Diversion Cruel and Unseasonable.

A Close Illimited Friendship is a Divine Enjoyment: could it be always pure, Sincere and perfect. But so many thousand Things conspire as Ingredients to compose and make up a Perfect friend, that I shall sooner Expect an Angel to be Conversant here on Earth, then such a Person. A Friend must be infinitly Faithfull, Tender, Honorable, Learned, Meek, Couragious, Humble: Innocent: Deeply Affectionat; Loving beyond measure, and in All Things exactly like oneself, for wherin ever He is unlike there will be Jarring and Discord. Dislike and Dislikenesse go together. Especialy where Resentments[1] are Keen and Violent. And if the Temper be lively and vigorous in my friend, the Resentments will be: if it be flat and insipid, there is an Abatement of the Pleasure. I confess that a Golden and Complying Humor, will smooth and Polish many Asperities. However this Inconvenience will ever attend it. He that hath a friend hath two to please: two Judgements to Satisfy; and two Wills. His own and anothers. Which here upon Earth is Inconvenient. It is better only to hav an infinit Benevolence toward all the

World, a Moderate friendship with the Good and Excellent: an Intire Illimited friendship with God alone.

Inducements to Retiredness, II

1 Emotions, sentiments.

6

On Celibacy

One Great reason, why our Savior, who is rightly stiled THE GREAT EXEMPLAR, remained Single: was becaus in His Solitary and Virgin State, (as He was more fit to be Beloved) He could more easily apply Him self to many Persons. For it becoms Him that would be the Son of God to be wholy evry ones. And He that would be wholy evry ones it becomes him to keep Higher then Privat Engagements, that he might be the Right of all with a Great Indifference. This Rule is not Universal, but it holdeth infallibly in Public Ministers.

God is that first and Sovereign Friend whose it is to Supply all our Wants, in the Absence of other friends. And this if we Discharge our Office, He will certainly do, according to His Riches in Glory.[1] It is not therfore that I should fear any Poverty or Inconvenience, by withdrawing from Men. For He has shewd me His Fidelity abundantly already. And it is easier for Heaven and Earth to pass away, then Him to forsake me. My friends therfore I will lov in God, according to the Nature and Order prescribed, by their Estate and Vertues: but to Him only will I individualy cleav. And whatever Excursions I make in the World, to Him will I return as to my Proper Centre. Whose Lov is more High, Holy Divine and Blessed then all other Loves: more Great Wise and Immutable: more Honorable Sweet and Secure: in evry respect more Satisfactory Profitable and Delightfull.

Inducements to Retiredness, II

1 Philippians 4.19.

7

Behaving well towards all things

46

All Kingdoms and all Ages Shall see Thee Eternaly, And thou even the very Thoughts of all persons in all Kingdoms and all Ages. Clothe thy Selfe with Beauty that Thou mayst be a Delight unto them. Lov them Intirely. And in every Action Design their Happiness. Prepare to Enjoy them. And night and Day in evry place think thy selfe a mong them. For So Thou art and shalt be Eternaly.

47

Towards Forrein Nations be always venerable. Pitty Those that Lye yet in Darkness. Long and Pray For Pagan Kingdoms, That their Eys may be Opened, and they may Delight thy Soul by Building Temples unto Jesus Christ. Behave thy selfe in all their Eys, as if upon thy Actions of shame or vertue all the Glory of Religion did Depend. Greiv at the Prophaness and at the Idolatry of Christians, that offendeth Turks and Hindereth Infidels.

48

Let the Joy and Splendor of the citties wherin Thou Livest; the flourishing of the villages, the Beauty of thy Kingdom, ravish thy soul. Rejoyce in the order peace and majesty of its magestrates and ministers. O Pray for the Peace of Jerusalem, They Shall prosper that Lov Thee.[1]

49

Let the Heavens and the Earth appear before Thee in all their Glory. Let the Sun and stars minister unto Thee in Serving all Ages. Esteem the world the wonder of Eternity, the Hous of God thy Great Inheritance, the Temple of His Glory. Rejoyce in it as a Mirror wherin the Angels See his Glory, Let it minister unto Thee in all its Influences, as it serveth this and every Kingdom.

50

Be venerable to thy Selfe, and Let thy Person be Sacred in thine one Esteem. O Prize thy selfe as thy God prizeth Thee. And becaus he serveth thee Infinitly, in Tendering thy Selfe Rejoyce to Pleas Him.

Thou who art His Freind, and Sole Heir of Heaven and Earth: Admire
His wisdom that could make every one Sole, and becaus thou art more
then Sole infinitly, Infinitly more regard thy Happiness and welfare
then if Thou wert Sole, becaus thou art to keep thy selfe as a Sacred
Treasure unto many Thousand others: That are Heirs of the world,
and in Thee to Inherit the Similitude of God, and in that Treasure
beyond all Imagination. Then Shall men speak well of Thee, when
Thou dost well to thy Selfe. Keep thy selfe from Blots Fals and wounds.
And remember that every Sin is an Infinit Poyson: that the Laws of
God are the Laws of Lov, commanding onely those Things that are
Sweet and Beneficiall, wherin thy Happiness and Honor are concerned.

51

Look upon His Service as Perfect freedom. And rejoyce that Thou art
instituted in a Life fraught with Divine Employments. Lov to be a
Blessing and Joy unto all: feel thy Enjoyments. Sing Praises for them.

52

It is no small matter to Dwell in community or in a congregation, and
to convers there without complaint, and to Persevere Faithfully in it
untill Death. Blessed is He that hath there Lived well, And Ended
Happily, They are as so many Gods if we respect the Grandure and
Power of their Soul: and wheather Innocent or miserable it is a weighty
thing to be conversant a mong them and not to Erre. Innocent no man
is in this world, much Less a Congregation. If there were we ought to
be Spotless, and that is weighty, to revere their censure, to be Amiable
in their Eys, to enjoy their Persons, to hold them Sacred, to be the Sons
of God, to enjoy their Glory: Promote His, Establish our own. To walk
as Gods would be then our Duty, which would be no Small Inferior
Thing. But if they were miserable as the most are, to be filled with great
compassion, to retain the Sence of the Eternal Diety. to Lov them as
the Saviour of the world doth, not to follow their Opinion, not to be
Provoked by their censure, not to approve ones selfe to them, not to
give them occation of evill Speech, not to be swayed by their example,
are Difficult Things, and He that passeth Thorrow all thes Bryers well,
and is in evry moment prudent shall be more beautifull then if he had
never sinned nor been among them.

53

Towards thy neighbor thou must behave thy Selfe with as much candor and sweetness as if He were an unspotted Angel. Becaus He is the Redeemed of Christ, made and called to Inherit all Things, an object of compassion. Yea by How much the Greater His Glory is and He knows it not, by so much the more is He to be Lamented, Aided and Pittyed. Therefore to the works of men Shouldst thou always bear an Enflamed Lov, and Zealously thirst after His Eternal Happieness. Suffer thy Selfe to be Injured for His Greater Benefits, and to improve all the wrongs and Injuries He doth, to His Best Advantage: which is the Salvation of His Soul. O that my Heart might be made a Stepping Stone for any ones Ascent into the Kingdom of Heaven.

54

Remember the Estate that Thou art in, and consider all wayes that the world is Corrupted. Wonder not therefore that men do not their Duty: but rather, How Thou art permitted to Breath a-mong them. Expect not to find any Good among them, but all Disorder and Perversness and Confusion. And if Thou find any Better then thy Soul Expected, Let it be thy Amazement and Joy, and with Great Admiration ascribe all to thy Redeemers Love. If they Discharge not theirs, remember thou what is Thy Duty: to imitate Christ: and Discharg it faithfully. By the Benefit of His Love, these Disorders were Put into thy Hand, and given to Thee as Infinit Treasures. Which Thou by wisdom must more improve then Adam could the Soyl and flowers in Eden. As being objects of thy care, and fair occation of Enriching thy Soul [with all] Kind of vertues.

55

Consider, and well understand, that Among invisible Things vertues are the fairest, being therefore made the way of Rewards, and the End of Things, becaus they are the Interiour Treasures of the Soul, and wholsome Beings, wherewith we Delight our selves and Enrich Eternity. Till men are acquainted with Invisible Things, it is exceeding wonderfull vertues should be So Glorious. But when we know them, we see manifestly they are the onely Beings whose Influence Blesseth the Life of man, Enricheth the world, and Atcheiveth Happiness. Those Things may be Spoken of them which no Ey ever Saw, and which have not yet been uttered by man. They Satisfie the Soul ... clothe a man with

Beauty before all Ages, make Him the Treasure and the Joy of Angels, becaus He voluntarily doth those Things, And it is their Joy to see Him doing those Things, That crown Gods works, Satisfie Gods Desire, Compleat His Happiness. The world would be in vain were it not for vertues: for by them it is enjoyed. Without these it would be a Den of Theeves, and a Caos of Confusion.

56

Begin with wisdom.[2] Wisdom is the Light in which Happiness is Enjoyed, by which our safety is Established, and our Life Adorned. It is that which guides us to our Soveraign End, Discovers the value of all our Treasures, shews us our Interest and Propriety in them: Teaches us the Glory of Pleasing God, Forewarns us of Dangers, makes us to see the Fulness of the Earth, and the Blessedness of His Kingdom. It is that which Directs us in all Arduous Affaires, makes us to Aime at the Best of Ends, and Helps us to Atcheiv them. It renders us Amiable in the Eys of others, and is in all respects Better then Rubies.[3] It is the very Possession of felicity, one with Righteousness and true Holiness Divinity and Blessedness. Happy are they that are not troubled with the false Apprehension of Things. A clear Sight and Bright Knowledge is much, but wisdom more. For to Know all Things and not to Prize them is the Greatest Folly in the whole world, to Do them truly, and enjoy them all is the Highest wisdom. Wisdom includes Knowledg, and the Improvment of it. It is Impossible for one to be wise, that does not Effectually Discharge His Duty. Therefore does wisdom contain the Residue, and is by Eminence every vertue.

57

Prudence is a choys Selection of the means: wisdom Exercised in Particular Things, Removing obstacles, Improving Evils, Laying Hold of oppertunities, finding Advantages, shunning Extreams, Attaining the mean, and walking warily in it when it is Found. O that I could hold this celestial vertue, which hath So much Place here upon Earth, as if it had none in Heaven. The truth is there will be Little need of Prudence there among all Stable and Permanent Things, which will Shine there as Eternal Objects to perfect wisdom. But here upon Earth a-mong such Lubricities, variety of Dispositions Apprehensions and occurrences, Prudence is a Thing so Eminent and Illustrous: that it will Shine in Heaven for the Sake of the Benefit it did on Earth, and be far more Bright then the morning Star. Will you know How God Almighty made this vertue: By giving us a Power to see Advantages, and a Liberty to improve them; or which is the very same, By Commanding us to be considerat, and Leaving us to our selves. By which He did for us a most Glorious Thing: For He Enabled us as Gods by our own vertue to Rule the world, and to Please Him, with Admirable Deeds, While He as a Spectator Delighted in them. Of all vertues in the whole world this is that which I most want. Since therefore it is so Delightfull: and of Daily use in evry occurrence, Let me Labor more Industriously for it, clothe my selfe more Continualy with it. It is of universal Benefit in Finding vertues, nay in Framing composing creating them. For this alone Applies the Rule, and Discerns the Golden mean where vertue Lieth, So that if I will enrich the world or my Selfe with Actions, Prudence must be my Companion, Light and shadow. Once more becaus I am exceeding Dull in Apprehending this vertue (Through the Real Splendor of this celestial world, and the Standing Rules and objects there); becaus none but this and Pride are incident continualy, non that I want so infinitly as this and Humility: once more remember, that through Imprudence, in not Bounding and Methodizing Things, Thou hast seemed vicious.

58

Courage is a vertue of Little use in our First Estate, but of infinit Since. For in Innocence it was Exercised with infinit Ease in the Propelling of Temptations, and nothing more then an Habitual Resolution to forsake all Things for the Lov we owe to So infinit a Benefactor. But now it is a vertue a-mong Stronger Assaults, more frequent and more continual, in a time also wherin we are more weak. And Therefore needs to be assured with Greater Strength. And so it is. It is Aided with the Death of Jesus Christ, whose Love and Example Should more Enflame us then all the Gloryes of Heaven and Earth. When is courage but in the Time of fighting. Eternal Torments which we hope to Escape, Everlasting Enjoyments which we hope to Attain, and the infinit Glory of an Assured victory are her Magizines. And Gods Assistances her onely Second. Where Courage is High, and Heroick indeed Enemies and battles are her Jubilee and Delight notwithstanding she can enjoy her enjoyments. It is a Masculine vertue that is Lord of the world, calamities are its Trophies, oppositions Her Jubilee, She Thrives by Difficulties, And is ever Triumphant in all Distresses. Yet without Prudence to Moderate and Guide it, this Amazon and virago is but a Bruit: tho without it no man at all Dares at all to be vertuous. Courage is that which Animates and Actuates every vertue, Plucks off the vizzar from evry Bugbear and make a Laughing Stock of every Danger. In which I Long to be more Compleat: For the truth is it makes every Thing a Joy, and the Earth Heaven.

59

Justice is that vertue by which we render unto all Their Due. And of infinit use from the First moment even to the End in Heaven. For it is at once the Payment and Enlargment of our Selves in the Fruition of our Blessedness. The Enlargment of our selves because the Extention of our Selves unto all objects, the Payment of our Selves because we owe our Selves to all Beings, which we Accomplish in Rendering a Due Esteem. The Primativ Soul of spiritual Justice; the Root and Fountain of all the Particular Acts wherin Justice can Express it selfe. without which we retain the precious and Expend the vile: and Lose what we Retain. For all vertue is of that Nature that it is Lost by Retaining, becaus by being retained it is not Permitted to Come into Being. All Justice without rendering a Due Esteem is an Empty Carcase. But that Justice of Esteeming Duly by way of Eminence includeth all. And causeth all, and causeth all. when we render unto God His Due Esteem, we are Just to Him, Render Him that which is most Pleasing, value His Essence according to its worth, Rejoyce in the Benefits we receive of Him, Sacrifice our Being in Homage to Him. For in rendering to Him a Due Esteem we offer up our selves in that Esteem: and becaus He is infinit, Prizing infinitly we are Loth to Lose Him, Love to Enjoy Him, and for that cause Delight to Pleas Him. Render Him his Due, Obedience, Thanksgiving. And which is the whole of both and soul of both a Genuin Lov, infinit and Pure. Justice extendeth to other Things. We are just to men when we render unto men their Due Esteem. For by valuing them truly we Lov them according to the Excellency of the Goodness that was infused into their Natures. And Dedicat our selves to Serve them becaus they are So much honoured by God. nay we do Justice to God by serving them Whom He Loveth, for we owe Him that Duty. And when we lov them as we ought we shall Prize them as our Selves: Liv in them, Tender them with Care, Render them a Due regard in Striving alwayes to Promote their Happiness, be Exalted in them, and Delight always in their Glory. Justice is a vertue of vast Enlargments; and so Great that no Age, nor world can hold it. It extendeth our affections and Due Esteem to Angels, cherubims and men, men of evry Age Kingdom and Generation, Patriarchs Prophets

Apostles &c. who are all by being Prized, Embraced and Enjoyed. We Transfer our selves into them whom we Prize as our selves, and are Seated there, are there affected, feel and receiv, do the work of nature and Delight, are by them received. But Justice Extendeth further. Inanimat creatures are capable of it. We ought to do Right to the Sun and Sea and Stars, to the skie the Earth Beasts and Trees, to value the Services which they already do us, which are by being Prized all Enjoyed. To them also do we giv our selves (in Pondering their Excellencies) and in them to God Almighty. Justice is a Kind of Bartering of ware, a commutativ vertue Exercised in giving and receiving, to the Common Benefit and Good of all. we are Enlarged in the Sun while we are there Esteeming it, becaus each of them are our Second Selves in God Almighty, becaus He is more. And in all this is the work of Blessedness, becaus it is our Interest both to giv and receiv, to be a Blessing and to Inherit all.

60

Temperance is the Execution of what Prudence Advised. It relateth not onely to meats and Drinks, but to all our Behaviours Passions and Desires. It settles them Effectualy in the Golden mean. There is a Temperance in Gesture Speech and Lov. In the right Temparament and Proportion of which, the Health and Harmonie of our Life consisteth.

Sit modus in Rebus, modus est Pulcerrima virtus

A lesson which becaus boys are taught to season their minds at first with vertue, they Despise when they are men: and for most Part when they are Exceeding old, need go to school againe to Learn the Practice.

> All musick sawces Feasts Delights and Pleasures.
> Games Dancing Arts, consist in Governd measures.
> Much more do words and Passions of the mind,
> In Temperance their Sacred Beauty Find.

61

These 4 Cardinal vertues ought evermore to be united into one. Courage in Attempting, Prudence in Directing, Temperance in Proportionating and Justice in Resolving to Pay evry Thing its Due. They are all Exercised in the Light of wisdom, and founded in Love: Lov is the Ground of courage that fuels and Inspires it, Lov is the Light of Prudence, becaus it actuates and makes it tender, makes it wakefull watchfull cautious, Lov is the very Soul that Animates and Distributes Justice, and the very Debt it Selfe which Justice Pays, even a Lov Proportiond to the merit of its cause. Lov is the Hand and Rule of Temperance. for it must be Pleased, which it cannot be but by Hitting right for the welfare of its Beloved. Acts of Justice and Courage them selves are Things beloved, and so are mens Persons. And a mong these Justice must Excite us to every vertue.

62

Beside these moral the[re] are Theological vertues. Faith Righteousness Holiness and Humility. Faith is the First and the Basis of all, which hath its use and Being only a mong Sinners Since the Fall. That Knowledge wherby Adam in Innocency foresaw His Happiness and the Rewards in Heaven, was rather Sight, and a certain Sence in Reason then formal faith. So was that wherby He beleived Sin was Death. For He saw it Intuitivly. But in beleiving that Death Should follow upon His Eating the forbidden fruit He Exercised faith. And yet even there also God Haveing forbidden it Him, His reason told Him it must be so. But since the fall without faith it is impossible to Pleas God, it was impossible to be vertuous, for till God Discovered His new Lov we could not be wise: which Lov we must see before we can be Blessed. As Long as we Apprehend God implacable in His Hatred towards us, we must of necessity hate Him. Before we can Love Him, we must beleiv He Loveth us. That Jesus Christ is the Redeemer of the world we must needs beleive before we can enjoy Him, that there are Eternal Joys, and that we have Liberty to gain them, before we can be Discreet or vertuous. So that unto Sinners even faith it self is the mother of wisdom, the Light of vertues: and in its own nature necessary to the Attainment of Eternal Joys. It includeth the Begining of every Grace, and is of infinit value a mong the sons of men. How wonderfull is it that Sin Should be the Parent of so Amiable a vertue. Lov includeth all other vertues. This Preventeth it and is the foundation of it. but what Horrible Confusion do they make who remove that Lov which Preventeth this; the Lov of God which is the object of it. They Lock men up in the chains of Darkness, take a way their Glory, Exhibit God in a False Mirror and in the Dungeon of this world encreas their misery. This faith is a vertue that Glitters in obscure Darkness, Like a King in Gold, Invested and Shining in Sun Beams.

63

Righteousness is but another Denomination of Justice and is a vertue to be Exercised in all worlds. Justice seems to be Exercised in giving, this in receiving: both in either. Its Etymology is Right-wiseness, its operation the work of Right Reason, Its office the Answer of all obligations, and the fruition of all Treasures. Its Excellency consisteth in the fulfilling of all Laws, its Reward is the Goodness of what it Prizeth. It is never Perfectly attained, till all Things are infinitly rich and ours. For that they are ours is Part of their Goodness. And this Part we Rob them of, by not beleiving it. All Things in Heaven and Earth are ours which when we have Courage to beleive and wisdom to perceiv, we hav Great need of Temperance and Power to Govern ourSelves, of Prudence to Direct and Justice to Regard the Grandure of others that are as Great as we.

64

Holiness is more then Righteousness is. It [is] the Zeal wherewith we render unto Things their Sacred value, The infinit care Intention and Fervor where with we Discharge our Duty, whoe are so violently Addicted to Discharge it in evry part and tittle of it, that even for whole worlds we should not Omitt it in the Least Degree. And this Intension and vehemency of Lov, how far soever beside the Substance of Things it may Seem, yet is it the onely thing that Sanctifieth our Duty, the onely Grace that maketh it Acceptable. The very Holiness of God is the infinit Intension and Greatness of his Lov, which maketh all Things Easy, Himselfe infinitly Delightfull unto us, and us unto Him.

Select Meditations, IV

1 Psalm 122.6.
2 Proverbs 4.7.
3 Proverbs 8.11; Job 28.18.

8

Pastoral advice on the keeping of Rogation

Pitty then it is that out of pretended fear of Superstition, Men should
neglect Primitv & Excellent Devotion: or out of fals Groundless fear,
Endeavor to Disannul such Heavenly Constitutions; there are som
things that carry so much Light & Beauty in them, that they need not
be written in a Law, being Asserted by Reason & Taught by Nature.
Certainly the time of the Ceremonial law was the most Nice & Critical
for the Admitting of Inventions that ever was, yet even then was there
a Place left for the Products of Mature & Perfect Reason, as there is
now, ever was, & will be always. There was no Provision made in the
Ceremonial Law for Altering the Tabernacle, & Turning it into a
Temple. Yet Davids reason, upon which He founded the Intention of a
Change, was Excellently Good; & the Design Accepted. Lo I Dwell in
a Hous of Cedar, & shall the Ark of the Lord remain under Curtains.[1]
When Israel had Rest & a Settled Estate, it was Suitable than, not
withstanding the Divinity, Holiness & Glorious Antiquity of the Tabernacle, to hav a more Magnificent & Permanent Temple. It was no
where provided in the Levitical Law, that Levites should be Divided
into Courses, & Singers added to the Publick Worship but Reason saw
it Expedient both for Ornament & Joy. That the Ark should be Brought
up to Jerusalem in Triumph, & be Attended by all the Congregation
of Israel, in an Act of Worship & Reverence to God, was no where
ordained, yet Reason saw it for His Honor & Glory; & Piety delighted
in it. They might all hav been contented with one Way of Honoring
God, within the Temple; but without Doors also to do it was Beautifull,
& Added to the Lustre of the Heavenly Kingdom. When David had
Assembled all the Tribes together, & brought the Ark to its place in
Jerusalem, there were many profane people that understood not the
Mystery, & few of them that Danced, Danced with Davids Heart.[2] Yet
was it unreasonable from the Error of the Vulgar, to induce a Conclusion against the integrity of the Commander. And Therfore the many
were Gross. & Rude in the Action, & tho they might all Honor God
in the Court of his Holiness, tho that Procession of theirs were not
ordained nor commanded by a Law, yet being the Product of a Clear
Reason, Adding to the Splendor & Glory of their Church & conferring
more to the Visible honor of God upon Earth, David allowed it, &

Rejoyced in it. I hav seen thy Goings O God! nay Thy people, & thine Enemies; They hav seen the Goings even the Going of God my King in the Sanctuary. The Singers went before, the Players on Instruments followed after, amongst them were the Damsels playing with Timbrels: Bless ye God in the Congregations, even the Lord from the Foundation of Israel. There is little Benjamin with their Ruler, the Princes of Judah & their Counsel, the Princes of Zebulun & the Princes of Naphtali. It was no where commanded that upon Solemn Festivals, Jubilees & Thanksgivings the People should be clad in White in token of Triumph, yet Reason found that to be the Cheerfull & Delightfull colour, & therefore when the Almighty Scattered Kings, it was White as snow in salmon,[3] that is, all the thousands in Israel after the Victory, being clothed in White, covered the Grounds & rejoiced in it, from which Custom Solomon exhorting us to be Cheerfull borroweth the phrase, Let thy Garments be always white. Finaly that we may make an End of this Matter at once, The very Number of Feasts was among the Jews a matter of Worship. Yet upon solemn Occasions they might Adde others by Human Institution. As the Days of Purim, & the Feast of the Dedication. For Temporal Deliverances therefore, & signal Mercies, much more for such Spiritual Great Transcendent Blessings as the Nativity of our Savior, His Ascension into Heaven, the Conversion of Nations, the Labors of the Apostles, may the Church with Reason Institut Festivals. And with an Incomparable Wideness & Depth of Wisdom, adde an Exterior Beauty. As well as an Interior within the Temple. That both without & within, in the field & in the Churches, God being Honored, a Contemplating Ey might hav the fuller Prospects, through out all the Land seeing the sitting of His Servants, & the majestie of His Service beneath the Roof, & the Goings of His Horses abroad, I the open Sun. Where by Ocular Demonstration they might view His Works, & see His glory which they hear of in the Temple, & learn to hav a Sacred Esteem even of the very fields, because they are His who made the Heavens. That all the World might appear to be the House of God, by the Universality Variety & Beauty of His Servants Minstery. I conclude therefore with Learned Hooker. It grieveth me that Things of Principal Excellency, should be Bitten at by Men, whom God hath endued with Graces, both of Wit & Learning for Better purposes.

Church's Year-Book

1 2 Samuel 7.2–3.
2 2 Samuel 6.1–5, 14.
3 Psalm 68.14.

9

On the Bible

1

When Thou dost take
  this sacred Book into thy hand;
Think not that Thou
  th' included sence dost understand.

2

It is a signe
  thou wantest sound Intelligence;
If that Thou think
  thy selfe to understand the Sence.

3

Bee not deceived
  Thou then on it in vain mayst gaze
The way is intricate
  that leads into a Maze.

4

Heer's nought but whats Mysterious
  to an Understanding Eye:
Where Reverence alone stands Ope,
  And Sence stands By.

Early Notebook

10

How to Liv the life of Happieness

O my God teach me Things concerning Happieness Soe Divine, and So Illustrious in their Native Light: that it may be very certaine as soon as they are Named, that neither Angels nor cherubims can bring any tidings even from Heaven it selfe more Glorious. Nor any of the Blessed and celestial Hosts inform us with more Profitable or Divin Misteries.

Instructions Teaching us how to Liv the Life of Happieness

1

Remember that it was possible that thou alone mightest have been in the world: and that then there had been no cities no Temples no palaces no kingdoms, but an open wilderness of Briers and thornes, and Dole-full creatures Endangering thy Life. Yet that the Sun would rise and Set, the Day be Beautifull, the Starrs Shine by night and minister to Thee. And all these be wholy thine, as they were once Adams, that waters would be thine to Quench thy thirst, And corn where thou couldst find it, and that all these were in the wilderness nevertheless to be enjoyd, and that they ought to have been prized according to their value.

2

Remember that the world is the begining of Gifts. And that the Sons of men in destroying the wild Beasts and Dressing the feilds, take a way the Briers and Thorns and Restore the world to the Beauty of Paradice. In Adorning the meadows and building villages they Sweat for Thee. And make the wilderness an Habitable Kingdom full of Cities Trades Temples and Beautifull varieties, which were it not for these would be an horrid and an Empty Desert, that all these are Superadded Treasures, Yea that all their Trades and occupations are thine. For without them Thou must go Naked and Lie in a cave, who now hast comfortable clothes and Houses.

3

That Gods Laws Command them all to Lov Thee as themselves, by which He hath given Thee all their Riches Authority and Power. and that How ever Disobedient men are, Things are to be Accepted According as they are intended. And thou infinitly Enriched by this Promulgation in the Bosom of God.

4

That Thou art made to Live in the Image of God. To Lov them. To be a Joy a Blessing and Treasure to them. And that it is a Greater Happiness to be a Joy and a Blessing unto others, then to have Millions of Silent worlds in Quiet Possession.

5

That haveing all these by the Gift of God Thou art to Admire His wisdom Goodness and Power, for makeing thy Soul the End of all Things. And as the freind of God to Live in the Contemplation of his Eternall Love, and in the continual exercise of Singing Praises and Loveing God.

6

That Swerving from this Glorious and Happy Life Thou art faln into sin. And needest a saviour to make an Atonement and Reedeem thee from Hell. which by reason of the Infinitenes of the Guilt, and sin, no man could do but the son of God. Who therefore was incarnat and became man. whose Incarnation, since it is soe Difficult yet necessary to beleive; All the wayes of God in promises prophesies miracles Types and figures, Ceremonies of the Law, and Revelations from Heaven in the Ages before he came were Busied to confirme. And all his ways since in the Evangelists and Apostles, preists and Martirs, Bishops and fathers, in converting kingdoms, Erecting Temples, Translating the scriptures &c are busied to reveal.

7

That all these being requisite and ordained to confirm thy Faith in that Glorious person are thy Treasures, and Sacred Blessing in thine Inheritance.

8

That Jesus christ redeemed all mankind to be thy Treasures as well as his. And that He Himselfe is thy Soveraign and Supremest Treasure, who purchased all these.

9

That now thou art to Liv as the freind of God, in a more Glorious union and Communion with him then before. All things being thy Treasures of a double value, if not by a double Right. And that the Lov is double to what it was in the First creation. That therefore all Ages are Thine Inheritance and Thou Like Abraham Heir of the world and now to Liv in communion with him, as an High Preist to prais and offer Sacrifice.

10

That the works of Lov which Thou returnest are pleasing to his Eternal majesty, and to all his Hosts that see thee with him. And so much the more by how much the more precious, costly and desired.

11

That the works of Lov which Thou returnest to God, being sought by all these meanes, are more precious then Thousands of millions of worlds. And that thou art to enjoy thy selfe as the joy of all after this Manner.

12

That in this Life Thou art to Liv Eternaly, as the Holy one of God: Angels and men being better then ministers officers and Attendants, Freinds unto Thee. That all the Things in Heaven and Earth are thy Delight, for Pleasing them. And finaly that a time cometh when all Things Shall be Naked and open to thine eyes, all thy Sences and affections perfect, All Angels and men before Thee, as realy and more effectualy then now thy friends and companions are. Every one of them being as Great a Delight to thee as Thou art to God, and thou a delight to evry one of them in His Image.

The seeds of all wisdom Happines and Glory are here Included. And these Instructions So Great, that I would have given in my childhood Millions of worlds to have met with one teaching them, so earnestly

did I Long after them. How much therfore am I bound to Bless God
for haveing Satiated my soul and Replenished me with Good Things.
It makes us see the face of Religion as Bright as the Sun, as Fair as the
Heavens, as Real as the world.

It Discovereth an Infinit weight and Depth of concernment in evry
work in evry Person. And Lifts a Holy Man above Thrones and Kingdoms, as much as Stars are above Sands or Angels above Pismires.

It maketh a man at home in his own kingdom. And even as a Pilgrim
here to Liv in Heaven.

It Sheweth the Infinit Dreadfullness of any crime: and with what
profound affections we ought on all occations to walk with God.

It Shews the infiniteness of the Love of God in the contemplation of
which we ought to Liv for ever.

Select Meditations, III, 31

II

Practise the presence of God

The least Slip of our Heart (out of the Devine presence) is Like the fall
of Angels, So is the Least Cessation wherin we forget to make God our
Supreme End. I ought therefore evermore in the Beginning of evry
Enterprize; to remember God, and aime at His Glory as my Supreme
End. When I forget Him I walk in Darkness, when I aim at my Self it
is in vain Glory. For He Lifteth up Himselfe above God that maketh
Himself his Last End. In every Conference therfore Discours and
enterprize I must actually remember His presence, and Direct my Inten-
tions to His Glory. Not to do it, not to do it is the Beginning of Error
and of all Calamity. For by forbearing to do this I wander in the Dark,
and become Subject to all Transgression, for from the very first moment
wherein a man doth otherwise He is Alienated from God, made weak,
Apt to be Led into all Temptations.

Select Meditations, III, 75

12

Ministry among the Saints

80

My Excellent friend, you see that there are Treasures in Heaven and Earth fit to be Enjoyed, besides those of Kings Courts and Taverns. The Joys of the Temple are the Greatest Joys were they understood; they are the most Magnificent Solemn and Divine. There are Glorious Entertainments in this Miserable World, could we find them out. What more Delightfull can be imagined, then to see a Savior at this Distance Dying on the Cross to Redeem a man from Hell, and to see one self the Beloved of GOD and all Kingdoms, yea the Admired of Ages, and the Heir of the whole World? Hath not His Blood united you and me, Cannot we see and Lov and Enjoy each other at 100 Miles Distance? In Him is the only Sweet and Divine Enjoyment. I Desire but an Amiable Soul in any Part of all Eternity, and can lov it unspeakably: And if lov it, Enjoy it. For Lov implies Pleasure, becaus it is ever pleased with what is Beloved. Lov GOD and Jesus Christ and Angels and Men, which you are made to do as naturaly as the Sun is made to shine, and the Beauty of the Holy Ghost Dwelling in you will make you my Delight, and the Treasure of the Holy Angels. You will at last be seen by me and all the others, in all your Thoughts and in all your Motions. In the mean time, Delight only in the Lov of JESUS, and Direct all your Lov unto Him. Adore Him, Rejoyce in Him, Admire His Lov and Prais Him, Secretly and in the Congregation. Enjoy His Saints that are round about you, make your self Amiable that you may be Admitted to their Enjoyment, by Meekness Temperance, Modesty Humility Charity Chastitie Devotion Cheerfulness Gratitude Joy Thanksgiving. Retire from them that you may be the more Precious, and com out unto them the more Wise. So shall you make the Place wherin you live a Nest of Sweet Perfumes, and evry Soul that is round about you will be a Bed of Honor and Sweet Repose unto you.

81

My Goodness extendeth not to Thee O Lord, but to Thy Saints, and to the Excellent in the Earth in whom is all my Delight. To Delight in the Saints of God is the Way to Heaven. One would think it Exceeding easy and reasonable, to Esteem those whom Jesus purchased with his precious Blood. And if we do so how can we chuse but inherit all Things. All the Saints of all Ages and all Kingdoms are his Inheritance, his Treasures, his Jewels. Shall they not be yours since they are His whom you love so infinitly? There is not a cup of cold Water given to a Disciple in the name of a Disciple, but He accepteth it as don to Himself. Had you been with Mary Magdalen, would you not hav annointed his feet, and washed them in tears and wiped them with the Hairs of your head? His poor Servants, his Contemptible and Disguised Members here upon Earth are his Feet, yea more, the Apple of His Ey: yea more, for He gave his Eys and Heart and Hands and feet for them. O therfore universaly in all places tender them and at all times be ready and Willing to Minister unto them. And that with infinit Joy, Knowing the Excellency of your Duty · for you are Enjoying the World, and Communicating your self like God unto them. You are laying up Treasure in Heaven and Enlarging your Soul, Beautifying your Life, and Delighting the Holy Angels, Offering up sacrifices unto God, and perfuming the World; Embracing Jesus Christ, and caressing your Savior while you are Dispensing Charities among them. Every Alms Deed is a Precious Stone in the Crown of Glory.

82

But there are a sort of Saints meet to be your Companions, in another maner · But that they lie concealed. You must therfore make your self exceeding Virtuous, that by the very Splendor of your Fame you may find them out. While the Wicked are like Heaps of Rubbish, these few Jewels lie buried in the Ruins of Mankind: and must Diligently be Digd for. You may Know them by their Lustre, and by the very Desire and Esteem they hav of you when you are virtuous. For as it is the Glory of the Sun that Darkness cannot approach it, becaus it is always encompassed with its own Beams; so it is the Priviledge of Holy Souls, that they are always secure in their own Light, which driveth away Divels and Evil Men: And is accessible by none, but Lovers of Virtue. Beginners and Desirers will give you the Opportunity of infusing your self and your Principles into them. Practicers and Growers will mingle souls and be Delightfull Companions, The Sublime and Perfect, in the Lustre of their Spirit will shew you the Image of Almighty God and the Joys of Heaven. They will Allure Protect Encourage Comfort Teach Honor and Delight you. But you must be very Good, for that is the way to find them. And very Patient to endure som time, and very Diligent to observ where they are.

83

They will Prais our Savior with you and turn the World into Heaven. And if you find those of Noble and Benevolent Natures, Discreet and Magnanimous, Liberal and Cheerful, Wise and Holy as they ought to be, you will hav in them Treasures Greater then all Relations whatsoever. They will Exchange Souls with you, Divide Estates, Communicate Comforts, Counsels and Honors, And in all Tenderness Constancy Fidelity and Lov be more yours then their own. There are exceeding few such Heavenly Lovers as Jesus was, who imparted his own Soul unto us. Yet som may Doubtlessly be found. And half a Dozen such as these wisely chosen will represent unto us the New Jerusalem: Entertain us always with Divine Discourses, Pleas us always with Heavenly Affections, Delight us always with Melodie and Praises, and ever make us near unto our Savior.

84

Yet you must Arm yourself with Expectations of their Infirmities, and resolv nobly to forgive them: not in a sordid and Cowardly maner, by taking no notice of them: nor in a Dim and Lazy maner, by letting them alone: but in a Divine and Illustrious maner, by chiding them meekly, and vigorously rendering and showering down all kind of Benefits. Cheerfully continuing to do Good, and whatever you suffer by your Piety and charity, Confidence or Lov, to be like our Savior, Unwearied: who when he was abused, and had often been evil intreated among men, proceeded couragiously through all Treacheries and Deceits to die for them. So shall you turn their very Vices, into Virtues to you, and as our Savior did make of a Wreath of Thorns, a Crown of Glory. But set the Splendor of Virtues before you, and when som fail, think with your self, there are some Sincere and Excellent, And why should not I be the most Virtuous?

85

With all their Eys behold our Savior, with all their Hearts Adore Him, with all their Tongues and Affections praise him. See how in all Closets, and in all Temples; in all Cities and in all feilds; in all Nations and in all generations they are lifting up their hands and Eys unto his Cross; and Delight in all their Adorations. This will Enlarge your Soul and make you to Dwell in all Kingdoms and Ages: Strengthen your Faith and Enrich your Affections: fill you with their Joys and make you a

Lively Partaker in Communion with them. It will make you a Possessor Greater then the World. Men do mightily wrong themselvs: when they refuse to be present in all Ages: and Neglect to see the Beauty of all Kingdoms, and Despise the Resentments[1] of every Soul, and Busie them selvs only with Pots and Cups and things at home, or Shops and Trades and things in the street. But do not liv to God Manifesting Himself in all the World, nor care to see, (and be present with Him, in) all the Glory of his Eternal Kingdom. By seeing the Saints of all Ages we are present with Them. By being present with them becom too Great for our own Age, and near to our Savior.

86

O Jesu, Thou King of Saints, whom all Adore: and the Holy Imitat, I admire the perfection of thy Lov in evry soul! Thou lovest evry one Wholy as if Him alone: Whose Soul is so Great an Image of thine Eternal Father, that Thou camest down from Heaven to die for Him, and to Purchase Mankind that they might be his Treasures. I Admire to see thy Crosse in evry Understanding, thy Passion in evry Memory, thy Crown of Thorns in evry Ey, and thy Bleeding, Naked Wounded Body in evry Soul. Thy Death liveth in evry Memory, thy Crucified Person is Enbalmed in evry Affection, thy pierced feet are Bathed in evry ones Tears, thy Blood all droppeth on evry Soul: Thou wholy Communicatest thy self to evry Soul in all Kingdoms, and art wholy seen in every Saint, and wholy fed upon by evry Christian. It is my Priviledge that I can enter with Thee into evry Soul, and in evry Living Temple of thy Manhood and thy Godhead, behold again, and Enjoy thy Glory.

Centuries of Meditations, I

1 Sentiments.

13

On Patience

Patience then is that Vertue by which we behave our selves constantly and prudently in the midst of Misfortunes and Troubles: That Vertue whereby we do not only forbear to break out in Murmurings and

Repinings, or support our selves from sinking under Afflictions, or suppress our Discontentments, and refrain from Anger and Disquiet; but whereby we retain our Wisdom, and the goodness of our Mind, notwithstanding all the Confusions and Disorders that would disturb us, and demean our selves in a serene and honourable manner, surmounting the Pains and Calamities that trouble us, and that would otherwise overwhelm us. While we move in a quick and vigorous manner under our Burthen; and by a true Courage improve our Afflictions, and turn them into the *Spoils* of Invincible Reason.

It is an easie Observation, that Troublous Times are the Seasons of Honour, and that a Warlike-Field is the Seed-Plot of great and Heroical Actions. Men that live in quiet and peaceful Ages, pass through the World as insensibly as if they had all their daies been asleep. Hazards, and Calamities, and Battles, and Victories fill the Annals with Wonder, and raise Great Men to an eminent degree of Fame and Glory. It is Saint *Chrysostoms* opinion, That a Man shews far greater Bravery, that grapples with a Disease, or surmounts his evil Fortune, or behaves himself with Courage in distress, bears the burning of his House, or the loss of his Goods, or the death of his Children with an equal Spirit, in the midst of all Calamities retains his Integrity with Humility and Patience, and Blesses GOD, chearfully submitting with Resignation to his Will, and shews himself Constant in all Estates: then he that in the midst of a prosperous Condition, buildeth Hospitals and Temples, shineth in the exercise of Bounty and Magnificence, and obligeth all the World without any other Expence than that of his Monics. A *Pelican* that feeds her young ones with her Blood, is a more Noble Bird than an Eagle, that fills her Nest with *Ravine*, though taken from the Altar: For though that of a Sacrifice be the more Sacred food, that of ones own Blood is more near and costly.

Times of Affliction are Seed-times for a future Harvest. *We are made perfect through Sufferings*: though the Way be mysterious, and the Manner almost incomprehensible, whereby the Sufferings we endure conduce to our Perfection. *Consider the Patience of* Job, how great a spectacle his Sufferings made him *to GOD, Angels, and Men*, and how glorious he became by his Patience to all *Generations*.

Christian Ethicks, Ch. 24

14

Dare to be Good

A Remark

To be Couragious is the Easiest thing in the World, when we consider the certain success, which Courage founded on Goodness must needs attain. For he that makes his Fortitude subservient onely to the excess of his Love, has all the Powers of Heaven and earth on his side, and the Powers of Hell that are already subdued are the only foes that are to be vanquished by him. To dare to be Good, is the Office of true and Religious valour. And he that makes it his Business to oblige all the world, he whose design it is to be delightful to all mankind, has nothing to overcome, but their error & bitterness, which by meekness, and Kindness, and Prudence, and liberality will easily be accomplished. For they all love themselves, and cannot chuse but desire those that are kind and Serviceable to them, and must so far forth as they love themselves, honor & delight in their Benefactors. So that Courage thus guided by Prudence to the works of Charity and goodness must surely be safe and prosperous on earth, its Admirableness and its Beauty being a powerful Charm, an Invincible Armour.

Christian Ethicks, Ch. 21

15

Infinitely thirst after God's acceptance

Infinitly Thirst after GODS Acceptance, & Delight in it; for by Delighting in His Acceptance & Thirsting after it, Thou art united to Him.

Prize his Acceptance abov all Worlds: for it is Transcendent to them.

Beautify thy self that Thou mayest be Accepted of Him.

Despise not the meanest Creature, but Desire Worthily to be Accepted of all: And yet so prefer the Acceptance of GOD as to be willing to perish in the Esteem of all, that Thou mayst find a place in His Gracious Acceptance.

Remember these Scriptures:

My Servant Job shall pray for you, for him will I accept. Job 42:8.

Let the Words of my Mouth & the meditations of my Heart be Acceptable in thy Sight, O Lord my Strength & my Redeemer. Psalm 19:14.

Mordecai the Jew was next to King Ahasuares, & great among the Jews, & Accepted of the Multitud of his Brethren, seeking the Wealth of his people, & speaking Peace unto all His Seed. Esther 10:3.

I beseech you therefore Brethren, by the mercies of GOD. That ye present your Bodies a living Sacrifice, holy, Acceptable unto GOD, which is your reasonable Service.

And be not conformed to this World, but be ye Transformed by the renewing of your Minds, that ye may prov what is that Good & Acceptable & Perfect Will of GOD. Romans 12: 1, 2.

Now I beseech you Brethren, for the Lord Jesus Christs sake, & for the Lov of the Spirit, that you strive together with me, in your prayers to GOD for me. That I may be delivered from them that do not believ in Judea; & that my service which I hav for Jerusalem may be Accepted of the Saints. Romans 15: 30, 31.

Commentaries of Heaven, 'Acceptance'

16

Advice on Apparel

After exploring under the categories 'Its Original' (clothes became necessary as a result of the fall), 'Its Use' (to cover shame and guilt), 'Its Abuse' (the following of fashion), 'of Spiritual Apparel' (being clothed in the fruits of the spirit), 'Of the Spiritual Use of Apparel' (it reminds us of our fallen state), Traherne writes:

Instructions

God himself is clothed with Light as with a Garment, & did put on Zeal as a Cloak: well mayest thou covet Ornaments in Spirit, that will make thee like him.

When thou seest others insisting so much upon those Empty Appearances, rejoyce that GOD hath opened thine Eys to behold their vanitie: & that thou knowest the Beauty of Divine Attires.

Seek not to win Esteem by Clothes, tis a base Reputation that is gained therby: tis as empty as its Cause, as uncertain & perishing.

Clothes are pittifull Suiters; Dost thou esteem any Body the more for his Clothes?

A Couragious prudent Active Man, Meek & humble, faithfull & obliging, Witty & Cheerfull, Just, Holy, Temperate, ready & Service-able, one that can forgive Injuries, & die for his friend: one so Honest that Men may commit their famelies their Estates their Wives & chil-dren, their Honors & Lives in his hand, may profess Poverty like Phocion if he will; he has clothes enough; the more liberal & charitable he is, even in his Thredbare Coat he shall shine among Princes. But there is no Way to make one self here, but by doing that by which som men are undone, in their own Conceits at least. For Eminent virtu is that alone which makes a mans fame & face to shine, & prepares a place among Princes for him. Make thy self able to help, & be willing.

None but fools esteem a man the more for his Clothes. Noble Men & Wise ones deride such Glaring Gu-Gawes as have nothing in them.

It is eminent folly to spread forth Sailes to big for thy Ship.

Be not a Bubble; be solid like God, & let all thy Worth be within.

He that tempers virtue, wisely is only Excellent. He that is clothed with all hath all Attires.

Commentaries of Heaven, 'Apparel'

6

Prayers

The theme of this chapter will not seem an obvious one to many readers of Traherne; it certainly did not seem so to me. Apart from his long, detailed and fascinating *Thanksgivings*, it seemed to me that Traherne had not written many prayers. He must have prayed; after all, he was a priest. But he had not left behind a tidy bundle of prayers, tied up with a neat string, that I could untie and peruse. Once I started looking, however, I found that prayers were everywhere, short sentence prayers in little asides, unexpected confessional prayers at the end of a meditation on parish work or the love of God or the beauty of the earth. There were prayers on feast days, and prayers on ordinary days, prayers in which he had taken parts of the psalms and adapted them, and prayers straight from his heart. There were all kinds of prayers in all kinds of places, and I realized that for Traherne, if his life were like his writing, prayer was in fact woven into the fabric of everything. There is so much one could say about Traherne and prayer that this chapter, which is now too small to contain it, can do no more than open a door on this theme.

Traherne's prayers, as of course do all of his writings, occur within a particular historical context of Restoration religion. It should be no surprise, given the conflict he had seen, that frequent prayers appear for the maintenance of order in the realm, for the state of the nation, for the well-being of the king, for stability and prosperity and peace. One of the many theological concerns of this Restoration church that is reflected in Traherne's written prayers is the loss of auricular confession. If one had no need to confess to a priest one was certainly liberated, but one was also less secure about one's spiritual state. How was one to know if one was in a state of grace or not? A question that plagued lay people and clerics alike was simply this: how do we know we are ready to make our communion, that we do not come unworthily to the table of the Lord? One of the best known of George Herbert's poems, 'Love', is coloured with this anxiety. Love bids the poet welcome to the table, but he feels unworthy; even when he is assured of his worthiness he cannot feel sure that this is so. Plagued by shame and guilt, he lists his failings, argues with Love about Love's gift, refuses almost to the point of defiance the gift Love offers. Eventually he approaches the table as one who serves in gratitude. He sits to eat only when an imperative is used – when he is told that he *must* taste the meat. A beautiful poem, it is nonetheless an anxious one. Its long-lasting appeal suggests that it touches a nerve with many that is still raw; the question of worthiness has not disappeared. The same concern surfaces in many of Traherne's confessional prayers. And it is in his confessional prayers that we get glimpses of a very human Traherne, a person who tries hard, and feels himself often to be a failure, yet hopes and tries again. Such a person is easy to love. When we read 'I could be quickly weary, quickly weary both of repenting and of interceding' (*SM*, I, 84), we know we could be reading about ourselves. There is an unaffected blend of humility and integrity in such prayers that leaps the centuries on bounding legs.

Another concern of the Restoration church in England, alluded to earlier, was the question of whether the priest's primary duty was to be prayer or preaching. As we have seen, in the late sixteenth and early seventeenth century Calvinism was the dominant religious culture in the Jacobean church. Patrick Collinson notes that preaching, or preaching and catechizing, were the main function of the minister. He was a minister of the word. As the century wore on, those who rejected this dominant model and wanted to move the church towards a more Arminian position, away from the pulpit and towards prayer, who rejected what they might have considered an obsession with the ear and wanted to include the whole person in worship – voice, taste, touch, eye – faced certain challenges. Traherne could not remain aloof from this central question: were churches to be primarily *auditoria* for the Word or *oratoria* for prayer and praises? And how did these distinctions affect not only the architecture and furnishing of churches, but also personal devotion and public liturgy?[180]

Traherne, who as we have seen had been educated by Puritans, placed in his first living by Puritan ministers, and remained on good terms with staunchly Puritan families, would have been familiar with Puritan

180 For further exploration of these tensions see Stewart, *The Expanded Voice*, pp. 8ff. and Collinson, *From Cranmer to Sancroft*, pp. 64ff.

teaching that favoured spontaneous prayer and praise, and that saw the *Book of Common Prayer* as a popish invention and feast days as superstitious. His confessional prayers in such writings as *Select Meditations* and *Inducements to Retiredness* have a ring of Puritan piety about them, yet he came to love the *Book of Common Prayer*, the feasts and festivals of the church and its order and liturgy. His respect for those liturgies is both overt and implied – his spirited defence of infant baptism in *Commentaries of Heaven* stands alongside the more oblique defence of simply using the *Book of Common Prayer* liturgy as a standard for 'good practice', or his description of the Magnificat as the 'Ravishing Song of the blessed Virgin'. However, he never completely casts off his Puritan education; robust as his support for the national church is, one senses Traherne's need to justify his celebration of feast days to those of the 'sola scriptura' tradition who saw every day as hallowed. 'Why should we not spend som time upon Holy Days?' he asks.

> They are the Ornaments of Time . . .
> The Days of Heaven seen upon Earth . . .
> The Lucid Intervals and Lights of the Year . . .
> The Relicks of Eden . . .
> Wherein we antedate the Resurrection of the Dead
> And come from our shops to our Saviour's Throne,
> From plowing our fields to Manna in the Wilderness,
> From Dressing our Vineyards to the Wine of Angels,
> From Caring for our Children to be the Sons of God.
> They are . . . Market Days of Heaven.
> Appointed Season, wherin GOD keepeth Open House . . . (*CYB*)

Down to earth in his images here, he is also careful in his wording elsewhere. His meditation on Mary in the *Church's Year-Book* praises her, but he never prays to her. He thanks God for her and shows her falling down with all the saints before the throne of God, and he reminds us by her example that all human beings may become the place where God dwells.

His prayers surrounding feast days and holy days are not only important as a part of the practice of the church; they are important to him more personally and perhaps most joyously because of what they say about time and eternity. Donald Allchin calls Traherne's vision of the world 'a world in which time was held in the embrace of eternity, in which eternity was present in the midst of time'.[181] The feasts and holy days mark God's specific interventions, and that is cause enough for celebration, but alongside that it is the present participation in the joys of heaven that these feast days suggest that fire Traherne's love for them. In them we contemplate eternity. As 'Relicks of Eden . . . Lucid Intervals and Lights of the Year', they remind us of what was and what most truly is. But Traherne loves the less lofty in them too, what Herbert calls 'heaven in ordinary': They are 'Market Days of Heaven' in which we leave our labours and gather together to exchange blessings. They are 'Appointed Seasons, wherein GOD keepeth Open House'. This is because for Traherne the holy days, and their respective prayers, were not just about lifting our souls to heaven but also about the sanctification of our ordinary days, the life of labour and the fruits of toil.

Traherne's prayer life fed on scripture, on experience, and on the written prayers of others. Prayers from Lancelot Andrewes and from Jeremy Taylor appear in the *Church's Year-Book*. With Taylor, Traherne shares an anti-Augustinian view of original sin. Taylor's *Unum Necessarium* (1655) and its sequel *Deus Justificatus* (1656), which argued against the Augustinian view of the fall of man, denied 'total depravity' and refuted the belief that the unbaptized were damned, won him as many enemies as friends. It also resulted in a kind of optimism about humanity not unlike the hopefulness we find in Traherne. But it may be that Traherne also gleaned from Taylor specific images. One particular image from *Centuries* comes to mind: where Taylor likens Christ in the sacrament to the tree of life in paradise,[182] Traherne writes: 'but abov all these our Saviors Cross is the Throne of Delights. That Centre of Eternity, That tree of Life in the midst of the Paradice of GOD!' (C, I, 55), and 'that Cross is a Tree set on fire with invisible flame' (C, I, 60).

As we have noted, Andrewes was a formative voice in the preparation of Traherne's prayerful *Thanksgivings*, which follow the *Preces Privatae* closely in form and in subject matter. Andrewes prays 'for the whole Church Catholic, eastern western our own'; Traherne's *Thanksgivings* have a similarly broad scope. For Andrewes there was no area of life that was not filled with the presence of Christ; the human–divine was everywhere. As Nicholas Lossky writes: 'Everything begins and every-

181 Allchin, *Profitable Wonders*, pp. 26–7.
182 Taylor, *Works*, Vol. II, discourse XIX, section 9.

thing ends in Him ... There is no province of life that may not be illuminated by his divine-human person: the Church, the sacraments, public life, private life, and the whole creation'.[183] Traherne shares this God-filled vision of the world. In the 'Thanksgivings for God's Providence' (ll. 388–95) he writes:

> What infinite Depths may lie concealed,
> In the rude appearance of the smallest Actions.
> A world of Joys hid in a Manger,
> For me, for every one.
> His Cross, a prospect of eternal Glory,
> Sheweth, that
> All things are treasures infinitely Diffusive;
> Earthy Occurrences, celestial Joys.

This is a very different approach to the matter of divine providence from that we sometimes see in *A Sober View of Dr Twisse*, in which God's providence is about who is to be saved and who is to be damned. In the *Thanksgivings*, divine providence means that God's unflagging efforts to save us are writ large in all the world: 'O let me see into the deeper value of such glorious Treasures!' writes Traherne in the same 'Thanksgivings' (ll. 429, 432–4):

> ... Images of God,
> Labouring to death
> For our sakes.

It is no mere accident, but a reflection of Traherne's tone of life in general, that his largest body of prayers are thanksgivings. There is everywhere in his work – poetry, prose and polemic – a spirit of gratitude, and in his prayers much more praise and thanksgiving than supplication. Confession, supplication and intercession all have their place, but Traherne has a joyous heart; he lives his life aware of the giftedness of creation and his primary prayer is one of gratitude and praise.

Even his choice of psalms shows a tendency towards those that praise rather than those that berate God or bewail the psalmist's sorry state. Traherne's admiration for the psalmist has often been noted; his use of the psalms is prevalent throughout his work: they form the basis of

183 Nicholas Lossky, *Lancelot Andrewes the Preacher*, Oxford: Oxford University Press, 1991.

his psalmic 'resolves' at the end of each chapter of *Inducements to Retiredness*, and make up a large part of the third Century. The psalmist seems to have touched a deep nerve for Traherne who saw in him another person like himself, full of longing and praise, drawn to things godly by the beauty of the earth. He writes of his joy in finding this kindred spirit:

> When I saw those objects celebrated in his Psalms which God and nature had proposed to me, and which I thought chance only presented to my view, you cannot imagine how unspeakable I was delighted to see so glorious a person, so great a prince, so divine a sage, that was a man after God's own heart, by the testimony of God Himself, rejoicing in the same things, meditating on the same, and praising God for the same. For by this I perceived we were led by one spirit, and that following the clue of Nature into this labyrinth, I was brought into the midst of celestial joys ... (C, III, 70)

He claims that the only way to become a person after God's own heart is to contemplate the works of God. Such contemplation is Traherne's life's work;[184] it is no surprise then that the person of David is for him such a strong companion. Of course, Traherne is not alone in his admiration of the psalms. The influence of the psalms on seventeenth-century poetry is well documented[185] and the emergence and prevalence of metrical versons of the psalms in the vernacular meant that psalm singing was one of the most common religious practices of the day. The psalms were and remain a staple part of monastic liturgies around the world and continue in the weekday evensongs sung in cathedrals. Yet there is something particular about Traherne's attachment to and

184 For further development of the link between the psalmist David and Traherne see Michael Ponsford, 'Men after God's Own Heart: The Context of Thomas Traherne's Emulation of David', *Studia Mystica*, 9 (1986), pp. 3–11; and Raymond-Jean Frontain, 'Tuning the World: Traherne, Psalms, and Praise', in Jacob Blevins, ed., *Re-Reading Traherne: a Collection of New Critical Essays*, Arizona: Arizona Renaissance Studies, 2007, pp. 129–51. In *Inducements to Retiredness* Traherne refers to the psalmist as 'David, that Wise and Admired Jew, that Warlike and Glorius Prince, that Royal Singer, that Divine Philosopher, that Triumphant King, and yet more that heavenly man' (*ITR*, ll. 797–9).

185 See Barbara Lewalski, *Protestant Poetics and the Seventeenth-Century Lyric*, Princeton, NJ: Princeton University Press, 1979; Harold Fisch, *Jerusalem and Albion: The Hebraic Factor in Seventeenth-Century Literature*, London: Routledge, 1964.

appropriation of the psalms. It is as if they become so much part of him that he reiterates and paraphrases them as his own words, as if his mind had been so formed by them that they have become his thoughts.

Traherne's well-loved Athanasius and St John Chrysostom are among the church fathers who note the transforming power of psalm singing. It makes us into angels, or, as Athanasius writes, in the spirit of prayer, the singer may 'becom himself a stringful instrument' sending back to God the praises that are due. Becoming an instrument of praise is exactly what Traherne's converted soul is about, since for him happiness and holiness coexist in the circle of desire and the circle of praise.

Raymond-Jean Frontain's recent study of Traherne and the psalms highlights how from St Jerome's account of Christ's humble psalm-singing home to the psalm-singing community at Little Gidding, psalm singing changed the atmosphere of a place. Through the literature of writers as diverse as Erasmus, Bunyan and metrical psalter editors, Frontain asserts that poets, preachers and playwrights alike share a widely held belief in the power of the psalms to transform. One testimonial recounts how residents of York sang as Cromwell besieged the city, their voices making the very ground to shake and transporting the body of singers to heaven itself while the terrors of war fell about them.[186] From earliest Jewish and Christian days, psalms have been said to 'Calm passions ... chase demons away ... and heal the wounds that life has struck'.[187]

Seventeenth-century psalm singing had its more political side, of course. As Collinson notes, in the sixteenth and seventeenth century metrical psalms could be sung provocatively by evangelical Protestants as a form of demonstration against Catholics and crypto-Catholics.[188] And yet, the psalms retained a strangely unifying potential too, since even those arch-Protestants who saw the *Book of Common Prayer* as popish superstition and would shun the Te Deum, the Magnificat, the Creed, the Venite and the Litany would still consider the psalms as *de rigueur*, as would the monks in monasteries. They were a kind of

186 Frontain, 'Tuning the World' pp. 129–51, esp. 131–7.

187 Diodore of Tarsus in Eric Werner, *The Sacred Bridge: The Interdependence of Liturgy and Music in Synagogue and Church during the First Millennium*, New York: Columbia University Press, 1959, p. 148, quoted in Frontain, 'Tuning the World', pp. 129–51.

188 Collinson, *From Cranmer to Sancroft*; Christopher Hill, *The World Turned Upside Down: Radical Ideas During the English Revolution*, London: Penguin, 1975.

bottom line that no side in the religious disputes of the day would be willing to sacrifice. The psalms, therefore, I suspect, appealed to Traherne's sense of inclusion: they were a useful tool to anyone interested in the process of comprehending all within the church.

However, I believe Traherne's deep love of the psalms and his use of them in prayers has a more specific, personal and profound root. Like the psalmist, Traherne is filled with longing and with praise; like the psalmist he writes about this ecstatically. They both see the world as conceived for them; their relationship with God is intimate and personal: they are God's sons, kings and heirs. They both enjoy wonder-filled revelations of divine love in creation. However, Traherne imagined he alone had these experiences and thoughts of God: 'I was so ignorant that I did not think any man in the World had had such thoughts before,' he confesses in the third Century, 'but as I read the Bible I was here and there surprised with such thoughts, and found by degrees that these things had been written of before, not only in the Scriptures, but in many of the Fathers, and that this was the way of communion with God in all Saints, as I saw clearly in the person of David' (C, III, 66). When Traherne sees the same things he had experienced in the psalms a new light dawns, he understands perhaps for the first time that his infant revelations connect with the rest of the world; because David's utterances are the utterances of any heart turned towards God, so can his utterances be. 'O that I were as *David*, the sweet Singer of *Israel!*'[189] cries Traherne. The relief that Traherne expresses at having found a kindred spirit in David is therefore not merely the expression of a lonely person having found a friend; it is the relief of a hemmed-in person having found freedom.[190] As Frontain asserts, David delivered him from solipsism. He shows Traherne how the personal may speak across a broad spectrum and how the unique may in fact, by extrapolation and imagination, encapsulate the experience of many.

What is more, because the psalms have the power to draw us out of the purely private into the public by allowing the personal in the psalmist or in Traherne to relate to the personal in another and another and another, Traherne finds more than a kindred spirit, and a deliverance

189 *Thanksgivings for the Body*, ll. 341–2.
190 'Methought a new light darted in into all his psalms, and finally spread abroad over the whole Bible,' writes Traherne (C, III, 66). He goes on to expand on this new freedom of vision, quoting David off and on for the next 34 meditations.

from solipsism in David. He finds a key to harmonizing the intense struggle between the private and the public in prayer that marked seventeenth-century religious life. We have seen how the Reformation thrust towards personal piety, personal conversion and a personal relationship with God had brought with it a move away from established liturgy and towards spontaneous prayer and praise. In fact it had brought a deep suspicion of liturgy and a loathing of the *Book of Common Prayer* as instruments of imposed authority. Inasmuch as Traherne's voice is often deeply personal and frequently spontaneous he fits well with this radical reformed enthusiasm, but inasmuch as he adheres to the order and devotions of the church, its prayer book and holy days, its rites and its sacramental liturgies, he resists the most radical elements of reform. The intensity of this private and public prayer debate derived in part from the fact that it had powerful political and social implications. Christopher Hill has pointed out the connection between Puritan insistence on inner discipline and the experience of masterlessness. One's object cannot be to find a new master in oneself, a rigid self-control shaping a new personality, without previous experience of masterlessness.[191] The personalized form of conversion is one answer to an unsettled society: convert, repress, make people saints, practise collective discipline, or depend on an external authority to impose order. Traherne's way through this religious and political tangle is by maintaining a conviction of the importance of personal salvation that does not confuse personal with private. Personal in community with other persons is his model. And this he gleans, at least in part, from his intense encounter with the psalmist who first unlocks that door.

'Christ loves not singularity: he called not one alone', wrote John Donne, who was similarly taxed by the problem of private and public prayer, in one of his sermons. Donne encouraged his listener to believe that there were benefits in public or communal prayer for the individual: 'Whilst thou art a member of a congregation that speaks to God with a thousand tongues, believe that thou speakest to God with all those tongues'. Though your own thoughts are distracted and impure, 'yet believe that some honester man then they selfe stands by thee, and that when he prayes with thee, he prayes for thee; and that, if there be one

191 See Hill, *The World Turned Upside Down*, pp. 47–9; and M. Walzer, *The Revolution of the Saints*, Cambridge, MA: Harvard University Press, 1965, pp. 308–16.

righteous man in the congregation, thou art made the more acceptable to God by his prayers.'[192]

Here the model of prayer is one in which the private need and the public act merge, as the private thought surfaces in the midst of the public words and the public words fill the private lack. Such a model is exactly where Traherne stands when he writes of the salvation of the nation and of the person being shared, because for Traherne religion is essentially not accidentally a public matter: 'our Savior deals with nations in their National Capacitie, threatens Cities that reject his Disciples, as well as particular persons, & commands his Apostles to go & teach, (not single men, but) all Nations, baptizing them in the Name of the Father, & of the Son, & of the H. Ghost.' Therefore, concludes Traherne, 'if there be a National Church, it is one of the Greatest Impieties in the World to destroy it' (*COH*, fol. 194r).

In a series of talks in Australia Rowan Williams quoted the French Catholic poet Charles Peguy, saying, 'everything begins in mysticism and ends in politics'. Williams goes on to trace the lineaments of a developing Anglican identity that includes a particular vision of the relation between church and society in which the church is not a sect operating within society but some members of that society operating in a particular way. He cites theologians, poets and priests, from George Herbert to William Temple and among them Traherne, and asserts:

> the church is not about religion as a separable activity. And the commands of God, the ways in which we become not acceptable to God but aligned with God, are to do with our fundamental social relations. Replace that with a doctrine of special religious duties and you have undermined the whole point of a church which witnesses to the priority of and freedom of God's action.'[193]

For Traherne the 'personal' is only found in this interweaving of public and private. Private faith that has no social imperative means as little as public faith that has no beating heart. As Donald Allchin reminds us, in Traherne's view the welfare of a *people* and the welfare of a *person* are inextricably linked.

192 *The Sermons of John Donne*, ed. Evelyn M. Simpson and George R. Potter, 10 vols, Berkeley, CA: University of California Press, 1953–1962, 2:280 and 7:233, quoted in Frontain, 'Tuning the World', p. 130.

193 Rowan Williams, *Christian Imagination in Poetry and Polity: Some Anglican Voices from Temple to Herbert*, Oxford: SLG Press, 2004, p. 17.

This is seen most clearly in his 'Thanksgiving and Prayer for the Nation', a masterpiece of the private and public interwoven. He writes of

> The sweet combinations of private love and
>   Particular friendships,
> Carried in the Bark of our Nations welfare . . .
> Let me see, O Lord, the grand mystery of thy spiritual Building,
> The Union of Souls in the Government of Nations, the perfect closure
> of those living Stones; constituting a Temple, one Temple entire unto
> thee;
>   The Two Pillars of the Earth strengthening each other;
>   Religion rooting Justice within,
>   Justice fencing Religion without,
> And both making an Arch of Government immovable.
>   These two Pillars as steady as they are, will (except they have an
> upholder) cleave and bend.
>   And the whole frame sink with them.
>   Therefore, O Lord, do thou support him that beareth them up.
>   Thy Spirit hath compared our Princes to a nail driven into a wall,
> whereon are hanged all both the Vessels of service, and instruments
> of Musick,
>   Firm may this nail abide, and never stir, For if it should, all our
> Cups would batter with the fall, the musick of our Quire be marr'd.
>   Both Church and Country put into danger.
> Let me see the combination of our Christian state,
>   The Glory, and Beauty, and Sweetness of it.
>   Pardon mine Eyes that I see not better. (ll. 338–63)

Here, where the public and the private are inextricably linked, the king is a nail driven into the wall on which all things ornamental and serviceable hang. 'Firm may this nail abide', writes Traherne.

Traherne prayed everywhere and in all situations. Some of his prayers, particularly those of confession and adoration, read as spontaneous prayers in which he talks to God as one person to another. These are perhaps his easiest prayers to assimilate. Others are more restrained, and he gives careful thought to the wording of his prayers for use in public worship. His inspirations were many, but the psalms played a major role in the formation of his language of prayer. In keeping with his boundless spirit of gratitude, his longest, most frequent and most highly developed prayers are thanksgivings: for the body, for the soul, for God's works and ways and laws, for God's providence and his Word, and finally for the nation. Much of his theology is reflected in these prayers: his belief in the goodness of creation, in the infinite capacity of the soul and its propensity for desire, in the infinite and intimate love of God, and his belief that the welfare of the person and the welfare of a people are inextricably linked. Traherne's particular blend of private and public prayer reflects his belief that personal did not mean private, and that public meant neither impersonal nor superficial, but that the person was saved within the context of a community of persons, and that a parson's mission was to the whole nation. Rooted in the specific concerns of his day, many of his prayers have about them the flavour of an antique age. Yet their passionate appeals for mercy and grace, and their wonder at the depth of the love of God, are timeless. There is an expansiveness in his prayer, a sense of being connected to all times and all ages, part of a small slice of eternity, that many modern prayers have lost. He never rushes, because time is always there to be wasted as luxuriously as the moment requires if you live, like God, in eternity. Traherne savours the moments of his life and prays with gratitude in his heart: 'Thy Ways, O my God, are infinitely Delicious'.

The extracts

Adoration and praise

1 Praise for the beauty of the Soul

2 Lord Jesus what Lov shall I render unto Thee

3 I desire to Adore thy Glory!

Confession

4 The Return

5 Unite me unto Thee in the Bands of an Individual lov

6 It is my shame

7 In Dust and Ashes

8 As a prisoner returning from the pitt

I

Praise for the beauty of the Soul

It is an inestimable Joy that I was raised out of Nothing, to see and
Enjoy this Glorious World: It is a Sacred Gift wherby the children of
Men are made my Treasures, but O Thou who art fairer then the
Children of Men, how great and unconceivable is the Joy of thy Lov!
That I who was lately raised out of the dust, hav so Great a Friend,
that I who in this life am born to mean Things according to the world
should be called to inherit such Glorious Things in the way of Heaven:
Such a Lord, so Great a Lover, such Heavenly Mysteries, such Doings,
and such sufferings, with all the Benefit and pleasure of them in thy
Intelligible Kingdom: it amazeth, it transporteth and ravisheth me. I
will leave my fathers house and com unto Thee; For Thou art my Lord,
and I will Worship Thee.[1] That all Ages should appear so visibly before
me, and all thy Ways be so lively Powerfull and present with me, that
the Land of Canaan should be so near, and all the Joys in Heaven and
Earth so sweet to comfort me! This O Lord declareth thy Wisdom, and
sheweth thy Power. But O the Riches of thine infinit Goodness in
making my Soul an Interminable Temple, out of which nothing can be,
from which Nothing is removed, to which nothing is afar off; but all
things immediatly near, in Real true and Lively Maner. O the Glory of
that Endless Life, that can at once extend to all Eternity! Had the Cross
been 20 Millions of Ages further, it had still been equaly near, nor is it
possible to remov it, for it is with all Distances in my Understanding, and
tho it be removed many thousand Millions of Ages more is as clearly seen
and Apprehended. This Soul for which Thou diedst, I desire to Know
more perfectly, O my Savior. That I may prais thee for it, and believ it
worthy, in its Nature, to be an Object of thy Lov; tho unworthy by reason
of sin: and that I may use it in thy Service, and Keep it pure to thy Glory.

Centuries of Meditations, I, 92

1 Psalm 45.11.

2

Lord Jesus what Lov shall I render unto Thee

Lord Jesus what Lov shall I render unto Thee, for thy Lov unto me!
Thy eternal Lov! Oh what fervor, what Ardor, what Humiliation, what
Reverence, what Joy, what Adoration, what Zeal, what Thanksgiving!
Thou that art Perfect in Beauty, Thou that art the King of Eternal
Glory, Thou that reignest in the Highest Heavens camest down from
Heaven to Die for me! And shall not I liv unto Thee? O my joy! O my
Sovereign Friend! O my Life, and my All! I beseech Thee let those
Trickling Drops of Blood that run down Thy flesh drop upon me. O
let Thy Lov enflame me. Which is so deep and infinit, that Thou didst
suffer the Wrath of GOD for me: And Purchase all Nations and Kingdoms to be my Treasures. O Thou that Redeemedst me from Hell, and
when Thou hadst Overcom the Sharpness of Death didst open the
Kingdom of Heaven to all Believers; What shall I do unto Thee? What
shall I do for Thee, O Thou Preserver of Men. Liv, Lov, and Admire;
and learn to becom such unto Thee as Thou unto me. O Glorious Soul!
whose Comprehensiv understanding at once contains all Kingdoms and
Ages! O Glorious Mind! Whose Lov extendeth to all Creatures! O
miraculous and Eternal GODhead, now suffering on the Cross for me:
As Abraham saw thy Day and was Glad, so didst Thou see me and this
Day from all Eternitie, and seeing me wast Gracious and Compassionat
Towards me. (All Transeunt Things are Permanent in God) *Thou settest
me before Thy Face forever.*[1]) O let me This Day see Thee, and be united
to Thee in Thy Holy Sufferings. Let me learn O GOD such Lessons from
Thee, as may make me Wise, and Blessed as an Angel of GOD!

Centuries of Meditations, I, 62

1 Psalm 41.12.

3

I desire to Adore thy Glory!

O my God with infinite affections I desire to Adore thy Glory! O that
I could See and Answer thy Lov forever more. It is as Easy for a Mirror
to be Put against the Sun, and yet no Sun Shine upon it: as it is for a
clarified Soul, to see.

Select Meditations, III, 32

4

The Return

To Infancy, O Lord, again I com,
    That I my Manhood may improv:
    My early Tutor is the Womb;
        I still my Cradle lov.
    'Tis strange that I should Wisest be,
    When least I could an Error see.

Till I gain strength against Temptation, I
    Perceiv it safest to abide
    An Infant still; and therfore fly
        (A lowly State may hide
    A man from Danger) to the Womb,
    That I may yet New-born becom.

My God, thy Bounty then did ravish me!
    Before I learned to be poor,
    I always did thy Riches see,
        And thankfully adore:
    Thy Glory and thy Goodness were
    My sweet Companions all the Year.

5

Unite me unto Thee in the Bands of an Individual Lov

Lord I lament, and Abhor my self that I hav been the Occasion of these thy Sufferings. I had never known the Dignity of my Nature, hadst not Thou esteemed it: I had never seen, nor Understood its Glory, hadst not Thou Assumed it. Be Thou Pleased to unite me unto Thee in the Bands of an Individual Lov, that I may evermore liv unto Thee, and Liv in Thee. And by how much the more Vile I hav been, let my lov be so much O Lord the more Violent Henceforth and fervent unto Thee. O Thou who wouldst never hav permitted sin, hadst Thou not known how to Bring good out of Evil, hav Pitty upon me: Hear my Prayer. O my GOD since Pitty Enbalmes Lov, let thine com Enricht, and be more precious to me Miserable Sinner. Let the Remembrance of all the Glory wherin I was Created make me more Serious and Humble, more Deep and Penitent more Pure and Holy before Thee. And since the World is Sprinkled with thy Blood, and Adorned with all Kingdoms and Ages for me: which are Heavenly Treasures and Vastly Greater then Heaven and Earth · Let me see thy Glory in the Preparation of them, and thy Goodness in their Government. Open unto me the Gate of Righteousness, that I may enter in to the New Jerusalem.

Centuries of Meditations, I, 78

6

It is my shame

It is my shame and one of Actual and Infinit crimes: that I do not constantly Ascrib and Acknowledg unto Him the Glory. It is my Infinit Shame, and by confessing it I must Lie under it. But I will confess it that I may a voyd it; and Escape its causes. O my God pardon my vileness: And enable me with Infinit Desires Always to Thirst and Intend thy Glory.

Select Meditations, III, 70

7

In Dust and Ashes

O my Lord did I Lov thee Perfectly, surely I Should be Infinitly Greived when I offend Thee. For He that offendeth against Him that Loveth infinitly before and resolveth to Lov Him Equaly afterward, is infinitly Guilty tho He be forgiven. Yea So much the more by How much the more Gracious and kind that Lov is, which resolveth to forgive. O my God I abhor my Selfe in Dust and Ashes, that I Love Thee not more tenderly. And I pray thee giv me Such a Lov that I may fear Thee becaus of thy Lov and watchfully hearafter take care to please thee becaus I shall be forgiven. Above all things in Heaven and earth Let me Dread to need forgivness, for to offend against infinit Love is the greatest misery, shame and sin.

Select Meditations, III, 74

8

As a prisoner returning from the pitt

As a prisoner returning from the pitt, as a Malefactor Saved from the cross, yea as a Devill taken out of Hell, I return O Lord to the Glory of thy kingdom. For my crime hath been wors then Satans. Having Sinned more, O more, much more in Sinning against my Redeemers Lov! How Sweet then will the Glory be to which I am restored, and How Delightfull his Lov, by whom I was Redeemed. O prince of peace who sittest at the Right Hand of God in the Glory of the father I Adore Thee, and Desire to Dye for Thee, or to Liv to please Thee. Thy Lov, O thy Lov is Better then Heaven! It is indeed the very only Sun and Soul of Heaven.

Select Meditations, II, 36

9

As my Body without my Soul is a Carcase, so is my Soul without thy Spirit

As my Body without my Soul is a Carcase, so is my Soul without thy Spirit. A chaos, a Dark Obscure Heap of Empty faculties: Ignorant of it self, unsensible of thy Goodness, Blind to thy Glory: Dead in Sins and Trespasses. Having Eys I see not, having Ears I hear not,[1] having an Heart I understand not the Glory of thy Works and the Glory of thy Kingdom. O Thou who art the Root of my Being, and the Captain of my Salvation, look upon me. Quicken me O Thou Life-giving and Quickening Seed. Visit me with thy Light and thy Truth, let them lead me to thy Holy Hill: and make me to see the Greatness of thy Lov in all its Excellencies, Effects, Emanations Gifts and Operations. O my Wisdom! O my Righteousness, Sanctification and Redemption; let thy Wisdom Enlighten me, let thy Knowledg illuminat me, let thy Blood redeem me, wash me and Cleans me, let thy Merits justify me, O Thou who art Equal unto GOD, and didst suffer for me. Let thy Righteousness clothe me. Let thy Will imprint the Form of itself upon mine; and let my Will becom Conformable to thine: that thy Will and mine, may be united, and made one for evermore.

Centuries of Meditations, I, 93

1 Psalm 115.4–7; Mark 8.18.

10

Thanksgivings for the Body

. . . Thy Name be glorified
   For evermore.
For all the art which thou hast hidden
   In this little piece
     Of red clay.
For the workmanship of thy hand,
  Who didst thy self form man

    Of the dust of the ground,
   And breath into his Nostrils
     The breath of Life.
  For the high Exaltation whereby thou hast glorified every body,
     Especially mine,
   As thou didst thy Servant
    Adam's in *Eden.* . . .
  But why would the Lord take pleasure in creating an earthly Body?
why at all in making a visible World? Couldst thou not have made us
immortal Souls, and seated us immediately in the throne of Glory?
   O Lord, thou lover of Righteousness,
     Whose Kingdom is everlasting;
  Who lovest to govern thy Subjects by Laws, and takest delight to
distribute Rewards and Punishments according to right.
   Thou hast hidden thy self
       By an infinite miracle,
  And made this World the Chamber of thy presence; the ground and
theatre of thy righteous Kingdom. . . .
  But couldst thou not have remitted our Knowledge, and established
to thy self a righteous Kingdom, without composing our Bodies, or the
World?
  By the Fall of some, we know, O Lord,
    That the Angels were tried,
   Which are invisible Spirits,
    Needing not the World,
   Nor clothed in Bodies,
    Nor endued with Senses.
  For our Bodies therefore, O Lord, for our earthly Bodies, hast thou
made the World: Which thou so lovest, that thou hast supremely magni-
fied them by the works of thy hands:
  And made them Lords of the whole Creation.
   Higher than the Heavens,
    Because served by them:
  More glorious than the Sun,
    Because it ministreth to them:
  Greater in Dignity than the material World.
    Because the end of its Creation.
   Revived by the Air,
   Served by the Seas,
  Fed by the Beasts, and Fowls, and Fishes,

Our pleasure.
Which fall as Sacrifices to
Thy glory.
Being made to minister and attend upon us.
O Miracle
Of divine Goodness!
O Fire! O flame of Zeal, and Love, and Joy!
Even for our earthly bodies, hast thou created all things.

All things { Visible. / Material. / Sensible.

Animals,
Vegetables,
Minerals,
Bodies celestial,
Bodies terrestrial,
The four Elements,
Volatile Spirits,
Trees, Herbs, and Flowers,
The Influences of Heaven,
Clouds, Vapors, Wind,
Dew, Rain, Hail, and Snow,
Light and Darkness, Night and Day,
The Seasons of the Year.
Springs, Rivers, Fountains, Oceans,
Gold, Silver, and precious Stones.
Corn, Wine, and Oyl,
The Sun, Moon, and Stars,
Cities, Nations, Kingdoms.
And the Bodies of Men, the greatest Treasures of all,
For each other.

What then, O Lord, hast thou intended for our Souls, who givest to our Bodies such glorious things! . . .

What is man, O Lord, that thou art mindful of him! or the son of man, that thou visitest him!

Kings in all their Glory minister to us, while we repose in peace and safety.

Priests and Bishops serve at thine Altar, guiding our Bodies to eternal Glory.

Physicians heal us.

Courts of Judicature stand open for our preservation.

The Outgoings of the morning and evening rejoyce to do us service.

The holy Angels minister unto us.

Architects and Masons build us Temples.

The Sons of Harmony fill thy Quires.

Where even our sensible bodies are entertained by thee with great magnificence; and solaced with Joys.

Jesus Christ hath washed our feet.

He ministred to us by dying for us.

    And now in our humane body, sitteth at thy right hand, in the throne of Glory.

        As our Head,

        For our Sakes,

Being there adored by Angels and Cherubims.

    What is it Lord

      That thou so esteemest us!

Thou passed'st by the Angels,

        Pure Spirits;

    And didst send thy Son to die for us

      That are made of both

        Soul and Body.

    Are we drawn unto thee?

      O why dost thou make us

        So thy treasures?

Are Eyes and Hands such Jewels unto thee?

What, O Lord, are Tongues and Sounds,

      And Nostrils unto thee?

    Strange Materials are visible bodies!

Things strange even compared to thy Nature,

      Which is wholly spiritual.

For our sakes do the Angels enjoy the visible Heavens.

    The Sun and Stars,

      Thy terrestrial Glories,

    And all thy Wisdom

    In the $\begin{cases} \text{Ordinances of Heaven.} \\ \text{Seasons of the Year.} \end{cases}$

Wondering to see thee by another way,

So highly exalting dust and ashes.

    Thou makest us treasures

        And joys unto them;

Objects of Delight, and spiritual Lamps,
Whereby they discern visible things.
They see thy Paradise among the sons of men.
Thy Wine and Oyl, thy Gold and Silver,
By our Eyes.
They smell thy Perfumes,
And taste thy Honey, Milk, and Butter,
By our Senses.
Thy Angels have neither ears nor eyes,
Nor tongues nor hands,
Yet feel the Delights of all the World,
And hear the Harmonies, not only which
Earth but Heaven maketh.
The melody of Kingdoms,
The joys of Ages,
Are Objects of their joy.
They sing thy Praises for our sakes;
While we upon Earth are highly exalted
By being made thy Gifts,
And Blessings unto them:
Never their contempt;
More their amazement;
And did they not love us
Their Envy hereafter,
But now their Joy. . . .

Yet have I been wholly estranged from thee, by the sinful Courses of
this World, by the Delusions of vain Conversation.

Being unsensible of these things, I have been blind and dead, profane
and stupid, seared and ingrateful; and for living beneath such a glorious
Estate, may justly be excluded thine everlasting Kingdom.

Enable me to keep thy Temple sacred!
Which thou hast prepared for thy self.
Turn away mine Eyes
From beholding Vanity.
Enable me to wash my hands in Innocency.
That I may compass thine altar about,
And lift up my Hands
To thy Holy Oracle.
Put a Watch over the Door of my Lips,
That I speak not unadvisedly with my Tongue.

Let my Glory awake early in the morning,
  To bring praises unto thee.
Enter, O Lord, the Gates of my Heart.
  Bow down the Heavens, O Lord,
And break open those Everlasting Doors,
  That the King of Glory may enter in.
Let the Ark of thy Presence rest within me.

Let not Sin reign in our mortal Bodies, that we should obey it in the Lusts thereof.

Neither let us yield our Members as instruments of Unrighteousness unto Sin, but let us yield our selves to God, as those that are alive from the Dead: and our Members as Instruments of Righteousness to God. *Rom.* 6.

My Beloved put in his Hand by the Hole of the Door, and my Bowels were moved for him.

I rose up to open to my beloved, and my Hands dropped with Myrrh, and my fingers with sweet smelling Myrrh, upon the Handles of the Lock.

O my beloved be not as a Wayfaring Man, that turneth aside to tarry but for a Night.

Thou hast ravished mine Heart with one of thine Eyes.

How fair is thy Love my Sister, my Spouse! How much better is thy Love than Wine! and the smell of thine Oyntments than all Spices!

Thy Lips, O my Spouse, drop as an Hony Comb: Hony and Milk are under thy Tongue, and the smell of thy Garments is as the smell of *Lebanon.*

Or ever I was aware my Soul made me like the Chariots of *Aminadab.*
Return O my Love!
  I would lead thee, and bring thee
    Into my Mothers House.
  I would kiss thee, yet should I not be despised.
    O let me live in thy Bosom for ever.

O Infinite God, Center of my Soul, Convert me powerfully unto thee, that in thee I may take Rest, for thou didst make me for thee, and my heart's unquiet till it be united to thee. And seeing, O Eternal Father, thou didst create me that I might love thee as a Son, give me Grace that I may love thee as my Father. O only begotten Son of God, Redeemer of the World, seeing thou didst Create and Redeem me that I might Obey and Imitate thee, make me to Obey and Imitate thee in all thy imitable Perfection. O Holy Ghost, seeing thou didst create me to Sanctify me, do it, O do it for thine own Glory; that I may acceptably praise and serve the holy and undivided Trinity in Unity, and Unity in Trinity. Amen.

II

Prayers for the Nation

82

. . . I beseech Thee to hear my Daylie prayers. Save this Nation, Spare thy People, let me O Lord rejoyce in the felicity of thy chosen, and be glad with thine Inheritance. Remember I beseech Thee How much thou lovest me, Who lovest me so much, as if me a-lone. Yea more O Lord, for as much as by loving others, Thou Raisest them to be my freinds and Treasures. O remember how all Thy Lov Terminates in me: How I am made thy Bride, the End of all Things, A lover of all Things and in that like Thee. An Active ey, an Infinit Sphere in which thou Dwellest forevermore. They are not purses and Trunks of Jewels that I regard, but God and kingdoms. O let thy Glory Abide a-mong us, Thy praises in our Assemblies. Let Thy citties prosper, our vilages flourish, our children Grow up in fear of thy Name, like Oliv plants about thy Table. Soften our Kings Heart, Teach our Senators Wisdom, Heal the Abominable, cleans the Profane, giv our young Men and Maydens Knowledg, let our people walk in the light of thy Countenance, O Let the Ministers Mourn for the profanes of our Streets, And giv not Thy Turtle Dove the Beloved of thy Soul into the Enemies Hand. O Lord they will not regard the Glory of thy kingdom, nor mind the Hidden Riches of thy Benefits. They all are gon a way and refuse to return. They would not make Mention of thy loving kindness nor understand the Excellency of thy Holy laws nor be enflamd with thy lov nor sing praises unto Thee, yet O Lord pardon us, and make us not a Desolation, nor an Astonishment in the Earth. For Thy Tender Mercys sake which have been ever of old be favourable unto us, and Continue thy presence in the midst of us.

84

God tendereth his Saints as the Apple of his Eye. But he is terrible in his Anger against all his Enemies, becaus by How much the Greater his Goodness was, So much the Greater his Provocation is. Because he knows the Good things He Intends, He Deferreth them long and is many Ages before he is weary of Repenting. I admire and Tremble at the Height and Depth of his Infinite patience: I Adore the Riches of his long Suffering, extended unto Kingdoms from Generation to Generation. He that is Conversant with the Ancient Prophets shall See Him Contending, wooing and pursuing an Incorigible Nation many 100. years: before He Destroyes them, And tho he know all Ages to be alike from the Begining of the World, pervers and obstinat, yet is not Discouraged to forbear, and Intreat, but by his prophets and ministers endeavoureth to Melt them, Refine them, Gain them.

. . . O my God I Could be Quickly weary Quickly weary both of Repenting and Interceding. But thy Lov is the encourager of mine, the Soul and strength that Animates mine. Becaus thou lovest them with an infinit Love therefore art thou So long before thou art weary. O pardon my weakness, who am made in thine Image. Make me Great in patience and compassion and Lov to Thee. Tho they have been and are Rebellious against Thee and will be, yet let me Continually Intercede for them. As they are thy Garden, Jewels, Peculiar Treasures, So they are mine, Members of My Body as they are of Thine, more Dear to me, more Beautifull then Eden. O lay it not wast, Bereav us not O lord. Remember How thy Name is praised in our Temples, And How our children are taught the Knowledg of thy Son. Tho the whole Nation will Not Come in, yet like waters that sqweez in by Drops one of a family and two of a Tribe Return unto Thee. In every one of which Thou hast a nother Selfe, an Infinite Treasure, a freind, an IMAGE.

85

. . . Besids the Heaven and the Earth which the Heathen enjoy, Thou hast brought in the Gospel of thy Son into our land, Converted our Kings Senators and Nobles, Exalted thy name, Established thy word and worship by Laws, Builded thy Selfe Temples, and Apoynt[ed] Revenues for thy church and Ministers, Greatly are the Bishops [of] our Saviour Dignified, and our Cittys Beautified with those thy most Glorious and Beautifull Houses. wear all this to be Done againe Thou knowest the Sweat and Bloud wherewith it was Atcheived. But O the wickedness of Ignorant Zealots! who contemn thy mercies and Despise the union the Beautifull union of my Nationall church! every way thou art provoked to Anger, by Open profaness and Spirituall wickedness. And by the Ignorance of both, Despising thy mercies O lord when our citties and Teritories are united by Laws in the fear of thy Name: and are at one accord in Calling upon Thee; when they Move by Consent like an united Army. How Ravishing is their Beauty, How Sweet their Order! It is O my God as if the Nation had but one Soul. In all which while thy Glory Reigneth, She is made thy Throne; one Throne and Temple unto Thee. Be not wroth very Sore O Lord, neither remember Iniquity forever. Thy Holy Citties are a wilderness, Zion is a wilderness, Jerusalem a Desolati[on], our Holy and our Beautifull house where our fathers praised Thee is burnt up with fire and all our pleasant Things are layd wast. Wilt thou Refrain thy Selfe for these Things O Lord, wilt thou ho[ld] thy peace and afflict us very Sore: O profane not the Throne of thy Glory! let not the Heathen Trample it under foot! Much Less let Christians Defile it with their Bloud!

Select Meditations, I

12

Rogation

Traherne's instructions concerning prayers for Holy Days in general, here in particular Rogation.

Our Savior Comforting His Disciples against Tribulation by the Promise of the H. Ghost, assureth them that Prayers made in His Name should be Accepted. Whatsoever you shall Ask the Father in my Name He will giv it you. Ask, & Receiv, that your Joy might be full.

This Blessed Precept, Large Commission, & Beneficial Duty, which our Savior gav His Apostles, & in them to us, & to all Succeeding Ages, is the Strength, Hope Encouragement & Confidence of all our Prayers. Which are at all times to be performed in as full a Degree as the Ordinary Estate of our calling will permit: And yet H. Church hath wisely set apart these Rogation Days, as an Extraordinary Time, which cannot be always tho they may conveniently be som times, for more peculiar praying then upon other Days. As being prompted thereunto by the Contemplation & Memory of our Saviors Departure & Ascention. That our Minds by prayer may Ascend to Heaven, whither our Mediator Ascended in person.

To Ask Mercies in the Times of Common Miseries; Sympathizing with the Church in all her Calamities.

To Implore Gods Blessing upon the fruits of the Earth, which are then all in Springing.

To Deprecat His Judgement that neither the Catterpillar nor Palmer Worm, with the rest of the Army of the Lord of Hosts, fall upon us.

To implore His Mercy for our Safety & Protection.

To be Affected with the Great & Publick Concernments of the Nation & Kingdom in which we liv. Espousing the Benefits & Welfare of all which certainly is a Glorious Thing: for it will fill our Houses with privat Wealth, by making us to be concerned in All as Kings: & it will giv us a Communion with God Almighty, in all His Publick Ways & Blessings, Mercies & Judgments, His peoples Joys, & His Glorious Works which are abroad the World.

And certainly in this the Wisdom of the Church is Infinit. For She leadeth us in the Circuit of all his Mercies: And having upon other H. Days brought us by Degrees to Things past, our Saviours Nativity, Circumcision, Epiphany, or Manifestation & to other Divine Spiritual & Celestial Blessings in the Saints & Apostles, to the Commemoration of His Cross & Passion, to the Joyful Prospect of His Resurrection, & in all those to Spiritual Joys, Sublime Feasts, & Heavenly Treasures: she now leads us by the Hand to the Sight & Possession of Temporal Delight & Earthly Blessings even to present Affairs in the Dispensations of His Providence, & the Visible Beauties of His Works beneath, which in their proper Season com also to be Remembered. For it is not our Gold & Silver & the things in our Houses, that will make us Happy; without a lively Sight & Sense of the Benefits which He hath prepared abroad, & by giving which He hath Magnified the Greatness of His Wisdom & Lov to us. They hav Ordained also Procession at this Time, to view & Secure the Publick Bounds, which is an Act of Justice, being a fence against Wrong, an Act of Prudence in Removing Troubles, an Act of Charity by preventing Quarrels. And to Compleat all, they hav made it an Act of Thanksgiving by Joyning His Praises to so convenient a Season: And an Act of Triumph & Publick Joy, in Causing the Minister to go abroad with His People in Token & Memory of the victory of Christians. For it sheweth the vanquishing of Pagan idols, the Glorious conquest of Christian Religion, the Peace of His Church, & the Reign of Christians: whose flourishing Estate, & present happiness is there Evidently, in Beautifull Troops Exhibiteth before us.

To Prais God therefore for His Mercies, is another End for which this time is appointed. The Doing of which in Publick Solemnities with Scriptures & Prayers, is so H. a Duty, that it Sanctifieth the Land in all our Eys, & maketh it more Happy then the Kingdom of Canaan, by the manifest Appearance of our Saviors Soveraignty, & Gods Divinity acknowledged in it. The Prospect & Effect of which is Equaly Wonderfull Sweet & Delightfull. Therin we Acknowledg openly all Blessings to com from God, in whom as we live move & have our Being, so we Desire that all our Moving Living & Being may be to His Glory; that He Blessing the Creatures to us, we may in a Right Use of the Creatures, Bless & Prais & Magnifie Him forever more. . . .

But giv us Grace O Lord to Bruis the Serpents Head, & to cut off occasions of Sin.

To set apart Times for Prayers, & especially those Times which thy H. church hath set apart for us.

That we may be Glad of those Times to withdraw ourselves from Labors, to the Exercise of Repentance.

O Lord, Compell us to com in unto Thee, & to Practice Obedience to thy H. Church for Thee.

And let the Peoples Prophaneness be Healed, not by a Divestation, or Opression of Power, but by an Intelligent Persuasion of Interior Holiness.

That in the Midst of Decency Order & Beauty, retaining all the Marks of Peace of a flourishing Church, they may be Spiritual and Holy.

Church's Year-Book

13

Poem for Pentecost

I

Com Holy Ghost Eternal God
Our Hearts with Life Inspire
Inkindle Zeal in all our Souls
And fill us with thy Heavenly fire.

2

Send forth thy Beams, and Let thy Grace
        Upon my Spirit shine:
That I may all thy Works enjoy,
    Revive, Sing Praises, be Divine.

Church's Year-Book

14

A Prayer of Thanks for Mary

First among the saints Traherne remembers Mary.

And first O Lord I prais & Magnify thy Name
    For the Most H. Virgin Mother of GOD, who is the Highest of Holy
Saints.
    The most Glorious of all thy Creatures.
    The most Perfect of all thy Works.
    The Nearest unto Thee, in the Throne of God
        Whom Thou didst pleas to make
    Daughter of the Eternal Father.
    Mother of the Eternal Son.
    Spous of the Eternal Spirit.
    Tabernacle of the most Glorious Trinity.
    Mother of Jesus.
    Mother of the Messias.
    Mother of Him that was the Desire of all Nations.
    Mother of the Prince of Peace.
    Mother of the King of Heaven.
    Mother of our Creator.
    Mother of our Redeemer.
    Mother & Virgin.
    Mirror of Humility and Obedience.
    Mirror of Wisdom & Devotion.
    Mirror of Modesty & Chastity.
    Mirror of Sweetness & Resignation.
    Mirror of Sanctity.

Mirror of all Virtues.

The most Illustrious Light in thy Church, Wearing over all her Beauties here, the vail of Humility, to shine the more Resplendently in the Eternal Glory.

And yet this H. Virgin-Mother, stiled herself but the Handmaid of the Lord & falls down with all the Glorious Hosts of Angels, & with the Armies of Saints, at the foot of Thy throne, to worship & Glorify Thee forever & ever.

I prais Thee O Lord with all the Powers & faculties of my soul; for doing in Her all thy Mercifull Works for my sake, & the Benefit of Mankind.

For uttering the Glorious Word: yea rather Blessed are they that Hear the Word of God, & Keep it.

For looking round about upon thy Disciples & Saying, Behold my Mother & my Brethren. For whosoever shall do the Will of God, the same is my Brother & my Sister & Mother. Yea for what Thou wilt say, Inasmuch as ye hav don it to the least of these, ye hav don it unto me.

The most unworthy of all thy Servants falleth down to worship Thee for thine own Excellencies; even if O Lord, for thine own Perfections, & for all thos Glorious Graces, given & imparted to this Holy Virgin, & to all thy Saints.

I Prais Thee for them all, & comemorat them all with Joy & Thanksgiving.

Church's Year-Book

15

A Prayer for All Saints Day

To lov Thee is my Joy & my Crown.
O make my Soul Capable of Infinit Lov: that I might return all to thy Infinit Bounty.
I am sick of Lov, because I cannot lov enough. O that I were sick this Excess of Lov.
O that I could lov Thee as much as I desire: as much as Thou dost merit, as much as Thou oughtest to be Beloved!
O Divine Lov, turn me all into Lov.
Shew how much Lov Thou canst giv to an infinit Thirsty Longing soul.

Thou alone art wholly Amiable, wholy Desirable, wholly Beautifull wholy All Things, wholy Lov unto me.

I can hav no Lov but what I hav in thee: Therfore Great must be my Lov unto thy Saints, both Triumphant & Militant. Who hav given up their Lives, & do giv up their Names unto Thee.

For them all I prais Thee, I prais Thee for them most Exaltedly with all the Powers of my Soul & Body.

Church's Year-Book

16

Prayer of Thanks for the Patriarchs, Prophets and Disciples

And now O Lord I prais Thee, for the Patriarchs most Honorable Senate.

Who during their Abode in this Vale of Tears were the Salt of the Earth, & Light of the World.

Who in those Darker Times, & Scarcer Means of Grace before the Sun of Righteousness rose in the Morning & Twi-light of the World, believed in Thee. Hoping in thy Son, & walking in the Spirit: And with less Light of Divine Revelation safely passed thorow all Disadvantages: even to the State of Glory: for which infinit Lov, & Conduct of thy Mercy to them, I magnify thy Name, & Prais Thee forever.

I Prais Thee also for the Godly fellowship of thy Prophets; & their most Holy Quire:

Those Proto notaries of Heaven.

Those Registers of Divine Truths.

Those Mirrors of Divinity.

Whose Souls hav been the Organs of thy Truths.

Whose Mouths hav been the Instruments of thy Prais.

Whose Pens hav been the Conduits of thy Mercies.

Whose Hearts hav been the Rivers, & whose Books the Seas, which Thou hast filled with thy Wisdom, Ways, & Wonders.

I Humbly prais Thee for them, who are the Transcendent Witnesses of our Saviors Dietie: & who Ministerd unto us, the things which are now reported by the Preaching of the Gospel. I beseech Thee that I may see by faith, what they did fore see by the Inspiration of thy H. Spirit. And giv me Grace to imitat their close Adhesion unto Thee, (that

I may feel the Sweetness of those Extasies they enjoyed) while they were so Gloriously Inspired by Thee.

Church's Year-Book

17

O my God revive my Soul

O my God revive my Soul, and refresh it with the Stream of Liveing waters! Life, sence, affections, Zeal: these, O these are the Living waters flowing from thy Throne. Replenish me with these, and I shall no more be a stony well of Dust, but a spring and fountaine of Living waters, Enriching and Reviving all thy works; Satisfying the thirst of God Himselfe; to whom also the Angels may come with Golden Buckets. The Ages Drink and Let in their cisterns.

Select Meditations, III, 62

18

GOD never shewd Himself more a GOD, then when He appeared Man: A prayer for faithfulness

This Body is not the Cloud, but a Pillar assumd to manifest His Lov unto us. In these Shades doth this Sun break forth most Oriently. In this Death is His Lov Painted in most lively colours. GOD never shewd Himself more a GOD, then when He appeared Man. Never gained more Glory then when He lost all Glory. Was never more Sensible of our Sad Estate, then when He was bereaved of all Sence. O let thy Goodness shine in me! I will lov all O Lord by thy Grace Assisting as Thou doest: And in Death it self, will I find Life, and in Conquest Victory. This Sampson by Dying Kild all His Enemies.[1] And then carried the Gates of Hell and Death away, when being Dead, Himself was born to his Grave. Teach me O Lord these Mysterious Ascentions. By Descending into Hell for the sake of others, let me Ascend into the

Glory of the Highest Heavens. Let the Fidelity and Efficacy of my Lov appear, in all my Care and Suffering for Thee.

Centuries of Meditations, I, 90

1 Judges 16.21–31.

19

Let my Lov unto Thee be as Strong as Death

O Jesu Lord of Lov · and Prince of Life! who even being Dead, art Greater then all Angels Cherubims and Men. Let my Lov unto Thee be as Strong as Death: and so Deep that No Waters may be able to Drown it. O let it be ever Endless and Invincible! O that I could realy so lov Thee, as rather to suffer with S. Anselm the Pains of Hell then to Sin against Thee. O that no Torments, no Powers in Heaven or Earth, no Stratagems no Allurements might Divide me from Thee. Let the Length and Bredth and Height and Depth of my Love unto Thee be like Thine unto me. Let undreinable fountains, and unmeasurable Abysses be hidden in it. Let it be more vehement then flame, more Abundant then the sea, more Constant then the Candle in Aarons Tabernacle that burned day and night. Shall the sun shine for me; and be a Light from the Beginning of the World to this very day that never goeth out, and shall my Lov ceas, or intermit, O Lord, to shine or burn. O Let it be a Perpetual fire on the Altar of my Heart, and let my Soul it self be thy Living Sacrifice.

Centuries of Meditations, I, 91

20

Let my Lov unto all be Regular like thine

My Lord, Thou Head of the Holy Catholic Church I Admire and Prais Thee for Purchasing to thy self such a glorious Bride: and for Uniting us all by the Blood of thy Crosse. I beseech Thee let my Lov unto all be Regular like thine, and Pure, and Infinit. Make it Divine, and make it Holy. I confess I can see · but I cannot Moderat, nor Lov as I ought. I Pray Thee for thy Loving kindness sake supply my Want in this

Particular. And so make me to lov all, that I may be a Blessing to all: and welpleasing to Thee in all. Teach me Wisdom, How to Expend my Blood Estate Life and Time in thy service for the Good of all, and make all them that are round about me Wise and Holy as Thou art. That we might all be Knit together in GODly Lov, and united in thy service to Thy Honor and Glory.

Centuries of Meditations, I, 79

21

When I enter into Houses: A prayer for a moderate tongue

Keep my heart o lord always sencible of my created worthynes! And when I enter into Houses, let me remember the Glory I saw in the feilds and the Blessedness of thy Kingdom! it is imposible at once to be present with Men and Thee my God, unless we oppose and Greive at their Thoughts. For they are so far Like Runnagates run From Thee, that it is impossible by consent to goe a long with them, but their thoughts will lead us out of thy presence. The Heavens and the Earth are Annihilated in their understandings, Thy laws forgotten, and thy wayes unknown. They wander among weeds and gather vanities; They goe out into the wildernes and Hide them selves a-mong Bryers and Thornes; And know not How to return unto Thee. These Thinges, the Glory of thy kingdom, They cannot understand. There is a Great Gulph set between us, if they will not Come to me, O let not me goe back againe to them, but weep in my secret Places; and Pray for them. O my God make me faithfull, lively, constant; and Since Thou hast Given me a Tongue; Tho I am an Eternal Sphere in Communion with Thee, Teach me to use it moderately Prudently Seasonably to thy Glory. Amen.

Select Meditations, II, 100

22

A prayer that we may see our real treasures

97

When we hear or read of the Hypostatical union;[1] Divine Lov, or the Passion of our Lord: These objects appear as Divers, as the Eys are several, that behold the Same. The Things are open and obvious to all: but the Right Apprehension of them Inaccessible. To Some Eys they Seem False, to some Dubious and uncertain, to others Dim and to others Light and of Little value. To all the world distant and Sublime: to the most of all, Cold and unEffectual. Onely to the wise and holy they appear what they ought. . . . Let me my God see the Serious Profoundness of thine Eternal care, and while I Lament my Levity, Let me attain that fixed and Heavenly frame that may keep my Heart Close unto thee. O make [me] weighty in all my Deeds! and Let me be as Serious in enjoying my Treasures, as Jesus christ was in Redeeming Sinners! It is my tedious Shame that I am not Answerable to the Powerfull Bloodiness of his most Serious Passion.

98

O my God shall all the Things in Heaven and Earth be my Daily Treasures, and shall I be so much beloved of thee, and Shall I not Live as a son of God? O no more Shall Little Things take up my Life! Why Should Parlors and Jewels, Rents and clothes and monies, words and Injuries So Engage my Soul. Let the creation of the world and the Redemption of men, the Hypostatical union, and the Day of Judgment, the Laws of God and the Glory of His Lov, the Abundance of the Sea be converted unto me, and Eternal Joys in the Kingdom of Heaven be my Real weighty and [sub]Stantial Treasures. We are all undon by despiseing Great ones, and Regarding Little Things.

Select Meditations, III

---

1 The substantial union of two natures, human and divine, in One Person in Jesus Christ. This doctrine was accepted by the Church at the Council of Chalcedon (451).

23

O Let me be fast united unto Thee

O my God I am abundantly Satisfied with the Fatness of [thy] Hous; Thou hast made me to drink of the Rivers of thy Pleasures. My Honor and Happieness is Greater then I can Conceive. And the multitude of the Treasures wherewith Thou hast Enriched me are innumerable and Endless. I will now Liv as a son of God in communion with Thee: And above all these Things Delight in thy Glory. Being Enabled by thy Benefits So infinitly to Lov Thee, I will Liv a bove them all, Admiring the Lov which I see in them, abov them. All Exterior works will I Performe to Please Thee: but by Delighting in thy Love will be united to Thee. Thy Lov to me Shall Dwell within me, Return againe, be Lov unto Thee, Transform my Soul, and make us one. O my Father and the Bridgroom of my Soul, all these are Treasures, and thy Palace wonderfull, but thy Person is the Joy and Happines of my Soul, which exceedeth them all. Other Persons are made Amiable by Lov. Thy Person is Lov: the Fountaine of all Beauty Amiableness and Delight. O Let me be fast united unto Thee that nothing may Divert me from Contemplating thy Lov. Let me turn a way from the Thought of clothes, Rents, Houses, monies, Injuries, with all the Inferior Little Things which engage inferior and Feeble minds, and Liv above the Doubts of all Apostates in the Actual Fruition of thy Goodness Wisdom and Power. All which Thou has magnified in every Being in Heaven and Earth to Shew me thy Love. but thy Lov it Selfe is the GodHead which I Adore; the fountain and the End of all thy Benefits; fully manifested in all its Operations: in them and in it Selfe ever to be enjoyed. O make me feel How infinitly I am Beloved, and be the Rest of my Soul for ever.

Select Meditations, IV, 39

24

Shew me the Reasons of thy Lov

Why Lord Jesus dost Thou lov men; why are they thy Treasures? What Wonder is this, that Thou shouldst esteem them so as to Die for them? Shew me the Reasons of thy Lov, that I may Lov them too. O Goodness ineffable! they are the Treasures of thy Goodness who so infinitly lovest them that Thou gavest thy self for them. Thy Goodness delighted to be communicated to them whom thou hast saved. O Thou who art most Glorious in Goodness, make me Abundant in this Goodness like unto Thee, That I may as Deeply pitty others Miserie, and as Ardently Thirst their Happiness as Thou doest. Let the same mind be in me that is in Christ Jesus. For He that is not led by the Spirit of Christ is none of His. Holy Jesus I Admire[1] thy Lov I admire thy Lov unto me also. O that I could see it through all those Wounds! O that I could feel it in all those Stripes! O that I could hear it in all those Groans! O that I could Taste it beneath that Gall and Vinegre! O that I could smell the Savor of thy sweet Oyntments, even in this Golgotha or Place of a Skull. I Pray Thee teach me first thy Lov unto Me, and then unto Man Kind! But in thy Lov unto Mankind I am Beloved.

Centuries of Meditations, I, 63

1 Wonder, marvel at.

Bibliography and Further Reading

A. M. Allchin, *Participation in God: A Forgotten Strand in Anglican Tradition*, London: Darton, Longman and Todd, 1988.

A. M. Allchin, *Landscapes of Glory: Daily Readings with Thomas Traherne*, London: Darton, Longman and Todd, 1989.

A. M. Allchin, *The Joy of All Creation: An Anglican Meditation on the Place of Mary*, London: New City, 1993.

John Stewart Allit, *Thomas Traherne Il Poeta-Teologo*, Milan: Edizioni Villadiseriane, 2007.

Jacob Blevins, ed., *Re-reading Traherne: A Collection of New Critical Essays*, Arizona: Medieval and Renaissance Texts and Studies, 2007.

Margaret Botrall, *The Way to Blessedness*, Oxford: Mowbray, 1962.

David Buresh, ed., *Waking Up In Heaven: A Contemporary Edition of Centuries of Meditations*, New Jersey: Hesed Press, 2002.

A. L. Clements, *The Mystical Poetry of Thomas Traherne*, Cambridge, MA: Harvard University Press, 1969.

Patrick Collinson, *From Cranmer to Sancroft*, London: Hambledon Continuum, 2006.

Esther DeWaal, *Lost in Wonder: Rediscovering the Spiritual Art of Attentiveness*, London: Canterbury Press, 2003.

Graham Dowell, *Enjoying the World: The Rediscovery of Thomas Traherne*, London: Mowbray, 1990.

David Ford, *Christian Wisdom: Desiring God and Learning in Love*, London: Cambridge University Press, 2007.

Patrick Grant, *The Transformation of Sin: Studies in Donne, Herbert, Vaughan and Traherne*, Amherst: University of Massachusetts Press, 1974.

Christopher Hill, *Collected Essays. Writing and Revolution in Seventeenth Century England*, Amherst: University of Massachusetts Press, 1985.

Denise Inge, ed., *Thomas Traherne: Poetry and Prose*, London: SPCK, 2002.

Denise Inge, 'Thomas Traherne and the Socinian Heresy in *Commentaries of Heaven*', *Notes and Queries*, 252:4 (December 2007): 412–16.

Denise Inge, *Wanting Like a God: Desire and Freedom in the Work of Thomas Traherne*, London: SCM Press, 2008.

Belden Lane, *Landscapes of the Sacred: Geography and Narrative in American Spirituality*, Mahwah, NJ: Paulist Press, 1988.

Belden Lane, 'Thomas Traherne and the Awakening of Want', *Anglican Theological Review*, 81 (1999): 651–64.

Barbara Lewalski, *Protestant Poetics and the Seventeenth-Century Lyric*, Princeton: Princeton University Press, 1979.

Nicholas Lossky, *Lancelot Andrewes. Le Predicateur*, Paris: 1986.

Nabil Matar, 'The Political Views of Thomas Traherne', *Huntingdon Library Quarterly*, 57 (1994): 241–53.

Mark McIntosh, *Discernment and Truth: The Spirituality and Theology of Knowledge*, New York: Herder and Herder, 2004.

Helen Oppenheimer, *Making Good: Creation, Tragedy and Hope*, London: SCM Press, 2001

Anne Ridler, ed., *Poems, Centuries and Three Thanksgivings*, London: Oxford University Press, 1966.

Jan Ross, ed., *The Complete Works of Thomas Traherne*, Vols I and II, Cambridge: Boydell and Brewer, 2005, 2007.

Julia Smith, ed. *Select Meditations*, Manchester: Carcanet Press, 1997.

Julia Smith, 'Thomas Traherne and the Restoration', *The Seventeenth Century*, 2 (1988): 203–22.

Stanley Stewart, *The Expanded Voice: The Art of Thomas Traherne*, San Marino: Huntington Library, 1970.

Nicholas Tyacke, 'Religious Controversy', in Nicholas Tyacke, ed., *The History of the University of Oxford, Vol. IV, Seventeenth-Century Oxford*, Oxford: Oxford University Press, 1997, pp. 569–620, esp. 598–609.